INTERNATIONAL CRIMINAL LAW IN CONTEXT

International Criminal Law in Context provides a critical and contextual introduction to the fundamentals of international criminal law. It goes beyond a doctrinal analysis focused on the practice of international tribunals to draw on a variety of perspectives, capturing the complex processes of internationalisation that criminal law has experienced over the past few decades.

The book considers international criminal law in context and seeks to account for the political and cultural factors that have influenced – and that continue to influence – this still-emerging body of law. Considering the substance, procedures, objectives, justifications and impacts of international criminal law, it addresses such topics as:

- the history of international criminal law;
- the subjects of international criminal law;
- transitional justice and international criminal justice;
- genocide, crimes against humanity, war crimes and the crime of aggression;
- sexual and gender-based crimes;
- international and hybrid criminal tribunals;
- sentencing under international criminal law; and
- the role of victims in international criminal procedure.

The book will appeal to those who want to study international criminal law in a critical and contextualised way. Presenting original research, it will also be of interest to scholars and practitioners already familiar with the main legal and policy issues relating to this body of law.

Philipp Kastner is an Assistant Professor in International Law at the Law School of the University of Western Australia in Perth, Australia.

INTERNATIONAL CRIMINAL LAW IN CONTEXT

Edited by
Philipp Kastner

Routledge
Taylor & Francis Group

LONDON AND NEW YORK

First published 2018
by Routledge
2 Park Square, Milton Park, Abingdon, Oxon OX14 4RN

and by Routledge
711 Third Avenue, New York, NY 10017

Routledge is an imprint of the Taylor & Francis Group, an informa business

British Library Cataloguing-in-Publication Data
A catalogue record for this book is available from the British Library

Library of Congress Cataloging-in-Publication Data
Names: Kastner, Philipp, editor.
Title: International criminal law in context / edited by Philipp Kastner.
Description: New York, NY : Routledge, 2017. | Includes bibliographical
  references and index.
Identifiers: LCCN 2017021862| ISBN 9781138675476 (hbk) | ISBN
  9781138675513 (pbk)
Subjects: LCSH: International criminal law.
Classification: LCC KZ7000.I586 2017 | DDC 345—dc23
LC record available at https://lccn.loc.gov/2017021862

ISBN: 978-1-138-67547-6 (hbk)
ISBN: 978-1-138-67551-3 (pbk)
ISBN: 978-1-315-56068-7 (ebk)

Typeset in ITC Galliard Std
by Swales & Willis Ltd, Exeter, Devon, UK

CONTENTS

PREFACE

This book seeks to enhance the nexus between research and teaching in the field of international criminal law (ICL) by presenting the core topics of ICL through critical and contextualised analyses. I would like to express my sincere thanks to the authors who embarked with me on this endeavour. Without them, this book would obviously not have been possible, and I am very grateful for their faith in its relevance and feasibility.

My thanks also go to the editors at Routledge, who provided the first impetus for this publication and who supported the whole project patiently and constructively. The anonymous reviewers of the book proposal also offered valuable comments at an early stage.

Daniel McCluskey from the University of Western Australia conducted outstanding editorial assistance and provided very useful and critical comments on draft chapters, far beyond what I had expected from an advanced law student.

My special thanks go to Elisabeth Roy Trudel, with whom I had the privilege of discussing my ideas for this project on several occasions and who made insightful observations, including on the introduction and the chapter on hybrid tribunals. Elisabeth also transformed *International Criminal Law in Context* into an artwork, thus adding another dimension to the book. The cover image, entitled *Hope in red*, seeks to inspire and to make the viewer think about this field of law in various ways. The red dots or stains can be understood as a direct reference to blood and to the terrible atrocities that international criminal law attempts to deal with. Indeed, the dots can symbolise a crowd seen from far above, in which the usually unknown perpetrators and victims of international crimes must live close to each other, with the cloud-like surroundings conveying a complex context.

Yet the red, on a second look, is not the typical red of violence, crime and blood. It is cadmium red. This is a direct reference by the artist to the writer, art critic and artist John Berger and to his exchange of letters with John Christie that forms the text *I Send You This Cadmium Red. . .* Red, as Berger noted, is not usually innocent, but this one is. Cadmium red is the colour that one sees when staring at the sun with closed eyes, and in that sense, it conveys a sense of confidence, warmth and hope.

In a way, *Hope in red* hence reminds us that in the face of violence and oftentimes depressing developments, a dose of optimism is needed to pursue such projects as international criminal law. I hope that this book will provide some inspiration for this pursuit.

Philipp Kastner

ABBREVIATIONS

ACDEG	African Charter on Democracy, Elections and Governance
ACHPR	African Court on Human and Peoples' Rights
ACJHR	African Court of Justice and Human Rights
ACJ	African Court of Justice
ASP	Assembly of States Parties
ATCA	Alien Tort Claims Act
BNUB	United Nations Office in Burundi
CAR	Central African Republic
CDF	Civil Defence Forces
DDR	disarmament, demobilisation and reintegration
DRC	Democratic Republic of Congo
ECCC	Extraordinary Chambers in the Courts of Cambodia
ECtHR	European Court of Human Rights
FRY	Federal Republic of Yugoslavia
HOSG	heads of state and government
IAC	international armed conflict
ICC	International Criminal Court
ICCPR	International Covenant on Civil and Political Rights
ICJ	International Court of Justice
ICL	international criminal law
ICRC	International Committee of the Red Cross
ICT	international criminal tribunal
ICTJ	International Center for Transitional Justice
ICTR	International Criminal Tribunal for Rwanda
ICTY	International Criminal Tribunal for the former Yugoslavia
IHL	international humanitarian law

IL	international law
ILC	International Law Commission
IR	international relations
JCCD	Jurisdiction, Complementarity, and Cooperation Division
LOAC	laws of armed conflict
MICT	Mechanism for International Criminal Tribunals
NATO	North Atlantic Treaty Organization
NGO	non-governmental organisation
NIAC	non-international armed conflict
OAU	Organisation of African Unity
OTP	Office of the Prosecutor
PALU	Pan African Lawyers Union
QPN	Quaker Peace Network
RPF	Rwandan Patriotic Front
SADC	Southern African Development Community
SCSL	Special Court for Sierra Leone
SSR	security sector reform
STL	Special Tribunal for Lebanon
SWG	Special Working Group
TJU	Transitional Justice Unit
TRC	truth and reconciliation commission
UCG	unconstitutional change of government
UN	United Nations
UNMICT	United Nations Mechanism for International Criminal Tribunals
VWS	Victims and Witnesses Section

CONTRIBUTORS

Kamari Maxine Clarke is a professor of Global and International Studies at Carleton University. With a BA in Political Science-International Relations from Concordia University, a Masters in the Study of Law from Yale University, and a Ph.D. from the University of California-Santa-Cruz, her research is both multi-disciplinary and engaged in global and transnational formations. Her publications include *Fictions of Justice: The International Criminal Court and the Challenge of Legal Pluralism in Sub-Saharan Africa* (Cambridge University Press, 2009), *Mirrors of Justice: Law and Power in the Post-Cold War Era* (Cambridge University Press, 2010, with Mark Goodale), and *Africa and the ICC: Perceptions and Realities* (Cambridge University Press, 2016, with Eefje De Volder and Abel Knotterus).

Christian M. De Vos is an advocacy officer with the Open Society Justice Initiative and a co-editor of the volume *Contested Justice: The Politics and Practice of International Criminal Court Interventions* (Cambridge University Press, 2015). He has worked as a human rights advocate, attorney, and researcher for organizations including Amnesty International, the United States Institute of Peace, the War Crimes Research Office, and Leiden University's Grotius Centre for International Legal Studies. De Vos received his JD from the American University Washington College of Law and his PhD (Law) from the University of Leiden.

Mark A. Drumbl is the Class of 1975 Alumni Professor at Washington & Lee University, School of Law, where he also serves as Director of the Transnational Law Institute. He has held visiting appointments on several law faculties, including Oxford University, Université de Paris II (Panthéon-Assas), University of Melbourne, Masaryk University, University of Sydney,

Vanderbilt University, Free University of Amsterdam, University of Ottawa and Trinity College-Dublin. His book, *Atrocity, Punishment, and International Law* (Cambridge University Press, 2007) has won commendations from the International Association of Criminal Law (U.S. national section) and the American Society of International Law. In 2012, he published *Reimagining Child Soldiers in International Law and Policy* (Oxford University Press), which has been widely reviewed and critically acclaimed.

Sophie Gagné is an L.L.M. candidate at Université Laval in Québec City, Canada. Having graduated with honours from a Joint Bachelor in Public Affairs and International Relations, she is currently working on the qualification of armed conflicts by judges of international criminal tribunals. She is the recipient of various scholarships and awards, including from Canada's Social Sciences and Humanities Research Council and Québec's *Fonds de recherche Société et Culture*.

Rosemary Grey is a Postdoctoral Fellow at Melbourne Law School. Her research focuses on gender issues in international criminal law. Prior to her appointment at Melbourne Law School, Rosemary completed her PhD at the University of New South Wales (UNSW). Her PhD thesis was titled *Prosecuting sexual and gender violence crimes in the International Criminal Court: Historical legacies and new opportunities.* While completing her PhD, Rosemary taught international criminal law at UNSW, and worked and volunteered with a number of Hague-based organisations including Women's Initiatives for Gender Justice, the International Bar Association, and the International Criminal Court.

Philipp Kastner is an Assistant Professor at the Law School of the University of Western Australia and holds degrees in law from McGill University (LL.M. and D.C.L.) and the University of Innsbruck, Austria (Dr. iur. and Mag. iur.). His research and teaching interests include the resolution of armed conflicts, international criminal law, public international law, law of the sea, and legal pluralism. He is the author of *International Criminal Justice* in bello? *The ICC between Law and Politics in Darfur and Northern Uganda* (Martinus Nijhoff, 2012) and *Legal Normativity in the Resolution of Internal Armed Conflict* (Cambridge University Press, 2015).

Fannie Lafontaine is a lawyer and full professor at the Faculty of Law at Laval University and holder of the Canada Research Chair on International Criminal Justice and Human Rights. She is the project director of a major grant from Canada's Social Sciences and Humanities Research Council for a partnership between academia and civil society entitled 'Strengthening Justice for International Crimes: a Canadian Partnership'. Before joining Laval University, she worked for the Office of the United Nations High

Commissioner for Human Rights, for the International Commission of Inquiry on Darfur, for human rights NGOs and at the Supreme Court of Canada. Her publications include *Prosecuting Genocide, Crimes Against Humanity and War Crimes in Canadian Courts* (Carswell, 2012).

Wendy Lambourne is a Senior Lecturer in the Department of Peace and Conflict Studies, University of Sydney. Her interdisciplinary research on transitional justice and peacebuilding after genocide and other mass violence has a regional focus on sub-Saharan Africa and Asia/Pacific. Her recent publications include chapters in *Dimensions of Peace* (Palgrave Macmillan, 2016), *Restorative Justice in Transitional Settings* (Routledge, 2016), *Breaking Cycles of Repetition* (Budrich, 2016) and *Transitional Justice Theories* (Routledge 2014), as well as articles in the *Journal of Peacebuilding and Development, International Journal of Transitional Justice, Human Rights Review, Genocide Studies and Prevention* and *African Security Review*.

Eyal Mayroz is a Lecturer in the Department of Peace and Conflict Studies, University of Sydney, Australia. His research covers relationships between politics, ethics and the law in the prevention of genocide and other mass atrocities; focus on influences of US public opinion and the media on American foreign policy. His upcoming book is titled *'Ever Again?' America's Failure to Halt Genocide, From Bosnia to Darfur* (under review by University of Pennsylvania Press). Eyal is a member of the Genocide Prevention Advisory Network, an international network of experts on the causes, consequences, and prevention of genocide and other mass atrocities.

Yvonne McDermott is Associate Professor of Law at Swansea University, UK. She is an Academic Fellow of the Inner Temple, and a Door Tenant at Invictus Chambers, London. She holds a PhD from the Irish Centre for Human Rights and undergraduate and postgraduate law degrees from the National University of Ireland, Galway, and Leiden University. Yvonne is the author of *Fairness in International Criminal Trials*, published by Oxford University Press in 2016, and over 40 articles and book chapters on topics relating to international criminal law and procedure, evidence and proof, and international human rights law.

Frédéric Mégret is an Associate Professor and Dawson Scholar at the Faculty of Law of McGill University, where he teaches and researches international law, international criminal law, criminal justice and human rights law. From 2006 to 2015 he held the Canada Research Chair on the Law of Human Rights and Legal Pluralism.

Raphaëlle Nollez-Goldbach is a researcher at the French National Centre for Scientific Research (CNRS) and a member of the Center for Legal Theory and Analysis at the École Normale Supérieure (Ulm) in Paris. She is a specialist in international criminal law and the International Criminal Court. Her publications include *Quel homme pour les droits ? Les droits de l'homme à l'épreuve de la figure de l'étranger.*

Sean Richmond is a Canadian lawyer and political scientist who researches and teaches in the areas of international law and international politics. He currently works in the Legal Bureau at Global Affairs Canada in Ottawa. Prior to this position, he was an Assistant Professor in the Law Faculty at the University of Western Australia in Perth, and a Postdoctoral Fellow in the Munk School of Global Affairs at the University of Toronto. He completed his doctorate at Oxford University under a Commonwealth Scholarship and Doctoral Fellowship from Canada's Social Sciences and Humanities Research Council.

Gerry Simpson is a Professor of Public International Law at the London School of Economics and previously held the Kenneth Bailey Chair in Law at the University of Melbourne. He is the author of *Great Powers and Outlaw States* (Cambridge, 2004, awarded the American Society of International Law's annual prize for Pre-eminent Contribution to Creative Legal Scholarship) and *of Law, War and Crime: War Crimes Trials and the Reinvention of International Law* (Polity, 2007) as well as the co-editor of *Hidden Histories* (Oxford, 2014, with Kevin Jon Heller) and of *Who's Afraid of International Law?* (Monash University Press, 2017, with Raimond Gaita).

Stephen Smith Cody is a Visiting Assistant Professor of Law at the University of the Pacific, McGeorge School of Law, and a research fellow at the Human Rights Center at Berkeley Law. His research seeks to understand the experiences of victims and vulnerable witnesses in criminal trials. He holds a Ph.D. in sociology from the University of California, Berkeley, a J.D. from Berkeley Law, and an M.Phil. in social anthropology at Cambridge University. He teaches criminal law, civil procedure, and international criminal law.

Dale Stephens is a Professor at the University of Adelaide Law School. Prior to this appointment he served for 23 years as Legal Officer in The Royal Australian Navy attaining the rank of Captain. His operational deployments include East Timor and Iraq. He has been awarded the Conspicuous Service Medal, the (US) Bronze Star and the (US) Meritorious Service Medal. He holds a Master of Laws degree and a Doctorate in Law from Harvard Law School. He is the Director of the Adelaide Research Unit on Military Law and Ethics and Head of the SA/NT Navy Legal Panel.

Eric Stover is Faculty Director and Adjunct Professor of Law and Public Health at the Human Rights Center, School of Law, University of California,

Berkeley. He is the author and editor of several books, including *The Witnesses: War Crimes and the Promise of Justice in The Hague; My Neighbor, My Enemy: Justice and Community in the Aftermath of Mass Atrocity* (with Harvey Weinstein); *The Guantanamo Effect: Exposing the Consequences of U.S. Detention and Interrogation Practices* (with Laurel Fletcher); and *Witnesses from the Grave: The Stories Bones Tell* (with Christopher Joyce). In 2017, he co-produced a three-hour PBS documentary, 'Dead Reckoning: War, Crime, and Justice from World War II to the War on Terror'. The documentary is a companion film to his latest book, *Hiding in Plain Sight: The Pursuit of War Criminals from Nuremberg to the War on Terror* (with Victor Peskin and Alexa Koenig).

Timothy William Waters is Professor of Law and Associate Director of the Center for Constitutional Democracy, Indiana University Maurer School of Law. He holds a JD (*cum laude*) from Harvard; an M.I.A. from Columbia, with an Advanced Certificate in East Central Europe from the Harriman Institute; and a B.A. from UCLA. He was an Alexander von Humboldt Fellow at the Max-Planck-Institut in Heidelberg. He is the editor of *The Milošević Trial – An Autopsy* (Oxford, 2013). Waters has taught at Boston University, the University of Mississippi, Bard College, and Central European University and has worked for the International Criminal Tribunal for the Former Yugoslavia, the Organization for Security and Cooperation in Europe, the Open Society Institute, and Human Rights Watch.

Thomas Wooden is a Research Associate with the Research Unit on Military Law and Ethics at the University of Adelaide Law School. He holds a Bachelor of Laws (Hons) and Bachelor of International Studies from the University of Adelaide, and is admitted as a solicitor and barrister in the Supreme Court of South Australia. He has completed a six-month internship with the International Criminal Tribunal for the former Yugoslavia (ICTY) in The Hague, and a three-month internship with the United Nations Assistance to the Khmer Rouge Trials (UNAKRT) in Phnom Penh. Thomas currently works for the Australian Public Service.

INTRODUCTION

International criminal law in context

Philipp Kastner

In 1946, Nazi leaders were convicted by an international tribunal for their crimes committed during World War II. Famously stating that '[c]rimes against international law are committed by men, not by abstract entities',[1] the Nuremberg judgment transcended the sovereignty of states and their privilege to impose criminal sanctions, and held accountable individuals – not states – responsible for the most serious crimes of concern to the international community, including crimes against humanity and war crimes.

While the idea of international trials is hence not new, it is only recently that international criminal law (ICL), a body of law sitting between public international law and domestic criminal law, has established itself as an important field of study and research. It is in the 1990s and 2000s that institutions like the International Criminal Tribunal for the former Yugoslavia (ICTY), the International Criminal Tribunal for Rwanda (ICTR) and the International Criminal Court (ICC) further defined the substance and distinct procedures of ICL. Among others because of their focus on the individual as a subject under international law, these processes have had a significant impact on the broader field of international law. They have also intensified the complexity of the relationship between international law and politics on a global scale, as is exemplified by the persistent 'peace versus justice' debate and strong criticisms *vis-à-vis* the allegedly imperialist or neo-colonial outlook of international criminal courts and tribunals. In other words, despite the significant progress made over the past few decades, the ways in which international law criminalises certain forms of conduct are still not settled. Four sets of key questions can be identified.

---

1 *Nuremberg Judgement (International Military Tribunal, 1 October 1946)* in *Trial of the Major War Criminals before the International Military Tribunal* (Nuremberg, 1947) 223.

First of all, *what* is criminalised and, just as important, what is not criminalised? Is the list of crimes – genocide, crimes against humanity, war crimes and the crime of aggression – in the statute of the first permanent international criminal court, the ICC, exhaustive? Or are there other forms of conduct that the international legal order is, or should be, concerned with, and that would, therefore, also require transcending the sovereignty of states?

The second fundamental question is *who* should be held accountable. The current trend consists in focusing on the architects of mass atrocities, on political and military leaders who plan and order, or do not prevent, the perpetration of international crimes; the direct perpetrators, those who actually commit violent acts – kill unlawfully, rape, torture, persecute groups, destroy property on a large scale – are typically not the first priority for prosecutors. The focus on certain leaders also occludes, at least to some extent, the inherent collective dimensions of mass atrocities and of other forms of violence that create the conditions in which these atrocities are committed. This begs the question whether ICL, based on the premise that responsibility and guilt can always be individualised, has not gone too far in its focus on individual perpetrators and their acts.

Third, and closely related to the preceding queries, is the *how*. In which ways should ICL be administered and enforced? Although a number of different international and so-called hybrid criminal tribunals have been established since the 1990s, with national courts also applying ICL more and more frequently, no ideal institutional design has emerged. Indeed, the grand institutional experiments seem to be over: the *ad hoc* tribunals, namely the ICTY and ICTR, have more or less finished their work, and it is unlikely that similar tribunals will be established in the near future (if only because of their price tag); hybrid tribunals have not lived up to their promises; and the ICC, hailed as a milestone for international justice when its statute was adopted in 1998 and entered into force four years later, is under severe pressure and criticised from many sides, and some states parties recently even withdrew from its statute. As a result, ICL can certainly not be described as a field full of exciting opportunities anymore, as it was perhaps the case in the 1990s and 2000s when several newly established international criminal justice institutions held the promise of ending impunity for serious crimes, of preventing the perpetration of such crimes in the future and of possibly even stopping armed conflicts. While such effects are inherently difficult to measure, it is certain that genocide, crimes against humanity and war crimes are still being perpetrated with impunity around the world, as demonstrated by the well-documented atrocities committed during the armed conflict in Syria[2] that has been going on since 2011, to name just one example.

---

2 See, eg, the reports by the Independent International Commission of Inquiry on the Syrian Arab Republic, established by the United Nations Human Rights Council in 2011, <www. ohchr.org/EN/HRBodies/HRC/IICISyria/Pages/IndependentInternationalCommission. aspx>; for reports from non-governmental organisations, see, eg, Amnesty International

Finally, the sometimes very technical questions about the *what, who* and *how* hinge on a central, more philosophical question, namely *why* ICL exists. What are its objectives? What societal interests do we seek to protect through this body of law? Are we driven by a general quest for justice, by ideas of retribution, by the desire to deter future perpetrators? What about ICL's oftentimes claimed contribution to revealing the truth, to recalling a society's violent past, and to bringing about peace and reconciliation? Can and should ICL also have reparative, rehabilitative and restorative functions?

These are some of the questions surrounding the ICL project that will be explored in this book. Although many of these issues remain unresolved, and notwithstanding apparent setbacks for ICL in recent years, the premise that those responsible for the most serious crimes committed in this world should be held accountable has not withered away. Indeed, ICL continues to attract significant attention by scholars and practitioners as well as the media and the general public. This is, among others, related to its close relationship with politics; the issuance of arrest warrants by the ICC against sitting heads of state for their alleged involvement in the perpetration of genocide, crimes against humanity and war crimes is an obvious example.[3] From a more general transitional justice perspective, ICL can have a profound impact on societies emerging from violent conflict, among others because it contributes to framing the ways in which past atrocities are considered and dealt with on the domestic level.

In other words, ICL has become a reality, and it continues to fulfil potentially important functions. It would, for instance, seem inconceivable not to envisage some form of justice and accountability for the crimes committed by all sides in the Syrian conflict. This may take time and also require some creativity, but a comprehensive peace process will, in some form, have to deal with the crimes committed. In the meantime, the unprecedented establishment, in December 2016, by the United Nations General Assembly of a 'mechanism' to assist in the investigation and prosecution of those responsible for the most serious crimes committed in Syria,[4] while certainly not able to bring justice to Syrians by itself, suggests that ICL can be applied in many ways. The experimental phase of the institutional enforcement of ICL is not over, and there is space and need for creativity.

While ICL is hence well alive, it may have to reconsider itself, its claims and dominant modes of operation if it wants to play a more constructive role. One option consists in looking beyond the ICL system in a narrow sense and realise that this body of law does not exist in isolation, independently from

---

<www.amnesty.org/en/documents/mde24/5415/2017/en/> and Human Rights Watch <www.hrw.org/news/2017/02/13/syria-coordinated-chemical-attacks-aleppo>.

3 On the still outstanding arrest warrant against the Sudanese President Omar Al-Bashir, see Chapter 12 in this book.

4 GA Res 71/248, UN GAOR, 71st sess, 66th plen mtg, UN Doc A/RES/71/248 (21 December 2016).

external factors and forces. This means that any analysis of ICL can benefit from considering the context and from drawing on a variety of perspectives. 'Context' is therefore understood in a twofold way here: inside-out and outside-in. Inside-out refers to a consideration of the context as seen from an ICL perspective, such as an appreciation of the impact of ICL decisions on society and of the political will needed to establish international criminal tribunals; outside-in refers to a consideration of ICL from outside the system itself, i.e. as seen and assessed from neighbouring fields, such as international relations, peace and conflict studies, and criminology.

Consequently, this book not only offers an introduction to the fundamentals of ICL, its crimes and main modes of institutional enforcement, but it considers ICL both critically and contextually. By transcending a purely doctrinal analysis focused on the statutes and jurisprudence of international criminal courts and tribunals, and by taking into account the increasingly self-reflexive and critical turn in the field of ICL,[5] the 16 chapters that compose this book present original approaches through which some of the complex dynamics surrounding the recent internationalisation of criminal law can be captured.

Several themes resurface throughout the book. These include the historical trajectories of ICL, its embeddedness within international law, and its relationship with other branches of international law, such as international humanitarian law and international human rights law, as well as its relationship to politics. Questions as to who makes and applies ICL, who its main constituencies are and who may speak authoritatively on behalf of victims of serious crimes are also important concerns for several authors.

Part I discusses some of the historical and conceptual foundations of ICL and contextualises ICL within the larger fields of international law and transitional justice.

In *Chapter 1*, Gerry Simpson highlights that ICL developed from a variety of sources. While the usual linear narrative may be easier to tell – ICL started after World War II with the International Military Tribunals in Nuremberg and Tokyo, went dormant for decades until re-awakened in the 1990s with the establishment of the ICTY and the ICTR in the 1990s – this chapter proposes a more nuanced and complex account of ICL's history. Through his particular and engaging approach, writing style and further reading suggestions, Simpson also reminds us of the usefulness of reading widely, and certainly beyond statutes and court cases, to understand the ICL project.

Who commits international crimes? Who are ICL's subjects? Frédéric Mégret, in *Chapter 2*, revisits these fundamental questions, which are related

5 See, eg, Christine Schwöbel (ed), *Critical Approaches to International Criminal Law: An Introduction* (Routledge, 2014); Frédéric Mégret, 'The Anxieties of International Criminal Justice' (2016) 29(1) *Leiden Journal of International Law* 197; Sergey Vasiliev, 'On Trajectories and Destinations of International Criminal Law Scholarship' (2015) 28(4) *Leiden Journal of International Law* 701.

to the historical trajectories of ICL and its increasing focus on individual accountability to the detriment of state criminality. Indeed, celebrated as one of the main achievements of ICL, the development of individual legal subjectivity represents an important shift in international law. Yet there are both individual and collective dimensions to the responsibility for serious crimes, with genocide, crimes against humanity, war crimes and aggression typically being committed by individuals acting within larger structures. This is why the criminal responsibility of different non-state actors, including corporations, is a recurrent motif in the contemporary international legal debates.

In *Chapter 3*, Wendy Lambourne contextualises ICL by considering it as part of a larger transitional justice and peacebuilding discourse. In her very critical piece, she argues that while ICL plays a significant role in the context of radical political transformations and of societies emerging from violent conflict, its potential to deal effectively and comprehensively with grave crimes is inherently limited. The chapter considers critiques of the dominant transitional justice paradigm, discusses the complex relationship between such justice endeavours and peacebuilding – beyond the frequently assumed peace vs. justice dilemma – and concludes by presenting a model for transformative justice.

The chapters in **Part II** shed light on some of the normative dynamics and contemporary debates surrounding the core crimes under international law. The crimes are also contextualised in a methodological sense, with some of the authors drawing on various approaches developed in the social sciences, such as international relations and sociology.

The first two chapters offer two different perspectives on dealing with some of the darkest sides of humanity. While genocide and crimes against humanity are distinct crimes, they can be viewed as two different ways in which international law has responded to mass atrocities. In the case of genocide, this has led to the creation of a group-based crime that protects certain collectives, whereas the concept of crimes against humanity primarily seeks to protect the individual human being. Adopting a socio-legal approach, Eyal Mayroz, in *Chapter 4*, considers political and moral dimensions of the legal concept of genocide and asks the central question as to why, 70 years after the adoption of the Genocide Convention, we still fail to prevent genocide. Raphaëlle Nollez-Goldbach turns in *Chapter 5* to the concept of humanity, which appeared for the first time in nineteenth-century treaties on the law of war. While it recently began to spread with the development of international criminal law and the particular category of crimes against humanity prosecuted before international criminal tribunals, references to humanity remain largely implicit and vague in international norms and case-law. This chapter analyses the legal concept of humanity and its evolution from an abstract moral value to a conception of humanity as a victim as well as understandings of humanity centred on solidarity and biology.

In *Chapter 6*, Dale Stephens and Thomas Wooden address the relationship between ICL and international humanitarian law (also called the laws of armed conflict). Analysing both traditional and novel dilemmas of armed conflict, the authors provide a foundational understanding of what constitutes a war crime in the contemporary context and discuss whether there is a correlation between the prosecution of war crimes and adherence to IHL. In this context, they also consider the relevance of the traditionally salient distinction between international and non-international armed conflicts and its implications for ICL as well as ethical considerations in the context of increasingly automated warfare and resulting challenges for individual responsibility.

Rosemary Grey, in *Chapter 7*, focuses on the cross-cutting theme of sexual and gender-based crimes and their increased prosecution in recent years. Her analysis exposes inherent biases within ICL and broader gender norms and reveals shifting patterns – such as the recognition of rape as a weapon of war or as a means to commit genocide – that materialised because of the efforts of different actors both inside and outside international criminal courts and tribunals.

Chapter 8, by Sean Richmond, considers the recent adoption of a definition of the crime of aggression by the ICC Assembly of States Parties in the context of a broader debate about international peace, security and authority. He aims to stimulate reflection about why such interdisciplinary questions are relevant to debates within and outside ICL, and how they can be addressed in a methodologically rigorous and analytically reflective manner. Through this approach, the author hence clearly contributes to this book's broader objective of exploring the relationship of ICL to international relations and international law more generally.

In *Chapter 9*, Kamari Maxine Clarke invites us to reconsider the types of conduct criminalised under international law as well as the dominant narrative about their institutional enforcement through international criminal courts and tribunals, based on a now apparently widely accepted accountability norm. The author explores the establishment of a new regional judicial mechanism, namely the African Court of Justice and Human Rights, and repositions such new judicial formations as not only an example of new ways of recasting responsibility and accountability in Africa, but as a way to envision alternatives to the model of international criminal justice as embodied by the ICC. This chapter, while concluding Part II on crimes, thus also provides a critical introduction to the different institutions that will be discussed in Part III.

Part III turns to the implementation of ICL by analysing the establishment and practice of international and internationalised criminal justice institutions, the enforcement at the national level as well as some broader current trends in this context. The first three chapters follow a certain chronological order with respect to the establishment of international and internationalised criminal justice institutions (although such a presumably linear narrative of phases is critically reviewed in Chapter 11).

Timothy William Waters starts, in *Chapter 10*, with an assessment of the legacies of the ICTY and ICTR, which were among the great institutional initiatives of the early post-Cold War era, infused with great expectations. It is also through the experiences and choices of these tribunals that ICL has taken form.

The author surveys the *ad hoc* tribunals' origins, their jurisprudence and processes, the politics surrounding them, and their accomplishments and failings.

In *Chapter 11*, Philipp Kastner considers some of the lessons learnt from the hybrid, or internationalised, tribunals that have been established, among others, in Sierra Leone, Cambodia, Kosovo and Lebanon from the early 2000s onwards. The chapter also argues that we should try to resist the common impulse to draw any final conclusions on these institutional experiments; these tribunals rather manifest the continued potential for creativity within ICL. Moreover, they allow us to consider in a particular light a number of conceptual issues related to ICL, such as the multifaceted relationship between international and national criminal law and the legitimacy of the respective institutions.

Christian De Vos, in *Chapter 12*, considers some of the ICC's defining features – notably the principle of complementarity, which holds that the ICC is designed to complement, not supplant, national jurisdictions – as well as key aspects of its institutional architecture and emerging jurisprudence. Moreover, the chapter shows that the ICC, while celebrated as a milestone and embodiment of a new global accountability norm when it came into existence in 2002, has since struggled to realise the high expectations that accompanied its establishment. Keeping in mind ICL's close relationship with politics, with the ICC and its oftentimes controversial decisions being the most discernible embodiment of this relationship, the author also analyses the political objectives and effects that have defined the Court's operations to date.

Fannie Lafontaine and Sophie Gagné further explore the crucial theme of complementarity in *Chapter 13* by turning to the prosecution of international crimes at the national level. Both 'vertical complementarity', a central feature of the ICC regime having the potential to 'catalyse' domestic prosecutions, and 'horizontal complementarity', which refers to the general international legal obligations of states to prosecute international crimes, will be discussed. The chapter presents important gaps that currently exist in the international legal system, including with respect to interstate cooperation in the extradition of alleged perpetrators of international crimes, and discusses practical and political obstacles in this context.

The remaining chapters consider three particular issues of international criminal trials, namely the relevance of human rights law; sentencing, which exposes a number of explicit and implicit concerns and hierarchies in ICL (like longer sentences for certain crimes and for certain modes of liability); and the role of victims of international crimes, a group of actors that has received increasing attention in recent years. While closely related to an emerging international criminal procedure, and sometimes quite technical, these issues are also revealing of the broader objectives and justifications of ICL.

In *Chapter 14*, Yvonne McDermott discusses whether international criminal tribunals are formally bound by international human rights standards and examines the institutional interplay between international criminal tribunals and international human rights courts. Through an analysis of a number of distinct areas of international criminal procedure, this chapter demonstrates that human rights law has had a remarkable influence over the moulding and interpretation of international criminal procedure.

Mark Drumbl, in *Chapter 15*, explores *how* and *why* individuals convicted of international crimes are punished by international criminal courts and tribunals. His chapter summarises the governing legal texts of representative institutions and reviews sentencing practices, jurisprudence and enforcement. It also assesses penological aspirations in the context of mass atrocity and, in particular, the ability of custodial sentences to attain retributive and deterrent goals, arguing that other aspirations, including reparation, rehabilitation and restoration, have been side-lined.

Chapter 16 posits that international criminal justice depends on victims. Stephen Smith Cody and Eric Stover trace the evolution of the participation of victims in trial proceedings and claim that greater attention to the inclusion of victims has expanded opportunities for survivors to join cases and to seek reparations. However, as empirical research shows, victim participants have expressed frustration with the length of trials, the acquittal of defendants and the lack of support services. The chapter argues that while international criminal trials will never be a panacea for the diverse needs of survivors, international tribunals must support national and international efforts to protect and restore communities affected by mass violence.

This call for more comprehensive responses and efforts resonates with the main premise of this book, namely that ICL, regarding its substance and procedures, its objectives, justifications and impacts, needs to be considered in context. In this sense, the contributions in this book do not content themselves with explaining 'facts' about ICL; rather, by considering the context of ICL and of the establishment and decisions of international criminal courts and tribunals as well as of national courts applying ICL, they seek to critically analyse the current ICL framework and present trends in the field.

PART I

Contextualising international criminal law

1

THE CONSCIENCE OF CIVILISATION, AND ITS DISCONTENTS

A counter history of international criminal law

Gerry Simpson

'Tell me, tall man, where would you like to be overthrown?
Jerusalem or Argentina?'
Bob Dylan, 'Angelina', *Shot of Love* (1981)

'Reitlinger: minimum 4,194,400 ; maximum 4,581,200
The Anglo-American Committee: 5,721,500
Leszczynsky: 6,093,000
Blumenthal: 6,500,000'.
Hanna Yablonka, *The State of Israel v Adolf Eichmann* (Schocken Books, 2004) 83

'The Divine Architect of the World
He didn't create mankind
as a uniform entity ...'
Tom Paulin, 'Locarno III', *The Invasion Handbook* (Faber and Faber, 2002)

I Introduction

At the heart of international criminal law (ICL) lie three projects: a project to end 'impunity' by punishing the perpetrators of war crimes using the methods of legalism (trial, conviction, punishment),[1] a project to console

---

1 On the need to end impunity see the extensive works of Cherif Bassiouni. For critiques of this obsession with impunity see Frédéric Mégret, 'Three Dangers for the International Criminal Court: A Critical Look at a Consensual Project' (2001) 12 *Finnish Yearbook of International Law* 244; Gerry Simpson, 'The Pro-Death League: Anti-Anti-Anti-Impunity' (forthcoming, 2018).

victims (through procedures of vindication, reconciliation, reparation and pedagogy),[2] and a project to consolidate something I have called, elsewhere, 'juridical humanity', by responding to an imagined 'conscience of mankind' and by giving that 'conscience' institutional and doctrinal shape through the punishment of 'enemies of mankind'.[3] Of course, ICL has many other stated and unstated purposes that have been dissected by a generation of writers.[4] But these three ideas anchor the system and give it the meaning it has today. In this opening chapter I want to offer a history of ICL that understands that history as an effort to bring these various imperatives into some sort of equilibrium or, at least, relationship, and I do this through exploring some of the less familiar aspects of ICL's past at Versailles during the negotiations over the trial of the Kaiser, at Moscow where the show trials of the 1930s offer a counterpoint to the Nuremberg and Tokyo Trials that followed, and in Lyon where Klaus Barbie was tried.[5] An examination of these trials will bring out, too, some of the dominant sub-themes of the paper: the question of memorialisation through law, the apparent linearity of the trial narratives, and the spectre of *ad hoc* 'provisionalism' that hangs over ICL.

When does history begin? Or the history of a particular field? In the case of ICL, the contenders are various. Scholars have pointed to a number of historical trials that might serve as precursors to modern ICL. These include the *von Hagenbach* Trial in 1474 or the Mixed French-Siamese Arbitral Tribunal in 1893–94.[6] But beyond specific trials, it could be argued that ICL began

---

2 The literature on victims is enormous. For clear thinking, see Mark A Drumbl, 'Victims who Victimise' (2016) 4 *London Review of International Law* 217; Sara Kendall and Sarah Nouwen, 'Representational Practices at the International Criminal Court: The Gap between Juridified and Abstract Victimhood' (2014) 76 *Law and Contemporary Problems* 235; Ann Sagan, 'African Criminals/African Victims: The Institutionalised Production of Cultural Narratives in International Criminal Law' (2010) 39 *Millennium* 3. On the didactic aspects of ICL see Lawrence Douglas, 'The Memory of Judgment: The Law, the Holocaust and Denial' (1996) 7 *History and Memory* 100; Lawrence Douglas, *The Memory of Judgment: Making Law and History in the Trials of the Holocaust* (Yale University Press, 2001); David Hirsh, *Law against Genocide: Cosmopolitan Trials* (Glasshouse Press, 2003); Alain Finkielkraut, *Remembering in Vain: The Klaus Barbie Trial and Crimes Against Humanity* (Columbia University Press, 1992).
3 The question of 'humanity' is taken up more frontally in this volume by Raphaëlle Nollez-Goldbach. See, too, Ruti Teitel, *Humanity's Law* (Oxford University Press, 2011); Samera Esmeir, *Juridical Humanity: A Colonial History* (Stanford University Press, 2012). For a searing assault on the hypocrisies of ICL see Tor Krever, 'Dispensing Global Justice' (2014) 85 *New Left Review* 67; Tor Krever, 'International Criminal Law: An Ideology Critique' (2013) 26 *Leiden Journal of International Law* 701. See also Sara Nouwen, 'Justifying Justice' in James Crawford and Martti Koskenniemi, *The Cambridge Companion to International Law* (Cambridge University Press, 2012) 327, 330 (ICL 'nurtures a sense of belonging to an "international community"').
4 For a useful overview, see Mirjan Damaška, 'What is the Point of International Criminal Justice?' (2008) 83 *Chicago-Kent Law Review* 329.
5 For a discussion of juridical humanity, see Raphaëlle Nollez-Goldbach's chapter in this collection.
6 See Kevin Heller and Gerry Simpson (eds), *The Hidden Histories of War Crimes Trials* (Oxford University Press, 2013).

with international law itself and the Roman split between the *ius civile* and the *ius gentium*: a law among Romans and a law to be applied to foreigners; or with Grotius's opening lines in *de jure praedae* (1604–5) where he denounces the Portuguese as 'cruel enemies' thereby casting them into the realm of enemies of mankind. Cicero is thought to be the originator of the idea that pirates are *hostes humani generis* or 'enemies of mankind', and this may well represent the first appearance of 'mankind' or humanity as a category capable of acting against enemies (as opposed to a political ideal to be strived for, or an immanent state or prospect to be identified among the entrails of the current imperfect order).[7] Grotius, in his *On the Law of War and Peace* speaks of the right to punish pirates:

> It is, therefore, a praiseworthy custom on the part of [some] peoples [that persons] who are about to set sail [are granted] warrants, by the public authority, to destroy whatever pirates they discover on the sea; so that if the occasion offers they may be able to act as public servants, and not upon their own initiative.[8]

This 'praiseworthy custom' it might be said, became the law of war crimes. The capture and punishment of pirates represents a highly plausible origin for ICL because for the first time individuals were held responsible for breaches of international law and that responsibility was effected through an extension of state's jurisdiction to areas beyond its territory. This combination, then, of extracurricular jurisdiction, individual liability and punishment acts as a model for the field.[9] The punishment, too – itself an alternation between violent liquidation and *ad hoc* trial – becomes a mark of the contemporary repression of enemies of mankind and the establishment of mankind as a juridical category.[10]

Of course, ICL has its roots in a number of other historical episodes and trajectories. The decision to exile Napoleon (despite a clamour from the Prussians for some sort of exemplary trial) represents both the final act of a diplomatic system committed to disposing of enemies through a form of political action and an act of proto-ICL (exile being a form of internationally-sanctioned punishment).[11] Alongside this, though, are long-range developments in the area of international

---

7 Is there a sense in which Cicero's stoicism works against his attitude to piracy? Or is humanity somehow established, as a category, in its engagements with its enemies?

8 Stephen C Neff (ed), *Hugo Grotius on the Law of War and Peace* (Cambridge University Press, 2012) 275.

9 Gerry Simpson, *Law, War and Crime* (Polity, 2007). See, too, Monique Cormier and Gerry Simpson, 'Piracy' in *Oxford Bibliographies* (23 March 2012).

10 Marcus Rediker, *Villains of All Nations: Atlantic Pirates in the Golden Age* (Verso, 2004); Daniel Heller-Roazen, *The Enemy of All: Piracy and the Law of Nations* (Zone Books, 2009).

11 Gary Bass, *Stay the Hand of Vengeance: The Politics of War Crimes Tribunals* (Princeton University Press, 2000).

law and the use of force where a just war tradition – distinguishing good and bad war and forming the basis for a later criminalisation of aggression – does not altogether recede; or in the humanitarian laws of war where misconduct in war is increasingly sanctioned through international law (the Lieber Code, the St Petersburg Declaration); or in the way in which anti-slavery efforts were internationalised while the slave-trader became the latest incarnation of the enemy of mankind.

ICL, of course, now has its own 'histories' of these and later developments and each of these offers a different perspective on such developments.[12] For Gary Bass, in his *Stay the Hand of Vengeance*, Napoleon's exile is the first step towards a liberal-legalist push for war crimes trials. Such trials, he argues, arise from a desire on the part of constitutional states to export liberal procedures to the international realm.[13] Four more recent histories each approach the origins of ICL differently. Mark Lewis's *Birth of the New International Justice* thinks of international war crimes trials as the culmination of several institutional and doctrinal developments in the fields of international humanitarian law, the law of war and peace and criminal law coupled with changes in the nature of democracy within states.[14] Kevin Heller's *The Nuremberg Military Tribunals and the Origins of International Criminal Law*, meanwhile, locates many of our present concerns in a series of trials (the Control Council Trials) held by the Americans at Nuremberg between 1946 and 1948, where a number of now-familiar doctrinal and historical quandaries emerged. Rob Cryer and Neil Boister have also sought to decentre the iconic Nuremberg Trial by directing us to its neglected cousin at Tokyo. The more familiar origin of ICL, of course, lies at the trial of the Major War Criminals at Nuremberg between October 1945 and November 1946 (*Göring et al*) when 22 leading Nazi War Criminals (including Hermann Göring, Albert Speer, Hans

---

12 This is hardly an exhaustive catalogue of these histories of ICL. Apart from the extensive histories of the Versailles proceedings (see, eg, Kirsten Sellars, 'Trying the Kaiser: The Origins of International Criminal Law' in Morten Bergsmo, Cheah Wui Ling and Ping Yi (eds), *The Historical Origins of International Criminal Law* (TOAEP, 2015) 195), the Nuremberg trials (see, eg, Ann Tusa and John Tusa, *The Nuremberg Trial* (Macmillan, 1983); Telford Taylor, *Anatomy of the Nuremberg Trials: A Personal Memoir* (Knopf, 1992); Christian Tomuschat, 'The Legacy of Nuremberg' (2006) 4 *Journal of International Criminal Justice* 830), and the Tokyo trials (Yuma Totani, *The Tokyo War Crimes Trial: The Pursuit of Justice in the Wake of World War II* (Harvard University Press, 2009); Madoka Futamura, *War Crimes Tribunals and Transitional Justice: The Tokyo Trial and the Nuremberg Legacy* (Routledge, 2008); Neil Boister and Rob Cryer, *The Tokyo International Military Tribunal: A Reappraisal* (Oxford University Press, 2008)) there have been other readable general histories (see, eg, Donald Bloxham, *Genocide on Trial: War Crimes Trials and the Formation of Holocaust History and Memory* (Oxford University Press, 2003)).
13 Bass, above n 11.
14 Mark Lewis, *The Birth of the New Justice: The Internationalization of Crime and Punishment, 1919–1950* (Oxford University Press, 2015); Kevin Jon Heller, *The Nuremberg Military Tribunals and the Origins of International Criminal Law* (Oxford University Press, 2011).

Frank and Joachim von Ribbentrop) were tried for committing war crimes, crimes against humanity and crimes against peace. Twelve were sentenced to death, seven received jail terms and three were acquitted.[15] This trial is the subject of two books published in 2016. In Andrew Williams' *A Passing Fury: Searching for Justice at the End of World War II*, the author traces the foundations of the system back to the numerous investigations and trials held in post-war-Germany after the war (trials and investigations since eclipsed by the main Nuremberg trial) and takes the familiar – perhaps even clichéd – view that such foundations were shaky, flawed and, sometimes, unjust but ultimately necessary: 'What else could they have done?', as he asks at the end of the book.[16] In *East West Street*, Philippe Sands offers up a highly personal and astutely (auto)biographical reading of the origins of ICL in the efforts of two men at Nuremberg: Raphael Lemkin, the Polish jurist and originator of the term 'genocide', and Hersch Lauterpacht, a Cambridge don and prominent international lawyer whose family perished in the Holocaust and whose articulation of the category 'crimes against humanity' was central to the whole proceedings and, indeed, the future of ICL.[17]

II Cavell, 1915

My own historical account begins on August 3, 1915 with the court martial of an English nurse, Edith Cavell. Cavell had been found guilty of aiding Allied prisoners in their escape from Belgium during the German occupation of Belgium. This, for me, represents the beginning of an effort to end impunity, provide redress for victims of atrocity and inaugurate a juridical humanity from the ruins of Empire. Cavell was convicted of a breach of German military regulations and an act of treason: a strange charge in this context – she owed no loyalty to the German state, after all – but a charge that has, as we shall see, an interesting history in this field of law. Despite a flurry of diplomatic protests – the German ambassador to the US, rather unhelpfully, said he would shoot five English nurses if he had them in custody – Cavell was executed on the morning of October 14 at the National Rifle Range in Brussels.[18] This marks a moment of origin for the field of ICL.

---

15 Of the two others, Robert Ley, the Labour Secretary, hanged himself and Gustav Krupp was declared unfit to stand trial. Martin Bormann, Hitler's *de facto* deputy in the bunker, and one of the twelve, was sentenced to death *in absentia*. His DNA remains were later identified in Germany.

16 Andrew Williams, *A Passing Fury: Searching for Justice at the End of World War II* (Jonathan Cape, 2016) 432.

17 Philippe Sands, *East West Street: On the Origins of Genocide and Crimes against Humanity* (Penguin Random House, 2016).

18 See Diana Souhami, *Edith Cavell* (Quercus Books, 2010). See also Rowland Ryder, *Edith Cavell* (Hamish Hamilton, 1975); Catherine Butcher, *Edith Cavell: Faith before the Firing Squad* (Monarch Books, 2015).

The execution sets off a train of events that leads to Article 227 of the Versailles Peace Treaty and then onwards to Nuremberg, Rome and Kampala.

The Germans, already accused, often falsely, of unspeakable crimes against the Belgian population, were immediately demonised further. Lloyd George went to the 1918 election with one of the most compelling election slogans of the twentieth century: 'Hang the Kaiser'. The promise was made, and though the Kaiser remained resolutely unhanged after the war, this promise became the foundation of ICL. Kaiser Wilhelm died peacefully on June 3, 1941 a month or so before Hitler's invasion of the Soviet Union, and these two events together conjoin two origins of the field at Versailles (the 1919 peace treaty between Germany and the Allied Powers) and later at Nuremberg where Hitler's march on Moscow is prosecuted as a crime against peace.

Back in 1918, though at the Imperial War Cabinet meeting, at 12 noon on November 20 Lloyd George presents his proposal to try the Kaiser for the crime of aggression. Lord Curzon, the Lord President of the Council, opens the meeting by remarking that there is no need even to argue for the trial of the Kaiser. He is after all, 'the arch-criminal'.[19] As Curzon reports, the French had not yet bothered to consult their own jurists about international law. No matter, the Kaiser could be put on trial and declared a 'universal outlaw'. Indeed, he goes on, wouldn't it be ideal to begin the League of Nations experiment on this note of trial and retribution? Lloyd George continues the discussion:

> With regard to international law, well [such a lot hanging on that word "well"], we are making international law and all we can claim is that international law should be based on justice ... there is a sense of justice in the world.[20]

It was not always thus. This commitment to ending impunity is a long way from the Peace of Westphalia in 1648 where a law of impunity or oblivion forms the basis for a new European political and religious order:

> That there shall be on the one side and the other a perpetual ... Amnesty, or Pardon of all that has been committed since the beginning of these Troubles ... but that all that has pass'd on the one side, and the other ... during the War, shall be bury'd in eternal Oblivion.[21]

The meeting of the Imperial War Cabinet though represents a transitional moment, and there is resistance to this retributive innovation. Billy Hughes,

19 Minutes of Imperial War Cabinet Meeting, No 37, November 20th, 1918, 6.
20 Ibid 7.
21 Treaty of Münster, Art. II.

the Australian Prime Minster, is puzzled by the whole idea of crimes against peace. As he famously puts it: 'why not try Alexander the Great and Moses'?[22] Hughes's point seems to be that what we call the 'crime of aggression' used to be known as 'history'. 'You cannot indict a man for making war', Hughes continues. And, in a supremely evocative phrase, he equates the whole idea of criminalising war with what he called: 'treason against mankind'. An absurd and eccentric idea for him, but a phrase that carries enormous weight now as we consider how un-selfconscious we have become about deploying the international community against outlaws, or about referring to 'crimes against humanity'. Hughes is, in the end, outvoted but not before he receives some support from the Minister for Munitions, only there in an advisory capacity. This minister, Winston Churchill, argues that the Allies would be 'within our rights to kill the Kaiser as an act of vengeance' but that it would be much more dubious to deal with him on the basis of 'what is called justice and law' (note the hesitant phrasing).[23] Churchill remained attached to this idea in 1945 when he, initially, seems to support summary execution for the defeated Nazi elites.

At Versailles, then, the law of war crimes begins with some familiar patterns: anxiety about the relationship between revenge and justice, a cavalier attitude to the role of actual lawyers, a belief on the part of proponents of trial that the justice of the cause renders unnecessary legal process and precedent, and permits a form of *ad hoc* justice, and the first sign that when it comes to war crimes and crimes against humanity, the identity of the perpetrators matters as much as the identity of the crime.

The three projects I began with are there at the origins of ICL at Versailles where the centrality of the victim as an engine or catalyst of punitive legalism is present, where the drift to legalism first manifests itself and where 'mankind' makes an early appearance as an agent of justice in relation to whom it is possible to commit 'treason'.

III Bukharin, 1937

Treason, of course depends less on what is done and more on where one stands. And where one stands can be a matter of chance. Or as Lenin once put it: 'he went to one room and found himself in another'.[24] Usually, the history of war crimes trials passes over the inter-war years in silence. This was a period in which the efforts of progressives seem to be directed at social and economic change or minority rights treaties or welfare or the sort of softer internationalism found in Geneva at the League of Nations.

---

22 Minutes of Imperial War Cabinet Meeting, No 37, November 20th, 1918, 9.
23 Minutes of Imperial War Cabinet Meeting, No 37, November 20th, 1918, 10.
24 Nathan Leites and Elsa Bernaut, *Rituals of Liquidation: The Case of the Moscow Trials* (Free Press, 1954) 153.

But are the Moscow Show Trials, perhaps, the missing link between Versailles and Nuremberg? Historians of ICL tend to think of Solferino or The Hague Peace Conference in 1899 or the German war crimes trials in Leipzig as the precursors to the trials in post-war Germany. Moscow, 1937 is an embarrassing antecedent after all. Judith Shklar describes show trials as the liquidation of political enemies using legal procedure.[25] Stalin knew all about that but, in this, he does not seem too far removed from Lloyd George and Lord Curzon. Establishing a tribunal for the specific purpose of liquidating or punishing an enemy? This is what the Imperial War Cabinet was debating in 1918.

Of course, the Moscow Show Trials were very unlike the Nuremberg War Crimes Trials in many important respects, but the idea that people's justice or humanity's justice or a sense of justice can somehow dispose of the need for proper procedure or legal precedent represents a sibling dark side of these trials. A show trial is one in which it is obvious that the guilty are guilty. The trial seems otiose: the mere performance of a justice already delivered elsewhere. Vishinsky, the Soviet Prosecutor at Moscow was also at Nuremberg. During dinner with the judges at Nuremberg he raises a toast: 'To the defendants, they will all hang'.[26] This was before the trial had begun. But Roosevelt, too, was worried about acquittals and his concerns made their way into the *Charter of the International Military Tribunal* where Article 19 states that:

> The Tribunal shall not be bound by technical rules of evidence. It shall adopt and apply to the greatest possible extent expeditious and non-technical procedure, and shall admit any evidence which it deems to be of probative value.

But then maybe these trials are as much about political spectacle as they are about legal propriety. For Hannah Arendt, a show trial is a 'spectacle with pre-arranged results' or the obliteration through compulsive staging of 'the irreducible risk' of acquittal.[27] The point of the trial is the trial itself: its ramifications, its warnings, its effluxions of terror. George Orwell understood this.

In his famous novel, *1984*, Mrs Parsons lives with her two little daemonic children at Victory Mansions. Her drains are blocked, as they often are, and she calls Winston Smith down to help her unblock the sink.

25 Judith Shklar, *Legalism: Law, Morals and Political Trials* (Harvard University Press, 1964) 149.

26 Telford Taylor, *Anatomy of the Nuremberg Trials* (Knopf, 1992) 211.

27 Hannah Arendt, *Eichmann in Jerusalem: A Report on the Banality of Evil* (Penguin, 1994) 266. The concept of 'irreducible risk' is from Otto Kirchheimer, *Political Justice* (Princeton University Press, 1961).

The two children torment Winston, calling him a Eurasian spy, threatening to vaporise him and shouting 'Goldstein' as he leaves the flat. Mrs Parsons is apologetic; the children are furious, she explains, because she failed to take them to the hanging: 'Some Eurasian prisoners, guilty of war crimes, were to be hanged that evening . . . this happened once a month and was a popular spectacle'.[28]

It strikes me as important to think about trials in this way; not as depoliticised programmes of management designed to end impunity or assuage the pain of victims but as slightly wild-eyed theatres of revenge: human rights with a vengeance. As one of the observers of the Moscow Show Trials eerily put it: these were 'dramas of subjective innocence and objective treason'.[29] This 'objective treason' was repeatedly enunciated in the months preceding the major trials at Nuremberg and Tokyo where, in Germany, the Nazis were described as the world's worst criminals and where, before both trials, the defendants were chosen with great care and on the basis of political impact.

The Soviet-era show trials, themselves, continued into the 1950s, most famously in Prague where the purpose was not to determine guilt or innocence, nor, even, to remove political opponents but rather to create them. The trials there were initially conceived as trials of fairly low-level *apparatchiks*. Under pressure from Moscow, President Gottwald found a higher level defendant, Otto Sling, a district party secretary. Under torture, Sling implicated Rudolf Slansky, the General Secretary of the Czech Communist Party, in a fantastic and implausible conspiracy. Finally the Soviet advisers had a defendant of sufficient seniority. The Czechs were initially shocked and bemused. What about the evidence? One Soviet legal adviser, soon to be himself purged, said: 'We have been sent here to stage trials not to check whether the charges are true'.[30]

As for the existence of legal norms, again this didn't matter. *Ad hoc*-ery and improvisation were the preferred methods. The instincts of the proletariat would stand in for what Kyrlenko, one of the Moscow prosecutors, called '[b]ourgeois sophistry'. And this recalls, too, a Nazi Law of June 28, 1935 referring to the need to punish criminals and deviants according to 'the sound perceptions of the people'. Ten years later, though, President Roosevelt was worrying about acquittals on technicalities and Robert Jackson – pressed on the existence of crimes against humanity or aggression – replied by saying '[w]e can save ourselves from these pitfalls [of definition] if our

---

28 George Orwell, *1984* (Penguin Books, first published 1949, 1974 edn) 22.
29 Maurice Merleau-Ponty, *Humanism and Terror: An Essay on the Communist Problem* (John O'Neill trans, Beacon Press, 1969) 202.
30 Meir Cotic, *The Prague Trial* (Herzl Press, 1987) 69.

test of what is a crime gives recognition to those things which fundamentally outrage the conscience of the American people'.[31] The victims of war crimes had become the people in general. Legalism remained the only viable solution. This became at trial the idea of 'shocking the conscience of mankind'.

IV De Menthon, 1945, Poincaré, 1919

Mankind, of course, has now become humanity. Just as the old language of enemies of mankind has been reworked as 'crimes against humanity'. When someone at the Imperial War Cabinet asks what crime the Kaiser is being charged with, Lloyd George replies: 'The crime of plunging this country into war'. Sir Robert Borden, the Canadian PM, smoothly offered a gloss on this by interjecting that 'it was a crime against humanity'.[32] And there it is, the moment when the Great Powers begin to think of themselves as 'humanity' rather than a coalition of victorious powers. At least the victors at Vienna 100 years earlier merely thought of themselves as 'Europe'. But the idea of 'crimes against Europe', while far more accurate as a description of extra-textual law, might seem too openly self-serving.

François de Menthon, one of the French Prosecutors at the Nuremberg war crimes trial in 1945, was assigned the task of defining humanity. The context was a trial in which a more or less new legal category – crimes against humanity – had to be created to encompass the system of abuse and murder instituted by the Nazis in the mid-1930s. De Menthon invoked three distinguishable concepts. The first two were familiar enough but the third, and most radical, concept of humanity saw it as a unified and indivisible category, a moral or juridical agent. There is a paradox at the heart of international criminal justice though. While its core animating idea is the abolition of all distinctions within humanity, some of its most energetic practices are dedicated to punishing 'inhumane' acts (acts committed by individuals who have lost their humanity?) and acting on behalf of humanity against those who are deemed to have stepped outside or defied humanity (think of Leon Bourgeois, at the Versailles Peace Conference, insisting on 'penalties to be imposed for disobedience to the common will of civilized nations'[33] or the editorial in the *Canberra Times* on October 3, 1946, p. 3 which thundered that the Nuremberg trial was '. . .a landmark from which the United Nations must press on to police and enforce world peace against all potential or actual disturbances of the peace or crimes against humanity').[34]

31 Quoted in Richard Minear, *Victor's Justice* (Princeton University Press, 1971) 7.
32 Minutes of Imperial War Cabinet Meeting, No 37, November 20th, 1918, 11.
33 Papers relating to the Foreign Relations of the United States, *The Paris Peace Conference Papers 1919* (1942) 185.
34 Quoted in Paul Bartrop, 'Nuremberg Trials as Viewed from Australia' (1994) 12 *Australian Jewish Historical Society Journal* 606.

Its favoured penalties, indeed, often come in the form of extreme violence applied to these outsiders (historically, the quartering of pirates, the beheading of tyrants; more recently, the hanging of war criminals and the waging of 'humanitarian wars'). But this history of violence does not appear to have unseated or even qualified humanity's self-confidence. Speaking very much in this vein, Raymond Poincaré, the French President, announced, also at Versailles: 'Humanity can place confidence in you, because you are not among those who have outraged the rights of humanity'.[35] But humanity here included the Belgians, French and British each of whom were, by this time, responsible for three centuries of sometimes violent, certainly racially-inflected, Empire.

Though the Imperial War Cabinet meeting on November 20th, 1918 began at noon, there was a lot to get through. The main line of business was the disposition of the Kaiser. What were the representatives of humanity going to do about this outlaw? But first, there were some minor matters to take care of. Lloyd George: 'there are two or three questions we are not clear about . . . Palestine, East Africa . . . questions of that kind'.[36] 'We have not quite settled in our minds *what sort of government we will set up* in Mesopotamia'. It was ever thus. Here are the representatives of civilisation, just prior to elaborating the idea that aggressive war would be a crime against humanity, reordering their imperial outposts, themselves, as Justice Pal (the Indian judge) remarked at Tokyo, the result of three centuries of aggressive war.

How did the Imperial War Cabinet get from its own imperial consolidations and restructurings to the enemy's crimes against humanity? After all they each seemed to be grounded on precisely the same combination of non-consensual territorial acquisition and mass violations of human rights. Was there a hint of self-consciousness? What was the hinge?

Between the surprisingly cursory discussion of Palestine, Syria and Iraq and the lengthier debate about the Kaiser there is one short announcement. A telegram is read out from the Association of Universal Loyal Negroes of Panama. It reads:

> Negroes throughout Panama send congratulations on your victory and in return for services rendered by the negroes throughout the world in fighting ... beg that their heritage wrested from Germany in Africa may become the negro national home with self-government.[37]

This is passed over in silence and the discussion moves on to the Kaiser's terrible crime of making war on Europe and the shock this delivered to the conscience of mankind and the newly minted idea of 'humanity'.

35 Papers relating to the Foreign Relations of the United States, *The Paris Peace Conference Papers 1919* (1942) 159.
36 Minutes of Imperial War Cabinet Meeting, No 37, November 20th, 1918, 2.
37 Minutes of Imperial War Cabinet Meeting, No 37, November 20th, 1918, 12–13.

V 'Lolita' in Jerusalem, 1961

Mankind is, of course, shocked by many different things at different times, something the US advisors, Robert Lansing and James Brown Scott argued at Versailles when they resisted the whole idea of crimes against humanity claiming that there was no such thing as humanity, only nations with different moral outlooks. On April 11, 1961, the District Court of Jerusalem purported to be acting in the name of a shocked humanity when it began hearing the trial of the head of Gestapo Unit IVB4 (responsible for 'Jewish matters and for the evacuation of the population') for crimes against humanity. The defendant, Adolf Eichmann (abducted from Argentina in May 1960 by Israeli agents and later to be found guilty and executed) seemed unshockable. His thoughtlessness, indeed, was his most remarkable quality.

Arendt, again:

> The longer one listened to him the more obvious it became that his inability to speak was closely connected to his inability to think ... he was genuinely incapable of uttering a single sentence that was not a cliché.[38]

He seemed curiously affectless, in other words. At one point, he is handed some novels to read. One of them is *Lolita*. After two days Eichmann returned the novel, visibly indignant; 'That is quite an unwholesome book', he tells the guard.

VI Klaus Barbie in Lyon, Duško Tadić in The Hague, Martin Bormann in Frankfurt: 'Nazis and others', 1987–1998

While Eichmann was running the Final Solution from an office in Berlin and then Budapest, Klaus Barbie was hunting down Jean Moulin, the French Resistance leader in Lyon in 1942. Barbie might have found Moulin in François de Menthon's house where he occasionally spent time. De Menthon at this time had become a resistance sympathiser. Barbie tortured Moulin to death but de Menthon went on to develop the concept of crimes against humanity at Nuremberg, a category of criminality that would be later applied to Barbie himself during his trial in Lyon in 1985. The Barbie case ought to be given its full name: *The Federation of Resistance Fighters v Klaus Barbie*.[39] This was to be the trial that established a judicial record of the heroism of the French resistance.

---

38 Arendt, above n 27, 328–9.
39 *Fédération Nationale des Déportés et Internés Résistants et Patriotes v Barbie* (1985) 78 ILR 124 (Cour de Cassation, France, 20 December 1985).

There was a small problem though. At ten past eight in the morning of April 6, 1944, Klaus Barbie had sent a telex to the Office for Jewish Affairs in Paris. It reads: 'This morning, the Jewish children's home "colonie enfant" in Izieu was cleaned . . . total 41 children aged 3 through 13 years were apprehended . . . Transport to Drancy to follow'.[40] The children were transported in manacles to Paris and then sent east to the camps. All of them were murdered (two of the boys were executed in Tallinn, Estonia).

But the trial was a curious affair. What was it about? And how does a state memorialise war crimes? From the perspective of the French state, it was about French resistance to Nazi occupation. Jewish groups in Lyon, needless to say, believed that the trial would provide some reckoning for Barbie's micro-Holocaust at Izieu. Barbie's defence lawyer, Jacques Vergès – later to defend Carlos the Jackal and Saddam Hussein – believed the trial was an opportunity to embarrass the French by pointing to crimes against humanity closer to home: institutionalised torture in Algeria and fascist collaboration in war-time Vichy. And so, a problem emerged. From the perspective of the prosecuting state, crimes against humanity in its then standard definition was a category both over- and under-inclusive. Over-inclusive in the sense that it threatened to encompass French colonialism in Algeria, under-inclusive in that it seemed to be about attacks on civilians and therefore could not encompass Barbie's murderous behaviour towards the French resistance. But as someone once said, every war crimes trial is saying this of the prosecuting state: 'We, at least, and whatever we have done in the past or might do in the future, are not Nazis'. And so, crimes against humanity in the Barbie trial were defined as crimes committed in furtherance of a policy of racial discrimination. Broad enough now to cover the resistance crimes, narrow enough to exclude Algeria where the French, at least, were not Nazis.

The narrowing was quite explicit. Recalling the original French draft at Nuremberg, crimes against humanity were defined as crimes committed by a state practising an ideology of racial discrimination. Though the Court in *Barbie* seemed to narrow the reach of crimes against humanity improperly, this simply reflected a long-standing tendency to equate crimes against humanity with a very particular genre of crimes against humanity, namely the crimes of Nazis.[41] Indeed, from 1945 to 1997 (Tokyo apart), it would have been possible to figure the history of war crimes as a history of Nazi war crimes. In the Australian War Crimes Amendment Act 1989 (Cth), for example, war crimes are defined as those crimes committed in Europe between 1939 and 1945. So, in a way, ICL often begins in the spirit of

---

40 Serge Klarsfeld, *The Children of Izieu: A Human Tragedy* (Harry N Abrams, 1984) 95.

41 See, eg, Leila Sadat Wexler, 'The Interpretation of the Nuremberg Principles by the French Court of Cassation: From Touvier to Barbie and Back Again' (1994) 32 *Columbia Journal of International Law* 289.

universalism but ends in the practice of particularism. Crimes against humanity are acts committed anywhere by anyone against anyone at any-time but not here, not now, not before 1988 (in the case of the *Pinochet* decision), not in relation to this person who is protected by her official position, not in relation to these peacekeepers immunised through Security Council Resolution 1422, only if the perpetrators acted in the name of national socialist ideology and so on.

An orthodox account of the history of ICL inverts this trajectory: think-ing of the practice of tribunals as having begun with the particular (victors' justice at Nuremberg) and ended in the universal (the International Criminal Court with its broad ranging jurisdiction).[42] So, we might say that modern de-nazified retributive legalism begins on May 8, 1997, the day that Duško Tadić is convicted of murder as a crime against humanity: the first non-Nazi to be tried before an international criminal court in Europe since 1946, and one of the first non-Nazis to be tried anywhere for crimes against humanity. Or maybe it begins a year later when a set of human remains are subject to DNA testing in Frankfurt and determined to be those of Martin Bormann, the last Nazi, or at least the last of the Nuremberg defendants to be unac-counted for. Bormann's ashes are scattered in the Baltic just as Eichmann's are disposed of in the Mediterranean (these removals at sea anticipating the burial of Osama Bin Laden and perhaps gesturing back to the roots of war crimes law and anti-terrorism jurisdiction in the original crime of crimes, namely that of piracy on the high seas).

VII Conclusion: un-creating mankind

The question might be: has modern ICL somehow cleansed itself of the moral obtuseness and political opportunism of those early trials? The legal principles certainly *seem* more transparent yet the institutions are engineered in a way that makes even facially apolitical prosecution and trial unlikely. 'We are objects of history' as Varenc Vagi said on his way to the gallows in Prague after his show trial.[43] The practice of international war crimes law suggests that only those on the wrong side of history get prosecuted: Ghaddafi, the Lord's Resistance Army, Radovan Karadžić, Omar Bashir, Laurent Gbagbo.

To situate the development of ICL in its historical setting, then, is to reveal also that crimes against humanity do not simply exist in some supervening

---

42 Antonio Cassese, 'On the Current Trends towards Criminal Prosecution and Punishment of Breaches of International Humanitarian Law' (1998) 9 *European Journal of International Law* 2; Theodor Meron, 'The Humanization of Humanitarian Law' (2000) 94 *American Journal of International Law* 239.

43 Simpson, *Law, War and Crime*, above n 9, 114.

ethical space to be picked off by appropriately articulated rules. Crimes against humanity are violent acts committed by enemies of mankind in concrete circumstances. And the enemies of mankind change depending on the exigencies of the situation. Every legal rule expressed in neutral, generally applicable language seems to have another more particular norm hovering, ghost-like, around it. At first the transparency of these ideological commitments is almost touching. At Versailles, the Kaiser is specifically indicted in Article 227 of the Peace Treaty.[44] By Nuremberg, there is a softening of this language; a not-very-good faith effort to make it sound like a universally-applicable legal rule. Remember the French wanted this definition of aggression at Nuremberg: 'Aggression is an act carried out by the European Axis Powers in breach of treaties and in violation of international law'.[45] In *Barbie* and *Eichmann*, these tendencies continue. There is less of this around now but the most recent articulation of a legal rule came in 2010 with the definition of aggression added to the Rome Statute by the Kampala Amendments. The crime of aggression is now defined as 'a manifest violation of the UN Charter'. 'Manifestness' will depend on scale, gravity and character. Character will depend on the existence of an arguable legal case. The existence of an arguable legal case will at least partly depend on the particular position of the state making that case.[46]

So, what should we make of this history? This is a matter that requires enormous delicacy. Thousands of people work conscientiously in the field of war crimes law (investigating, prosecuting, helping victims, trying to reform the system, calling for universal forms of justice, arguing against Great Power immunity), many more victims of horrible atrocities view a trial as their last great hope for justice. No-one can read about the moral strenuousness of the witnesses in the Eichmann Trial or the personal anguish of a man like Hersch Lauterpacht (struggling in Cambridge to develop a workable theory of crimes against humanity while his family disappears into the Polish and Ukrainian bloodlands) or the bravery of those testifying in the Balkan trials in The Hague, without stopping to acknowledge that the law of war crimes has become a site of great courage and the bearer of some of the ethical hopes of 'humanity'.[47]

Yet, there is something deeply awry with this system of justice. Indeed, one could justifiably describe it as a system of injustice. And these are not just remediable defects of the sort one might encounter in the way Family Law is administered in France. Rather they go to the question of what it might

---

44 Treaty of Peace between the Allied and Associated Powers and Germany (28 June 1919) 225 ConTS 188, arts 227–30 ('Treaty of Versailles').

45 Maurice Hankey, *Politics, Trials and Errors* (Pen-In-Hand, 1950) 21.

46 Gerry Simpson, '"Stop Calling it Aggression": War as Crime' (2008) 61 *Current Legal Problems* 191.

47 On Lauterpacht, see Sands, above n 17.

mean to live under the rule of law in a particular society. The history I have recounted leads to a possible conclusion that crimes against humanity are those crimes committed by enemies of mankind. Let me put the two problems in this way: the identity of the violator seems more significant – decisive even – than the identity or nature of the violation. But, more than this, the identity of the violations is already too narrowly imagined, creating morally suspect distinctions between different types of violence.

The question always asked of the critic is 'well, what instead?'. In 2002, I participated in a debate about the legality of the Iraq War. I offered several arguments against the war. During the question and answer period, a man stood up at the back and asked me what *I* would do about Iraq? I replied that if not intervening in Iraq constituted doing nothing, then I would prefer to do nothing. Not creating a war crimes tribunal to specifically investigate, say, the downing of MH 17 over the Ukraine might strike many people as the right thing to do. But the objections one might have to such an initiative bleed into the whole edifice of ICL. Certainly, *not* doing ICL might help us attend to other things. How helpful is it to demonise Russia using ICL? Haven't we been here before at Versailles? In Baghdad? The world is very complicated but international criminal justice can be very simple-minded and linear.

How should we respond to atrocity? The truth is I don't really know. I am not even sure that war crimes law isn't sometimes the right answer: maybe in North Korea, maybe in Colombia or Georgia. In 1944, Georg Schwarzenberger was already anticipating the objections I have made here in his book *Totalitarian Lawlessness*. 'The human mind revolts at the idea of covering these deeds with an all-forgetting mantle of oblivion . . . and the alternative of indiscriminate vengeance I hardly find more pleasant'.[48] But law often is experienced as incongruous or technocratic or literal. Could it be that the more we memorialise through elaborate legal ritual, the less we are capable of remembering as moral event?

As I have written before, what Primo Levi, the Italian chemist and Auschwitz survivor, feared most of all on his release from the death camps was disbelief. In one of his earliest books he describes a meeting with a lawyer shortly after the liberation of Auschwitz. The interview is marked by awkwardness on the part of Levi and, on the lawyer's side, incredulity. At the conclusion of the meeting, the lawyer gets up, shakes the writer's hand and 'urbanely excuses himself'.[49] There was nothing the lawyer could do in the face of this survivor testimony. He could neither believe it nor find a

---

48 Georg Schwarzenberger, *International Law and Totalitarian Lawlessness* (J Cape, 1943) 57.
49 Primo Levi, *The Truce* (Four Square Books, 1966).

legal response to it. Perhaps, then, we might consider sometimes electing the agonising uncertainties of Primo Levi over the solemn and definitive judgments of international criminal justice.[50]

Further reading

Geras, Norman, *Crimes Against Humanity: Birth of a Concept* (Manchester University Press, 2011).

Heller, Kevin and Gerry Simpson (eds), *The Hidden Histories of War Crimes Trials* (Oxford University Press, 2013).

Hill, Barry, *Peacemongers* (University of Queensland Press, 2015).

Lewis, Mark, *The Birth of the New Justice: The Internationalization of Crime and Punishment, 1919–1950* (Oxford University Press, 2014).

Moyn, Sam, *The Last Utopia* (Harvard University Press, 2010).

Sands, Philippe, *East West Street: On the Origins of Genocide and Crimes against Humanity* (Weidenfeld, 2016).

---

50 See Gerry Simpson, 'Satires of Circumstance: Some Notes on Irony and War Crimes Trials' in Carsten Stahn and Larissa van den Herik (eds), *Future Perspectives on War Crimes Trials* (TMC Asser Press, 2010) 11.

2

THE SUBJECTS OF INTERNATIONAL CRIMINAL LAW

Frédéric Mégret

I Introduction

The question of who commits international crimes may sound like a question of fact but it is, in fact, mostly a question of law. Since there are no crimes outside what the law describes as such (at least as far as the law is concerned),[1] the designation of who can commit them under the law is also a legal one. In that respect, making a particular actor into a subject of international criminal law (ICL) is a decision loaded with ambiguous meaning, both designating said category of agents to potential infamy yet simultaneously affirming that they are significant enough to at least be subjects of international law.

To make matters more complex however, the answer to the question in law is also heavily based on assessments about evolving factual questions, such as an evaluation of the degree of nefariousness of various actors on the international stage. For example, some have suggested that non-state actors have become relatively more toxic for international relations and therefore ought to be recognized as subjects, whereas others argue that the state's capacity to commit crimes remains unequalled. The debate is rife with substantive, procedural, jurisdictional, transitional and policy implications.[2] For instance, not all those who are considered to be substantively liable for international crimes may be worth prosecuting to the same extent.

---

1 Criminologists for example may define their object more liberally and see as precisely the problem, for example, the state's attempts to put its own deviance beyond the reach of the criminal law. Herman Schwendinger and Julia Schwendinger, 'Defenders of Order or Guardians of Human Rights?' (2014) 40 *Social Justice* 87.
2 Frédéric Mégret, 'Is the ICC Focusing Too Much on Non-State Actors?' in Margaret de Guzman and Diane Marie Amann (eds), *Mélanges in Honor of Bill Schabas, Arcs of Justice* (Oxford University Press, forthcoming in 2017).

It is important to note that neither domestic criminal law generally nor ICL is defined by who has been determined to be their subjects. The criminal law is first and foremost that body of law that attaches broadly punitive consequences to certain violations of norms that are considered of higher social interest, and whose breach affects public order or fundamental matters of morality. This in and of itself tells us nothing about who its subjects are or ought to be, and a variety of subject-based systems of criminal law are conceivable. In fact, although ICL's notion of who its principal subjects are has by now significantly stabilized, it has experienced various takes on international legal subjectivity. From both a legal and sociological point of view, it is nonetheless true that a system's general complexion will vary considerably depending on what are perceived to be its subjects. A system of criminal law based on individuals, for example, stands to be quite different from one based on legal entities (the state, non-state groups), or whatever hybrid system might be produced at the intersection of the two.

This chapter is a succinct introduction to the main subjects of international criminal law. It begins with the State, long the leading target of the projects of international criminal justice (II). It then charts the emergence and increased centrality of the individual as a subject of international law (III). Finally it looks more briefly at emerging developments targeting various non-state actors for a form of corporate criminal responsibility (IV).

II States

The idea of state international responsibility is among the most accepted and central elements of the international legal order. That responsibility, however, is typically understood as a responsibility for harm caused – what domestically would be referred to a as a civil (tortious or contractual) responsibility – not a responsibility for violation of public order – i.e. of a criminal kind – as such. Its fundamental rationale is to compensate those who have suffered for injury as a result of a violation of international law, not to particularly "punish" the violator or express social condemnation against the violation. This is even though some of the historically primitive means of enforcement of international law (reprisals, war) may be mistaken for a form of punishment; and it is irrespective of the fact that a population may feel "punished" as a result of broad determinations of reparations for certain violations of international law.

The historical absence of a criminal responsibility of the state reflects a broad morally agnostic attitude of international law to violations. It thrives on a non-hierarchic conception of international law and the attendant tendency to see all violations as equally problematic (a violation of a trade treaty is equally grave as a violation of the Genocide Convention). It is characteristic of an international society that remains little integrated and does not exhibit the state-like characteristics that are generally seen to be conducive to the emergence of criminal repression.

Nonetheless, in the 1920s many early international criminal law authors considered that the primary target for efforts at international criminal justice should be none but the state itself.[3] Although the expression "state crimes" is sometimes used loosely to describe crimes that have a sovereign organizational component, it tends to be strictly understood under international law as the idea of crimes committed by the state as such, qua legal person. It is this possibility, long the focus of political scientists,[4] criminologists[5] and human rights activists, that was famously discussed from 1976 onwards by the International Law Commission (ILC) as part of its effort to draft Articles on state responsibility,[6] as well as the related effort to elaborate a Code of Crimes Against the Peace and Security of Mankind. Whilst the idea of state criminality traditionally aroused scepticism in a domestic context (how could the state make its own behaviour criminal and how therefore could one cogently speak of "state crimes"?), inscribing it within international law would have dealt with this problem of circularity. Moreover, the idea of state crime in international law certainly arose against a background of increasing hierarchization of international norms (e.g. norms of *jus cogens*), perceived growth of world communal interests (e.g. *erga omnes* norms), and gradual centralization of enforcement resources. Finally, proponents of the notion helpfully dispensed with much of the psychological-cognitive apparatus of the criminal law, making crimes of state if anything the consequence of violations of particularly important norms rather than of subjective "evil."[7]

The issue was debated passionately. Its defenders saw it as potentially the crowning jewel of the international law of state responsibility, one that would have further crystallized the international legal order as having a strong *ordre public* and community dimension. Many commentators nonetheless voiced early concerns that the debate had got off on the wrong foot by having even described the issue as that of state "crimes," which confusingly brought to mind the analogue notion of individual crimes. Instead, all that was at stake was distinguishing between ordinary and extraordinary violations of international law. Ultimately, much of the original plan was eviscerated by foregoing the concept of state crime as such and replacing it by the more

---

3 Vespasien V Pella, *La guerre-crime et les criminels de guerre: réflexions sur la justice pénale internationale, ce qu'elle est et ce qu'elle devrait être* (Éditions de la Baconnière, 1964).

4 Jeffrey Ian Ross, *Controlling State Crime* (Transaction Publishers, 2000).

5 The idea of crimes of state as a distinct component of criminality has gained currency in criminology even beyond the debate on strictly international crimes, leaving little doubt that states can be fundamentally criminogenic in a variety of ways.

6 See Articles 40 and 41 of the ILC Articles on State Responsibility. Also Joseph H Weiler *et al, International Crimes of State: A Critical Analysis of the ILC's Draft Article 19 on State Responsibility* (Walter de Gruyter, 1989) Vol. 10.

7 A similar course, incidentally, has been charted in moral theorizing about collective responsibility. Marion Smiley, 'From Moral Agency to Collective Wrongs: Re-Thinking Collective Moral Responsibility' (2010) 19 *Journal of Law and Policy* 171.

neutral "serious breach of an obligation under a peremptory norm of international law." This also led to a reinterpretation of the problem not as one of repression per se but of increased international community reaction to certain breaches, important as this may be.[8] The idea that punishing states is a cumbersome and morally blunt tool has since become part of the basic common sense of ICL. For example, according to the ICTY Appeals Chamber "[u]nder present international law it is clear that states, by definition, cannot be the subject of criminal sanctions akin to those provided for in national criminal systems."[9]

It is true that states have been held liable for engaging in international crimes. For example Serbia was found by the ICJ liable for acts of genocide for failing to prevent it in conformity with its obligations under the Genocide Convention.[10] The Court also found that in theory a state could be liable even more directly for the acts of its de facto or de jure agents, although that was not the case here. This is often hailed as a progress. But it is also interesting for what it clearly does not welcome. Although the Court said that a state could "commit" genocide, the term is confusing because it is so evocative of the criminal law.[11] But, in effect, the ICJ did not give credence to the idea of a crime of state and went on to only deal with Serbia from the point of view of ordinary international responsibility. The clear message was that Serbia had not *committed* genocide at least in any criminal sense of the term, only violated peremptory norms for whose "civil" consequences it would be held liable.[12] Although the judgement depended heavily on the circumstances of the case and notably the fact that Serbia was not found to have controlled the perpetrators of genocide in Bosnia, this has been described as the "second death" of the ILC's notion of state crimes.[13]

---

8 In that respect, the final version of the Articles on state responsibility is if anything more interested in reinforcing the notion of obligations *erga omnes* than it is in entrenching a new category of state responsibility. It is not just that crimes of state are not called crimes of state, but that a collective and decentralized reaction to a violation would not typically be thought as sufficient domestically to qualify the corresponding norm as criminal in nature.

9 *Prosecutor v Blaškić* (Judgement on the Request of the Republic of Croatia for Review of the Decision of Trial Chamber II of 18 July 1997) (International Criminal Tribunal for the former Yugoslavia, Appeals Chamber, Case No IT-95-14-AR 108, 29 October 1997) [25].

10 *Application of the Convention on the Prevention and Punishment of the Crime of Genocide* (*Bosnia and Herzegovina v Yugoslavia (Serbia and Montenegro)*) (Request for the Indication of Provisional Measures) [1993] ICJ Rep 3 [52A(1)].

11 The Court's reasoning was not helped by a tendency to invoke concepts from international criminal law such as complicity. Antonio Cassese, 'On the Use of Criminal Law Notions in Determining State Responsibility for Genocide' (2007) 5 *Journal of International Criminal Justice* 875.

12 Marko Milanović, 'State Responsibility for Genocide' (2006) 17 *European Journal of International Law* 553, 562. In fact, aggravated responsibility was not even mentioned in passing, obiter dictum.

13 Pierre-Marie Dupuy, 'A Crime without Punishment' (2016) 14(4) *Journal of International Criminal Justice* 879, 880.

Indeed, even the state's ordinary international responsibility for genocide, grave as it may be, is clearly sui generis and distinct from the criminal responsibility of the individual: the state does not even have to have an intent to commit genocide, it only needs to have had effective control over agents who did, or to have failed in preventing a genocide that it could reasonably have prevented.[14] The state's international obligations may thus be broader (they include an obligation, for example, to prevent international crimes which individuals typically do not have) but they are also shallower, so that their violation is met by a less drastic social reaction.

In short, the idea that states would assent to recognizing their own criminal responsibility was always a dubious political proposition beyond the debates of a few international lawyers, and hopes that even aggravated responsibility would have a marginal role have so far been dashed. The state is an indispensable ally in enforcing individual criminal responsibility, and thus in a strong bargaining position to off-load responsibility on a different genus of actors such as individuals (significant as that concession may be, as we will see, from the point of view of state sovereignty). Nonetheless, normative and policy arguments for some kind of criminal regimen for states remain strong. Most international crimes are effectively committed within the ambit of states, even if one is reluctant to call them state crimes. If the argument for having individual responsibility directly in ICL is that the state cannot always be relied on to prosecute its own, then a fortiori given that the state cannot be relied on to prosecute itself, a criminal responsibility of the sovereign should exist in international law. In fact, unbeknownst to most commentators, the idea of state crimes has at least survived with force in the lengthy separate opinions of a one-time judge at the Inter-American Court of Human Rights.[15] Moreover, the incongruous reality that the European Union can *fine* states for their failures to comply with certain EU laws has to be squared with shrill denials that states can commit any offense.[16]

---

14 When it comes to a failure to prevent, one is on particularly shaky grounds to characterize this in terms of criminal responsibility. Some authors, in criticizing the ICJ's reasoning, have gone further, arguing that there is no prohibition as such in the Genocide Convention on states committing genocide. See Paola Gaeta, 'On what Conditions Can a State Be Held Responsible for Genocide?' (2007) 18 *European Journal of International Law* 631.

15 Judge Cançado-Trindade has frequently resorted to the notion to describe particularly grave and malicious human rights violations. See Frédéric Mégret, 'Le renouveau de la notion de crime d'État devant la Cour inter-américaine : San José reprend le flambeau abandonné à Genève et négligé à La Haye?' in Hélène Trigoudja and Ludovic Hennebel (eds), *Le particularisme interaméricain des droits de l'homme* (Pedone, 2009). Judge Cançado-Trindade considerably moderated his stance once nominated at the International Court of Justice, however.

16 Gerda Falkner, 'Fines against Member States: An Effective New Tool in EU Infringement Proceedings?' (2015) 14 *Comparative European Politics* 36.

III Individuals

International law has a deep and long-term resistance to the notion that individuals might be anything but "objects" of international law,[17] and international criminal law's own production of the individual as a subject must be questioned in that context. For a long time, international law recognized at best that certain behaviour should be criminalized domestically, but international lawyers would not typically have thought that such criminality was synonymous with *international* criminality (i.e. criminality directly under international law).[18] It is true that the resistance to individuals being subjects is historically mostly tied to reservations about their ability to claim their rights directly under international law, only a secondary consideration of ICL which is primarily concerned with imposing onerous obligations on individuals.[19] The wariness towards making the individual into a subject is nonetheless anchored in the perceived need to restrict subjecthood to states when it comes to developing, enforcing or even simply being bound by international law. Part of the reason for this is that targeting individuals directly means that whatever once stood as the *domaine réservé* of states is likely to be all the more scrutinized; another reason is that addressing individuals directly, "above" their state and effectively instructing them to ignore or even violate domestic orders or laws is more than many states could historically countenance.

If anything, both criminal and individual liability belonged, as far as classical international law was concerned, to domestic law. International law might objectively encourage and promote the imposition of domestic criminal law for international law purposes (this is the case in relation to a range of transnational criminal offences), going as far as to create international tribunals that partly enforce domestic norms (as in the case of the Special Court for Lebanon's jurisdiction over terrorism under Lebanese law or the Special Court for Sierra Leone's jurisdiction over arson and pillage under Sierra Leonean law). States may be internationally liable for crimes committed by their citizens or persons within their jurisdiction but this is irrespective of the criminal responsibility of the individual in either domestic or international law. Domestic crimes appear at best in international law as acts imputable to the state, raising questions of fact regardless of their characterization under domestic law.

17 George Manner, 'The Object Theory of the Individual in International Law' (1952) 46 *American Journal of International Law* 428.
18 In fact this internationally-mandated domestic criminality can be, strictly speaking, an alternative rather than a complement to direct responsibility under international law, based as it is on a recognition that the state is primarily responsible for reining in individuals within its jurisdiction.
19 Obviously the "international criminal defendant" is entitled to procedural rights as part of his or her trial, but these are very much limited and derivative of the otherwise rather unenviable status as a defendant.

It is against this inhospitable background that individual responsibility in ICL has nonetheless come to assume a domineering position. Debates on the status of individuals in international law do have an old pedigree in international legal history in a context where the general and exclusive focus on the state is a relatively late international legal development, and where concerns with a broader "civitas maxima" or Humanity are as old as the discipline. Moreover the idea that individuals might commit international crimes has long been accepted in relation to at least one very specific category of individuals in international law: pirates. Pirates by definition commit offences in their own name and not for or as part of a state (in which case their behaviour would immediately be classified as something else such as privateers, corsairs, buccaneers, etc.). They are thus in a sense not only the original but also the quintessential "international criminal." Piracy's universal jurisdiction regime, however, was always a bit of an anomaly, created less because pirates had somehow shattered the glass ceiling of international subjecthood by the sheer malevolence of their ways, than to solve a more conventional problem of jurisdiction in a space subject to no state jurisdiction.[20]

This precedent nonetheless made the case that nothing in principle barred individual criminal responsibility in international law. Individual responsibility emerged from this background where states were and are still seen as the principal subjects of international law (regardless of whether they can commit crimes). Several factors no doubt precipitated its emergence. Senior Nazis at Nuremberg "helpfully" provided a case where the sheer evil of a few individuals had had a larger than life impact on the destinies of a state. As the narrative goes, in punishing individuals international criminal justice would avoid blaming an entire population through broad collective guilt, in ways that might have sown the seeds of future conflicts, as the Versailles settlement had arguably done. Moreover, the general rise of human rights in the second half of the twentieth century increasingly highlighted the individual as a beneficiary and agent of human rights in ways that meshed well with the newfound focus on individual responsibility in ICL.[21]

More contingent factors no doubt played and continue to play a role: for example, whilst sovereign immunity (the immunity of states as such) remains very much alive, the immunity of individuals before the courts of third-states has proved to be much more fragile. If at all applicable in the case of sitting heads of states and senior officials, it is not effective once they are no longer in office and therefore do not enjoy the trappings of personal immunity. This makes prosecutions against individuals a likelier remedy than suing,

20 Eugene Kontorovich, 'The Piracy Analogy: Modern Universal Jurisdiction's Hollow Foundation' (2004) 45 *Harvard International Law Journal* 183.
21 Louis B Sohn, 'The New International Law: Protection of the Rights of Individuals Rather than States' (1982) 32 *American University Law Review* 1.

not to mention prosecuting (if it were even possible), states. Where criminal responsibility of the individual could once only be domestic, it can henceforth lie with international law alone, even (and perhaps most importantly) in cases where it is not actionable domestically. If anything, international humanitarian law or human rights law have now made the prosecution of certain individuals accused of grave crimes (torture, war crimes) into a state obligation with a view to fighting impunity and upholding victims' right to an effective remedy.[22]

Here individual responsibility has clearly not only preceded and survived the debate on state crime in international law, but in practice been wildly more successful as a political-legal construct. Especially when it comes to atrocity offences, offences that from a criminal law point of view are characterized by a high degree of "evil" and commonly associated with subjective mens rea, the individual, already the natural target of most domestic criminal systems, may always have been a more natural repository of criminal responsibility. In fact, there is a sense in which the rediscovery of individual responsibility in the early 1990s has coincided with and maybe helped precipitate the abandonment of a strong notion of "crimes of state."[23] Individual criminal responsibility for international crimes may even be increasingly separate from state responsibility of the ordinary variant, as individuals engage in international crimes as part of non-state actors or perhaps even as agents of the state acting ultra vires.[24]

The emergence of individual responsibility was not simply consumed with its proclamation at Nuremberg. Rather, it required the slow, multi-decade dismantling of structures of thought inherited from international law, and which had traditionally framed the relationship of sovereigns to their agents. The substantive imbrication of individual criminality within state structures, in particular, led to the frequent invocation of a particular genus of defences known as defences of "superior order." Indeed, individuals working for states have long sought to draw on this association to deny their own specific responsibility. This is relatively harder to do, for instance, in the case of an individual war crime or act of torture committed ultra vires (although the state's responsibility might still be engaged under its broad obligation to implement the Geneva Conventions or its obligations to "protect" in

22 Diane F Orentlicher, 'Settling Accounts: The Duty to Prosecute Human Rights Violations of a Prior Regime' (1991) *Yale Law Journal* 2537.
23 Frédéric Mégret, 'Epilogue to an Endless Debate: The International Criminal Court's Third Party Jurisdiction and the Looming Revolution of International Law' (2001) 12 *European Journal of International Law* 247.
24 Gaeta, above n 14. Although the latter possibility may seem remote in the sense that one would expect the state to quickly realize or at least negligently fail to realize that international crimes are being engaged in by one of its agents, the scenario is not entirely unlikely if for example the state agent is complicit with a non-state actor or a foreign state.

human rights law); but it is relatively easier when, for example, the crime was committed in service of, with the full knowledge of, indeed at the instigation and under the orders of the state. For all intents and purposes, the graver crimes under international law certainly fit into that description.

Indeed, for a long time not even war crimes, if they were officially condoned, could be attributed to their individual perpetrators. This is what was traditionally known in international law as the "act of state" doctrine which existed in the early days as a strong substantive (as a defence) rather than merely procedural (as part of the justification of ratione materiae immunity) construct, allowing both the state to oppose prosecutions of individuals for acts that it considered to be its own, and for individual defendants to reciprocally claim that they had acted on the state's behalf. It is worth noting that, although states have in specific circumstances been only too happy to assign individual responsibility to individuals in ICL "abandoning them to their fate" as it were, they also have a vested interest pulling in the opposite direction to ensure that the state as such is the only one that can theoretically be made answerable – even if that means that in practice no one is. A contrario, certain individuals, notably civil servants and particularly those working for the armed forces, may traditionally have expected that a quid pro quo for their relatively blind obedience to orders would be a commitment by the state to take responsibility for their (its) acts.[25]

It should nonetheless be clear that the starkness with which the act of state doctrine constructed the opposition between state and individual responsibility rested on rather arbitrary doctrinal foundations, not to mention an improbable psycho-social construction and a not very defensible policy framework. For example, if individuals can only be guilty of war crimes to the extent that they committed such crimes "independently" of the state or any group structure, one may well wonder when and how such circumstances might arise given that war is almost by definition engaged in by troops associated with states. The strict focus on the state contemplated by the doctrine also does not do justice to the fact that one can defer to a notion of corporate agency – seeing the sum as bigger than the part – yet be attentive and sensitive to the very real and dynamic role that certain individuals play within larger structures. Finally, from a policy point of view, the point of *making* individuals responsible is also to constitute a reality that will then encourage them to be more attuned to the consequences of their acts even as they operate within larger corporate structures.

---

25 It is worth noting that the failure by a state to take responsibility for the acts of its agents can entirely modify the nature of what those agents are doing. For example, if an individual is recognized as a state's soldier, then his or her killing of enemy troops may be privileged under the laws of war; if he or she is not so recognized, he or she then must be considered to have acted in a purely private capacity and to be solely answerable for what then becomes an evident crime under the domestic law of the country where the killing occurred.

As a result, it is probably the case today that a state could not invoke the theory of the act-of-state even if it wanted to forcefully endorse conduct committed by its agents, thereby "re-collectivizing" responsibility. Individual criminal responsibility in international law obviously has a strong *ordre public* dimension so that the state could not "take the blame" for its agents and absorb their guilt into its responsibility.[26] One might argue that individual responsibility for international crimes has acquired *jus cogens* status: two states, for example, could not agree to its exclusion by holding each other liable qua states, any more than a state could grant immunity to its agents domestically in exchange for recognizing its responsibility. Once the substantive defence of "act of state" was rejected, it was only a matter of time before its residual jurisdictional corollary in the form of immunities was rejected as well. In effect, developments in universal jurisdiction[27] make it increasingly hard for officials to claim ratione materiae immunity from third-party domestic courts (a fortiori international courts): if an act is not an act of state for the purposes of substantive law, then nor can it be an act of state for the purpose of immunity.

In retrospect, ICL as a project of cosmopolitan individual responsibility for the gravest offences against mankind needed to challenge the act of state doctrine head on, or risk most individual "crimes" being absorbed back into state responsibility. As a result, ICL has been nothing but steadfast, when it comes to individual responsibility, in its insistence that the act of state notion has no place at least as a substantive defence. Perhaps first and foremost, obedience to state laws and orders, simply being an agent of the state or even having the state endorse one's acts are not *defences* for the individual subject. The idea that the act of state doctrine cannot be invoked as a defence originated at the Nuremberg tribunal in relation to, notably, war crimes and crimes against humanity. As the tribunal put it: "The authors (of criminal acts) cannot shelter themselves behind their official position in order to be freed from punishment in appropriate proceedings. . . The very essence of the Charter is that individuals have international duties".[28]

Over time, we thus witness the emergence of a strong notion of individual criminal responsibility in international law. The individual is responsible irrespective of the responsibility of his or her state, even if the state is not liable under international law and, as it were, in his or her own name. However, the irreducibility

---

26 Indeed, the state's ability to do so has been challenged even in ordinary spying cases. Michael Pugh, 'Legal Aspects of the Rainbow Warrior Affair' (1987) 36 *International & Comparative Law Quarterly* 655; JJ Carlisle, 'Extradition of Government Agents as a Municipal Law Remedy for State-Sponsored Kidnapping' (1993) *California Law Review* 1541.

27 Dapo Akande and Sangeeta Shah, 'Immunities of State Officials, International Crimes, and Foreign Domestic Courts' (2010) 21 *European Journal of International Law* 815, 839–46.

28 Nuremberg Judgement (International Military Tribunal, 1 October 1946) in *Trial of the Major War Criminals before the International Military Tribunal* (Nuremberg, 1947) 223.

of that responsibility should not be over emphasized. Most international criminals today are, effectively, not "pirates." They only commit their crimes as part of their embeddedness in larger structures and neither "in their own name" nor, primarily, for private gain. This is quite evident for example in the very definition of crimes, most of which require an organizational element that for most intents and purposes will be synonymous with a "state policy" or at least the policy of significant collectives.

For example, crimes against humanity require a state policy or, since the Rome Statute, at least an organizational policy.[29] The state-dependency of certain crimes is also particularly evident in the case of aggression, a crime that by definition needs to result from state behaviour even if individuals can be made accountable for it. Even when it comes to war crimes, it is implicit that they are committed in international armed conflicts as a result of two states engaging in hostilities and in non-international armed conflict, a state or a non-state actor doing the same. In other words, the responsibility of individuals is a responsibility for leading or obeying the state or an organized armed group, not a responsibility for engaging in crimes in isolation. For some, the state-centric character of international crimes is so obvious that the rule of individual responsibility is itself presented as merely a secondary rule of the regime of state responsibility,[30] a view that has become quite unfashionable[31] but which in its excesses does capture a long-existing and still relatively influential train of thought in international law.

Even as substantively the organizational or collective criteria of definition of international crimes have been loosened, it arguably should remain a priority to prosecute those most responsible for heinous crimes, and they are even more likely to operate at the helm of broad structures of which the state remains the most typical. It is hard in particular to imagine the ICC devoting much time to prosecuting "Dr Strangelove, Goldfinger, and the Joker."[32] The story of individual responsibility in international law, in other words, is one of imperfect emancipation from the state matrix and, in a sense, the continuing shadow that the sovereign casts on its success.

IV Non-state actors

The criminal responsibility of non-state actors in international law faces a double challenge: like states, they are collectives which may face scepticism about

---

29 William A Schabas, 'State Policy as an Element of International Crimes' (2008) *Journal of Criminal Law & Criminology* 953.

30 Rafaëlle Maison, *La responsabilité individuelle pour crime d'État en droit international public* (Bruylant 2004).

31 Beatrice I Bonafé, 'Maison, Rafaëlle. La responsabilité individuelle pour crime d'État en droit international public' (2006) 17 *European Journal of International Law* 312.

32 William A Schabas, 'Prosecuting Dr Strangelove, Goldfinger, and the Joker at the International Criminal Court: Closing the Loopholes' (2010) 23 *Leiden Journal of International Law* 847.

their responsibility; but unlike states they are not subjects of international law and some are not even subjects of domestic law, decreasing the odds that they would be considered significant or legitimate enough for international legal cognizance. A criminal system, needless to say, can only punish persons that "exist."

As a matter of fact, the criminal responsibility of non-state actors has received only limited and partial recognition so far. On the one hand, some states do recognize the criminal responsibility of corporations, accrediting the idea that this is a legitimate and credible modality of criminalization. Moreover, the growing transnational practice of engaging the *civil* responsibility of corporations, although it cannot simply be assumed to translate automatically into the language of criminal law, suggests that an evolution is at least possible.[33] The language of transnational civil litigation, in fact, in ways reminiscent of the practice associated with state responsibility, often espouses criminal law concepts, as when plaintiffs in Alien Tort Claims Act (ATCA) cases invoke the complicity of corporations with state violations.[34] The more corporations are found liable in torts for what would otherwise be international crimes if they were committed by individuals, the more arguments about the possible international criminal liability of corporations will gain currency.[35] Finally, the fact that leading corporate agents (for example, CEOs) have been found individually liable domestically for committing international crimes, not only suggests that we are only one step removed from liability of the corporation itself,[36] but that this additional step should be embraced (just as the criminal liability of senior state leaders should be considered to be conducive to at least ordinary international if not criminal responsibility of the state).[37]

More developments may therefore be expected in a context where non-state actors are perceived as having an increasingly outsize role in harming international order, and where nothing in principle stands in the way of a further diversification of ICL's subjects. The fact that non-state actors are already considered to be bound by certain norms of customary international

---

33 Andrew Clapham, 'Extending International Criminal Law beyond the Individual to Corporations and Armed Opposition Groups' (2008) 6 *Journal of International Criminal Justice* 899.

34 Shriram Bhashyam, 'Knowledge or Purpose: The Khulumani Litigation and the Standard for Aiding and Abetting Liability under the Alien Tort Claims Act Note' (2008) 30 *Cardozo Law Review* 245.

35 There is a certain tendency to treat the talk of "complicity" as equally preparing the ground for arguments in favour of civil or criminal responsibility. See Anita Ramasastry, 'Corporate Complicity: From Nuremberg to Rangoon -- An Examination of Forced Labor Cases and their Impact on the Liability of Multinational Corporations' (2002) 20 *Berkeley Journal of International Law* 91.

36 Doug Cassel, 'Corporate Aiding and Abetting of Human Rights Violations: Confusion in the Courts' (2008) 6 *Northwestern University Journal of International Human Rights* 304.

37 Harmen van der Wilt, 'Corporate Criminal Responsibility for International Crimes: Exploring the Possibilities' (2013) 12 *Chinese Journal of International Law* 43.

law, notably as belligerents under the laws of war in non-international armed conflicts, suggests that there is nothing insuperable about recognizing them as subjects. With every obligation under international law should come consequences and even those who consider that non-state actors cannot "technically" engage in, say, crimes against humanity, they are still prohibited from doing so. Indeed, unlike states to which international law presumptively defers, there is at least no particular international *majestas* in corporations that would militate against their criminal liability. This means that prosecuting corporations would not raise issues of "act of state" or immunity. And although international law does not by itself anticipate criminal responsibility of non-state actors, it certainly does not prohibit it, including in relation to international crimes.[38] Corporate criminal responsibility, whatever it might be under international law, is a matter certainly left to the "general part" of the criminal law of every country, leaving a window open for certain domestic systems to forge ahead with domestic prosecutions of corporations for international crimes,[39] in ways that might well feed into an international self-fulfilling prophecy. Finally, there is no reason to think that situations of impunity would not arise in relation to non-state actors, so that in practice states and victims might at least in some cases require the support of international prosecutorial efforts.

On the other hand, it is important to be clear about the extent of these developments and the fact that, for the most part, although it would be theoretically and technically possible, the criminal responsibility of non-state actors remains elusive at this stage. For example, one may be a subject of international law for some purposes but not others, so that the argument that non-state groups are bound by certain principles of international law does not mean per se that they can be criminally punished. In fact, belligerent groups are if anything expected to become liable for their violations only if and when they become a state, through the medium of a sort of retroactive state responsibility, thus suggesting that outside this hypothesis their juridical status remains very uncertain. As to international criminal responsibility of corporations, it suffers from the lack of evident international jurisdictional forums and was rejected specifically in Rome.[40] Its dynamism as a domestic law concept will not translate easily into international law. Moreover, this is

---

38 W Cory Wanless, 'Corporate Liability for International Crimes under Canada's Crimes against Humanity and War Crimes Act' (2009) 7 *Journal of International Criminal Justice* 201.

39 James G Stewart, 'The Turn to Corporate Criminal Liability for International Crimes: Transcending the Alien Tort Statute' (2014) 47 *New York University Journal of International Law and Politics* 121.

40 Wolfgang Kaleck and Miriam Saage-Maaß, 'Corporate Accountability for Human Rights Violations Amounting to International Crimes: The Status Quo and its Challenges' (2010) 8 *Journal of International Criminal Justice* 699.

one area where legal systems are still very divided, making corporate criminal responsibility an unlikely candidate for universalization as a general principle of law or as a rule of customary international law.

Although loose talk of "complicity" of corporations in international crimes might lead one to conclude that corporate responsibility is already a feature of ICL, the term is better understood as part of an effort, typically emanating from the human rights sector and quite focused on domestic (albeit typically transnational) litigation, to emphasize the not particularly controversial fact that corporations can, if nothing else, contribute to harm that may otherwise be criminal if committed by certain more conventional international law subjects (i.e. states or individuals). Findings under domestic laws such as the ATCA that individuals have been complicit in international crimes remain, in essence, civil findings, a bit in the way a state might be found to have engaged its international responsibility for violating the Genocide Convention whilst not actually having – criminally speaking – committed the crime of genocide. For "complicity in harms" to become "complicity in crimes" in any given system of domestic law or international law will require more than semantic slippage.

Prodding the reasons for this relative neglect may nonetheless yield interesting insights about the dynamics of subjecthood in international law. To begin with, some of the arguments in support of making non-state actors criminally liable qua non-state actors may be half-hearted given the relative ease with which specific individuals within non-state actors can be targeted for prosecution in their own name anyhow.[41] The original Nuremberg "corporate" trials were, in effect, prosecutions of corporate *officials*, such as those working for IG Farben, Flick and Krupp.[42] Criminologically, it is easier to think of these individuals (e.g. a CEO or a rebel leader) as having had an outsize role within their respective collective structures, given how non-state actors operate at relatively close-quarters compared to states. One might say that individual agency is "just below the surface" in the relatively less complex corporate structures of non-state actors. Moreover, individuals will have joined non-state actors willingly and should a priori be more at liberty to leave them than the state under whose jurisdiction they fall, leaving much less scope for superior orders as a defence.[43] As to individuals

---

41 Pammela Q Saunders, 'Rethinking Corporate Human Rights Accountability' (2014) 89 *Tulane Law Review* 603.

42 Indeed, in the months preceding Nuremberg, the possibility of prosecuting corporations was seen as entirely available but prosecutions of individuals were preferred on largely pragmatic grounds. Jonathan A Bush, 'The Prehistory of Corporations and Conspiracy in International Criminal Law: What Nuremberg Really Said' (2009) 109 *Columbia Law Review* 1094, 1198–1200.

43 It is difficult to divest oneself of one's nationality, but it is relatively easier to not join an armed group or to put an end to an employment contract.

working for collectives (e.g. an armed group) that do not have legal personality, concerns with paying heed to these collectives will evaporate ab initio. Of course, the criminal responsibility in international law of individuals working for non-state actors, whilst it tells us something about the scope of *individual* responsibility and the circumstances in which it is likely to occur, is not as such determinative of (and may in fact detract from) the question of corporate responsibility.

From a more substantive point of view, some of the arguments against criminal responsibility of the state surely apply mutatis mutandis to non-state actors. If one is sceptical of state criminal responsibility on the grounds that individuals are never far behind the levers of crime even in the most complex of human organizations and should rightly be the focus of international efforts, then a fortiori one is likely to be wary of the corporate responsibility of simpler human organizations in which individual agency is much closer to the surface. Any criminal theory fixated on the centrality of mens rea and moral fault as psychological concepts is likely to find continuing problems with imputation to corporate actors.

But the arguments for excluding the criminal responsibility of non-state actors also include deeper and more specific reservations about endowing them with direct subjecthood under international criminal law. First, this is one area where concerns with the state-centric majesty of international law are at their highest. It is one thing to consider that individuals may incur criminal responsibility but the recognition of non-state actors as autonomous subjects of international law would endow them with a paradoxical legitimacy that would more directly clash with the state's monopoly of subjecthood. In other words, the point is that the interest in not granting them subjecthood at all trumps the interest of granting them one even for the otherwise desirable goal of punishing certain crimes. That interest in denying subjecthood is of course magnified when it comes to armed groups which more directly challenge states' monopoly of legitimate violence. It is here that ICL's more general international legal guardianship function appears.[44]

Second, some non-state actors are clearly unfit for attribution of criminal responsibility qua non-state actors. This is especially the case with non-state actors such as rebel movements or terrorist groups which are merely actors in the social rather than legal sense, and who do not have legal existence under domestic law. This means that either it is impractical to punish such groups

---

44 For the similar argument, notably in the context of the laws of war, that one should not recognize, even indirectly, terrorist groups as belligerents lest one legitimize them in the process of fighting them, see Mary Ellen O'Connell, 'The Legal Case against the Global War on Terror Symposium: Terrorism on Trial' (2004) 36 *Case Western Reserve Journal of International Law* 349.

as such because the law has no hold on them or that punishing them would paradoxically entail recognizing a certain legal quality that they have never otherwise been able to lay claim to. This is unlike individuals for example who are not subjects of international law ordinarily, but are evidently subjects of domestic law with a legal existence and who are therefore, all other things being equal, a more natural candidate for international legal subjecthood. The non-legal character of terrorist groups, by contrast, means that as far as ICL is concerned, they might as well not exist.

Third, even when it comes to legal non-state actors and even if one is sympathetic to the notion that they may commit crimes, arguments may be made to the effect that, at least on grounds of opportunity, it is not useful to think of them as directly subjected to international law. Such arguments include the notion that corporate crime ought and should be punished domestically as part of a natural division of labour between domestic and international law. Whereas state responsibility (criminal or not) and individual criminal responsibility associated with the state make sense in international law as pragmatic responses in order to circumvent the problem of impunity, states may at least be less likely to accept that they would systematically tolerate the criminal doings of corporations in their midst.

V Conclusion

This chapter has sought to present a sketch of the main subjects of ICL. The story of ICL's grappling with the notion of subjecthood shows a dramatic evolution from a focus on the state, to a radically different emphasis on the individual. That emphasis is only very marginally contested by either the now quasi-moribund idea of crimes of state or the emerging suggestion that non-state actors, at least those endowed with legal personality, should be held criminally accountable under international law. Neither the effort to make states or non-state actors criminally liable have been terribly successful at least so far, for reasons that are not dissimilar.

The focus on the individual may reflect the increasing dominance of penal modes of thought that are led naturally to think of criminal responsibility as individual, as opposed to international ones whose starting point is the state or at least significant non-state actors. But the individual's responsibility is a peculiar one that is in practice and probably also in law almost entirely derivative of the acts of broader, corporate or non-natural actors, first and foremost among which is the state. As to the responsibility of non-state actors, it sits oddly between these two extremes: close enough to individual responsibility that it may not seem worth the bother to prosecute the corporate actor as such; too far from the magnitude of state harm and too vulnerable to state prosecutions for their crimes to raise the right kind of international alarm.

Thinking about the evolution from state to individual responsibility as well as emerging debates on the criminal responsibility of non-state actors suggests a discipline that is evolving dynamically and shaped by more than court decisions, treaties and customs. There is an intellectual substratum to all of these questions that is rarely acknowledged but is nonetheless tremendously present. The "production" of a particular theory of international subjecthood is reliant on ontological ideas about who is most responsible as well as instrumental ideas about who it makes most sense to make responsible. Understandings of history have a role, as does moral theory and our evolving concepts of the criminal law. Emphasizing the responsibility of some actors under ICL has implications for other actors as well as other forms of responsibility. For example, the criminal responsibility of a head of state is likely to have implications for state responsibility; conversely, individual responsibility will rely at least tangentially on determinations of wrongdoing by the state or non-state groups even as their criminal liability is hard or impossible to engage.

There is much need, it would seem, for a unified and integrated theory of subjecthood in ICL that is then better integrated with general international law. One of the great unsolved riddles of international criminal law, in this context, is the fundamental nature of international criminality. If international crimes are not strictly committed by individuals, or rather if they are committed by individuals only to the extent that they participate in larger organizational designs, what is actually the gravity of individual responsibility? Is the individual not being made to pay for atrocities that largely transcend him?[45]

It would seem that, criminologically speaking, the most promising avenue is to see international criminality as symbiotic, as always involving individuals preying on structures and structures reciprocally preying on individuals. The degree will vary in each case, but fundamentally individuals need the force-multipliers that are states or large organizations, whereas obviously states and organizations need individuals to execute their deeds. State or non-state actor responsibility, then, especially in its elusive criminal dimension, might be reframed not as merely the international act of wronging "others," but as the much more intimate one of abusing one's own agents in the pursuit of criminal collective ends. Individual criminal responsibility, in turn, is the responsibility of either leading a state (or a non-state group), even though leading a state is never exhaustive of the state's own responsibility; or it might be the guilt implicit in allowing oneself to be abusively led by the state (or a non-state actor) down a path of international criminality. Theories of "system criminality" seem to capture this peculiar configuration of the individual and the collective.

---

45 Frédéric Mégret, 'Les angles morts de la responsabilité pénale individuelle en droit international' (2013) 71 *Revue interdisciplinaire d'études juridiques* 83.

Further reading

Bush, Jonathan A, 'The Prehistory of Corporations and Conspiracy in International Criminal Law: What Nuremberg Really Said' (2009) 109 *Columbia Law Review* 1094.

Dupuy, Pierre-Marie, 'A Crime without Punishment' (2016) 14(4) *Journal of International Criminal Justice* 879.

Van der Wilt, Harmen, 'Corporate Criminal Responsibility for International Crimes: Exploring the Possibilities' (2013) 12 *Chinese Journal of International Law* 43.

3

THE IDEA OF TRANSITIONAL JUSTICE

International criminal justice and beyond

Wendy Lambourne

I Introduction

In this chapter, international criminal law (ICL) is considered as part of a larger transitional justice discourse where it plays a significant role in the context of radical political transformations and societies emerging from violent conflict.[1] Transitional justice is concerned with the twin aims of dealing with the past in order to build peace and democracy for the future, and therefore intent on attaining 'peace with justice' in the long term rather than being stuck in the presumed binary dilemma of 'peace versus justice'.[2] Whilst not denying the real choices that sometimes need to be made about whether to prioritise the pursuit of war criminals or a peace agreement at a particular point in time,[3] this chapter sees transitional justice as being more inclusive in terms of both the types of justice and actors involved, and the time period over which these different types

---

1 This chapter draws in part on my original theoretical and empirical research published previously including especially Wendy Lambourne, 'Transitional Justice and Peacebuilding after Mass Violence' (2009) 3 *International Journal of Transitional Justice* 28; Wendy Lambourne, 'What Are the Pillars of Transitional Justice? The United Nations and the Justice Cascade in Burundi' (2014) 13 *Macquarie Law Journal* 41; Wendy Lambourne, 'Transformative Justice, Reconciliation and Peacebuilding' in Susanne Buckley Zistel *et al* (eds), *Transitional Justice Theories* (Routledge, 2014) 19-39.
2 Ruti Teitel refers to the early debates over 'peace versus justice', 'truth versus justice' and 'punishment versus impunity' as being derived from 'a somewhat artificial zero sum and dichotomous framework'. Ruti G Teitel, *Globalizing Transitional Justice: Contemporary Essays* (Oxford University Press, 2014) xiii.
3 As was perceived to be the case in Cambodia, for example, where the decision was made as part of the Paris Peace negotiations to forego accountability for the Khmer Rouge atrocities in order to pursue peace. Suzannah Linton, *Reconciliation in Cambodia* (Documentation Center of Cambodia, 2004) 42.

of justice can be sought and attained. In some cases, prosecutions may follow years after the negotiation of a peace agreement, as in Cambodia, for example; or a criminal tribunal may be established at the same time as a truth commission, as in Sierra Leone where both mechanisms were envisaged to contribute to peacebuilding after the end of the civil war. Transitional justice is thus an interdisciplinary and multifaceted enterprise, requiring coordination over time and across different mechanisms between international law and other disciplines, where justice and peace are seen as inextricably intertwined.

ICL is intended to ensure individual accountability for past war crimes, genocide and crimes against humanity, and to deter the perpetrators of future mass human rights violations.[4] However, ICL's potential to deal effectively and comprehensively with such grave atrocity crimes is inherently limited. This is especially so when the entire population of a country has been affected and there is widespread trauma and societal breakdown, with large numbers of victims and perpetrators, as in post-genocide Rwanda, for example. A broader, more comprehensive or holistic approach to justice is required in such circumstances of political and socioeconomic transition, as suggested by the transformative approach to transitional justice discussed in this chapter. In addition to legal accountability and retribution for past human rights violations, as provided by international criminal justice, transformative justice is concerned with the socioeconomic and political transformations regarded as necessary for building a sustainable peace. The transformative justice model proposed here also emphasises the need for psychosocial transformation and healing in local communities to support peacebuilding and reconciliation through restorative as well as retributive justice.[5]

In settings as diverse as Timor Leste and Sierra Leone, for example, empirical research has found that survivors of mass violence view socioeconomic justice as necessary for transitional justice to address the root causes of the conflict and thus to build a sustainable peace.[6] In South Africa, the Chair of the Truth and Reconciliation Commission (TRC), Archbishop Desmond Tutu, called for forgiveness and reconciliation as part of transitional justice, while in Timor Leste the Commission for Reception, Truth and Reconciliation incorporated indigenous rituals in its community reconciliation process.[7] In both cases, transitional justice went far beyond its

---

4 See Part II of this book for an explanation and discussion of the crimes covered by ICL.

5 Lambourne, 'Transitional Justice and Peacebuilding after Mass Violence', above n 1.

6 See, for example, Lambourne, 'Transformative Justice, Reconciliation and Peacebuilding', above n 1.

7 See, for example, Desmond Tutu, *No Future without Forgiveness* (Rider, 1999); Wendy Lambourne, 'Unfinished Business: The Commission for Reception, Truth and Reconciliation and Justice and Reconciliation in East Timor' in Lilian A Barra and Steven D Roper (eds), *Development of Institutions of Human Rights* (Palgrave Macmillan, 2010) 195.

traditional remit as international criminal justice associated with international lawyers, diplomats and human rights advocates.[8]

Arguments about what constitutes transitional justice commonly rely on normative goals and assumptions, such as what transitional justice should or must comprise, coming from (international) law as a normative endeavour and a focus on the liberal democratic peace paradigm and human rights norms. Sometimes these normative arguments may be supplemented or replaced by arguments derived from theories about sustainable peace, conflict transformation, democracy or development. The limits of transitional justice can also be defined based on empirical or praxis-based evidence, drawing on observations of *what people do* and inquiry about *what people say they want*, or on evidence of impact or effectiveness of different transitional justice interventions. My research and perspective on transitional justice has entailed a critique of normative assumptions drawing on empirical evidence of what people do and say they want, combined with the application of theories of peacebuilding and conflict transformation, as will be discussed later in this chapter.[9]

After starting with an overview of the origins and evolution of transitional justice in theory and practice, including definitions and models of transitional justice from the United Nations (UN) and other key actors and scholars, the chapter provides a critique of the dominant paradigm of transitional justice as international criminal justice. The limitations of a solely retributive, prosecutorial model of justice are highlighted and particular mention is made of the impact on scholarship of a criminal justice approach as compared with other disciplines and research methods in transitional justice. The discussion then moves to consideration of the relationship between peacebuilding theory and transitional justice, and concludes with discussion of a model of transformative justice which encompasses the multiple justice needs of transitional societies and the engagement of local populations in a long-term process of social transformation.

---

8 Despite these developments in practice, some scholars have argued against the expansion of the transitional justice field, including Christine Bell, 'Transitional Justice, Interdisciplinarity and the State of the "Field" or "Non-Field"' (2009) 3 *International Journal of Transitional Justice* 27; Lars Waldorf, 'Anticipating the Past: Transitional Justice and Socio-Economic Wrongs' (2012) 21 *Social & Legal Studies* 171. Scholars who have argued for an expanded definition of transitional justice include Lambourne, 'Transitional Justice and Peacebuilding after Mass Violence', above n 1; Paul Gready and Simon Robins, 'From Transitional to Transformative Justice: A New Agenda for Practice' (2014) 8 *International Journal of Transitional Justice* 339. See also Teitel, above n 2, for a discussion of the implications of the expanded focus of transitional justice.

9 Empirical evidence is derived from field research interviews conducted with survivors and perpetrators of mass violence, civil society and some government representatives in Rwanda (1998, 2005 & 2012), Cambodia (1999 & 2009), Timor Leste (2004), Sierra Leone (2006 & 2016) and Burundi (2012-2016).

II Origins and historical development of transitional justice

Transitional justice is a distinct field of theory, research and practice which has emerged and developed significantly primarily since the end of the Cold War. While some methods of transitional justice were pioneered in the form of the post-World War II Nuremberg and Tokyo trials, it was the democratic transitions in Europe, South Africa and Latin America that led to the first use of the term 'transitional justice' in a three-volume set edited by Neil Kritz of the US Institute of Peace in 1995 entitled 'Transitional Justice: How Emerging Democracies Reckon with Former Regimes'.[10] This was followed by the seminal work by Ruti Teitel *Transitional Justice* in 2000,[11] the creation of the international non-governmental organisation (NGO) the International Center for Transitional Justice (ICTJ) in 2001, and the launch of the field's flagship journal, the *International Journal of Transitional Justice*, in 2007.

Transitional justice was thus originally associated with the justice that was needed to deal with the past human rights violations perpetrated by autocratic or authoritarian regimes which had been discredited, defeated or overthrown to make way for a new democratic government. Common methods of dealing with the past, especially in post-Communist Europe, included restitution and lustration, or removal of those implicated in the perpetration of human rights violations from holding public office.[12] In Latin America, as well as in South Africa, historical inquiries or truth commissions were created in order to uncover the past violations and establish the truth of what had occurred in the country prior to the transition.[13] In order to enable a peaceful transition, amnesties were often granted, either blanket amnesty or conditional amnesty as in South Africa, where the TRC pioneered a more forward-looking approach focusing on restorative justice rather than retributive justice through prosecutions.[14]

10 Neil J Kritz, *Transitional Justice: How Emerging Democracies Reckon with Former Regimes* (United States Institute of Peace Press, 1995).
11 Ruti G Teitel, *Transitional Justice* (Oxford University Press, 2000).
12 Melissa S Williams and Rosemary Nagy, 'Introduction' in Melissa S Williams, Rosemary Nagy and Jon Elster (eds), *Transitional Justice* (New York University Press, 2012) 3.
13 For a comprehensive study of truth commissions see Priscilla B Hayner, *Unspeakable Truths: Transitional Justice and the Challenge of Truth Commissions* (Routledge, 2nd ed, 2011). See also Andrew G Reiter, 'Difficult but Ultimately Rewarding: Lessons from Transitional Justice in Latin America' in Kirsten J Fisher and Robert Stewart (eds), *Transitional Justice and the Arab Spring* (Routledge, 2014) 76.
14 Charles Villa-Vicencio, 'Restorative Justice in Social Context: The South African Truth and Reconciliation Commission' in Neil J Biggar (ed.), *Burying the Past: Making Peace and Doing Justice after Civil Conflict* (Georgetown University Press, 2001) 207. For a discussion of truth-telling and amnesties as transitional justice alternatives see David Bloomfield, Theresa Barnes and Luc Huyse, *Reconciliation after Violent Conflict: A Handbook* (International IDEA, 2003).

After the end of the Cold War, and the freeing up of the UN Security Council to act without the constraints of East–West tensions, the formation of the two ad hoc international criminal tribunals for the former Yugoslavia (ICTY) and Rwanda (ICTR) ushered in a new era of transitional justice where prosecutions took over from amnesties as the norm for dealing with past mass human rights violations.[15] The two ad hoc international tribunals were followed by a number of hybrid international-domestic courts, most notably the Special Court for Sierra Leone (SCSL) and the Extraordinary Chambers in the Courts of Cambodia (ECCC), and eventually in 2002 the establishment of the first permanent International Criminal Court (ICC).[16] The principle of universal jurisdiction has also been applied in the context of transitional justice to indict and prosecute war criminals, and increasingly domestic courts have put in place legislation to enable the prosecution of international crimes such as genocide in Rwanda.[17]

At the same time, the use of truth commissions as a transitional justice mechanism has also expanded, sometimes in tandem with prosecutions, while a third significant focus of transitional justice has been on the use of traditional or indigenous, informal approaches to justice and reconciliation.[18] Official and unofficial amnesties continue to prevail in some contexts, although this is becoming harder to sustain in the era of the ICC with its potentially wide reach to charge, if not arrest and prosecute, alleged perpetrators of mass atrocity crimes if states fail to do so.

Thus, like international criminal justice, transitional justice can occur in international, hybrid or domestic or, indeed, regional courts such as the European Court of Human Rights or African Court on Human and Peoples' Rights. The venue for transitional justice can be a court applying ICL, but it can also be other venues such as a truth commission or measures such as reparations or memorialisation. The context for transitional justice has expanded to include political or post-war transitions where there may not be a regime change, such as in Sri Lanka. Indeed, some scholars have argued for the applicability of transitional justice concepts and processes even when there has been no political transition, as in the case of existing democracies and dealing with violations against indigenous peoples, such as Canada's TRC.[19]

---

15 See Chapter 10 in this book. In the preceding decades, even national prosecutions were rare, despite obligations under international law to punish grave breaches of the Geneva Conventions and genocide. Rachel Kerr and Eirin Mobekk, *Peace and Justice: Seeking Accountability after War* (Polity Press, 2007) 24.

16 See Chapters 11 and 12 in this book.

17 Kerr and Mobekk, above n 15, 104.

18 Ibid 128-172.

19 See especially Rosemary L Nagy, 'The Scope and Bounds of Transitional Justice and the Canadian Truth and Reconciliation Commission' (2013) 7 *International Journal of Transitional Justice* 52; Jennifer Balint, Julie Evans and Nesam McMillan, 'Rethinking Transitional Justice, Redressing Indigenous Harm' (2014) 8 *International Journal of*

III Definitions and models of transitional justice

As discussed above, transitional justice is broader than the application of ICL in the form of prosecutions. It also incorporates methods and mechanisms such as truth commissions, lustration or purges, amnesties and traditional indigenous approaches to justice and reconciliation, as well as memorialisation, restitution or reparations, and institutional and constitutional reform. It has also moved beyond the original context of democratic transition to focus on interventions by the international community to promote peacebuilding after mass violence. These goals and methods are reflected in the 2004 definition of transitional justice provided by the former UN Secretary-General, Kofi Annan, as comprising:

> the full range of processes and mechanisms associated with a society's attempts to come to terms with a legacy of large-scale past abuses, in order to ensure accountability, serve justice and achieve reconciliation ... [these] mechanisms may be judicial or non-judicial, and may include individual prosecutions, reparations, truth-seeking, institutional reform, vetting and dismissals, or a combination thereof ... [Transitional justice] must balance a variety of goals, including the pursuit of accountability, truth and reparation, the preservation of peace and the building of democracy and the rule of law.[20]

Scholars and practitioners have more recently included such peacebuilding processes as security sector reform (SSR) and disarmament, demobilisation and reintegration (DDR) linked to development as part of the transitional justice agenda.[21]

The UN, meanwhile, has narrowed its perspective on transitional justice to five key pillars: prosecution initiatives, truth-seeking processes, reparation programmes, institutional reform and national consultations.[22] The first four of these key pillars are drawn directly from the Joinet principles of the right to justice, right to know, right to reparation and guarantee of non-recurrence.[23]

Transitional Justice 194; Stephen Winter, *Transitional Justice in Established Democracies: A Political Theory* (Palgrave Macmillan, 2014).

20 *Report of the UN Secretary-General on the Rule of Law and Transitional Justice in Conflict and Post-Conflict Societies*, UN Doc S/2004/616 (3 August 2004) 8, 25.

21 See especially Pablo de Greiff and Roger Duthie (eds), *Transitional Justice and Development: Making Connections* (Social Science Research Council, 2009); Chandra Sriram *et al* (eds), *Transitional Justice and Peacebuilding on the Ground: Victims and Ex-combatants* (Routledge, 2013).

22 United Nations, *Guidance Note of the Secretary-General: United Nations Approach to Transitional Justice*, DPA/UNSG/2010-00904 (10 March 2010).

23 The 'principles against impunity' were developed by Louis Joinet and presented to the United Nations Commission on Human Rights in 1997. United Nations Economic and Social Council, 'The Administration of Justice and the Human Rights of Detainees: Question

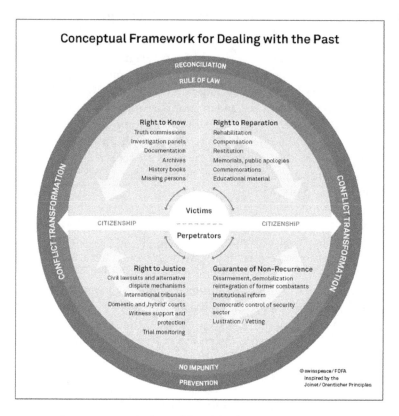

Conceptual Framework for Dealing with the Past

RECONCILIATION

RULE OF LAW

CONFLICT TRANSFORMATION

CONFLICT TRANSFORMATION

Right to Know
Truth commissions
Investigation panels
Documentation
Archives
History books
Missing persons

Right to Reparation
Rehabilitation
Compensation
Restitution
Memorials, public apologies
Commemorations
Educational material

Victims

CITIZENSHIP

CITIZENSHIP

Perpetrators

Right to Justice
Civil lawsuits and alternative
dispute mechanisms
International tribunals
Domestic and 'hybrid' courts
Witness support and
protection
Trial monitoring

Guarantee of Non-Recurrence
Disarmement, demobilization
reintegration of former combatants
Institutional reform
Democratic control of security
sector
Lustration / Vetting

NO IMPUNITY

PREVENTION

© swisspeace/ FDFA
Inspired by the
Joinet / Orentlicher Principles

FIGURE 3.1 swisspeace model of transitional justice

Also inspired by the Joinet principles, swisspeace has developed a model of transitional justice which lists a number of activities included under each of the four key pillars, and placing them all within a surrounding circle of the over-arching goals of conflict transformation and reconciliation (see Figure 3.1).[24]

A number of scholars and practitioners have offered theories and models of transitional justice which overlap with the UN and swisspeace approach, but there are some crucial differences which I would argue are critical to distinguishing transitional justice from international criminal justice. Alex Boraine and Stephan Parmentier, for example, include accountability rather than prosecutions and both also include reconciliation as a key pillar.[25]

of the impunity of the perpetrators of human rights violations (civil and political)', UN Doc E/CN.4/Sub.2/1997/20 (26 June 1997).

24 swisspeace, *A Conceptual Framework for Dealing with the Past: Holism in Principle and Practice* (swisspeace, 2012).

25 Stephan Parmentier, 'Global Justice in the Aftermath of Mass Violence. The Role of the International Criminal Court in Dealing with Political Crimes' (2003) 41 *International*

Pablo de Greiff has also offered a more holistic theory of transitional justice including the four goals: recognition of the agency and suffering of the victims of wrongdoing; civic trust between citizens and public institutions based on shared norms and values, including the rule of law; reconciliation as trust between citizens; and democracy.[26]

As I have argued elsewhere,[27] the inclusion of prosecutions rather than accountability by the UN has limited its approach to transitional justice and, as discussed in the following section, helped to create the impression that transitional justice can be equated with international criminal justice. By contrast, more holistic and transformative approaches which place an emphasis on reconciliation as a process as well as an outcome further help to explain how transitional justice is concerned with a much larger agenda than the significant but insufficient contribution of ICL.

IV The limits of international criminal law in transitions

Even though international criminal justice is thus but one aspect of transitional justice, at times it seems that those working in transitional justice consider these two distinct fields to be synonymous or, at least, to be integrally connected such that the latter is seen to be impossible to contemplate without the former. This bias towards international criminal justice is reflected in the focus on prosecutions rather than accountability as the first key pillar of transitional justice, as discussed above. In other words, transitional justice is equated with international criminal justice because of the dominant normative paradigm which prioritises ICL as a method of countering impunity and imposing Western legal forms of punishment in societies transitioning from past mass human rights violations.

Following the end of the Cold War, the international community increasingly prioritised Western-style criminal trials to prosecute war crimes, genocide and crimes against humanity. As observed by Mark Drumbl, there has been a 'mainstreaming of criminal justice in international relations' and a continuing 'hegemonic imperative to implement criminal trials' derived from the perceived 'duty to prosecute'.[28] At the same time, globalisation has led to an increase in demand for Western-style international criminal justice in the

---

Annals of Criminology 203; Alex Boraine, 'Defining Transitional Justice: Tolerance in the Search for Justice and Peace' in Alex Boraine and S Valentine (eds), *Transitional Justice and Human Security* (International Center for Transitional Justice, 2006).

26 Pablo de Greiff, 'Theorizing Transitional Justice' in Melissa S Williams, Rosemary Nagy and Jon Elster (eds), *Transitional Justice* (Nomos Li, 2012) 31.

27 Wendy Lambourne, 'What Are the Pillars of Transitional Justice?', above n 1.

28 Mark Drumbl, 'Restorative Justice and Collective Responsibility: Lessons for and from the Rwandan Genocide' (2002) 5 *Contemporary Justice Review* 8; Diane F. Orentlicher, '"Settling Accounts" Revisited: Reconciling Global Norms with Local Agency' (2007) 1 *International Journal of Transitional Justice* 10.

increasing number of locations where transitional justice is being implemented. This 'justice cascade'[29] has been reinforced by the creation of the ICC and its investigations, charges and trials for alleged crimes committed in countries such as Kenya, Sudan, Uganda and Democratic Republic of Congo, without the need for state consent or public support, far less ownership or participation. In many cases there has not even been a transitional process. So, in other words, international criminal justice has been taking precedence over transitional justice as a framework for dealing with the past, without considering the potential impact on peacebuilding and/or democratic transition. Questions have been raised about the timing and approach to transitional justice being imposed by the international community through the ICC without consideration of local alternatives, such as traditional Acholi justice in northern Uganda, and the perception of bias in the ICC's activities has culminated in the withdrawal of a number of African countries from the ICC.[30]

Hideaki Shinoda has warned that the application of ICL as part of a rule-of-law approach to peacebuilding can be accused of representing a new brand of Western imperialism, in which political theories of democratic liberalism are imposed on non-Western societies.[31] Rosemary Nagy argues further that 'steeped in Western liberalism, and often located outside the area where conflict occurred, transitional justice may be alien and distant to those who actually have to live together after atrocity'. [32] She notes that the 'international legalist paradigm' focuses on 'generating elite and mass compliance with international humanitarian norms' and 'channels transitional justice towards a fairly narrow interpretation of violence within a somewhat artificial time frame and to the exclusion of external actors'.[33]

Ruti Teitel similarly observes the increasing dominance of international law and what she calls the 'bureaucratic model' of transitional justice.[34] She raises the question of how to reconcile the 'normative commitments and obligations' of human rights law and ICL 'with other transitional values and context on the ground', and argues that 'bureaucratic decisionmaking regarding

---

29 Kathryn Sikkink, *The Justice Cascade: How Human Rights Prosecutions Are Changing World Politics* (WW Norton, 2011).

30 Tim Allen, *Trial Justice: The International Criminal Court and the Lord's Resistance Army* (Zed Books, 2006); Errol P Mendes, *Peace and Justice at the International Criminal Court: A Court of Last Resort* (Edward Elgar, 2010) 97; 'Why an African Mass Withdrawal from the ICC Is Possible' (2 November 2016) *Newsweek*, <http://europe.newsweek.com/icc-international-criminal-court-africa-gambia-south-africa-burundi-515870?rm=eu>.

31 Hideaki Shinoda, 'Enforcing International Criminal Law as a Tool for Peace-Building: An Exploration of the Rule of Law Approach to Peace-Building' (paper presented to the 43rd Annual ISA Convention, New Orleans, Louisiana, 25 March 2002).

32 Rosemary Nagy, 'Transitional Justice as Global Project: Critical Reflections' (2008) 29 *Third World Quarterly* 275.

33 Ibid.

34 Teitel, above note 2, xvii.

transitional justice being formulated by technocratic elites' in the UN, ICTJ and NGOs driven by human rights norms is 'not sufficiently informed by local politics'.[35] While she sees these developments primarily in terms of a dangerous disassociation of international law from the politics and timing of transition, she also identifies the limitations of ICL as a potential means of support for peacemaking and reconciliation:

> Although international criminal justice offers some degree of individual accountability, and hence affirms the liberal response to wrongdoing, it lacks the supportive national structures that are necessary for the true realization of reconciliation and the rule of law.[36]

In terms of reconciliation, international criminal justice can be seen as inadequate for a number of reasons, especially in the context of genocide or other situations where a significant proportion of the population has been involved directly or indirectly in the mass violation of human rights. These reasons include the emphasis on punishment or retributive justice which excludes the perpetrator from society and offers no chance for reintegration, and the potential for reinforcement of the identity of perpetrator and victim rather than survivors who need to live together in close proximity and engage in the new polity as equal citizens.

This critique highlights the importance of involving national governments and local civil society in developing mechanisms of transitional justice that are consistent with local priorities, cultures and needs. For example, by incorporating indigenous customary law and rituals in the transitional justice programme, local communities may be more likely to accept a new era of law and order that precludes the use of violence. Respect for the rule of law cannot be imposed from outside. As I have argued elsewhere, conflict participants need to become players in the process of transitional justice in order to counter claims of cultural imperialism, as well as to ensure that the needs of both victims and perpetrators are met.[37] Referring to the challenges of transitional justice following the Arab Spring, for example, Kirsten Fisher and Robert Stewart wonder whether inclusive societal healing can be fostered at the same time as imposing a liberal democratic model of transitional justice.[38]

---

35 Ibid.
36 Ibid 91.
37 Wendy Lambourne, 'Justice in the Aftermath of Mass Crimes: International Law and Peacebuilding' in Ustinia Dolgopol and Judith Gardam (eds), *The Challenge of Conflict: International Law Responds* (Martinus Nijhoff, 2006) 261.
38 Kirsten J Fisher and Robert Stewart (eds), *Transitional Justice and the Arab Spring* (Routledge, 2014) 6.

In an effort to understand the needs and priorities of individuals and local communities most affected by the mass violation of human rights, transitional justice scholars have embarked on research applying ethnographic and psychosocial methods and investigating topics that differ significantly from the narrow legal assessments of international criminal justice.[39] International criminal justice research, by contrast, emphasises the global implications and legacy of transitional justice mechanisms and jurisprudence on 'wider norms for international and domestic criminal law and procedures'.[40] And in terms of practice, Stacey Mitchell and Henry Carey argue similarly that 'norm change at the level of international criminal law is the clearest contribution accruing from international prosecution'.[41] They illustrate their argument with reference to experiences from the ICTY, ICTR, ICC and SCSL.

The SCSL, as one example, has been judged as successful more in terms of its contribution to global justice norms than to justice and peacebuilding for the local population. Its achievements in terms of the application of ICL were significant, having been the first to prosecute and convict a former head of state, Charles Taylor; to prosecute attacks against UN peacekeepers and forced marriage as a crime against humanity; and the first to deliver convictions for the recruitment of child soldiers.[42] Assessments of the SCSL's contribution to transitional justice have been less favourable, however, ranging from critiques of the cultural inappropriateness of the imposition of a 'one-size-fits-all' model of Western legal justice to questioning of the resources invested in a temporary institution which tried only nine people who were categorised as those most responsible for the past mass human rights violations. Its legacy in terms of contribution to developing the rule of law and rebuilding the justice system in Sierra Leone has been questioned.[43] The potential of the Sierra Leone TRC to provide a full accounting of the truth was adversely affected by the parallel functioning of the SCSL, and the promised reparations programme was delayed and perceived as inadequate.[44]

---

39 See especially Lambourne, above note 1; Laura Stovel, *Long Road Home: Building Reconciliation and Trust in Post-War Sierra Leone* (Intersentia, 2010); Phil Clark, *The Gacaca Courts, Post-Genocide Justice and Reconciliation in Rwanda: Justice without Lawyers* (Cambridge University Press, 2010).

40 Kirsten Ainley, Rebekka Friedman and Chris Mahony, 'Transitional Justice in Sierra Leone: Theory, History and Evaluation' in Kirsten Ainley, Rebekka Friedman and Chris Mahony (eds), *Evaluating Transitional Justice: Accountability and Peacebuilding in Post-Conflict Sierra Leone* (Palgrave Macmillan, 2015) 3.

41 Stacey M Mitchell and Henry F Carey 'Introduction: Current Issues Confronting International Criminal Prosecutions' in Henry F Carey and Stacey M Mitchell (eds), *Trials and Tribulations of International Prosecution* (Lexington Books, 2015) 4.

42 Charles C Jalloh (ed), *The Sierra Leone Special Court and Its Legacy: The Impact for Africa and International Criminal Law* (Cambridge University Press, 2014).

43 Ainley, Friedman and Mahony, above n 40, 4.

44 Field research conducted by the author in Sierra Leone over three weeks in November–December 2006 and again in December 2016.

Although it was relatively successful in achieving its short-term legal justice mandate, the SCSL has not contributed to long-term peace and reconciliation and has even undermined these objectives being pursued by the TRC.

Both international criminal justice and transitional justice are thus seemingly tied to a Western legal and human rights lens. The Western, liberal tradition of criminal accountability is seen as promoting an adversarial, prosecutorial, retributive model of formal legal justice. It not only privileges a juridical form of criminal justice, it ensures an individualistic approach to guilt and punishment.[45] By contrast, truth commissions and informal customary mechanisms are seen as focusing on restorative justice and reconciliation. In societies such as Timor Leste and Mozambique, for example, indigenous spirit-based approaches have been applied which focus on community restoration and bear little resemblance to the legal rights-based approach to transitional justice which draws on ICL.[46] However, this distinction is not always so clear cut in practice. Not all traditional indigenous processes are restorative and communitarian; many are indeed autocratic, power-based and focused on retribution. For example, punishments may be quite severe, including banishment or revenge in the case of serious or 'blood' crimes. Similarly, not all international criminal justice processes are viewed as purely retributive, with a legal discourse that includes ideas of restorative justice being pursued through the provision of reparations and victim participation as in the ECCC, for example.[47]

Furthermore, traditional informal justice mechanisms and indigenous reconciliation rituals may treat restorative and retributive justice as interdependent rather than mutually exclusive processes.[48] For example, the traditional *gacaca* community justice in Rwanda required the offender to

---

45 Michelle Burgis-Kasthala, 'Rethinking the International Criminal Justice Project in the Global South' (Australian National University, 2016) <http://asiapacific.anu.edu.au/regarding-rights/2016/12/16/rethinking-the-international-criminal-justice-project-in-the-global-south/>.

46 D Babo-Soares, '*Nahe biti*: Grassroots Reconciliation in East Timor' in Elin Skaar, Siri Gloppen and Astri Suhrke (eds), *Roads to Reconciliation* (Lexington Books, 2005) 225; Victor Igreja and B Dias-Lambranca, 'Restorative Justice and the Role of Magamba Spirits in Post-Civil War in Mozambique' in Luc Huyse and Mark Salter (eds), *Traditional Justice and Reconciliation after Violent Conflict: Learning from African Experiences* (International IDEA, 2008) 61.

47 Impunity Watch, *Victim Participation and Transitional Justice in Cambodia: the Case of the Extraordinary Chambers in the Courts of Cambodia (ECCC)* Research Report (Impunity Watch, April 2016).

48 Finca also argues that restorative and retributive justice should be seen as complementary rather than contradictory, and Kathleen Daly suggests that 'we should stop comparing "retributive justice" and "restorative justice" in oppositional terms' as 'such a strong, oppositional contrast cannot be sustained empirically'. Bongani Finca, 'They treat the wounds of my people cheaply' in Alex A Boraine and Sue Valentine (above n 25); Kathleen Daly, 'Revisiting the Relationship between Retributive and Restorative Justice' in Heather Strang and John Braithwaite (eds), *Restorative Justice: Philosophy to Practice* (Ashgate, 2000) 33, 34.

'appreciate the gravity of the damage s/he had caused' and the agreed outcome was construed as a form of punishment albeit not one so severe that it would interfere with the primary goal of reconciliation.[49] Thus *gacaca* could be experienced as both retributive and restorative at the same time.[50] As argued by Joanna Quinn: 'while the more formalized Western models often allow for only one form of justice – retributive, restorative, or reparative – these traditional institutions seek to combine various of these and other elements in keeping with the values of the community'.[51]

I argue, therefore, that the pluralistic solution of organising legal trials and a truth commission as complementary strategies to support both retributive and restorative justice in transitional settings is inadequate because it fails to break out of the dominant Western worldview of justice.[52] Instead, I have proposed that a more successful approach might be to take a lead from indigenous customary practices in order to design a more syncretic and locally relevant transitional justice mechanism that creatively combines retributive and restorative elements.[53] Such an approach to combining retributive and restorative justice is incorporated in the model of transformative justice presented later in this chapter, drawing on theories, goals and principles of sustainable or transformative peacebuilding as outlined in the next section.

V Transitional justice and peacebuilding

Transitional justice has become associated with a process implemented by the state with the assistance of the UN in the context of peacebuilding after mass

---

49 Arthur Molenaar, *Gacaca: Grassroots Justice after Genocide: The Key to Reconciliation in Rwanda?* African Studies Centre Research Report No 77 (African Studies Centre, 2005), 14. Furthermore, Kathleen Daly argues that we cannot presume to judge whether restorative justice processes are also perceived as punishment by the participants. Daly (ibid).

50 However, some argue that in its modern form, *gacaca* became a branch of the formal retributive legal system and all but completely lost its restorative justice character. See, for example, Wendy Lambourne, 'Transitional Justice after Mass Violence: Reconciling Retributive and Restorative Justice' in Helen Irving, Jacqueline Mowbray and Kevin Walton (eds), *Julius Stone: A Study in Influence* (Federation Press, 2010) 214; Lars Waldorf, 'Mass Justice for Mass Atrocity: Rethinking Local Justice as Transitional Justice' (2006) 79 *Temple Law Review* 53. By contrast, Phil Clark, while acknowledging the challenges of *gacaca*'s hybridity, suggests that it has been relatively successful in navigating the balance between reconciliation and retribution. See Clark, above n 39.

51 Joanna R Quinn, 'The Role of Informal Mechanisms in Transitional Justice', paper presented at Canadian Political Science Association Annual Meeting, June 2005 <http://cpas-acsp.ca/papers-2005/Quinn.pdf> 10.

52 By contrast, Waldorf concludes his review of local justice for mass atrocities by arguing for a legally pluralistic solution for transitional justice. Waldorf, above n 50, 87.

53 Lambourne, above n 50; Mark Findlay and Ralph Henham have also made the radical argument for the 'harmonization of restorative and retributive justice' within international criminal justice. Mark Findlay and Ralph Henham, *Transforming International Criminal Justice: Retributive and Restorative Justice in the Trial Process* (Willan Publishing, 2005) xiv.

violence, often resulting from the terms of a peace agreement. According to the UN, peacebuilding encompasses a wide range of political, developmental, humanitarian and human rights programmes and mechanisms designed to prevent the outbreak, recurrence or continuation of armed conflict.[54] Peacebuilding has short-term as well as long-term objectives aimed at ensuring sustainability in the security, political, economic and justice sectors. These objectives include the promotion of democracy and accountable governance, as well as eradication of poverty and sustainable development, and respect for human rights and the rule of law.[55]

Justice as part of peacebuilding may therefore be seen as something broader than ensuring legal accountability, and as a process that goes beyond the short-term notion of a political transition. Transitional justice thus becomes the first stage in a long-term process of constitutional and institutional transformation of the state in order to support a comprehensive or holistic and sustainable peace, incorporating both the ending of armed conflict ('negative peace') and the building of a 'positive peace' or 'peace with justice'.[56]

Transitional justice in the context of building a positive peace implies the inclusion of socioeconomic and political justice, as well as legal justice that combats a culture of impunity and sets up structures to ensure ongoing respect for human rights and the rule of law. A sustainable peace, furthermore, requires attention to both the 'software' and 'hardware' of peacebuilding, incorporating relational in addition to structural or institutional transformation, and a focus on local ownership, empowerment and contextualisation.[57] It requires a transdisciplinary mindset and a holistic and comprehensive approach to societal as well as state transformation incorporating insights and methods from multiple disciplinary perspectives and experiences which go beyond the dominant Western liberal peace versus justice paradigm. A narrow legal mindset, by contrast, limits our understanding of transitional justice both in theory and practice and its ability to support peacebuilding. This is illustrated in the following example from Burundi where the UN's approach to transitional justice has conflicted with that of the government and civil society.

54 United Nations Security Council, 'Statement by the President of the Security Council', UN Doc S/PRST/2001/5 (20 February 2001).
55 Ibid; Ho-Won Jeong, *Peacebuilding in Postconflict Societies: Strategy and Process* (Lynne Rienner, 2005).
56 Johan Galtung, 'Violence, Peace and Peace Research' (1969) 6 *Journal of Peace Research* 166.
57 Luc Reychler, 'Challenges of Peace Research' (2006) 11 *International Journal of Peace Studies* 1; John Paul Lederach, 'Journey from Resolution to Transformative Peacebuilding' in Cynthia Sampson and John Paul Lederach (eds), *From the Ground Up: Mennonite Contributions to International Peacebuilding* (Oxford University Press, 2000) 45.

The Arusha Peace and Reconciliation Agreement of 2000, which contributed to ending the civil war in Burundi, called for the establishment of transitional justice mechanisms including both a TRC and a tribunal for prosecuting past mass human rights violations. The Government of Burundi, however, steadfastly refused to contemplate the possibility of prosecutions, not surprisingly given the likelihood that members of the government would be implicated, including the President, Pierre Nkurunziza, who was himself a rebel leader during the civil war. The President also delayed in creating the TRC, despite expectations arising from the Arusha peace agreement and the results of national consultations conducted in 2009.[58]

In implementing the Arusha peace agreement, the UN peacebuilding and political missions maintained a mandate to support transitional justice, including through the Transitional Justice Unit (TJU) of the UN Office in Burundi (BNUB) created in 2011. UN Security Council resolution 2137 of 13 February 2014, which extended the mandate of BNUB to the end of 2014, included the following in relation to transitional justice:

> 15. *Calls upon* the Government of Burundi to work with international partners and BNUB for the establishment of transitional justice mechanisms, including a credible and consensual Truth and Reconciliation Commission to help foster an effective reconciliation of all Burundians and durable peace in Burundi, in accordance with the results of the work of the Technical Committee, the 2009 national consultations, Security Council resolution 1606 (2005) as well as the Arusha agreement of 28 August 2000.

At the same time as pledging its support for the TRC as part of building peace and reconciliation in Burundi, however, the TJU representative continued to push the Burundian government to pursue prosecutions.[59] Concerned by the imposition of a single UN model of transitional justice, the local Quaker Peace Network (QPN) in Burundi developed its own model of transitional justice which emphasised reconciliation and accountability rather than prosecutions. The public launch of the QPN Burundi model in July 2014 generated controversy because of its apparent downplaying of the call for an end to impunity emphasised by the UN. Meetings of QPN civil society leaders with the TJU failed to make any impression on the UN's attitude to transitional justice priorities in Burundi, despite assurances that they were not trying to replace the UN model, but rather to propose a complementary model that could be more effective in the cultural, socioeconomic and political context of Burundi.[60]

---

58 The TRC was finally established in March 2016.
59 Interview with UN TJU representative, Bujumbura, Burundi, June 2014.
60 Wendy Lambourne, 'Cooperation and Conflict: Civil Society Resistance and Engagement with Transitional Justice in Burundi' in Jasmina Brankovic and Hugo van der Merwe

The experience in Burundi thus demonstrates the tensions between international norms derived from the Joinet principles, which emphasise prosecutions and the ending of a culture of impunity, and state power and priorities which were intent on avoiding any form of accountability for the past. It also reflects apparent contradictions between the UN's mandate for peacebuilding and its approach to transitional justice in practice, and the potential for local civil society to take greater ownership of the transitional justice process in a way that may be more consistent with building peace and reconciliation.[61]

I argue, therefore, that peacebuilding and transitional justice become transformative when they emphasise the principles of local participation and empowerment which take into account local perspectives and priorities. Simon Robins similarly maintains that transitional justice practice has been 'both ritualized and subordinated' to the broader 'liberal peace' agenda and calls for a more 'elicitive approach grounded in the realities with which the citizens of transitional states live'.[62]

The sustainability of a transformative peacebuilding process therefore requires attention to the needs and expectations of local affected populations, as well as a coordinated focus on the multidimensional or multidisciplinary aspects of peacebuilding incorporating attention to all the dimensions of human security. It requires attention to psychosocial as well as political, economic, and law and order aspects of peace and justice. In the next section I will explore further how this model of transformative peacebuilding can be applied to the transitional justice sector.

VI Transformative justice

Several scholars have proposed the concept of transformative justice to replace or complement transitional justice, including Erin Daly, Paul Gready and Simon Robins, in addition to my own previous work on the topic. Thomas Bundschuh provides the most radical claim that 'ultimately, genuine transitional justice *is* transformative justice'.[63] Based on a conceptualisation of

---

(eds), *Advocating Transitional Justice in Africa: The Role of Civil Society* (Springer, 2017) (forthcoming).

61 Ibid.

62 Simon Robins, 'Mapping a Future for Transitional Justice by Learning from the Past' (2015) 9 *International Journal of Transitional Justice* 181, 190. See also Rosalind Shaw and Lars Waldorf with Pierre Hazan (eds), *Localizing Transitional Justice: Interventions and Priorities after Mass Violence* (Stanford University Press, 2010); Kieran McEvoy and Lorna McGregor (eds), *Transitional Justice from Below: Grassroots Activism and the Struggle for Change* (Hart, 2008).

63 Thomas Bundschuh, 'Enabling Transitional Justice, Restoring Capabilities: The Imperative of Participation and Normative Integrity' (2015) 9 *International Journal of Transitional Justice* 28.

human rights as capability rights, he proposes the need for 'sufficient and equal agency' as a fundamental principle in addition to 'inclusive participation' as part of a required normative shift in transitional justice. Bundschuh explains that this normative shift connects what he calls 'trans-normation' or formal change of law with its 'substantive impact' in terms of the 'trans-formation evidenced in victims' lives and reflected in the recovery of participatory capabilities'.[64] He goes on to explain how these two fundamental principles

> ground and inform the other three operative principles: the principle of nonselective factual acknowledgement of pretransitional injustice as a basis for responsive and cooperative change; the principle of legislation to incorporate formal legal change; and the principle of transformation, focusing on individual and collective redress as well as on structural transformation to make redress durable and sustainable.[65]

Bundschuh joins a number of scholars in advocating for a focus on structural transformation and socioeconomic justice as part of transitional justice. Gready and Robins, for example, define transformative justice as 'transformative change that emphasizes local agency and resources, the prioritization of process rather than preconceived outcomes and the challenging of unequal and intersecting power relationships and structures of exclusion at both the local and the global level'.[66] Gready and Robins also advocate a 'shift in focus from the legal to the social and political, and from the state and institutions to communities and everyday concerns'.[67] Erin Daly's concept of transformative justice is focused more on the psychosocial aspects of transformation including the need to transform the culture and values that 'tolerated or pursued the prior injustices', and how transformative justice can therefore contribute to reconciliation and deterrence.[68] Nevin Aiken similarly argues that transitional justice can contribute to intergroup reconciliation by keeping 'socioemotional, instrumental and distributive ends in mind' or at least working 'in tandem with other ongoing societal efforts to rebuild trust, cooperation and equality between former enemies'.[69]

Drawing on my field research and theories of peacebuilding outlined in the previous section, the model of transformative justice I have developed proposes four key elements of justice: accountability, or legal justice;

---

64 Ibid 24.
65 Ibid 28.
66 Ibid; Gready and Robins, above n 8, 340.
67 Ibid.
68 Erin Daly, 'Transformative Justice: Charting a Path to Reconciliation' (2001-2002) 12 *International Legal Perspectives* 73.
69 Nevin T Aiken, 'Learning to Live Together: Transitional Justice and Intergroup Reconciliation in Northern Ireland' (2010) 4 *International Journal of Transitional Justice* 166.

psychosocial justice, including truth and healing; socioeconomic justice; and political justice.[70] These four elements reflect the aspects of transformative justice highlighted by other scholars as outlined briefly above, but in a more holistic way which links them all into one model.

Legal justice in this model incorporates the potential for accountability provided by international criminal law which results in the punishment of perpetrators of mass human rights violations, and sometimes the accompanying provision of reparations to victims. However, accountability is defined more broadly than prosecutions, thus allowing for non-Western and non-formal legal approaches, such as a truth and reconciliation commission, in which perpetrators may be more likely to accept responsibility for their crimes through a restorative justice process in addition to, or in place of, retributive justice. As argued earlier in this chapter, a syncretic process combining elements of both restorative and retributive justice may be seen as most conducive to transformative justice and peacebuilding.

Psychosocial justice encapsulates the dimensions of justice that promote healing and address the need for truth in terms of both knowledge and acknowledgement of the human rights violation and its human and relational impact: knowledge of who was responsible, how it happened, where the bodies or remains are located, and acknowledgement of the loss, pain, hurt and suffering caused. Both knowledge and acknowledgment can contribute to a psychological process of healing and building of inner peace. Combining this inner transformation with relational transformation provides the foundation for reconciliation and a sense of psychosocial justice. Reconciliation is thus seen as a process of relationship-building as part of conflict transformation, as well as an outcome that is part of the experience of sustainable peace and development.[71]

I argue that 'truth', whether expressed as truth-seeking, truth-telling or truth recovery, is an inadequate concept to encapsulate the full meaning of truth, knowledge and acknowledgement to the various conflict participants in a transitional justice context, including both victims and perpetrators. The word 'truth' is also misleading, as it is often interpreted as the finding of a single truth of what happened, who was responsible and why. I draw on the distinction between four different types of truth made by the South African TRC: forensic or factual truth; personal or narrative truth; social or dialogue truth; and healing or restorative truth.[72] All four of these dimensions of truth are important to a holistic approach to transitional justice which promotes

---

70 For more details about the development of this model, please see Lambourne, 'Transitional Justice and Peacebuilding *after* Mass Violence', above n 1.

71 John Paul Lederach, *Building Peace: Sustainable Reconciliation in Divided Societies* (United States Institute of Peace Press, 1997).

72 Alex Boraine and Sue Valentine, above n 25.

psychosocial transformation. Whilst ICL can contribute to establishing part of the truth, namely knowledge and a forensic or factual truth, criminal trials are less likely to encourage acknowledgment from those accused of crimes nor to enable personal or narrative truths to be told. In order to create a social or dialogue truth and foster a healing or restorative truth, other transitional justice methods are also needed.

Socioeconomic justice incorporates the various elements of justice that relate to financial or other material compensation, restitution or reparation for past violations or crimes (historical justice) and distributive or socioeconomic justice in the future (prospective justice). The idea is to establish both an experience of justice about what occurred in the past and to ensure that structural violence in the future is minimised in order to promote a sustainable peace. Whilst most models of transitional justice include the idea of reparation, international criminal justice and thus transitional justice in practice tend to focus on historical reparations rather than the need for future socioeconomic justice as a conflict preventive measure. My emphasis on socioeconomic justice as decisive in transitional justice draws on Rama Mani's model that includes distributive justice as one of three critical dimensions of reparative justice.[73] Based on my field research and consideration of conflict theory, I concur with Mani's argument that alleviating impact and targeting causes through distributive justice are important for transitional justice to contribute to peacebuilding.

Political justice is necessary to ensure the successful implementation of transitional justice measures including institutional reform, rule of law and respect for human rights, addressing socioeconomic needs, and avoiding the appearance of victor's justice or a culture of impunity. As argued by Mahmood Mamdani, political justice requires a delinking of political identity from cultural identity and a move towards democracy that involves institutional reform, and separates and makes accountable the powers of the executive, legislature, judiciary and administration.[74] In other words, political justice involves transforming both institutions and relationships to eliminate corruption and promote a sense of fair representation and participation for the general population. Without political justice, transformative justice is therefore incomplete and peace unsustainable.

I have proposed six principles which apply to these four aspects of justice. The first two principles emphasise the significance of transformation – of both structures and relationships – to promoting transitional justice that supports transformative peacebuilding, as discussed in the previous section. The third principle indicates that transformative justice not only deals with the past, it also establishes conditions and structures to ensure justice in the

---

73 Rama Mani, *Beyond Retribution: Seeking Justice in the Shadows of War* (Polity Press, 2002).
74 Mahmood Mamdani, *When Victims Become Killers: Colonialism, Nativism, and the Genocide in Rwanda* (Princeton University Press, 2001).

present and the future, creating a longer-term vision and commitment than suggested by the term 'transitional justice'.[75] This applies to legal justice that promotes accountability for past violations and 'truth' that creates a historical record, as well as structures and relationships to ensure procedural justice in the present, and future respect for human rights and the rule of law. It also suggests the necessity of considering not only reparative or restitutive justice for past inequities, but also distributive or socioeconomic justice for the future. Factual or forensic truth dealing with the past may be needed as well as healing or restorative truth that creates the conditions for transformation of relationships necessary for sustainable peace. This focus on both retrospective (rectificatory or corrective) and prospective (distributive or restorative) justice is a distinction also made by Jeremy Webber who identifies the importance of linking these two forms of transitional justice.[76]

Transformative justice is thus about recognising the continuity of human rights violations before, during and after the peace agreement or political transition. As argued by Wendy Lambourne and Vivianna Rodriguez Carreon in the context of responding to gender-based violence:

> transformative justice is both backward and forward looking at the same time, and thus makes the connection between addressing the 'extraordinary' violations experienced by women during genocide, war and other mass violence and the 'ordinary' violations experienced by women during so-called peacetime.[77]

According to the fourth principle, transformative justice recognises the significance of symbolic and ritual processes to ensuring the local, cultural and personal relevance of transitional justice mechanisms. In Timor Leste, for example, local community reconciliation processes were experienced as personally meaningful because of the inclusion of the traditional *nahe biti* rituals.[78] Political structures and accountability processes need to be designed

---

75 Jennifer Balint *et al* take this further by explaining how 'transitional justice assumes a linear notion of time as progress, in which the past and the future are seen as separable and successive, instead of intertwined and co-implicated' which 'makes it difficult for transitional justice adequately to acknowledge, and hence redress, the enduring structural arrangements that may have resulted in past as well as present injustice and the ongoing effects of past inequities on present and future generations'. Jennifer Balint, Julie Evans and Nesam McMillan, 'Rethinking Transitional Justice, Redressing Indigenous Harm' (2014) 8 *International Journal of Transitional Justice* 194, 201.

76 Jeremy Webber, 'Forms of Transitional Justice' in Melissa S Williams, Rosemary Nagy and Jon Elster (eds), *Transitional Justice* (New York University Press, 2012) 98.

77 Wendy Lambourne and Vivianna Rodriguez Carreon, 'Engendering Transitional Justice: A Transformative Approach to Building Peace and Attaining Human Rights for Women' (2016) 17 *Human Rights Review* 71, 72.

78 Lambourne, above n 7.

for local conditions and with local ownership and inclusive participation, according to the fifth principle, in order to support capacity-building and meaningful personal and societal transformation.[79] Finally, the sixth principle maintains that transformative justice must be holistic, integrated and comprehensive, covering multiple approaches to justice and ensuring a coordinated process that is consistent with peacebuilding and reconciliation.

VII Conclusion

This chapter has critically assessed the norms and assumptions of transitional justice discourse and practice which are limited in their ability to effect transformation in societies recovering from mass violence because of the over-identification of transitional justice with international criminal justice. In particular, the UN's imposition of a model of transitional justice which prioritises prosecutions and fails to explicitly promote reconciliation has been seen as a major impediment to societal transformation and peacebuilding. The model of transformative justice advocated in this chapter reinforces transitional justice scholarship which argues for cultural and conflict contextualisation, local ownership and civil society participation, in order to promote sustainable peace and reconciliation whilst countering the dominant Western liberal democratic philosophy behind transitional justice policy and practice.[80]

As explained by Ruti Teitel, law's role in transitional justice is 'deeply and inherently paradoxical': 'in its ordinary social function, law provides order and stability, but in extraordinary periods of political upheaval, law maintains order even as it enables transformation'.[81] My research suggests that we need to go further than regarding transitional justice as playing a role in transforming societal norms in relation to constitutional and legal regimes, as proposed by Teitel. In order to contribute to building a sustainable peace and democratic transition, this chapter has argued that transitional justice needs to be seen as transformative in socioeconomic and psychosocial as well as legal and political terms.

The practicality and advisability of taking such a holistic and transformative approach to transitional justice has been questioned from a normative and theoretical perspective, but as discussed in this chapter, empirical evidence of

79 As a result of my previous research I proposed a focus on 'inreach' to complement 'outreach' in the activities of criminal courts as well as other transitional justice mechanisms, as a means of ensuring local ownership and civil society participation and thus local resonance and meaningfulness of transitional justice for those most affected by the violence and violations. Wendy Lambourne, 'Outreach, Inreach and Civil Society Participation in Transitional Justice' in Nicola Palmer, Phil Clark and Danielle Granville (eds), *Critical Perspectives in Transitional Justice* (Intersentia, 2012) 235.

80 Chandra Lekha Sriram, 'Transitional Justice and the Liberal Peace' in Edward Newman, Roland Paris and Oliver P Richmond (eds), *New Perspectives on Liberal Peacebuilding* (United Nations University Press, 2009) 123.

81 Teitel, above n 11, 6.

the complexity of justice needs and practices in transitional societies suggests that it is a reality that cannot be ignored. The challenge then becomes one of coordination and the management of expectations so that these multiple justice needs can be addressed, or at least acknowledged, in the transitional justice process. The transformative justice principles presented in this chapter promote means for combatting the risks of transitional justice and maximising its effectiveness as a way to promote peace, democracy and reconciliation.

Further reading

Buckley Zistel, Susanne *et al* (eds), *Transitional Justice Theories* (Routledge, 2014).

Corradetti, Claudio, Nir Eisikovits, and Jack Volpe Rotondi (eds), *Theorizing Transitional Justice* (Routledge, 2016).

Gready, Paul and Simon Robins, 'From Transitional to Transformative Justice: A New Agenda for Practice' (2014) 8 *International Journal of Transitional Justice* 339.

McAuliffe, Padraig, *Transformative Transitional Justice and the Malleability of Post-Conflict States* (Edward Elgar, 2017).

Report of the UN Secretary-General on the Rule of Law and Transitional Justice in Conflict and Post-Conflict Societies, UN Doc S/2004/616 (3 August 2004).

Simić, Olivera (ed), *An Introduction to Transitional Justice* (Routledge, 2017).

Sriram, Chandra Lekha, 'Transitional Justice and the Liberal Peace' in Edward Newman, Roland Paris and Oliver P Richmond (eds), *New Perspectives on Liberal Peacebuilding* (United Nations University Press, 2009) 123.

Teitel, Ruti G, *Globalizing Transitional Justice: Contemporary Essays* (Oxford University Press, 2014).

PART II
International crimes

4

GENOCIDE

To prevent and punish 'radical evil'

Eyal Mayroz

I Introduction

The 1948 Convention on the Prevention and Punishment of the Crime of Genocide (hereafter the Genocide Convention, or 'the Convention') was drafted on the basis of a premise, a vision, that by harnessing the global abhorrence of the Holocaust and other World War II catastrophes, and codifying it into international law, states could prevent future genocides. How is it, that even after the Convention entered into force, occurrences of genocide did not diminish but increased in number?

This chapter integrates legal observations and findings regarding the role of the term 'genocide' in international law with political and moral dimensions of its significance to real life situations. For example, we ask: could the genocidal massacre in Srebrenica, Bosnia in 1995 – where up to 8,000 Muslim men and boys were killed because of their ethnic identity – be considered more morally deplorable, and more worthy of political response than non-genocidal massacres with the same or greater numbers of victims?

Despite widespread perceptions of genocide as the most extreme violation of human rights, discussions of failures to prevent or halt perpetrations of the crime have often overlooked these questions. While legally speaking, no 'hierarchy of crimes' exists in international criminal law (ICL),[1] it has been argued that for 'everyone in the world' genocide *is* the crime of crimes.[2] Notably, this

---

1 For arguments in favour of such a hierarchy, see Alison M Danner, 'Constructing a Hierarchy of Crimes in International Criminal Law Sentencing' (2001) 87 *Virginia Law Review* 415, 472.

2 David Luban, 'Calling Genocide by its Rightful Name: Lemkin's Word, Darfur, and the UN Report' (2006) 7(1) *Chicago Journal of International Law* 303, 306. The term 'crime of crimes' was used even by the trial chambers of the ICTY and the ICTR.

was not the understanding of the UN International Commission of Inquiry on Darfur, which concluded in 2005 that crimes against humanity, and war crimes, had been committed in the region that *'may be no less serious and heinous than genocide'.*[3] Important divergences thus exist between perceptions of the term genocide, which seem to spill into legal proceedings,[4] and potentially into political decision-making.

To better understand the influence of these divergences, this chapter explores the complex and often contentious associations between legal obligations, moral imperatives and political decision-making in relation to genocide. We commence with an overview of the normative foundations of the term and the debates surrounding it since its inception. We then explore the motivations, hopes, and disappointments behind the legal obligation to prevent and punish in the Genocide Convention, and the capacity of international law to influence political action. Finally, we raise some points and questions about the capacity of the 'genocide' label to help prevent or halt the commission of mass atrocity crimes.

II The legal foundations of genocide

The term genocide originated as a legal concept. It was coined in 1943[5] by Raphael Lemkin, a Polish-Jewish jurist and refugee who escaped the Holocaust, by merging together the Greek word *genos* (race, tribe) and the Latin-derived -*cide* (from *caedere to* kill). In his seminal work, *Axis Rule in Occupied Europe,* Lemkin described genocide as 'an old practice in its modern development', and argued that new conceptions required new terms.[6]

In the introduction to his chapter on genocide, Lemkin summarised the essence of the concept as 'the destruction of a nation or of an ethnic group'.[7] However, as an amateur historian, he keenly studied the origins of mass murder, and his conception of his 'linguistic brainchild' extended well

---

3 United Nations, *Report of the International Commission of Inquiry on Darfur to the United Nations Secretary General* (25 January 2005) 518-19, 522 (emphasis added). See also Julie Flint and Alex De Waal, *Darfur: A Short History of a Long War* (Zed Books, 2006) 132; Luban, above n 2, 304-9.

4 For example, while the trial chambers of the Yugoslav and Rwanda Criminal Tribunals referred to genocide as the 'crime of crimes', this depiction was not upheld by their respective Appellate Chambers on the very same ground: that there is no hierarchy among international crimes. Luban, above n 2, 306.

5 The text was published a year later in 1944.

6 Raphael Lemkin, *Axis Rule in Occupied Europe. Laws of Occupation. Analysis of Government. Proposals for Redress* (Carnegie Endowment for International Peace, Division of International Law, 1944) 79.

7 Ibid.

beyond the events unfolding at that time in Europe.[8] His wider definition of the term described:

> a coordinated plan of different actions aiming at the destruction of essential foundations of the life of national groups, with the aim of annihilating the groups themselves. The objectives of such a plan would be disintegration of the political and social institutions, of culture, language, national feelings, religion, and the economic existence of national groups, and the destruction of the personal security, liberty, health, dignity, and even the lives of individuals belonging to such groups.[9]

A few years later, in 1948, the UN General Assembly adopted a legal definition of genocide as part of the Genocide Convention. Whereas Article I of the Convention established genocide as an international crime in times of peace and war, Article II defined it to mean:

> [A]ny of the following acts committed with intent to destroy, in whole or in part, a national, ethnical, racial or religious group, as such:
>
> (a) Killing members of the group;
> (b) Causing serious bodily or mental harm to members of the group;
> (c) Deliberately inflicting on the group conditions of life calculated to bring about its physical destruction in whole or in part;
> (d) Imposing measures intended to prevent births within the group;
> (e) Forcibly transferring children of the group to another group.[10]

Article III then enumerated a list of five punishable acts:

> (a) Genocide;
> (b) Conspiracy to commit genocide;
> (c) Direct and public incitement to commit genocide;
> (d) Attempt to commit genocide;
> (e) Complicity in genocide.

---

8 Dirk Moses, 'Raphael Lemkin, Culture, and the Concept of Genocide' in Donald Bloxham and A Dirk Moses (eds), *The Oxford Handbook on Genocide Studies* (Oxford University Press, 2010) 19, 21, 26-7.

9 Lemkin, *Axis Rule in Occupied Europe*, above n 6, 79.

10 *Convention on the Prevention and Punishment of the Crime of Genocide*, opened for signature 9 December 1948, 78 UNTS 277 (entered into force 12 January 1951) Art. II.

The definition of genocide in Article II fell short of Lemkin's original conception in at least two ways. First, the political calculations and interests of key states led to a narrow definition of the targeted groups (national, ethnical, racial and religious), and to the omission of some other groups, most importantly social, economic and political.[11] Second, the emphasis in the definition came to rest mainly on physical manifestations of the crime, and included only narrowly construed biological elements: i.e. measures intended to prevent births within the group.[12] Moreover, the cultural aspect of 'genocide', which was integral to Lemkin's thought, was narrowed down to cover only the forcible transferring of children to another group (2.e). While as many as fourteen states supported the insertion of 'cultural genocide' clauses into the definition,[13] the final motion still failed. As a lawyer and advisor to the drafting committee of the Genocide Convention, Lemkin was said to have understood the need to compromise in order to reach state consensus.[14] Whether or not he understood the implications of some of the compromises made in the final draft is another question.

In the decades that followed the signing of the Convention, controversies over the legal definition of the term genocide only increased. The following summary briefly expands upon three of them: the meaning and implications of 'the intent to destroy', 'protected groups', and 'in whole or in part'.

A The intent to destroy

Proceedings to convict individuals of genocide, or find a state guilty of genocide or of a failure to prevent or punish genocide require demonstration that genocide has taken place, is taking place, or was intended to take place. In these undertakings, proving intent is a key requisite. Some have linked the demonstration of intent to the issue of whether or not there was a state policy or plan to destroy a protected group.[15] The difficulty of doing so early enough to inspire,

11 According to Schabas, opposition to the inclusion of political groups was widespread and included even Lemkin himself. In William Schabas, 'What Is Genocide? What Are the Gaps in the Convention? How to Prevent Genocide?' (2009) 47(2) *Politorbis* 33, 38. Adam Jones argues that Lemkin did not support the inclusion of political groups because he did not consider them to be 'bearers of human culture' in the same way as ethno-national groups. See Adam Jones, *Genocide: A Comprehensive Introduction* (Taylor & Francis, 2nd ed, 2010) 319. Genocidal campaigns against political, social or economic groups are labelled sometimes nowadays 'politicides', a term coined by Barbara Harff. Barbara Harff, 'No Lessons Learned from the Holocaust? Assessing Risks of Genocide and Political Mass Murder since 1955' (2003) 97(1) *American Political Science Review* 57.

12 Schabas, above n 11, 39.

13 Support came from non-Western states, the Soviet Union, Yugoslavia, Byelorussian Soviet Socialist Republic, China, Czechoslovakia, Haiti, Lebanon, Liberia, Pakistan, Philippines, Poland, Saudi Arabia and Syria (see UN Doc A/PV.179 (9 December 1948) 847).

14 Moses, above n 8, 37-8.

15 William Schabas, 'Article 6. Genocide' in Otto Triffterer and Kai Ambos (eds), *Commentary on the Rome Statute of the International Criminal Court* (Beck/Hart, 2015) 127, 130.

encourage or dictate international prevention efforts was perhaps the greatest handicap imposed on the Genocide Convention by its drafters. So far the restrictive test used by international tribunals and courts to demonstrate the requisite intent has been that of 'specific intent' (*dolus specialis*). However, absent outward expression, intent is very difficult to establish.[16] Many have thus been calling for a more moderate, knowledge-based approach to perpetrators' intent.[17] Central to the knowledge-based argument is the primacy the Genocide Convention drafters assigned to protecting human groups. Failure to establish specific intent rapidly enough to engender preventive or reactive actions, based on a preliminary political finding of genocide, supported the view that the requirement of *dolus specialis* is incompatible with the object and purpose of the Convention.

B Protected groups

The decision to limit the groups protected in the Convention to four – national, ethnical, racial and religious – excluded other types of group against whom genocide can be readily committed. The best-known example was Cambodia, where an estimated two million people were murdered or starved to death by the brutal Khmer Rouge.[18] As most victims were targeted because of their social or political affiliations, the prosecution of 'genocide' by the Extraordinary Chambers in the Courts of Cambodia (ECCC) was confined to the atrocities perpetrated against Vietnamese and other ethnic minority groups.[19] Notably, some attempts have been made at a more liberal interpretation of the Convention's definition in relation to protected groups; for instance, by the Trial Chamber of the International Criminal Tribunal for Rwanda (ICTR), allegedly in an effort to resolve challenges involving the classification of the Tutsi minority as a clear ethnic group in the sense of the Genocide Convention.[20] An unresolved question that follows from this is whether stable and permanent groups not specified explicitly in Article II could still be considered protected under the Convention.[21] While excluding

---

16 Katherine Goldsmith, 'The Issue of Intent in the Genocide Convention and Its Effect on the Prevention and Punishment of the Crime of Genocide: Toward a Knowledge-Based Approach' (2010) 5(3) *Genocide Studies and Prevention* 238, 250. See also William Schabas, 'Semantics or Substance: David Scheffer's Welcome Proposal to Strengthen Criminal Accountability for Atrocities' (2007) 2(1) *Genocide Studies and Prevention* 31, 35.

17 For a review of the debate, see Goldsmith, above n 16, 241-8.

18 Tom Fawthrop and Helen Jarvis, *Getting Away with Genocide: Elusive Justice and the Khmer Rouge Tribunal* (Pluto Press, 2004) 4.

19 For example, see René Lemarchand, 'Comparing the Killing Fields: Rwanda, Cambodia and Bosnia' in Steven LB Jensen (ed), *Genocide: Cases, Comparisons and Contemporary Debates* (The Danish Center for Holocaust and Genocide Studies, 2003) 141, 142-5.

20 See William Schabas, 'The "Odious Scourge": Evolving Interpretations of the Crime of Genocide' (2006) 1(2) *Genocide Studies and Prevention* 93, 98-9.

21 Fanny Martin, 'The Notion of "Protected Group" in the Genocide Convention and its Application' in Paola Gaeta (ed), *The UN Genocide Convention: A Commentary* (Oxford University Press, 2009) 112, 118-20.

such a group may seem unjust, it has been noted that attempts to amend or 'liberally' interpret the definition risk diluting it and potentially 'trivializing the horror of the real crime'.[22]

C 'In whole or in part'

Considerable debate has focused on the meaning of 'in part' in Article II. Since the Genocide Convention did not elaborate further, it has been left for the courts to interpret the term. Schabas distinguished two basic approaches among jurists: a 'substantial part' and a 'significant' part'.[23] The word 'substantial' was interpreted by the Appeals Chamber of the International Criminal Tribunal for the Former Yugoslavia (ICTY) as primarily numeric: i.e. the size of the targeted part in relation to the overall size of the group. However, the Chamber specified also a second consideration of prominence or significance: i.e. how emblematic the targeted part of the group was and how essential it was to the survival of the entire group.[24] Despite concerted efforts, mainly by the ICTY,[25] no court ruling has conclusively resolved the definition, and disagreements remain.

To summarise, a genocide finding by a court is conditioned upon the court being satisfied that special intent existed; that the group targeted was one of the four specified in the definition; and that the intent to destroy extended to a substantial and/or significant part of the group. In addition, one or more of the acts carried out, attempted, or incited by the perpetrators, must match one of those enumerated in Article II of the Convention.[26]

The four elements described above comprise the essence of what many call 'the genocide debate': i.e. legal or political debates over the applicability of the genocide label to a specific crisis. Reluctance to bear the risks and costs of strong action is said to have led states to point to, or use, these debates as pretexts for inaction. They did so based on two assumptions: (a) that the absence of broad domestic and/or international agreement over the applicability of the 'genocide' label to a specific crisis reduces both the

---

22 William Schabas, 'Groups Protected by the Genocide Convention: Conflicting Interpretations from the International Criminal Tribunal for Rwanda' (2000) 6 *ILSA Journal of International & Comparative Law* 375, 386-7.

23 See discussion in Schabas, 'What Is Genocide?', above n 11, 40-1.

24 *Prosecutor v Krstić (Judgement)* (Trial Chamber, Case No IT-98-33-T, 2 August, 2001) [12]. See also Schabas, 'Article 6. Genocide', above n 15, 134-5.

25 See David Scheffer, 'Genocide and Atrocity Crimes' (2006) 1(3) *Genocide Studies and Prevention* 229, 239-42; and Schabas, 'Groups Protected by the Genocide Convention', above n 22, 13.

26 Killing, causing serious physical or mental harm, inflicting on the group conditions calculated to bring its destruction, preventing births, or transfers of children.

moral and legal obligation to act[27]; and (b) that a focus on the 'genocide debate' distracts politicians and publics from the need to take real action.[28] Finally, in spite of the definitional controversies that impeded the implementation of the vision at the heart of the Genocide Convention, half a century later the drafters of the Rome Statute of the International Criminal Court (ICC) ended up incorporating the exact same definition into Article 6 of the treaty.[29]

III The moral significance of genocide

For centuries, scholarly consensus has belittled the importance of ethical considerations in international politics.[30] Similar assertions have been made in recent decades in relation to the moral significance of the 'genocide' label. However, few efforts have been made thus far to explore this question empirically, and the political ramifications of invoking the term have remained largely hypothetical. In his 2000 report, *We the Peoples: The Role of the United Nations in the 21st Century,* the then UN Secretary-General Kofi Annan wrote:

> [I]f humanitarian intervention is, indeed, an unacceptable assault on sovereignty, how should we respond to a Rwanda, to a Srebrenica – to gross and systematic violations of human rights that offend every precept of our common humanity?[31]

The statement has often been cited to highlight the clashing imperatives which mired the 'humanitarian intervention' debates of the 1990s. But it was also an example of the recurring use of genocide, or well-known examples of

---

27 See Eyal Mayroz, 'Ever Again? The United States, Genocide Suppression, and the Crisis in Darfur' (2008) 10(3) *Journal of Genocide Research* 359, 367, 370.
28 Martin Mennecke, 'What's in a Name? Reflections on Using, Not Using, and Overusing the "G-Word"' (2007) 2(1) *Genocide Studies and Prevention* 57, 62, 66; Gareth Evans, 'Genocide or Crime? Actions Speak Louder than Words in Darfur', *The European Voice,* 18 February 2005; Gerard Prunier, *Darfur: The Ambiguous Genocide* (Cornell University Press, 2005) 129, 156; Scott Straus, 'Rwanda and Darfur: A Comparative Analysis' (2006) 1(1) *Genocide Studies and Prevention* 41, 51; Juan E Mendez (interview), 'United Nations Report from the Special Advisor on Genocide Prevention', *Voices on Genocide Prevention,* 16 February 2006; Samantha Power, 'Dying in Darfur: Can the Ethnic Cleansing in Sudan be Stopped?', *The New Yorker,* 23 August 2004.
29 There were but a few modest and unsuccessful attempts by states to introduce changes to the definition. A more substantive discussion was included in the Elements of Crimes document of the Rome Statute. See Schabas, 'Article 6. Genocide', above n 15, 127-43.
30 Famously, the philosophers of ancient Greece, Niccolò Machiavelli, Cardinal Mazarin, Oliver Cromwell, and in more recent times realist thinkers such as Hans J Morgenthau, Reinhold Niebuhr, and EH Carr.
31 Kofi Annan, *We the Peoples: The Role of the United Nations in the 21st Century* (United Nations, 2000) 48.

genocide, to argue that in certain extreme situations no justification could excuse international inaction in the face of mass atrocities. The humanitarian intervention literature, in prioritising questions such as who should intervene, when and how to intervene and what to do if there were no collective political will to authorise or carry out interventions, has failed frequently to distinguish genocidal instances of mass atrocities from non-genocidal ones.[32] In some of the studies which did assert explicit focus on 'genocide', the definition of the term was not always precise.[33] In short, there has been much confusion and few answers concerning the moral significance of the label in policymaking. What *could* be argued with considerable certainty is that in just a few decades the term genocide had acquired a notoriety which placed it at the pinnacle of immoral criminal behaviour.

What attributes single out genocide as the 'crime of crimes'? It has been noted that in situations of genocide victims are targeted simply because they exist. However, this characteristic is shared by other extreme examples of crimes against humanity.[34] In such instances, the perpetrators are said to be offending against humanity as a whole.[35]

A unique attribute of genocide is the perpetrators' intent to destroy, not only individuals as human beings, or as members of a particular group, but the *group* itself, in whole or in part.[36] Lemkin placed great emphasis on the diversity of the human race and the cultural loss to the world if human groups were to be annihilated.[37] As noted by Roger Smith in a succinct depiction of the crime, genocide has the inherent potential to:

> distort and alter the very meaning for 'humankind', erasing for all time particular biological and cultural possibilities...For a particular group to claim for itself a right to determine what groups are, in effect, human, possessing the right to life, is a threat to the existence of all other humans.[38]

32 For a parallel treatment of genocide and non-genocide, see Michael J Smith, 'On Humanitarian Intervention' in Neal Riemer (ed), *Protection Against Genocide – Mission Impossible* (Praeger Westport, 2001) 123, 123; Shannon Peterson, *Stories and Past Lessons: Understanding U.S. Decisions of Armed Humanitarian Intervention and Nonintervention in the Post-Cold War Era* (Dissertation, Ohio State University, 2003) 1-36; Robert C DiPrizio, *Armed Humanitarians: U.S. Interventions from Northern Iraq to Kosovo* (Johns Hopkins University Press, 2002) 157.

33 For example, see Jack Donnelly, 'Genocide and Humanitarian Intervention' (2002) 1(1) *Journal of Human Rights* 93, 99; Kenneth J Campbell, *Genocide and the Global Village* (Palgrave, 2001).

34 Alain Destexhe, *Rwanda and Genocide in the Twentieth Century* (New York University Press, 1995).

35 See the preamble to the Genocide Convention.

36 Destexhe, above n 34.

37 Raphael Lemkin, 'Genocide: A Modern Crime' (1945) 4 *Free World* 39, 39-43, <www.prevent genocide.org/lemkin/freeworld1945.htm>.

38 Roger W Smith, 'As Old as History' in Carol Rittner, John K Roth and James M Smith (eds), *Will Genocide Ever End?* (Paragon House, 2002) 31, 33.

A particularly reprehensible characteristic of genocide is the indelibility of membership in the targeted group. That is, in many cases individuals are not allowed to discontinue their membership to escape persecution or extermination.[39] In Nazi Germany, as in 1994 Rwanda, the decision to classify a person as a member of a targeted group – Jewish/Roma or Tutsi – was entirely in the hands of the perpetrators.

While the destruction of a human group may be viewed as more serious than the murdering of as many group members without destroying the group as such,[40] this so-called collectivist position has been increasingly challenged by those prioritising the lives of group members over the survival of the group. Thus, genocide does not *necessarily* affect more individuals in terms of magnitude, death-toll or level of suffering than other mass atrocity crimes.[41] The US bombings of Hiroshima and Nagasaki in 1945 – arguably, war crimes and crimes against humanity – could be said to have resulted in more casualties and no less grief than some genocidal campaigns. The same applied to non-genocidal killings of millions of Russians and Chinese citizens during the twentieth century by their own governments.[42] It is thus not statistics, or even suffering, which have made genocide stand out.

The ethical debates are ongoing, but in international politics the tendency has been to pay more attention to the legal aspects of genocide than to its moral distinctiveness. If a state were to ever again consider invoking the Genocide Convention in relation to a situation, the difficulty of satisfying all four key elements of the definition of genocide – particularly the requirement to demonstrate 'special intent' – would act as a discouraging factor. But is there really a need for a legal genocide determination to activate the Convention? And if the Convention *were* activated: what then? Who bears the responsibility to 'do something', and what is that 'something'? Would a state party's duty to prevent genocide be satisfied merely by referring the case to the UN? And what does the undertaking to punish entail? The following discussion covers these questions, to better understand the nature and scope of the obligations triggered by the Genocide Convention.

IV The obligations imposed by the Genocide Convention

Following a number of assertions made over the years by the International Court of Justice (ICJ), the undertakings to prevent and punish genocide

---

39 John K Roth, 'The Politics of Definition' in Carol Rittner, John K Roth and James M Smith (eds), *Will Genocide Ever End?* (Paragon House, 2002) 23, 26.

40 As proposed in Prunier, above n 28, 156.

41 See Steven P Lee, 'The Moral Distinctiveness of Genocide' (2009) 18(3) *Journal of Political Philosophy* 335, 335-56.

42 See, eg, Rudolph J Rummel, *Death by Government* (Transaction Publishers, 1994).

constitute *erga omnes* obligations.[43] *Erga omnes* obligations are owed by states toward the community of states as a whole.[44] While the details of these obligations are contested, it has been argued that each state has, or should have, a legal interest in maintaining respect for them and their implementation.[45] This notwithstanding, the jurisprudence has assigned lesser legal prominence to the punishment and prevention of genocide than to the prohibition on the crime, as the latter is considered a peremptory (*jus cogens*) norm of customary international law.[46] While peremptory norms are said to attract *erga omnes* obligations, the latter do not automatically and necessarily amount to *jus cogens*.[47]

The late Judge Cassese noted once that the Genocide Convention was designed to deal mainly with the criminal liability of individuals.[48] Indeed, despite the precedents set in Nazi Germany and other state-run genocides, the risk that states would continue to engage in acts of genocide was not appropriately addressed in the treaty. Apart from the categorisation of genocide as an international crime in times of peace and of war, the responsibilities of states parties – to the degree these are explicated in the Convention's provisions – relate mostly to their dual obligations under Article I to *prevent* and *punish* the crime. Yet by excluding stronger prevention and enforcement measures from the text, the drafters produced a woefully weak document.

---

43 *Application of the Convention on the Prevention and Punishment of the Crime of Genocide* (*Bosnia and Herzegovina v. Serbia and Montenegro*) (Preliminary Objections) [1996] ICJ Rep 595, [31]. See also Marco Longobardo, 'Genocide, Obligations *Erga Omnes*, and the Responsibility to Protect: Remarks on a Complex Convergence' (2015) 19(8) *International Journal of Human Rights* 1199, 1201-2.

44 See on the duty to prevent genocide as *erga omnes*, Mark Toufayan, 'The World Court's Distress When Facing Genocide: A Critical Commentary on the Application of the Genocide Convention Case' (2005) 40 *Texas International Law Journal* 233, 249-50; Marko Milanovic, 'State Responsibility for Genocide' (2006) 17(3) *European Journal of International Law* 554, 570.

45 This is because all states could be affected by the violation of these obligations. Longobardo, above n 43, 1202.

46 See discussions in Manuel J Ventura, 'The Prevention of Genocide as a *Jus Cogens* Norm? A Formula for Lawful Humanitarian Intervention' in Charles C Jalloh and Olufemi Elias (eds), *Shielding Humanity: Essays in International Law in Honour of Judge Abdul G. Koroma* (Martinus Nijhoff, 2015) 289, 289-351; Paola Gaeta, 'On What Conditions Can a State Be Held Responsible for Genocide?' (2007) 18(4) *European Journal of International Law* 631, 632. For a more general discussion, see M Cherif Bassiouni, 'International Crimes: *Jus Cogens* and *Obligatio Erga Omnes*' (1997) 59(4) *Law and Contemporary Problems* 63, 63-74.

47 Bassiouni, above n 46, 73.

48 Antonio Cassese, 'Taking Stock of the Genocide Convention and Looking Ahead' in Paola Gaeta (ed), *The UN Genocide Convention: A Commentary* (Oxford University Press, 2009) 531, 531-3, 535-6.

A The undertaking to prevent

As shown in the title of the Convention, the idea of prevention was central to the vision of its drafters.[49] However, despite their good intentions, the treaty's final text focused mainly on punishment. There are two explicit references to 'prevention' in the document, in Articles I and VIII. Article I reads: 'The Contracting Parties confirm that genocide, whether committed in time of peace or in time of war, is a crime under international law which they *undertake to prevent* and to punish'.[50] Unfortunately, the rest of the text did little to clarify which events would trigger these undertakings, or what preventative measures states had to take if the Convention were activated.[51]

The second mention of 'prevention' is in Article VIII, which reads:

> Any Contracting Party may call upon the competent organs of the United Nations to take such action under the Charter of the United Nations as they consider appropriate for the prevention and suppression of acts of genocide or any of the other acts enumerated in Article III.[52]

The common interpretation of this provision is that it does not go beyond conferring the right on states parties to refer a situation – deemed by them genocidal, or likely to become genocidal – to one of the 'competent organs' of the UN.[53] Moreover, the drafters did not specify what actions would have to be taken, if at all, by the UN.[54]

Why is the Genocide Convention so vague? Part of the answer is historical. Firstly, as is common in the drafting of international treaties, the intergovernmental committees that worked on the text felt obliged to produce a document conservative enough to allow most states to sign on.[55] Secondly,

---

49 See also the General Assembly's instructions to the drafting committee in GA Res 96(I), 55th plen mtg, UN Doc A/RES/96(I) (11 December 1946).

50 *Genocide Convention*, Art. I (emphasis added).

51 Ben-Naftali notes that Article III offers implicit support for prevention by criminalising early acts as incitement and conspiracy. Orna Ben-Naftali, 'The Obligations to Prevent and to Punish Genocide' in Paola Gaeta (ed), *The UN Genocide Convention: A Commentary* (Oxford University Press, 2009) 27, 28, 30.

52 *Genocide Convention*, Art. VIII.

53 See Luban, above n 2, 305n; Flint and De Waal, above n 3,131; Straus, above n 28, 51; William Schabas, *Genocide in International Law: The Crime of Crimes* (Cambridge University Press, 2nd ed, 2009) 85. For a different view, see Samantha Power, '*A Problem from Hell*': *America and the Age of Genocide* (Flamingo, 2003) 58.

54 The drafting committees left these decisions to political negotiations. See, in relation to the UNSC discussions, Mark Toufayan, 'Deployment of Troops to Prevent Impending Genocide: A Contemporary Assessment of the UN Security Council's Powers' (2002) 40 *Canadian Yearbook of International Law* 195, 222, 226-7.

55 Such concerns were frequently voiced by delegates during the deliberations. For example, see US delegate to the Ad Hoc Committee in UN Doc E/AC.25/SR.6 (18 April 1948) 13; Peruvian delegate to the Sixth Committee in UN Doc A/C.6/SR.79 (20 October 1948) 60.

the global realities of 1947-8 and the prevailing norms of the time impeded international consensus, particularly since an emerging bipolar divide was already reducing the willingness of states to act in the 'common good'.[56] Thirdly, the sanctity of state sovereignty was merely dented at Nuremberg, and, so shortly after the end of World War II, the focus was still on the dangers of interstate rather than domestic conflicts.[57] Finally, the link between domestic violations of human rights and the maintenance of international peace and security was much less clearer than it is today, and early prevention was still an underdeveloped concept.[58]

B Failures to implement the undertaking to prevent

During the Cold War, international responses to genocide were characterised by neglect.[59] No serious attempts were made to prevent genocide; to rescue the millions who were dying in genocidal outbreaks; or even to address the legal ambiguities which crippled the implementation of the Genocide Convention.[60]

The first significant development took place in March 1993. Eleven months into the civil war in Bosnia, the government of Bosnia-Herzegovina took the Federal Republic of Yugoslavia (Serbia and Montenegro, hereafter FRY) to the ICJ on charges of violations of the Genocide Convention and requested provisional measures for protecting its citizens.[61] In addition to committing genocide it also accused the FRY of failing to prevent genocide under Article I of the Convention.[62]

Fourteen years later, in February 2007, the ICJ issued its final judgement on the Application of the Genocide Convention Case. In it, the Court described the Convention's provision of 'undertaking to prevent' as normative and compelling, unqualified, and as bearing direct obligation on

---

56 Alex Alvarez, 'The Prevention and Intervention of Genocide during the Cold War Years' in Samuel Totten (ed), *The Prevention and Intervention of Genocide: Genocide: A Critical Bibliographic Review* (Transaction Publishers, 2008) Vol. 6, 7, 10.

57 Ibid 10-11.

58 Eyal Mayroz, 'The Legal Duty to Prevent: After the Onset of Genocide' (2012) 14(1) *Journal of Genocide Research* 79, 90.

59 Benjamin Whitaker, *Revised and Updated Report on the Question of the Prevention and Punishment of the Crime of Genocide* ('the Whitaker Report'), UN Doc E/CN.4/ Sub.2/1985/6 (2 July 1985) [55], [65].

60 In the decades following the signing of the Genocide Convention, very little jurisprudence and commentaries appeared about its provisions, apart from the Bosnia-Herzegovina case. Two exceptions were the ICJ case *Reservations to the Convention on the Prevention and Punishment of the Crime of Genocide (Advisory Opinion)* [1951] ICJ Rep 15, and some work by the UN International Law Commission.

61 *Application of the Convention on the Prevention and Punishment of the Crime of Genocide (Bosnia and Herzegovina v Serbia and Montenegro) (Provisional Measures) (Order of 8 April)* [1993] ICJ Rep 3.

62 Mayroz, 'The Legal Duty to Prevent', above n 58, 81.

states parties.[63] It noted also that a referral to the Security Council did not relieve states parties of the general obligation of prevention.[64] The Court then concluded that the obligation to prevent was one of conduct rather than of result, in the sense that compliance is to be measured by action and not by outcome.[65] Furthermore, states parties' obligations could vary according to their capacity 'to influence effectively the action of persons likely to commit, or already committing, genocide'.[66]

The judgement also addressed the politically thorny question of when a state's obligation to prevent genocide begins. Discounting the widespread notion that activation of the Convention required a legal determination of genocide, the ICJ argued:

> [To suggest] that the obligation to prevent genocide only comes into being when perpetration of genocide commences... would be absurd *since the whole point of the obligation is to prevent, or attempt to prevent, the occurrence of the act.*[67]

It therefore determined that '[a] State's obligation to prevent, and the corresponding duty to act, arise at the instant that the State learns of, or should normally have learned of, the existence of a *serious risk* that genocide will be committed'.[68] Importantly, the definition of what a 'serious risk' is was left open to case by case interpretations by states or courts.[69]

V Punishing to deter genocide

In its final judgement on the Application of the Genocide Convention Case, the ICJ affirmed the binding nature of states parties' obligation to *punish* genocide, under Article I and 'other relevant provisions of the Convention',[70] and noted the close links between the undertakings to prevent and to punish.[71]

---

63 *Application of the Convention on the Prevention and Punishment of the Crime of Genocide (Bosnia and Herzegovina v Serbia and Montenegro) (Judgment)* [2007] ICJ Rep 43, [427], [162], [165].
64 Ibid [427].
65 Ibid [430], [461]. States have to manifestly take all the measures within their power that would contribute to preventing genocide. Their obligation is not to succeed but to exercise 'due diligence' in employing all means *reasonably* available to them to prevent genocide, *so far as possible*. The justification was that the combined efforts of different states could succeed in situations where efforts by one state could not.
66 Ibid [430].
67 Ibid [431] (emphasis added). See similar argument in Scheffer, above n 25, 231.
68 *Application of the Genocide Convention,* above n 63, [431] (emphasis added).
69 See a more detailed discussion in Mayroz, 'The Legal Duty to Prevent', above n 58, 82-5.
70 *Application of the Genocide Convention,* above n 63, [439]. The ICJ pointed to Articles III–VII as 'fairly detailed provisions concerning the duty to punish'. Ibid [426].
71 The ICJ noted that 'simply by its wording, Article I of the Convention brings out the close link between prevention and punishment'. It also pointed out 'that one of the most effective ways of preventing criminal acts, in general, is to provide penalties for persons

The institutional arrangements for the obligation to punish were set out in Article VI of the Convention:

> Persons charged with genocide or any of the other acts enumerated in Article III shall be tried by a competent tribunal of the State in the territory of which the act was committed, or by such international penal tribunal as may have jurisdiction with respect to those Contracting Parties which shall have accepted its jurisdiction.[72]

Central to the provision were attempts by the drafters to reconcile contentious jurisdictional debates concerning territoriality, complementarity and universality, some of which have not been fully settled yet – particularly in relation to situations where the territorial state was behind the genocide.[73]

Article V offered implicit support for prevention by obliging states parties to enact the necessary legislation to give effect to the Convention's provisions; particularly to provide effective penalties for persons guilty of genocide.[74]

Under Article IV, 'Persons committing genocide or any of the other acts enumerated in Article III shall be punished, whether they are constitutionally responsible rulers, public officials or private individuals'. By including rulers and public officials, the provision continued efforts from the Nuremberg trials to limit the immunity provided to state officials by various other treaties.[75] Indeed, genocide, like other 'core crimes' of ICL[76] had been perpetrated mostly by state officials in their official capacity, and with acquiescence or direct support from the state apparatus.[77] But as state responsibility does not attract criminal liability – not even for genocide – legal sanctions against the state cannot replace the deterring function of ICL, even as the two are complementary in nature.[78]

The abstract language of the Genocide Convention, typical of international treaties, required a great deal of interpretation and explication to begin to meet the detailed and precise requirements of ICL and its system of justice.

---

committing such acts, and to impose those penalties effectively on those who commit the acts one is trying to prevent'. Ibid [426].

72 *Genocide Convention*, Art. VI.

73 See the discussion in Ben-Naftali, above n 51, 48-54.

74 Ibid 28, 30.

75 See Paola Gaeta, 'Immunities and Genocide' in Paola Gaeta (ed), *The UN Genocide Convention: A Commentary* (Oxford University Press, 2009) 310, 310-33.

76 Crimes against humanity, war crimes and the crime of aggression.

77 Paola Gaeta, 'International Criminal Law' in Basak Cali (ed), *International Law for International Relations* (Oxford University Press, 2010) 258, 259.

78 See the extended discussion in Anja Seibert-Fohr, 'Accountability of States for Genocide' in Paola Gaeta (ed), *The UN Genocide Convention: A Commentary* (Oxford University Press, 2009) 349, 349-72.

After a few decades of near standstill, the process commenced in earnest in the 1990s under the *ad hoc* Tribunals, and later the ICC. In 2007, the ICJ issued its significant contribution to the jurisprudence on the Genocide Convention. The obligation to punish, the ICJ has noted, was distinct yet connected to the obligation to prevent genocide[79]; connected in the sense that criminal proceedings are intended, among other things, to deter would-be *génocidaires*.[80] The minutes (*travaux préparatoires*) of the Genocide Convention's drafting process also indicate that the majority of states' delegations prioritised criminal repression during the negotiations over other means of prevention.[81]

Legal minds tend to be better equipped than others to bear the long maturing period for international criminal law and its instruments. The same cannot be said for political actors who are constrained by short election cycles, humanitarian actors, and certainly not victims. With many of the legal questions still unresolved, it is only fair to ask which considerations should guide future efforts to prosecute genocide.

Looking at the rate of successful genocide convictions, the picture is far from rousing. Aside from Rwanda's domestic criminal courts (which have managed to convict – sometimes controversially – thousands of genocide and genocide-related cases[82]) the combined numbers for all other domestic and international convictions, including by the ICTR, are estimated at only a few dozen.[83] For a nearly seven-decades-long enterprise, during which dozens more alleged cases of genocide were perpetrated globally, and, given the amount of effort and resources invested by the international community since the 1990s, this is not much.

However, convictions are not and should not be our main concern. As noted, it was deterrence which constituted the primary incentive and central link between punishment and prevention in the Genocide Convention.[84] It is deterrence which has the potential to help bring would-be perpetrators to rethink their plans. Therefore, assessing the challenges and benefits of genocide prosecution as part of the term's overall deterrent capacity is important.

---

79 *Application of the Genocide Convention*, above n 63, [425].
80 Ibid [426]. See also discussion in Ben-Naftali, above n 51, 29-32.
81 Ben-Naftali, above n 51, 31.
82 See, eg, Human Rights Watch, 'Rwanda: Justice after Genocide – 20 Years On' (March 2014), <www.hrw.org/news/2014/03/28/rwanda-justice-after-genocide-20-years#_ftn12>. These numbers do not include over a million and a half convictions, mostly of 'less serious' crimes by the *Gacaca* courts. On the latter, see Anne-Marie de Brouwer and Etienne Ruvebana, 'The Legacy of the *Gacaca* Courts in Rwanda: Survivors' Views' (2013) 13(5) *International Criminal Law Review* 937, 937-76.
83 See Patricia M Wald, 'Genocide and Crimes Against Humanity' (2007) 6 *Washington University Global Studies Law Review* 621, 628-9.
84 See discussion of the drafters' purpose, as manifested in the *travaux préparatoires*, in Ventura, above n 46, 289-351.

William Schabas has argued that the legal utility of genocide has declined in favour of crimes against humanity.[85] Taking perpetrators to court on charges of genocide is more difficult than on charges of crimes against humanity, he says, as the latter does not require proof of specific intent.[86] Moreover, prosecuting under crimes against humanity became particularly advantageous once the scope of the crime was extended in the Rome Statute of the ICC to times of peace – long the unique prerogative of genocide.[87]

On the other end of the argument is the normative force, or notoriety, integrated into political, legal and popular conceptions of the term 'genocide'. Schabas himself noted that defendants before international criminal tribunals preferred being convicted of war crimes or crimes against humanity to being labelled *génocidaires*, writing: 'Plea agreements systematically involve[d] withdrawing charges of genocide in favour of convictions for crimes against humanity'.[88] It is unclear whether such concerns could deter would-be perpetrators during the early preparatory stages of genocide.

If deterrence through prosecution *is* useful to genocide prevention, occurrences in recent years have been far from heartening. The failure to bring to justice Sudan's sitting President Omar al-Bashir, indicted by the ICC in 2010 for genocide and crimes against humanity in Darfur,[89] provides little hope (not to speak of the considerable damage to the reputation of the Court). This is particularly so since the referral of the case to the ICC was made by the UN Security Council, the only UN organ qualified to impose binding and enforceable decisions on states.[90]

In a similar vein, one cannot help being troubled by recent efforts on the part of certain African governments to introduce immunity clauses for high level state officials under the plan for a revamped African court of justice and

---

85 Schabas, above n 11, 33, 39.

86 William Schabas, 'Genocide, Crimes against Humanity, and Darfur: the Commission of Inquiry's Findings on Genocide' (2006) 27(2) *Cardozo Law Review* 1703, 1719-20.

87 It was the nexus to armed conflict, imposed by the great powers in Nuremberg on 'crimes against humanity', which led to the internationalisation of the term genocide in 1946. While the powers feared being targeted for repressive acts by a peace-time crime, emerging states, specifically India, Cuba, Panama and Saudi Arabia, were pushing for an instrument that could protect them, and settled on genocide. See Schabas, above n 22, 6-7.

88 Schabas, *Genocide in International Law*, above n 53, 11, n 32. See also Ventura, above n 46, 321.

89 In June 2015, during a visit to South Africa for an African Union Summit, al-Bashir was allowed to leave the country in defiance of a South African court order. Conor Gaffey, 'South Africa Loses Appeal over Sudan President Al-Bashir Arrest Warrant', *Newsweek*, 15 March 2016 <www.newsweek.com/south-africa-omar-al-bashir-darfur-genocide-appeal-436928>.

90 There is sufficient evidence to suggest that the UNSC's failures to ensure al-Bashir's arrest were influenced by self-interest calculations of some of the Council's most powerful members. See, eg, Peter Cluskey, 'Efforts to Arrest Sudan President Foiled by UN veto: International Criminal Court Is Weakened by the UN Security Council, *Irish Times*, 22 March 2015 <www.irishtimes.com/news/world/efforts-to-arrest-sudan-president-foiled-by-un-veto-1.2148911>.

human rights. These arrangements, if realised, are likely to include immunity for egregious international crimes such as genocide.[91]

VI The significance of the 'genocide' label to policymaking

Earlier in the chapter, we pointed to the potential influence of 'genocide debates' on states' behaviour. Rooted in the global abhorrence of the term, such debates pertained at different times to current, burgeoning or earlier alleged cases of genocide. A notable example are enduring efforts by successive Turkish governments to convince states not to apply the term 'genocide' to the extermination campaign which the Young Turks government conducted during World War I (1915-1918) against the Armenian people. Over decades, Turkey had invested significant political and economic capital in these attempts.[92] In the case of Darfur, squabbles since 2004 over the applicability of the term genocide to the crisis were said to have forestalled more meaningful international responses to the violence.[93] Consequently, it has been suggested that shifting public and political focus away from the term may help to circumvent some of the obstacles created by its 1948 definition. An initiative advanced by David Scheffer[94] attempted to resolve some of these complications. Scheffer's idea was to separate the public and political usage of the word 'genocide' from its legal definition to allow states and international organisations 'to publicly describe precursors of genocide and react rapidly either to prevent or to stop mass killings or other seeming acts of genocide'.[95] He argued that governments:

> should not be constrained from acting by the necessity of a prior legal finding that the crime of genocide in fact has occurred or is occurring and, once that legal finding has been made, that governments are somehow obligated to use military force in response.[96]

Instead of labelling a crisis as genocide, Scheffer recommended using a broader term, 'atrocity crimes', which would amalgamate four types of international crimes: genocide, crimes against humanity, war crimes and

---

91 Amnesty International, 'Malabo Protocol: Legal and Institutional Implications of the Merged and Expanded African Court' (22 January 2016) <www.amnesty.org/en/documents/afr01/3063/2016/en/>. See also Chapter 9 in this book.

92 Nikolaus Schrodt, *Modern Turkey and the Armenian Genocide: An Argument about the Meaning of the Past* (Springer, 2014).

93 Mennecke, above n 28, 62, 66; Evans, above n 28; Prunier, above n 28, 156; Straus, above n 28, 51; Mendez, above n 28; Power, above n 28.

94 Former US Ambassador at Large for War Crimes Issues in the Clinton Administration (1997-2001).

95 Scheffer, above n 25, 229.

96 Ibid.

the emerging crime of ethnic cleansing.[97] In his opinion, the 'unification' of crimes would lead to greater clarity in public discussions, news coverage and decision-making.[98]

The idea of reducing focus on the term 'genocide' challenges long-held assumptions about its 'unmatched' ability to draw crucial attention from journalists, the wider public and politicians[99]; 'create irresistible public pressures on governments to act'[100]; and 'motivate and mobilize' for intervention.[101] If these expectations were factual, so goes the argument, then abandoning the label would remove a powerful political tool for action. Notably, this claim may be at odds with the fact that most humanitarian interventions have taken place in response to clearly *non*-genocidal events (e.g. Somalia, Haiti, Kosovo, Sierra Leone and East Timor). The historical record thus poses a distinct question mark over the normative capacity of 'genocide' terminology to meaningfully affect official policies.

VII Conclusion

Apart from rare hypothetical scenarios, genocide is not a single event. It results from a series of interconnected deliberate actions taken by many individuals over an extended period, which, if successful, have the potential to bring about the partial or complete destruction of a human group. For these same reasons, preparations for genocide could be detected early and prevention be pursued through various means.

Still, failures to prevent genocide have occurred despite repeated pledges by states and intergovernmental organisations to avert, or halt, the perpetration of the crime ('never again' rhetoric). These failings had various causes. First, although the Genocide Convention imposed a binding obligation on states parties to prevent genocide, the nature and many specifics

97 The proposal included the designation of a new field in international law: atrocity law, which would deal with 'atrocity crimes'. See Scheffer, above n 25, 229. The scope suggested for 'atrocity crimes' was similar to that of Responsibility to Protect's 'mass atrocity crimes', and (with the inclusion of the crime of aggression, instead of 'ethnic cleansing') to the jurisdiction assigned to the ICC in the Rome Statute.

98 David Scheffer, 'Atrocity Crimes: Framing the Responsibility To Protect' (2008) 40(1-2) *Case Western Reserve Journal of International Law* 111, 111.

99 William FS Miles, 'Labeling "Genocide" in Sudan: A Constructionist Analysis of Darfur' (2006) 1(3) *Genocide Studies and Prevention* 251, 252, 257, 260.

100 Michael P Scharf, 'International Law in Crisis: A Qualitative Empirical Contribution to the Compliance Debate' (2009-2010) 31 *Cardozo Law Review* 45, 78.

101 See Madeleine K Albright and William S Cohen, *Preventing Genocide: A Blueprint for U.S. Policymakers* (United States Holocaust Memorial Museum, 2008). Schabas noted that the definition of genocide in the report was broad enough to represent all atrocity crimes. William Schabas, *The Genocide Convention at 60* (6 February 2009) <www.crimesofwar.org/commentary/the-genocide-convention-at-60/>.

of this obligation remained uncertain until at least 2007. What *has* been clear from the start is that in line with Article VIII, states parties were permitted but not obligated to invoke the Convention. Second, many states have been confused by the notion that the existence of genocide had to be legally proven *prior to* referring the case to the 'competent organs' of the UN. The consequences of the ICJ's 2007 ruling that a 'serious risk' of genocide is sufficient to invoke the Convention are yet to be internalised and realised. Third, during many genocidal situations states were not keen to invoke the Convention, fearing that doing so would oblige them to take part in an international intervention. Some of the legal uncertainties have now been addressed by the ICJ, though, arguably, more so for legal minds than for politicians and citizenries. Fourth, the Security Council – rightly regarded as the appropriate UN organ to be called upon by state parties – retains wide autonomy over the decision of how to give effect to the Convention. Fifth, while Security Council membership consisted over the years overwhelmingly of states parties to the Convention, their obligations under the treaty were never linked – by courts or by the UNSC itself – to their responsibilities, or enhanced capacity to act as Council members.[102] Their failure to translate the UN referral of the situation in Darfur into a robust international action, beyond forwarding it to the ICC prosecutor, is a case in point.[103]

Finally, the significance of the 'genocide' label to political processes has been documented much more systematically in relation to Western nations. Efforts should be taken to learn about the dynamics and influence of the term elsewhere in the world, particularly in Russia and China, as both powers continue to be in a strong position to either contribute to, or to frustrate the battle against genocide and other mass atrocity crimes.

Further reading

Abtahi, Hirad and Philippa Webb (eds), *The Genocide Convention: the Travaux Préparatoires, Volumes 1 and 2* (Brill, 2008).

Application of the Convention on the Prevention and Punishment of the Crime of Genocide Case (Bosnia and Herzegovina v Serbia and Montenegro) (Judgment) [2007] ICJ Rep 43.

Gaeta, Paola (ed), *The UN Genocide Convention: A Commentary* (Oxford University Press, 2009).

Goldsmith, Katherine, 'The Issue of Intent in the Genocide Convention and Its Effect on the Prevention and Punishment of the Crime of Genocide: Toward a Knowledge-Based Approach' (2010) 5(3) *Genocide Studies and Prevention* 238.

---

102 Mayroz, above n 58, 'The Legal Duty to Prevent', 79-98.
103 Eyal Mayroz, *'Ever Again?' America's Failure to Halt Genocide, From Bosnia to Darfur* (forthcoming 2017).

Jones, Adam, *Genocide: A Comprehensive Introduction* (Taylor & Francis, 2nd ed, 2010).

Mayroz, Eyal, 'The Legal Duty to Prevent: After the Onset of Genocide' (2012) 14(1) *Journal of Genocide Research* 79.

Moses, Dirk A, 'Raphael Lemkin, Culture, and the Concept of Genocide' in Donald Bloxham and A Dirk Moses (eds), *The Oxford Handbook on Genocide Studies* (Oxford University Press, 2010).

Power, Samantha, '*A Problem from Hell*': *America and the Age of Genocide* (Flamingo, 2003).

Schabas, William, *Genocide in International Law: The Crime of Crimes,* (Cambridge University Press, 2nd ed, 2009).

Scheffer, David, 'Genocide and Atrocity Crimes' (2006) 1(3) *Genocide Studies and Prevention* 229.

5

CRIMES AGAINST HUMANITY

The concept of humanity in international law

Raphaëlle Nollez-Goldbach

From the first appearance of the term 'humanity' in nineteenth-century treaties on the law of war to its current use as a basis for a new category of crimes – crimes against humanity –, the concept of humanity has undergone a radical development.[1] Its purpose henceforth is to protect all human beings from the most serious crimes concerning the international community.

With the development of international criminal courts and tribunals, the concept of humanity developed considerably at the end of the twentieth century and the beginning of the twenty-first century to ground crimes against humanity. For the first time in international law, a permanent and supranational criminal court, the International Criminal Court (ICC), was set up to try the perpetrators of these crimes. By their nature (as an attack against the essence of human beings), extent and gravity, crimes against humanity affect the entire international community and must therefore be punished in its name. The concept of humanity thus embodies the world community in its entirety, transcending individual rights and lives and including present and even future generations.

Yet the reference to humanity remains largely implicit and vague in international norms and case-law. It is not properly defined, nor is its nature or content developed. The legal concept of humanity firstly refers, in the law of war, to an abstract moral value directed at limiting war atrocities (I). The conception of humanity as a victim thus characterises crimes against humanity (II), while a biological understanding of it is currently developing as a result

---

1 This paper builds on a previous study that sets out my preliminary research on the concept of humanity: Raphaëlle Nollez-Goldbach, 'Les paradoxes de l'humanité juridique' in Olivier de Frouville (ed), *Le cosmopolitisme juridique* (Pedone, 2014) 127-135.

of bioethics (IV). Humanity also points to the existence of a worldwide community of interests underlying a concept of humanity centred on solidarity (III). This results, finally, in a fundamental transformation of the international system that is now grounded on the protection of humanity. It did not lead though to a paradigm shift from the traditional centrality of State sovereignty (V).

I The birth of humanity in the law of war: an abstract moral value

The legal concept of humanity first appeared in the law of war at the end of the nineteenth century. It was created in connection with war and its atrocities as a means of limiting them. Humanity was first used in international treaties to call for a treatment based on the 'humanity'[2] of prisoners and wounded persons. It was later sanctioned as a general principle by the International Court of Justice (ICJ).

The 'laws of humanity' were first introduced in international law[3] with the Declaration of Saint Petersburg[4] in 1868, with the purpose of renouncing the use of certain explosive projectiles in times of war. They next appeared in the preamble to the Hague Convention of 1899, in which States Parties agreed to serve the 'interests of humanity' even during armed conflicts and, consequently, to protect populations and belligerents under the 'laws of humanity' (as stated in the Martens clause[5] included in that preamble). These humanity laws were then incorporated into the new Hague Conventions[6] in 1907, which revised the former convention and formed the basis of the law of war, as well as into the Geneva Conventions[7] in 1949, which established humanitarian law.

---

2 *Geneva Convention for the Amelioration of the Condition of the Wounded and Sick in Armed Forces in the Field of August 12, 1949 (Geneva Convention I)*, opened for signature 12 August 1949, 75 UNTS 31 (entered into force 21 October 1950) Art. 5.

3 See Raphaëlle Nollez-Goldbach, 'Le crime contre l'humanité et la protection de la vie' (2008) 2 *Revue Aspects* 85.

4 This has been considered by the ICJ as part of 'a body of legal prescriptions' governing the conduct of military operations and 'cardinal principles' of humanitarian law. See *Legality of the Threat or Use of Nuclear Weapons (Advisory Opinion)* [1996] ICJ Rep 226 [77]–[78].

5 The 'Martens clause', named after the Russian delegate at The Hague Conference who proposed it, reads: 'Until a more complete code of the laws of war has been issued, the High Contracting Parties deem it expedient to declare that, in cases not included in the Regulations adopted by them, the inhabitants and the belligerents remain under the protection and the rule of the principles of the law of nations, as they result from the usages established among civilized peoples, from the laws of humanity, and the dictates of the public conscience'.

6 *Hague Convention for the Protection of Cultural Property in the Event of Armed Conflict*, opened for signature 14 May 1954, 249 UNTS 240 (entered into force 7 August 1956) preamble.

7 *Geneva Convention I*, above n 2, Art. 63; *Geneva Convention for the Amelioration of the Condition of Wounded, Sick and Shipwrecked Members of Armed Forces at Sea of August 12, 1949*

The relative extension of this new legal concept was being pursued by the ICJ in its case-law. Indeed, the Court referred in several cases to some 'elementary considerations of humanity'[8] that are to be observed by all States in the fields of the law of war and humanitarian law.[9] In the *Corfu Channel* case in 1949, the Court relied 'on certain general and well-recognized principles, namely: elementary considerations of humanity, even more exacting in peace than in war'.[10] In this particular case, the ICJ judges based a State's obligation to declare the existence of a minefield within its territory on this principle of 'elementary considerations of humanity' that they established for the first time.

The ICJ founded further State international obligations regarding humanitarian law and the law of war on the principle of humanity. In the *Nicaragua* case in 1986, the Court referred both to the 'elementary considerations of humanity' included in the Geneva Conventions that expressed the fundamental general principles of humanitarian law, and to 'the laws of humanity' binding States to fulfil obligations resulting from humanitarian law and the law of war.[11] Furthermore, in the *Legality of the Threat or Use of Nuclear Weapons* case in 1996, the Court based the obligation to observe the fundamental rules of humanitarian law – the Geneva Conventions – and of the law of war – the Hague Conventions – on 'the respect of the human person and "elementary considerations of humanity"'.[12] The legal concept of humanity is therefore used in ICJ case-law as a general principle of international law and

---

(Geneva Convention II), opened for signature 12 August 1949, 75 UNTS 85 (entered into force 21 October 1950) Art. 62; *Geneva Convention relative to the Treatment of Prisoners of War of August 12, 1949 (Geneva Convention III)*, opened for signature 12 August 1949, 75 UNTS 135 (entered into force 21 October 1950) Art. 142; *Geneva Convention relative to the Protection of Civilian Persons in Time of War of August 12, 1949 (Geneva Convention IV)*, opened for signature 12 August 1949, 75 UNTS 287 (entered into force 21 October 1950) Art. 158.

8 *Corfu Channel (United Kingdom of Great Britain and Northern Ireland v Albania)* (Judgment) [1949] ICJ Rep 22; *United States Diplomatic and Consular Staff in Tehran (United States of America v Iran)* (Judgment) [1980] ICJ Rep 43; *Military and Paramilitary Activities in and against Nicaragua (Nicaragua v United States of America)* (Judgment) [1986] ICJ Rep 14 [215], [218]; *Legality of the Threat or Use of Nuclear Weapons*, above n 4, [35], [79].

9 See Gilbert Guillaume, 'La Cour internationale de justice et les droits de l'homme' (2001) *Droits fondamentaux* <http://droits-fondamentaux.u-paris2.fr/article/2001/cour-internationale-justice-droits-homme> 26-27.

10 See *Corfu Channel*, above n 8.

11 *Military and Paramilitary Activities in and against Nicaragua*, above n 8, [218]. The Court was referring here to the respective Articles in the Geneva Conventions, including the 'laws of humanity'. See note 6.

12 *Legality of the Threat or Use of Nuclear Weapons*, above n 4, [35], [79]. See Pierre-Marie Dupuy, 'Les considérations élémentaires d'humanité dans la jurisprudence de la Cour internationale de justice' in Nicolas Valticos, René Jean Dupuy and Linos-Alexandre Sicilianos (eds), *Mélanges Nicolas Valticos* (Pedone, 1999) 122.

as a basis for States' international obligations regarding humanitarian law and the law of war.

Yet the first normative appearance of humanity and its development at the level of case-law concerns only the restriction of the means of war and the enforcement of humanitarian law. The emerging principle of humanity is not limited merely to conflict situations but also remains vague since no further definition is provided. In particular, the 'laws of humanity' and the 'elementary consideration of humanity' point toward a legal concept of humanity shaped as a moral value.

The 1928 Kellogg–Briand Pact, which is considered as one of the first international treaties for the renunciation of war, illustrates this use of humanity as an abstract moral guideline. Its preamble's first sentence grounds this new ban on States Parties' 'solemn duty' – a clear moral reference[13] – to develop the 'welfare of mankind'. This is a very general assertion that offers no specifications as to the content of such an abstract and polysemous notion. Likewise, the ICJ Advisory Opinion in the *Reservations to the Genocide Convention* case in 1951 referred to 'moral law' when defining the crime of genocide that 'shocks the conscience of mankind and results in great losses to humanity which is contrary to moral law'.[14] Specifically, the Court linked humanity and morality by asserting that the Genocide Convention is based on 'moral and humanitarian principles'. The French version is even clearer, establishing a connection between the 'moral and humanity principles which are its basis'.[15] The first appearance of the concept of humanity in international law thus appears to point to an abstract moral value aimed at limiting war, without any substantial development of its nature or content.

II Crimes against humanity: humanity as the basis of an international crime

The concept of humanity only recently began to spread, especially with the development of international criminal law and the particular category of 'crimes against humanity', both of which were born at the end of the Second World War. The Nuremberg trial legally gave birth to crimes against humanity. The International Military Tribunal tried major war criminals (of the European Axis countries) for the first time and, under Article 6(c), its

---

13 It is also worth noting that the French version adds that this duty 'incombe' – is incumbent upon – the States Parties, underlying the idea of a moral obligation.
14 *Reservations to the Genocide Convention (Advisory Opinion)* [1951] ICJ Rep 23. See Gleider I Hernández, 'A Reluctant Guardian: The International Court of Justice and the Concept of "International Community"' (2012) 83(1) *British Yearbook of International Law* 13.
15 Translation from the original French version: 'des principes de morale et d'humanité qui sont à sa base', *Reservations to the Genocide Convention (Advisory Opinion)* [1951] ICJ Rep 23, [24].

Charter of 8 August 1945 introduced crimes against humanity as those acts or persecutions committed against a civilian population, 'in connection' with other crimes within the jurisdiction of the Tribunal (crimes against peace and war crimes).[16] The decision to grant the Nuremberg Tribunal jurisdiction over such new crimes against humanity resulted from the allies' will to extend trials to those 'who committed not only war crimes but also those who committed other serious crimes that fall outside the ambit of traditional war crimes'.[17] That is why the inclusion of crimes against humanity in the Nuremberg Charter was justified by their relation to war, a link illustrated by the Tribunal's observation that

> from the beginning of the war in 1939 war crimes were committed on a vast scale, which were also crimes against humanity; and insofar as the inhumane acts charged in the indictment, and committed after the beginning of the war, did not constitute war crimes, they were all committed in execution of, or in connection with, the aggressive war, and therefore constituted crimes against humanity.[18]

This was the first time that the category of crimes against humanity had been included in international law. It had been used only once before 'in a non-technical sense'[19] in 1915, in which it was employed by the Governments of France, Great Britain and Russia to denounce the massacres of the Armenian population in Turkey as 'crimes against humanity and civilization'.[20] It was subsequently included, on the basis of the Nuremberg Charter, in Article 5.c of the International Military Tribunal for the Far East Charter of 19 January 1946.

16 Article 6 (as amended by Protocol of 6 October 1945) reads: '... The following acts, or any of them, are crimes coming within the jurisdiction of the Tribunal for which there shall be individual responsibility: . . . c) crimes against humanity: namely, murder, extermination, enslavement, deportation, and other inhumane acts committed against any civilian population, before or during the war, or persecutions on political, racial or religious grounds in execution of or in connection with any crime within the jurisdiction of the Tribunal, whether or not in violation of the domestic law of the country where perpetrated'.
17 *The Prosecutor v Duško Tadić a/k/a "Dule" (Opinion and Judgement)* (International Criminal Tribunal for the former Yugoslavia, Trial Chamber, Case No IT-94-1-T, 7 May 1997) [619].
18 *Trial of the Major War Criminals before the International Military Tribunal*, Nuremberg, 1947, Vol. 22, 30 September 1946, 497.
19 *The Prosecutor v Duško Tadić a/k/a "Dule"(Opinion and Judgement)* (International Criminal Tribunal for the former Yugoslavia, Trial Chamber, Case No IT-94-1-T, 7 May 1997) [618].
20 Declaration of 28 May 1915 of the Governments of France, Great Britain and Russia denouncing the massacres of the Armenian population in Turkey as 'crimes against humanity and civilization for which all the members of the Turkish Government will be held responsible together with its agents implicated in the massacres'. Quoted in Egon Schwelb, 'Crimes Against Humanity' (1946) 23 *British Year Book of International Law* 178, 181. It is also worth noting that Robespierre called for the French king Louis XVI to be declared 'a traitor to the French nation, a criminal against humanity', Robespierre's discourse to the National Convention, 3 December 1792.

By creating this new crime category, the international community 'was widening the category of acts considered of "meta-national" concern'.[21] This clearly constitutes a turning point in international law.

However, the notion of humanity only arose markedly from the 1990s and the first decade of the twenty-first century. It has developed in international law with the increase in international criminal courts and tribunals and the judgement of international crimes. Confronting mass crimes and gross human rights violations, the new international criminal order that was set in place by the international community is thus responsible for its protection. Crimes *against* humanity are tried *in the name of* humanity.

The first international criminal tribunals were established[22] by resolutions of the Security Council of the United Nations acting under Chapter VII of the Charter to try the individuals responsible for 'serious violations of international humanitarian law' committed in the former Yugoslavia (ICTY, 1993) and in Rwanda (ICTR, 1994). Subsequently, international courts and tribunals multiplied, be it on the grounds of agreements between the UN and the domestic governments (the so-called hybrid tribunals) of East Timor (2000), Sierra Leone (2002) and Cambodia (2006) or through a Security Council resolution under Chapter VII for Lebanon (2007). The ICC was created by the Rome Treaty in 1998 – which entered in force on 1 July 2002 – as the first permanent and supranational international criminal court. Under the terms of the preamble to its Statute, the Court seeks to put an end to impunity for the perpetrators of 'the most serious crimes of concern to the international community as a whole': crimes of genocide, crimes against humanity, and war crimes. Its prosecutor calls for judgements in the name of the international community and has jurisdiction to initiate an investigation on his or her own initiative.

The ICC Statute's definition of crimes against humanity, under Article 7, is currently the most complete, incorporating the Nuremberg Statute as well as both the ICT Statutes and case-laws. It quotes a broad list of acts,[23] some of which are mentioned for the first time, such as 'sexual slavery, enforced prostitution, forced pregnancy, enforced sterilization, or any other form of sexual violence of comparable gravity', as well as the 'national, ethnic, cultural, religious, gender or other grounds that are universally recognized as impermissible under international law' that reinforced the crimes of rape and persecution, respectively. Article 7 also lists crimes that were only defined

21 Antonio Cassese, *International Law* (Oxford University Press, 2005) 440.
22 As will be discussed in more detail in Part III of this book.
23 'Murder; extermination; enslavement; deportation or forcible transfer of population; imprisonment; torture; rape, sexual slavery, enforced prostitution, forced pregnancy, enforced sterilization, or any other form of sexual violence of comparable gravity; persecution against any identifiable group or collectivity; enforced disappearance of persons; the crime of apartheid; other inhumane acts'.

in international treaties as crimes against humanity: 'apartheid' and the 'enforced disappearance of persons'.

All the acts listed in the first paragraph of Article 7 constitute crimes against humanity when 'committed as part of a widespread or systematic attack directed against any civilian population, with knowledge of the attack'. Therefore, the elements required to characterise a crime against humanity are, firstly, that it be an attack against a civilian population which is either widespread or systematic (of note, a crime against humanity no longer needs to be linked to the existence of an armed conflict). The alternative conjunction 'or' was chosen by the States over the cumulative one 'and'. Secondly, the attack requires a policy to organise the perpetration of the crimes. However, this policy could result from either a State or an organisation (*i.e.* non-State actor). Ultimately, the authors' intent must be demonstrated, both in terms of their knowledge of the broader context, namely the existence of a widespread or systematic attack, and of their intention to commit the crime.

It is worth noting that from the first appearance of humanity in the law of war, as an abstract moral value, to its current use in international criminal law, the legal concept of humanity is based on a victim-centred notion of humanity. This is a reaction to the horrors of armed conflicts and aims to protect human beings against mass crimes and the most serious violations of their rights. Indeed, States only accepted some limitation to their sovereignty in reaction to 'the most serious crimes of concern to the international community as a whole', as stated in the ICC Statute's preamble. It is almost as if humanity only existed when attacked, embodying that smaller universal: the defence of human beings against genocide, crimes against humanity, and war crimes. The universal value of humanity is reduced to its smallest common denominator. The humanity which is thus guaranteed by the international criminal order is focused on a victim-centred humanity. It represents only the defensive face of humanity.[24]

Two different kinds of humanity[25] are in fact emerging nowadays. On one hand, there is the victim-centred concept of humanity, which needs to be protected and rescued. This is embodied by crimes against humanity, the right of humanitarian intervention, and the responsibility to protect. This defensive face of humanity is coupled with the notion of humanity centred on solidarity.[26] This aspect of the concept of humanity is meant as a community of interests, embodied in the common heritage of humanity and global public goods. Yet this part of the concept is still on hold since the common heritage of humanity and global public goods are not well-developed categories. The concept of humanity which is today the most

---

24 Nollez-Goldbach, above n 3, 92.
25 Danièle Lochak, *Le droit et les paradoxes de l'universalité* (PUF, 2010).
26 Ibid.

advanced is the victim-centred one. This is guaranteed by the international criminal order that has been growing increasingly over the past two decades and it is enforced by the decisions of both the ICTs and the ICC. Nonetheless, nowhere is this understanding of humanity defined; it is only implied. Yet it constitutes the basis of an international crime. Herein lies a real paradox.

III Humanity in international criminal case-law

To provide a more specific answer to the question of how to define the legal concept of humanity and to find some indications as to the nature and constitutive elements of that understanding of humanity, one needs to dig further into international criminal case-law.

The Nuremberg case-law is the first example of the occurrence of humanity in international criminal case-law. The International Military Tribunal referred to the 'principles of humanity' in the trial of Wilhelm von Leeb and thirteen others. For the Tribunal, humanity constitutes the ground for the mode of responsibility of high-level commanders, which 'is fixed according to the customs of war, international agreements, fundamental principles of humanity'.[27] Humanity also became a legal basis for defining the criminality at stake during the Second World War: 'from an international standpoint, criminality may arise by reason that the act is forbidden by international agreements or is inherently criminal and contrary to accepted principles of humanity as recognized and accepted by civilized nations'.[28] An act becomes criminal because it is contrary to the principle of humanity, making humanity the legal basis for crimes against humanity in a kind of tautological definition. At the time, these new crimes were indeed non-existent in international law and punished by the Tribunal without any positive legal ground. The international community therefore had to establish a basis for them. The concept of humanity stands as a meta-legal value that allows an act to be punished by the International Tribunal and that constitutes the moral horizon of international criminal justice.

A more specific definition of humanity was later provided by the ICTY in its first case. This marked a change in the use of humanity, which established it as a global community transcending individuals. In the *Drazen Erdemovic* case, the Tribunal first declared that

27 The United Nations War Crimes Commission, *Law Reports of Trials of War Criminals*, Vol. XII, 1949, 75. Quoted by Elena Carpanelli, 'Principles of International Law: Struggling with a Slippery Concept' in Laura Pineschi (ed), *General Principles of Law – The Role of the Judiciary* (Springer, 2015) 125.
28 Ibid.

crimes against humanity are serious acts of violence which harm human beings by striking what is most essential to them: their life, liberty, physical welfare, health, and or dignity. They are inhumane acts that by their extent and gravity go beyond the limits tolerable to the international community, which must perforce demand their punishment.[29]

By their very nature (as an attack against the essence of human beings), such acts affect the international community as a whole, and it is therefore in the name of the international community that they must be punished. The Tribunal also considered

> that the life of the accused and that of the victim are not fully equivalent. As opposed to ordinary law, the violation here is no longer directed at the physical welfare of the victim alone but at humanity as a whole.[30]

The extent and gravity of the crimes raised them from a violation of the rights of individuals to that of the rights of humanity. The concept of humanity thus embodies the world community, a universal collective group transcending individual rights and lives: 'crimes against humanity also transcend the individual because when the individual is assaulted, humanity comes under attack and is negated'.[31] Finally, the ICTY definition of humanity matched the victim-centred one developed in international law since the nineteenth century, in a formulation that could not be clearer: 'it is therefore the concept of humanity as victim which essentially characterises crimes against humanity'.[32]

ICC case-law, for its part, does not at first offer any further clarifications. When using the concept of humanity, the Court seems to do so implicitly, without digging any deeper into its content and material substance. It mainly points either to an abstract moral value or to a victim-centred understanding of humanity, although it may in some cases refer to a global community sharing common interests.

When the ICC alludes to humanity, it is firstly to refer to an abstract humanity as a moral value, whether this is on the part of the judges calling for 'the

---

29 *The Prosecutor v Drazen Erdemovic (Sentencing Judgement)* (International Criminal Tribunal for the former Yugoslavia, Trial Chamber, Case No IT-96-22-T, 29 November 1996) [28].

30 Ibid [19].

31 Ibid [28].

32 Ibid. The ICTR referred to this definition in *Prosecutor v Jean Kambanda (Judgement and Sentence)* (International Criminal Tribunal for Rwanda, Appeals Chamber, Case No ICTR-97-23-S, 4 September 1998) [15].

conscience of humanity',[33] or the prosecutor,[34] or representatives of the victims urging the judges to decide 'to the advantage of humanity'.[35] The reference to the conscience of humanity comes directly from the preamble to the ICC Statute, for which the atrocities of this century 'deeply shock the conscience of humanity'.[36] ICC case-law offers no development on the concept of humanity, though, and its occurrence is limited to the basic quotation of the Statute. Yet it is worth noting that if humanity has a conscience (which is debatable), it should be more a subject than an object of international law. That conscience underpins, in any case, humanity's presumed capacity to bear moral judgements.

Another interpretation of the concept of humanity was then interestingly developed by ICC case-law. The reference to humanity embodies the 'interest of the world community'[37] to put the perpetrators of the most serious crimes against humanity to trial. These semantics originate not only in the Hague Convention, which referred to the 'interests of humanity' to preserve peace, but also in more recent treaties regarding the protection of the environment. The latter point out the 'common interest of all mankind'[38] in

33 *Prosecutor v Uhuru Muigai Kenyatta (Decision on Defence Request for Conditional Excusal from Continuous Presence at Trial)* (International Criminal Court, Trial Chamber V(B), Case No ICC-01/09-02/11-830, 18 October 2013) [2]; *Prosecutor v William Samoei Ruto and Joshua Arap Sang (Decision on Prosecutor's Application for Witness Summonses and resulting Request for State Party Cooperation)* (International Criminal Court, Trial Chamber V(A), Case No ICC-01/09-01/11-1274-Corr2, 17 April 2014) [63], [64], [124], [128], [129]; *Prosecutor v Abdallah Banda Abakaer Nourain (Decision on the defence request for a temporary stay of proceedings and Concurring Separate Opinion of Judge Eboe-Osuji)* (International Criminal Court, Trial Chamber IV, Case No ICC-02/05-03/09-410, 26 October 2012) [28], [83], [109], [133]; *Prosecutor v Uruhu Muigai Kenyatta (Corrigendum of Concurring Separate Opinion of Judge Eboe-Osuji)* (International Criminal Court, Trial Chamber V, Case No ICC-01/09-02/11-728-Anx3-Corr2-Red, 2 May 2013) [92]; *Prosecutor v Jean-Pierre Bemba Gombo (Judgment on the appeal of Mr Aimé Kilolo Musamba against the decision of Pre-Trial Chamber II of 14 March 2014 entitled "Decision on the 'Demande de mise en liberté provisoire de Maître Aimé Kilolo Musamba'",* dissenting opinion of Judge Anita Ušacka) (International Criminal Court, Case No ICC-01/05-01/13-559-Anx2, 11 July 2014) [6].
34 Oral Closing Statement of the Office of the Prosecutor in *Prosecutor v Jean-Pierre Bemba Gombo* (International Criminal Court, Trial Chamber III, Case No ICC-01/05-01/08, 12 November 2014).
35 Oral Closing Statement of the Victims' Legal Representative in *Prosecutor v Jean-Pierre Bemba Gombo* (International Criminal Court, Trial Chamber III, Case No ICC-01/05-01/08, 13 November 2014).
36 This expression was first used in the Preamble to the *Universal Declaration of Human Rights*, GA Res 217A (III), UN GAOR, 3rd sess, 183rd plen mtg, UN Doc A/810 (10 December 1948), stating that barbarous acts 'have outraged the conscience of mankind'.
37 *Prosecutor v Lubanga (Judgment on the Appeal of Mr. Thomas Lubanga Dyilo against the Decision on the Defence Challenge to the Jurisdiction of the Court pursuant to Article 19(2)(a) of the Statute of 3 October 2006)* (International Criminal Court, Appeals Chamber, Case No ICC-01/04-01/06-772, 14 December 2006) [39].
38 See the preambles of the *Treaty on Principles Governing the Activities of States in the Exploration and Use of Outer Space, Including the Moon and Other Celestial Bodies,*

the peaceful exploration and protection of outer space, for example, or 'the interests and needs of mankind as a whole'[39] and the 'benefit'[40] it derives from the protection of the maritime environment and the maintenance of peace, justice, and progress. The interests of humanity are thus focused on justice, peace, and environmental protection for the world community and point to a concept of humanity centred on solidarity.

One final interpretation of humanity appeared in ICC case-law. It relates humanity to the 'sake of present and future generations', again quoting the preamble to the Statute. The ICC was indeed created in favour of these present and future generations (comprising all human beings including those not yet born). This is a collective[41] and transtemporal[42] humanity, which transcends space (wherever the crime is committed, by its very nature, extent and gravity, it concerns humanity as a whole) and time (a crime committed today could affect human beings not yet born). The first sentence issued by the ICC, in the *Lubanga* case, underscored, as a purpose of punishment, the fact that the Court was established 'for the sake of present and future generations'.[43]

This normative concept of humanity derived from the United Nations Charter, the preamble of which opens with its determination to save 'succeeding generations' from war, which has already brought 'sorrow to mankind', drawing a line between present and future generations. The link

opened for signature on 27 January 1967, 610 UNTS 205 (entered into force 10 October 1967); of the *Convention on International Liability for Damage Caused by Space Objects*, opened for signature on 29 March 1972, 961 UNTS 187 (entered into force 1 September 1972); and the *Convention on Registration of Objects Launched into Outer Space*, opened for signature on 14 January 1975, 1023 UNTS 15 (entered into force 15 September 1976).

39 *United Nations Convention on the Law of the Sea*, opened for signature 10 December 1982, 1833 UNTS 396, (entered into force 16 November 1994) Preamble.

40 Ibid Arts 140, 143, 149, 150(i) and 246(3).

41 Catherine Le Bris, 'Esquisse de l'humanité juridique' (2012) 29(2) *Revue interdisciplinaire d'études juridiques* 21.

42 René-Jean Dupuy, 'Réflexions sur le patrimoine commun de l'humanité' (1985) (1) *Droits* 69.

43 *Prosecutor v Thomas Lubanga (Decision on Sentence pursuant to Article 76 of the Statute)* (International Criminal Court, Trial Chamber I, Case No ICC-01/04-01/06-2901, 10 July 2012) [16] and Dissenting Opinion of judge Odio Benito, for whom the crimes for which Mr Lubanga has been convicted 'caused serious damage which may continue to date and may extend into the future, even affecting future generations', 41 [19]. See also *Prosecutor v William Samoei Ruto and Joshua Arap Sang (Decision on Prosecutor's Application for Witness Summonses and resulting Request for State Party Cooperation)* (International Criminal Court, Trial Chamber V(a), Case No ICC-01/09-01/11-1274-Corr2, 17 April 2014) [63]. This declaration was confirmed by the Appeal Chamber in its judgement on the appeals against that sentence: *Prosecutor v Thomas Lubanga Dyilo (Judgment on the appeals of the Prosecutor and Mr Thomas Lubanga Dyilo against the "Decision on Sentence pursuant to Article 76 of the Statute")* (International Criminal Court, Appeals Chamber, Case No ICC-01/04-01/06-3122, 1 December 2014) [16].

between generations was then emphasised by treaties recognising 'the duty'[44] to protect present and future generations of mankind[45] and asserting 'the necessity for establishing new, equitable and global links of partnership and intra-generational solidarity, and for promoting inter-generational solidarity for the perpetuation of humankind'.[46]

The ICJ also referred to this notion of transtemporal humanity. It defined humanity as all present and future generations, in one of the rare case-law occurrences of the concept of humanity. In the *Gabčíkovo-Nagymaros Project* case, the Court recognised that new norms have emerged to protect the environment because of 'a growing awareness of the risks for mankind', which it defined as 'present and future generations'.[47]

Humanity has hence emerged in international law as a link between all human beings, even those yet to be born, constituting a united global community with shared interests. This humanity needs to be protected at the level of each individual everywhere in the world and whenever it is attacked, even in the unknown future.

IV Humanity in bioethics: a biological humanity

When examining the conceptualisation of humanity, it is striking to note how it has focused increasingly on the protection of the biological aspect of the human being. Humanity is intended as a defence against gross rights violations and consequently as a protection of the biological life of the human being. This approach is generating an evolution in the concept towards a humanity centred on life and biology.

In France, for instance, the legal definition of humanity was overturned by the bioethics laws of 2004. Since only crimes against humanity were part of the criminal code, a new category of crimes against all human beings was created: crimes against the human species.[48] These include eugenics crimes and reproductive cloning.[49] This crime against the human species was introduced

---

44 *Convention for the Protection of the World Cultural and Natural Heritage*, opened for signature 16 November 1972, 1037 UNTS 151 (entered into force 17 December 1975) Art. 4.

45 *United Nations Framework Convention on Climate Change*, signed 4 June 1992, 1771 UNTS 107 (entered into force 21 March 1994) Preamble, Art. 3; 1992 *Convention on Biological Diversity*, opened for signature 5 June 1992, 1760 UNTS 79 (entered into force 29 December 1993) Preamble, Art. 2.

46 *Declaration on the Responsibilities of Present Generations Towards Future Generations*, UNESCO GC Res 44, 27th plen mtg, UNESDOC 28 C/INF.20 (12 November 1997) Preamble.

47 *Hungary v Slovakia (The Gabčíkovo-Nagymaros Project)* (Judgment) [1997] ICJ Rep 78, [140].

48 This is to my knowledge the only example in domestic law of this new category of crimes against the human species, as distinct from crimes against humanity.

49 *Loi n° 2004-800 du 6 août 2004 relative à la bioéthique* [Law No 2004-800 of August 6, 2004] (France) JO 6 August 2004, Art. 28.

into French criminal law through its distinction from humanity. Humanity is henceforth split into two parts: a moral one and a biological one.[50]

This division of the notion of humanity into these two categories aims at providing the best possible protection of natural persons facing the new scientific and technological progress that is now allowing for genome modification and the sequencing of human DNA. This serves as a means of fighting eugenics policies and practices such as the ones once set in place in Nazi Germany. The legal concept of the human species thus affords the necessary protection for the genetic specificity of human beings. It is also, however, a way to introduce a biological aspect into the concept of humanity, by linking the protection of natural persons with their belonging to an animal species. The concept of the human species should not be introduced into criminal law through its distinction from humanity.

It is indeed extremely important to draw a distinction between the human being emerging from human rights[51] and the one from biology. Two rationalities are at stake here:

> on the one hand, the biological rationality that places life as the supreme value denying the notions of person and humanity and, on the other hand, the rationality of human rights. The human being of human rights is not the same as that of the biologist. It is a human being whose primary characteristic is not life.[52]

The genome is even defined today as the 'common heritage of humanity' by the Universal Declaration on the Human Genome and Human Rights of 11 November 1997. It has entered the common heritage of humanity 'in a symbolic way'[53] as the representation of the unity and diversity of the human species. The genome is only the biological code of the living production of the human species[54] though. The same transformation of the concept of humanity was adopted in the French proposal for the adoption by the United Nations of the Declaration of the Rights of Humankind. It proclaims the rights of humanity by defining the latter as one species

---

50 Mireille Delmas-Marty, *Le relatif et l'universel. Les forces imaginantes du droit* (Le Seuil, 2004) 84.
51 Raphaëlle Nollez-Goldbach, *Quel homme pour les droits? Les droits de l'homme à l'épreuve de la figure de l'étranger* (CNRS Éditions, 2015).
52 Mireille Delmas-Marty and Olivier Mongin, 'L'homme des droits de l'homme n'est pas celui du biologiste. Entretien avec Mireille Delmas-Marty' (1989) 156 *Esprit* 121 [author's translation].
53 *Universal Declaration on the Human Genome and Human Rights*, UNESCO GC Res 16, 29th sess, UNESDOC 29 C/Res. 66 (11 November 1997) Art. 1.
54 Numa Murard, 'La figure de l'homme en trop' (2005) 25 *Tumultes* 105.

among 'all living species'.[55] The introduction of the biological aspect of human beings is thus giving rise to a deep transformation of the concept of humanity.

V The political basis of humanity

In the context of a 'biologisation' of humanity – an evolution of humanity towards a biological-centred status – the concept of humanity needs to be developed through the inclusion of its political aspect. The basis of the legal concept of humanity should not exclusively be the life and dignity of natural persons. The concept of humanity should also embody the idea of an international living together to form the basis of global law.

The development of a biological vision of humanity makes sense in the context of the defence of a victim-centred one. Indeed, it is even inevitable in the context of crimes committed against that humanity. However, this cannot constitute the entire notion. Humanity must be defined not only as a state of belonging, a legal status focused on a being that needs to be defended, but also as a participation in a common and plural world, as formulated by the philosopher Hannah Arendt.[56] The concept of humanity should embody the construction of a common and global community allowing for an international political space and citizenship; as such, it could form the basis of a global and common law.

Immanuel Kant founded the concept of cosmopolitan law, as the law of world citizens aiming at establishing perpetual peace in the face of the 'inhospitable conduct' of States. Kant proposed a 'right to hospitality' based on the common possession of the land and of the surface of earth by all human beings.[57] This right to hospitality allows foreigners entering a State not to be treated as enemies and entitles them to a right of visit so that they can become members of that society.[58]

Nowadays, this idea can be found in the 'non-refoulement' principle[59] in international law. Incorporated into the Convention Relating to the Status of Refugees, it forbids, under Article 33, the expulsion or return of a refugee to the frontiers of territories where his/her life or freedom would be threatened. Cosmopolitan law also aims at allowing for the inclusion and political

---

55 Arts 6, 11.
56 Hannah Arendt, *The Origins of Totalitarianism* (Harcourt, Brace & Co, 1951) and Hannah Arendt, *The Human Condition* (University of Chicago Press, 1958).
57 Immanuel Kant, *Perpetual Peace: A Philosophical Essay* (1795, French edition – Le Livre de Poche, 2002) 62-63.
58 Ibid.
59 See Raphaëlle Nollez-Goldbach, *Quel homme pour les droits?*, above n 51, Ch. 5, sub-s 2.2.

participation of the other, who embodies the claim to the rights of humanity[60] and global citizenship 'in order to achieve the public law of humanity'[61] expected by Kant. Therefore, humanity could point toward the creation of a common and global law.

To a certain extent, the creation of international criminal courts and tribunals arose from this conception of humanity, constituting a breach in the history of international law. After the Second World War, international law changed from a law of coexistence – a simple frame for State relations – into a law of coordination, involving a stronger cooperation between interdependent States. This change in the structure of international law[62] led to the creation of the United Nations in 1945, which was directed at building lasting peace between States, and to the universal proclamation of human rights by the Universal Declaration of Human Rights of 1948.

The creation of the first permanent supranational criminal court, the ICC, which is responsible for trying 'the most serious crimes of concern to the international community as a whole', is in line with this structural evolution. This is a major step in international law because it draws the lines for some supranational law. Crimes under the jurisdiction of the ICC can be referred to the Court by States Parties, or the Security Council of the UN acting under Chapter VII of the Charter (even if the crimes were committed on the territory of a Non-State Party or by a Non-State Party national). They can also be referred by the ICC prosecutor, who can initiate an investigation on his or her own initiative in the name of the international community (but only if the crimes were committed on State Party territory or by a State Party national).

The existence of the ICC results in a fundamental transformation of the international system by influencing the role of the individual at the international level. The Universal Declaration of Human Rights already granted international rights to the individual. With the development of international criminal law, individuals now bear certain obligations; they are internationally responsible. If human beings are only passive subjects of international law, because they cannot take legal action at the international level – individuals cannot refer situations to international courts and

60 Seyla Benhabib, *The Rights of Others: Aliens, Residents, and Citizens* (Cambridge University Press, 2004) 28; Étienne Tassin, *Un monde commun. Pour une cosmo-politique des conflits* (Le Seuil, 2003) 271.
61 Kant, above n 57, 64.
62 Wolfgang Friedmann, *The Changing Structure of International Law* (Columbia University Press, 1964).

tribunals, with the noteworthy exception of European and American Human Rights Courts – they now possess international rights and obligations. This is a major turning point.

VI Conclusion

The key question remains: has the development of a legal concept of humanity led to a real paradigm shift in international law? This new status of humanity needs to be questioned. The creation of the ICC constitutes a big step in putting an end to impunity for the perpetrators of the most serious crimes and in achieving the goal of bringing peace through law and universal justice. However, the international criminal justice set in place by the ICC can still be blocked by one of the big powers of the UN Security Council that holds the right to veto. It can forbid the Court from investigating a situation, as is illustrated by Russia and China's vetoes to the UN Security Council resolutions to refer the crimes committed in Syria to the ICC. The Security Council can also request, under Article 16 of the ICC Statute, that the Court refrain from investigating or prosecuting a crime for a year (which is renewable). Moreover, the members of the Security Council hold the power, in the name of the international community, to refer situations to the Court or to prevent it from investigating, even though some of them have not themselves recognised the Court. Three of the five permanent members of the Security Council – the United States, Russia, and China – have not ratified the ICC Statute (the United States and Russia even 'unsigned' it to mark their disapproval). The humanity that is being expressed here clearly does not point to universality but only to a selective humanity.

If the ICC constitutes a major progress for a common and global law, by trying the perpetrators of the most serious crimes of concern to humanity in the name of humanity, its jurisdiction was immediately limited by the opposition of sovereign States. A situation, for example, was referred to the Court by the Security Council on 26 February 2011 – resolution 1970 was adopted unanimously, setting a precedent in international law – regarding the crimes committed in Libya. The ICC prosecutor issued warrants of arrest in June 2011 against Mouammar Kadhafi – who died while being arrested –, his son Saïf Al-Islam, and the head of secret services, Abdullah Al-Senussi. However, these suspects are currently being held in Libya, which refuses to transfer them to the Court and is contesting the Court's jurisdiction to try them. The ICC even ended the proceedings against Al-Senussi on 24 July 2014 declaring the case inadmissible in favour of the jurisdiction of the Libyan domestic courts. This illustrates the limits of the international criminal order, which lacks its own armed forces and police to enforce its decisions and is based on the will of sovereign States to cooperate.

The same remark can be made concerning immunities in ICC proceedings. Immunity does not bar the Court from exercising its jurisdiction, and official capacity as (active or former) Head of State does not exempt an individual from their criminal responsibilities. This is an important step in international law. The charges against the Kenyan President and the Vice-President were confirmed by the Court in 2012, as were the charges against the former President of Côte d'Ivoire, Laurent Gbagbo, whose trial was initiated on 28 January 2016. Yet both proceedings against the Kenyan Heads of State ended without a conviction, with the charges being vacated in the *Ruto* case on 5 April 2016 and withdrawn in the *Kenyatta* case on 5 December 2014. This was due to insufficient evidence in both cases. This underscored the limits of the Court and the international community when confronted with the will of an opposing sovereign State. In the Kenya situation, the Office of the Prosecutor was prevented from investigating properly and some witnesses died in unclear circumstances.[63] Likewise, warrants of arrest were issued against the active President of Sudan on 4 March 2009 and 12 July 2010, for his alleged involvement in the perpetration of genocide, crimes against humanity, and war crimes in Darfur. However, he has still not been arrested, which illustrates the absence of enforcement of Court decisions when States refuse to execute them.

This clearly highlights the paradoxes of the concept of humanity and of the international order underlying it. There is a major contradiction between an international system ruled by State sovereignties and the concept of humanity as the basis of supranational law. The sovereignty principle is clearly still central to international law. The tension between States' sovereignty and humanity has not been resolved in favour of humanity, which is far from being sovereign.[64]

The political basis of humanity is currently non-existent. The concept of humanity is limited to a reaction in the face of common global crimes, risks, and dangers[65] and still needs to be adequately formulated[66] in order to form

---

63 International Criminal Court, Office of the Prosecutor, 'Statement of the Prosecutor of the International Criminal Court, Fatou Bensouda, on the withdrawal of charges against Mr. Uhuru Muigai Kenyatta' (5 December 2014) <www.icc-cpi.int/Pages/item.aspx?name=otp-statement-05-12-2014-2>.

64 For an opposite view, see Olivier de Frouville, who proposes a model of 'sovereign humanity', Olivier de Frouville 'La Cour pénale internationale: une humanité souveraine?' (2000) 610 *Les Temps Modernes* 257; and Ruti Teitel, for whom 'sovereignty is no longer a self-evident foundation for international law' and is being replaced by a new normative discourse 'constructed more along humanity law lines', Ruti Teitel, *Humanity's Law* (Oxford University Press, 2011) 10.

65 Tassin, above n 60, 190.

66 Mireille Delmas-Marty, *Vers un droit commun de l'humanité ? Entretien avec Philippe Petit* (Textuel, 2005).

the basis of a common and global law of humanity. It has, however, initiated a movement, which would now seem impossible to obstruct, towards a normative international order grounded on the protection of humanity and towards 'the reconception of the law in terms of the primacy of the individual [. . .] building a sense of shared global community'.[67]

Further reading

Delmas-Marty, Mireille *et al, Le crime contre l'humanité* (PUF, Que-sais-je, 2013).
Le Bris, Catherine, *L'humanité saisie par le droit international* (LGDJ, 2012).
Luban, David, 'A Theory of Crimes against Humanity' (2004) 29 *Yale Journal of International Law* 85.
May, Larry, *Crimes against Humanity: A Normative Account* (Cambridge University Press, 2004).
Teitel, Ruti, *Humanity's Law* (Oxford University Press, 2011).
Vernon, Richard, 'What Is a Crime against Humanity?' (2002) 10 *Journal of Political Philosophy* 231.

67 Teitel, above n 64, 9-11.

6

WAR CRIMES

Increasing compliance with international humanitarian law through international criminal law?

*Dale Stephens and Thomas Wooden**

I Introduction

Traditionally, states were held responsible for the actions of their nationals during international armed conflict. Moreover, before the Nuremberg and Tokyo Trials, universal jurisdiction had not yet extended to individual criminal responsibility by an international court. Despite this, it was accepted that states could prosecute their own nationals for crimes committed during wartime, even if committed abroad.

The prosecution of war criminals by the state was customary in nature, with the 1899 and 1907 Hague Conventions[1] failing to regulate or even provide a framework for the prosecution of individuals. This meant there existed no treaty-based instructions or enforcement mechanisms to provide punishment of war criminals. To remedy this, and after two world wars, the 1949 Geneva Conventions included provisions for states to prosecute grave breaches of the Geneva Conventions,[2] now accepted as 'war crimes'.

---

* The authors would like to acknowledge the invaluable research assistance provided by Ms Caitlyn Georgeson.
1 *Convention (II) with Respect to the Laws and Customs of War on Land and its annex: Regulations concerning the Laws and Customs of War on Land*, The Hague, 19 July 1899 (entered into force 04 September 1900); *Convention (III) relative to the Opening of Hostilities*, The Hague, 18 October 1907 (entered into force 26 January 1910); *Convention (IV) respecting the Laws and Customs of War on Land and its annex: Regulations concerning the Laws and Customs of War on Land*, The Hague, 18 October 1907 (entered into force 26 January 1910).
2 *Geneva Convention for the Amelioration of the Condition of the Wounded and Sick in Armed Forces in the Field of August 12, 1949*, opened for signature 12 August 1949, 75 UNTS 31 (entered into force 21 October 1950) ('GC I') arts 49, 50; *Geneva Convention for the*

International individual criminal responsibility was not established by the 1949 Geneva Conventions or its 1977 Additional Protocols,[3] though they were later used as the basis for the international criminal tribunals and courts that were subsequently established. Instead, it was envisaged that prosecution would occur in a decentralised manner, namely by national law and national courts.[4] With the obligation resting on states to prosecute grave breaches of the Geneva Conventions, it has been held that '[i]nternational law does not predetermine the proper penalization of war crimes at the national level. It establishes, however, an obligation to effectively guarantee the criminal prosecution of grave breaches of international humanitarian law'.[5]

As established in Chapter 1, the creation of the Nuremberg and Tokyo Trials marked a turning point for international criminal law (ICL). For the first time, individuals were to be held accountable under international standards according to international humanitarian law and were no longer protected by state sovereignty. War crimes, in particular, were an important feature of the Nuremberg and Tokyo Trials.[6] While acknowledging that these trials have been criticised for representing 'victor's justice' and imposing retrospective concepts of criminal liability,[7] they nonetheless represent a key benchmark in the evolution of ICL dealing with war crimes.

Despite the significance of the trials which followed the Second World War, it was not until 1993, during the breakup of the former Yugoslavia, that the international community (albeit through the agency of the

Amelioration of the Condition of Wounded, Sick and Shipwrecked Members of Armed Forces at Sea of August 12, 1949, opened for signature 12 August 1949, 75 UNTS 85 (entered into force 21 October 1950) ('GC II') Arts 50, 51; *Geneva Convention relative to the Treatment of Prisoners of War of August 12, 1949*, opened for signature 12 August 1949, 75 UNTS 135 (entered into force 21 October 1950) ('GC III') Arts 129, 130; *Geneva Convention relative to the Protection of Civilian Persons in Time of War of August 12, 1949*, opened for signature 12 August 1949, 75 UNTS 287 (entered into force 21 October 1950) ('GC IV') Arts 146, 147.

3 *Protocol Additional to the Geneva Conventions of 12 August 1949, and relating to the Protection of Victims of International Armed Conflicts*, opened for signature 8 June 1977, 1125 UNTS 3 (entered into force 7 December 1978) ('AP I'); *Protocol Additional to the Geneva Conventions of 12 August 1949, and relating to the Protection of Victims of Non-International Armed Conflicts*, opened for signature 8 June 1977, 1125 UNTS 609 (entered into force 7 December 1978).

4 Rüdiger Wolfrum, 'The Decentralized Prosecution of International Offences through National Courts' in Yoram Dinstein and Mala Tabory (eds), *War Crimes in International Law* (Martinus Nijhoff, 1996) 233, 242.

5 Ibid 243.

6 *Charter of the International Military Tribunal – Annex to the Agreement for the Prosecution and Punishment of the Major War Criminals of the European Axis* (8 August 1945) Art. 6(b) ('Nuremberg Charter'); General Douglas MacArthur, *Special Proclamation by the Supreme Commander for the Allied Powers at Tokyo* (19 January 1946) Art. 5(b) ('Tokyo Charter').

7 Judith Shklar, *Legalism: Law, Morals and Political Trials* (Harvard University Press, 1964) 181-183, who was highly critical of the trials due to their largely non-criminalised status in pre-war conceptions.

UN Security Council) found the capacity to create another international criminal tribunal to try individuals for, *inter alia*, war crimes – namely, the International Criminal Tribunal for the former Yugoslavia (ICTY).[8] Former President of the ICTY held, acknowledging the critique of the former international trials as 'victor's justice', that

> the United Nations Security Council has established the first truly international criminal tribunal for the prosecution of persons responsible for serious violations of international humanitarian law [...] and gives a new lease on life to that part of international criminal law which applies to violations of humanitarian law.[9]

One year later, in 1994, the International Criminal Tribunal for Rwanda (ICTR) was established to try individuals for grave breaches of the Geneva Conventions, crimes against humanity, and genocide.[10]

For the first time in over 45 years, individuals were to be held criminally responsible by an international forum for war crimes committed during armed conflict. Despite pertaining to specific conflicts, these two tribunals significantly contributed to the development of a corpus of generally applicable rules in international criminal law, specifically that of war crimes. However, it was not until the adoption of the Rome Statute founding the International Criminal Court (ICC) in 1998 that (potentially) universal jurisdiction was fully realised. For the first time, the world finally had a permanent international forum possessing universal jurisdiction in which it could try, *inter alia*, alleged war criminals.

II Establishing a war crime

A *What is a war crime?*

There is no exhaustive list or definition of what is specifically a war crime, though the Geneva Conventions and jurisprudence from international criminal tribunals and courts are instructive. War crimes are commonly described as 'serious violations' of customary or treaty law, which come from the laws of armed conflict (LOAC, or international humanitarian law – 'IHL'), attracting individual criminal responsibility. The foundational ICTY Appeals Chamber decision of *Prosecutor v Duško Tadić* sets out a general guide of what may constitute a justiciable war crime under the ICTY statute where this is not specifically prescribed in the relevant treaty or rule of customary international law:

8 SC Res 827, UN SCOR, 48th sess, 3217th mtg, UN Doc S/RES/827 (25 May 1993).
9 Theodor Meron, *War Crimes Law Comes of Age* (Oxford University Press, 1998) 210.
10 SC Res 955, UN SCOR, 49th sess, 3453rd mtg, UN Doc S/Res/955 (8 November 1994).

(i) the violation must constitute an infringement of a rule of international humanitarian law;

(ii) the rule must be customary in nature or, if it belongs to treaty law, the required conditions must be met [. . .];

(iii) the violation must be "serious", that is to say, it must constitute a breach of a rule protecting important values, and the breach must involve grave consequences for the victim;

(iv) the violation of the rule must entail, under customary or conventional law, the individual criminal responsibility of the person breaching the rule.

It follows that it does not matter whether the "serious violation" has occurred within the context of an international or an internal armed conflict, as long as the requirements set out above are met.[11]

The Chamber distinguished a 'serious violation' from a non-serious violation with an example:

a combatant simply appropriating a loaf of bread in an occupied village would not amount to a "serious violation of international humanitarian law" although it may be regarded as falling foul of the basic principle [...] of the Hague Regulations [and] customary international law whereby "private property must be respected" by any army occupying an enemy territory.[12]

Gaeta further elaborates on what may constitute a war crime, demonstrating the high threshold of 'seriousness':

It would therefore be incorrect to believe that the individual who breaches a rule of IHL commits *ipso facto* a war crime. Further elements must be added, namely: (i) the conduct must be contrary to a rule protecting fundamental values; (ii) the breach must have caused grave consequences to the victims; (iii) the illegal conduct must have been carried out with the requisite criminal mind, that can be expressly or implicitly provided by the rule of IHL that was breached, or be identified through other means.[13]

11 *Decision on the Defence Motion for Interlocutory Appeal on Jurisdiction* (International Criminal Tribunal for the former Yugoslavia, Trial Chamber, Case No IT-94-1-T, 2 October 1995) [94].

12 Ibid.

13 Paola Gaeta, 'War Crimes and Other International "Core" Crimes' in Andrew Clapham and Paola Gaeta (eds), *The Oxford Handbook of International Law in Armed Conflict* (Oxford University Press, 2015) 737, 748.

B *How to identify war crimes*

Evidently, not all violations of IHL constitute a war crime. Only violations of IHL which are 'serious' may constitute a war crime attracting international criminal jurisdiction, with less serious violations being subject only to national law and potentially giving rise to international responsibility on behalf of the party and not the individual. Although the decision in *Tadić* is instructive, it is not exhaustive, and not all war crimes are codified in the Geneva Conventions and their Additional Protocols. In order to determine what constitutes a war crime, various other sources must be analysed. These include recourse to consistent state practice and *opinio juris* (whether found in national legislation or courts) demonstrating a violation is considered a war crime, decisions or statutes of international courts and tribunals, military manuals, and legislation or practice of the state to which the accused belongs or on whose territory the crime has allegedly been committed.[14]

C *Nexus with armed conflict*

Just as not all violations of IHL constitute a war crime, so too must there be a nexus between the alleged violation and its occurrence within armed conflict. For a war crime to be constituted, it must be closely related to the hostilities in which it occurs.[15] This relationship serves to distinguish between war crimes and 'ordinary' criminal conduct that falls under the law applicable in the relevant territory.[16] This principle has been reflected in Article 8 of the Rome Statute of the ICC,[17] as further explained in the ICC's Elements of Crimes document.[18]

---

14 Antonio Cassese, *Cassese's International Criminal Law* (Oxford University Press, 2013) 68; Gaeta, above n 11, 745.

15 *Prosecutor v Akayesu (Judgement)* (International Criminal Tribunal for Rwanda, Trial Chamber I, Case No ICTR-96-4-T, 2 September 1998) [630]–[634], [638]–[644]; *Prosecutor v Clément Kayishema and Obed Ruzindana (Judgement)* (International Criminal Tribunal for Rwanda, Trial Chamber II, Case No ICTR-95-1T, 21 May 1999) [185]–[189], [590]–[624]; *Prosecutor v Alfred Musema (Judgement and Sentence)* (International Criminal Tribunal for Rwanda, Trial Chamber I, Case No ICTR-96-13-A, 27 January 2000) [259]–[262], [275], [974]; *Prosecutor v Duško Tadić a/k/a "Dule"(Opinion and Judgement)* (International Criminal Tribunal for the former Yugoslavia, Trial Chamber, Case No IT-94-1-T, 7 May 1997) [573]; *Prosecutor v Zejnil Delalić et al (Judgement)* (International Criminal Tribunal for the former Yugoslavia, Trial Chamber, Case No IT-96-21-A, 20 February 2001) [193]; Guénaël Mettraux, 'Nexus with Armed Conflict' in Antonio Cassese (ed), *The Oxford Companion to International Criminal Justice* (Oxford University Press, 2009) 435.

16 Cassese, above n 14, 77.

17 *Statute of the International Criminal Court*, opened for signature 17 July 1998, 2187 UNTS 90 (entered into force 1 July 2002) ('Rome Statute').

18 International Criminal Court, *Elements of Crimes* (2011) 13-43.

Identifying this nexus with an international armed conflict (IAC) is relatively simple, as two belligerent states oppose one another, with consequent offences typically against parties of the other state. In non-international armed conflict (NIAC), however, ambiguities arise more often, as there can be difficulties in identifying whether the alleged violating party is a civilian or combatant. Regardless of these differences, the standard of a nexus is an objective one, linking the armed conflict with the crime and not the criminal.

The ICTY Appeals Chamber Judgment in *Prosecutor v Dragoljub Kunarac et al* explains the difference between a war crime and a domestic offence:

> What ultimately distinguishes a war crime from a purely domestic offence is that a war crime is shaped by or dependent upon the environment – the armed conflict – in which it is committed. It need not have been planned or supported by some form of policy. The armed conflict need not have been causal to the commission of the crime, but the existence of an armed conflict must, at a minimum, have played a substantial part in the perpetrator's ability to commit it, his decision to commit it, the manner in which it was committed or the purpose for which it was committed. Hence, if it can be established, as in the present case, that the perpetrator acted in furtherance of or under the guise of the armed conflict, it would be sufficient to conclude that his acts were closely related to the armed conflict.[19]

Critically, this nexus is not necessary when individuals commit violations, serious or not, against their own party. Although the offence may occur in the context of the conflict, it is not of the conflict itself, and is therefore not subject to international prosecution. This kind of offence is typically an 'ordinary' or 'normal' crime, where individuals are subject to their own nation's law and prosecutorial process. In circumstances such as that found in the former Yugoslavia, there existed a number of issues concerning: identifying whether the armed conflict was within one of the two categories of international or non-international, and what role ethnicity played within those two categories when violations occurred. Multiple layers may exist within any given conflict, which serve to complicate the identification of a war crime.

D *War crimes in international armed conflict and non-international armed conflict*

War crimes were once distinguished according to whether they were committed in international armed conflict between two or more states, or

---

19 *(Judgment)* (International Criminal Tribunal for the former Yugoslavia, Appeals Chamber, Case No IT-96-23 & IT-96-23/1-A, 12 June 2002) [58].

non-international armed conflict, where conflict occurs within a state that involves large-scale armed violence, thus precluding riots, isolated and sporadic acts of armed violence, or conduct of a similar nature.[20]

Serious violations of IHL constituting war crimes occurring in NIAC were traditionally not criminalised. This distinction between responsibility in IAC and NIAC has been described as 'glaring and preposterous',[21] with the view commonly held that '[p]erpetrators of atrocities in internal wars should not be treated more leniently than those engaged in international wars'.[22]

Following the Appeals Chamber decision in *Tadić*,[23] it has become widely accepted that serious violations of IHL, constituting war crimes, are applicable both in IAC and NIAC, rendering the distinction between IAC and NIAC 'obsolete'.[24]

III Relationship between international humanitarian law and international criminal law

Contemporary warfare exhibits a distinct shift from the classic battle space and the frameworks envisaged to provide the necessary boundaries around such conflict. Hence contemporary warfare increasingly confronts dense legal regulation that may or may not cleanly apply to the modalities of such conflict where there are fused public and private legal spheres and with new and unanswered questions regarding modern weapons systems. As new weapons are developed and conflicts increasingly become internal or hybrid in nature, legal ambiguities arise. Kennedy states that 'lines are now harder to draw, both because the world of war has become more mixed up and because ambiguities, gaps and contradictions in the materials we use to draw the lines have become more pronounced'.[25]

IHL has attempted to regulate the use of newly developed weapons, with treaties created specifically to deal with: chemical weapons, biological weapons, anti-personnel landmines and cluster munitions, laser weapons and soon, nanotechnology and autonomous weapons systems. These weapons are regulated by IHL in conflicts occurring on land, ocean, air, cyberspace, and soon enough in outer space.[26]

---

20 The preclusion of internal small-scale armed violence when determining if a violation is a war crime is enshrined in Arts 8(d) and (f) of the Rome Statute.
21 Cassese, above n 14, 71.
22 Meron, above n 9, 217.
23 *Prosecutor v Duško Tadić* (International Criminal Tribunal for the former Yugoslavia, Appeal Chamber, Case No IT-94-1-A, 15 July 1999) [94]–[137].
24 Gaeta, above n 13, 746.
25 David Kennedy, 'Lawfare and Warfare' in James Crawford and Martti Koskenniemi (eds), *The Cambridge Companion to International Law* (Cambridge University Press, 2012) 158, 161.
26 See work being undertaken on the *Manual on International Law Applicable to Military Uses of Outer Space* (2016) <www.mcgill.ca/milamos/home>.

It is within this new world of war, and our new world of international criminal courts and tribunals, that the international criminal justice system must adapt. Although the existing regime of international criminal institutions provides a level of accountability for decision-making in armed conflict, questions of clarity when dealing with complex concepts of proportionality and distinction continue unresolved. These two principles, which will be explored in more detail below, underpin all modern IHL and enable the conduct of armed conflict in all contexts to be managed and violence contained to the greatest extent. It is in the context of ICL that IHL may be interpreted in an authoritative manner.

Whilst the ICC continues to develop and evolve its own early corpus of international criminal legal standards, state military forces and non-state armed groups must continue to look to the jurisprudence of the ICTY and ICTR for guidance on the tests and limits when engaging in armed conflict. These forums have not, however, prevailed in exacting a calculable test for the principles of proportionality and distinction. It is these two principles, unlike others, that are enduring in all armed conflicts, and become increasingly complex where weapons are used that have the potential to harm more than one individual during any one attack.

A *Ambiguity between IHL and ICL: the principles of proportionality and distinction*

The ICTY Appeals Chamber judgment in the case of *Prosecutor v Ante Gotovina* is a prime example of the difficulties in devising a test for distinction and proportionality. In the Trial Chamber Judgment of this case, the Chamber held that a 200-metre Impact Analysis was determinative of deciding criminal guilt concerning distinction and proportionality assessments, relating to artillery attacks on four separate towns. It was held that the attackers 'may have determined in good faith that firing at the [relevant target] would have offered a definite military advantage'.[27] Using the 200-metre Impact Analysis, the Chamber held that all impact sites located more than 200 metres from a target deemed legitimate were evidence of an unlawful artillery attack.[28] In this case, a mathematical test was devised, with distance as the workhorse of the principles of distinction and proportionality.

On appeal, this mathematical determination of acceptable distinction and proportionality was contested by Gotovina,[29] to which the Appeals Chamber

---

27 *Prosecutor v Ante Gotovina et al (Judgement)* (International Criminal Tribunal for the former Yugoslavia, Trial Chamber, Case No IT-06-90-T, 15 April 2011) [1899]–[1902].
28 Ibid [1903]–[1906], [1919]–[1921], [1932]–[1933], [1940]–[1941].
29 *Prosecutor v Ante Gotovina and Mladen Markač (Judgement)* (International Criminal Tribunal for the former Yugoslavia, Appeals Chamber, Case No IT-06-90-A, 16 November 2012) [29]–[35], [44].

chiefly agreed, rejecting the Trial Chamber's Impact Analysis and acquitting the accused.[30] It was thus held:

> The Appeals Chamber finds that there was a need for an evidentiary basis for the Trial Chamber's conclusions, particularly because these conclusions relate to a highly technical subject: the margin of error of artillery weapons in particular conditions. However, the Trial Chamber adopted a margin of error that was not linked to any evidence it received; this constituted an error on the part of the Trial Chamber. The Trial Chamber also provided no explanation as to the basis for the margin of error it adopted; this amounted to a failure to provide a reasoned opinion, another error.[31] [...]
>
> The Trial Chamber's Impact Analysis, which the Appeals Chamber, Judge Agius and Judge Pocar dissenting, has now found to be erroneous, was at the very core of its finding that the artillery attacks on the Four Towns were indiscriminate, and thus unlawful. The Trial Chamber deemed almost all the additional evidence of unlawful attacks as equivocal when considered independent of the Impact Analysis.[32]

Although the Trial Chamber's mathematical equation was found not to have been based on proper evidence, it demonstrates an attempt to strictly define the limits of distinction and proportionality. This case leads to a broader discussion of whether there is a definitive measure to determine acceptable distinction and proportionality, and it illustrates ICL's attempts to provide strict guidelines when interpreting IHL.

In contrast to attempts to strictly limit and define distinction and proportionality, the case of *Prosecutor v. Stanislav Galić*[33] demonstrates the pervasive fluidity of ICL's interpretation of IHL. In this case, the Trial Chamber provided that the test of lawfulness for the concept of proportionality was based on 'reasonableness':

> The basic obligation to spare civilians and civilian objects as much as possible must guide the attacking party when considering the proportionality of an attack. In determining whether an attack was proportionate it is necessary to examine whether a *reasonably* well-informed person in the circumstances of the actual perpetrator, making *reasonable* use of the information available to him or her, could have expected excessive civilian casualties to result from the attack.[34]

30 Ibid [158].
31 Ibid [61].
32 Ibid [77].
33 *Prosecutor v Stanislav Galić (Judgement and Opinion)* (International Criminal Tribunal for the former Yugoslavia, Trial Chamber, Case No IT-98-29-T, 5 December 2003).
34 Ibid [58] (emphasis added).

This test was reaffirmed by the Appeals Chamber, where it cited with approval the Trial Chamber's test of 'reasonableness' when listing factors such as: relevant distances at play, identification criteria, relevance of surrounding combat activity, and visual issues.[35]

The yardstick of reasonableness is strewn throughout ICL for testing the lawfulness of various IHL principles. Although not an entirely dissimilar assessment when compared with a variety of national jurisdictions, this ostensibly objective assessment fails to provide definitive guidance during times of armed conflict. Koskenniemi aptly states that '[a]ll law is about lifting idiosyncratic ("subjective") interests and preferences from the realm of the special to that of the general ("objective") in which they lose their particular, political colouring and come to seem natural, necessary or even pragmatic.[36] The test of 'reasonableness' provides a useful mechanism to undertake this heavy lifting. For armed groups acting during NIAC who do not have a legal team on command, in particular, utilising such measures during armed conflict seems impossible. This is not to excuse armed groups from complying with IHL – far from it. But what these examples demonstrate is that there exists an ever-growing body of jurisprudence which armed groups (and states) are somehow expected to keep up with, comprehend, and comply and yet are somewhat vague and elusive in their stated boundaries.

B *Distinction and proportionality without measure: fully autonomous weapons*

What happens to the principles of distinction and proportionality when war crimes are committed by weapons that are not controlled by humans? Who does ICL apportion liability to, and can there be strict measures of reasonableness for a weapon that makes decisions without human control or interference? These are questions facing the international community consequent to the pursuit of fully autonomous weapons development.

Then-UN special rapporteur on extrajudicial, summary, or arbitrary executions, Philip Alston, held in regard to unmanned weapons systems that 'the rapid growth of these technologies, especially those with lethal capacities and those with decreased levels of human control, raise serious concerns that have been almost entirely unexamined by human rights or humanitarian actors'.[37]

---

35 *Prosecutor v Stanislav Galić (Judgement)* (International Criminal Tribunal for the former Yugoslavia, Appeals Chamber, Case No IT-98-29-A, 30 November 2006) [193].
36 Martti Koskenniemi, *From Apology to Utopia* (Cambridge University Press, 2005) 597.
37 Philip Alston, *Interim Report of the Special Rapporteur on Extrajudicial, Summary or Arbitrary Executions*, UN GAOR, 65th sess, Agenda Item 69(b), UN Doc A/65/321 (23 August 2010) 10.

This was in 2010. Since then, not only has weapons technology advanced further, but there has emerged a cascade of debate amongst members of the robotics, legal, ethics, philosophy, military, and science communities concerning the development of evolving weapons systems.

The debate chiefly revolves around weapons systems that will be fully autonomous. The International Committee of the Red Cross (ICRC) defines fully autonomous weapon systems as weapons that can 'independently select and attack targets, i.e. with autonomy in the "critical functions" of acquiring, tracking, selecting and attacking targets'.[38] In a 2012 Directive, the United States' Department of Defense defined autonomous weapons systems as:

> A weapon system that, once activated, can select and engage targets without further intervention by a human operator. This includes human-supervised autonomous weapon systems that are designed to allow human operators to override operation of the weapon system, but can select and engage targets without further human input after activation.[39]

Further to these definitions, Human Rights Watch has succinctly explained the three levels of autonomy a weapons system may possess, based on the level of human control of their actions, namely where: robots select targets and deliver force with human command (in the loop); robots select targets and deliver force under the oversight of a human operator who can override the robots' actions (on the loop); and robots that are capable of selecting targets and delivering force without any human input or interaction (out of the loop).[40] While fully autonomous weapons do not yet exist, states continue to develop their technologies with that goal in mind.

There are two extremes surrounding the debate. Firstly, it is argued that we should ban the development of fully autonomous weapons technology, and also ban fully autonomous weapons altogether. It has been held that the pursuit of fully autonomous weapons means '[w]e could be moving into the final stages of the industrialization of warfare towards a factory of death and clean-killing where hi-tech countries fight wars without risk to their own forces'.[41] Contrastingly, proponents of fully autonomous weapons hold they should continue to be developed and their limits explored.

---

38 International Committee of the Red Cross, *Autonomous Weapons Systems: Technical, Military, Legal, and Humanitarian Aspects* (March 2014) 7.
39 United States of America Department of Defense, *Directive 3000.09: Autonomy in Weapon Systems* (21 November 2012) 13-14.
40 See Human Rights Watch and International Human Rights Clinic, *Losing Humanity: The Case against Killer Robots* (2012) 2.
41 Noel E Sharkey, 'The Evitability of Autonomous Robot Warfare' (2012) 94(886) *International Review of the Red Cross* 787, 788.

The cause for debate lies primarily with three issues: distinction, proportionality, and accountability. Whilst fully autonomous weapons systems do not yet exist, we are in a rare period of time where the international community can shape the future use (or misuse) of these weapons. The 'vacuous and emotive'[42] debates persist, with little consensus achieved.

IV Distinction and proportionality

As already indicated, it is a central principle in IHL that an attacker must distinguish between a combatant and non-combatant. In addition to this principle, and possibly one of the most complex rules of IHL, the attack must be proportionate, which means that the harm to civilians through an attack must not excessively outweigh the anticipated military advantage.

There thus exists a question about the extent to which a fully autonomous weapons system could distinguish between civilians, combatants, or immune actors such as wounded combatants or those combatants who have surrendered. This argument has often been characterised by the change in armed conflict in recent decades from international to the increasing occurrence of non-international armed conflict. Typically, in non-international armed conflicts, 'urban battles [are] fought among civilian populations, [making] distinguishing between legitimate targets and noncombatants increasingly difficult', where 'combatants often do not wear uniforms or insignia. Instead they seek to blend in with the civilian population and are frequently identified by their conduct, or their "direct participation in hostilities"'.[43]

It has been argued that a fully autonomous weapons system does not have the inherent human qualities required to comply with the rules of proportionality and distinction.[44] Accordingly, it has been held that a fully autonomous weapons system would not have the human ability to distinguish between combatants and non-combatants, and would fail to comprehend the status of immune actors.[45]

In contrast, it has been held that by building these weapons systems, the goal to comply with IHL (and hence ICL) has not dissipated – instead, a class of robots should be created that not only comply with IHL restrictions, but which have the potential to 'outperform human soldiers in their ethical capacity

42 Michael N Schmitt, 'Unmanned Combat Aircraft Systems and International Humanitarian Law: Simplifying the Oft Benighted Debate' (2012) 30 *Boston University International Law Journal* 595, 596.
43 Human Rights Watch, above n 40, 30.
44 Human Rights Watch and International Human Rights Clinic, *Mind the Gap: The Lack of Accountability for Killer Robots* (2015) 7.
45 Sharkey, above n 41, 788.

under comparable circumstances'.[46] In this polarising debate, one side argues that the use of fully autonomous weapons will increase the risk of death or injury to civilians and unlawful loss of life,[47] whereas the other argues the complete opposite.[48]

V Accountability

The issues of distinction and proportionality are at the heart of the debate, but with no fully autonomous weapon system yet created to test its abilities, no answer exists. Putting aside these questions, if a fully autonomous weapons system did exist, who could be held accountable if it committed a war crime? This is more perplexing than whether principles of distinction and proportionality can be coded into a machine or not. This question relates to who is responsible when war crimes are committed by a weapons system that does not require any human control.

Potential defendants under ICL include the military commander, operator (who initiates the weapon, not controls it), programmer, or the manufacturer. Obviously the weapon itself is unpunishable.[49] However, holding any of these individuals accountable for an act they did not control faces problematic issues of criminal responsibility. Under current tenets of international criminal law, for a war crime to be committed, there must always be a physical and mental element. Any of these individuals could arguably have committed the physical element by ordering the weapon to mobilise, turning it on, programming the weapon to work, or to build the weapon in the first place, but it is likely none of these individuals possessed the intent or knowledge to conduct the attack which resulted in a serious violation of IHL. Command responsibility could be useful in determining accountability, but faces problems of its own.[50]

---

46 Ronald C Arkin, 'The Case for Ethical Autonomy in Unmanned Systems' (2010) 9(4) *Journal of Military Ethics* 332, 339.

47 Human Rights Watch, above n 40, 1; Human Rights Watch, above n 44, 8.

48 Schmitt, above n 42; Arkin, above n 46; Ronald Arkin, 'Ethical Restraint of Lethal Autonomous Robotic Systems: Requirements, Research, and Implications' in International Committee of the Red Cross, *Autonomous Weapons Systems: Technical, Military, Legal, and Humanitarian Aspects* (March 2014) 33.

49 'At the moment, it would obviously be nonsensical to do this, as any robot that exists today, or that will be built in the next 10-20 years, is too dumb to possess anything like intentionality or a real capability for agency. However, this might change in a more distant future once robots become more sophisticated and intelligent'. Armin Krishnan, *Killer Robots: Legality and Ethicality of Autonomous Weapons* (Ashgate, 2009) 105.

50 On this form of liability, see, e.g., Alejandro Kiss, 'Command Responsibility under Article 28 of the Rome Statute' in Carsten Stahn (ed), *The Law and Practice of the International Criminal Court* (Oxford University Press, 2015) 608.

If the fully autonomous weapon itself was somehow to be held liable, what benchmark would apply to assess criminal liability? Former UN special rapporteur on extrajudicial, summary, or arbitrary executions, Christof Heyns, held that while they 'cannot be required to be perfect, they will in practice be held to standards that are significantly higher than those posed for humans.[51] However, this statement was followed by the conclusion that 'without clear accountability for their use and inherent risks, it will be irresponsible and, I would argue, unlawful to use autonomous weapon systems'.[52]

Such weapons therefore pose a 'responsibility gap' where individuals could be held 'responsible for actions of machines over which they could not have sufficient control'.[53] If there is to be no legal accountability for the commission of war crimes, then there is no way to ensure the goals of ICL (compliance, deterrence, punishment, justice and/or peace) can be realised. Accordingly, Heyns states that '[w]ar crimes are not crimes if there cannot be prosecution'.[54] Lack of accountability is, evidently, an unacceptable conclusion. If states and private armed groups continue to work towards developing a fully autonomous weapons system there will be a need to devise a new criminal responsibility model that extends beyond traditional concepts.

VI Compliance and deterrence

Chief Prosecutor at the ICTY, Serge Brammertz, opines that '[d]eterring crime and strengthening compliance with the rules of international humanitarian law (IHL) have been principal expectations for contemporary international criminal justice'.[55] Emphasis of this statement is to be placed on *contemporary* international criminal justice. With a past focused on punishment and justice, contemporary international criminal law faces a dilemma in its goal of strengthening compliance as well as deterrence.

The Nuremberg and Tokyo Trials following the Second World War were established for punitive and justice purposes, with Article 1 in both founding charters holding that the tribunals were established 'for the just and

---

51 Christof Heyns, 'Increasingly Autonomous Weapon Systems: Accountability and Responsibility' in International Committee of the Red Cross, *Autonomous Weapons Systems: Technical, Military, Legal, And Humanitarian Aspects* (March 2014) 47.
52 Ibid.
53 Andreas Matthias, 'The Responsibility Gap: Ascribing Responsibility for the Actions of Learning Automata' (2004) 6 *Ethics and Information Technology* 175, 176, 183.
54 Heyns, above n 51, 45.
55 Serge Brammertz, 'The Impact of Criminal Prosecutions on Compliance with IHL: Challenges and Perspectives on the Way Forward' (2015) 39 *University of Western Australia Law Review* 4.

prompt trial and punishment of the major war criminals'.[56] Arguably, the establishment of the *ad hoc* ICTY and ICTR in the 1990s mirrored the first tribunals' purposes, with an added goal of restoring peace and reducing violence on the ground whilst the conflicts were ongoing.[57] Such broader social and political goals necessarily temper the character of the process and indeed of the application of the law itself. It is apparent that '[g]eneral deterrence does not seem to have been a primary goal of the architects of the *ad hoc* Tribunals'.[58] Despite the initial purposes for the establishment of the *ad hoc* tribunals, throughout their existence the idea that international criminal law can and should provide compliance and/or deterrence became widespread. In contrast to its predecessors, the ICC was established with the explicit goal of deterrence.[59] Klabbers has gone as far as stating that general deterrence 'is one of the main reasons (perhaps the main reason) underlying the creation of the ICC: the idea is to ensure punishment and, through punishment, to deter'.[60]

The central role of international criminal courts such as the ICC remain traditional, namely to ensure breaches of the law are punished and that IHL is enforced through judicial means. However, there is also this broader role that the international community expects these courts to assume, one of ensuring the diffusion of norms that will result in both compliance and also deterrence. Hence courts like the ICC are expected to play a broader social role in their representative and perhaps symbolic role of reflecting international standards that are then internalised to shape behaviour on the battlefield. But can the international criminal courts and tribunals ensure deterrence and compliance through their actions? It has been argued against the case of deterrence that the international criminal justice system is generally decentralised and has strict geographic, procedural, and temporal limits, precluding the system from influencing individuals from committing war crimes.[61] Contrastingly, Acquaviva states that each of the international criminal institutions should be looked at as part of an intertwined and mutually reinforcing network, with the potential to 'increase awareness of the primary rules for the protection of human dignity among

---

56 *Nuremberg Charter* and *Tokyo Charter*, above n 6, Art. 1.
57 This is evident in both resolutions which have almost identical preambulatory clauses: SC Res 827, above n 8; SC Res 955, above n 10.
58 Kate Cronin-Furman, 'Managing Expectations: International Criminal Trials and the Prospects for Deterrence of Mass Atrocity' (2013) 7 *International Journal of Transitional Justice* 434, 436.
59 *Rome Statute*, above n 17, preamble ('Determined to put an end to impunity for the perpetrators of these crimes and thus to contribute to the prevention of such crimes').
60 Jan Klabbers, 'Just Revenge? The Deterrence Argument in International Criminal Law' (2001) 12 *Finnish Yearbook of International Law* 249, 251.
61 Cronin-Furman, above n 58, 440.

the general public and, together with other institutions, foster compliance with the law and therefore, indirectly, general deterrence'.[62]

Both arguments possess merit, and the debate about whether the international criminal courts and tribunals can ensure compliance as well as deterrence is ongoing. This is bound up in a larger debate as to the purpose of the international courts and tribunals, and whether they be for general or specific deterrence, compliance, peace, or restorative, punitive and/or transitional justice.

A *Pursuing compliance, pursuing complementarity*

Looking deeper into the role of the international criminal justice system, one observes a relationship between the international and domestic frameworks which can ensure compliance and/or deterrence. War crimes are, generally, often well-regulated in domestic systems, with states undertaking the primary responsibility to prosecute their nationals. The importance of the role of the state in prosecuting its own nationals is seen repeatedly in the complementarity principle reflected in instruments such as the Rome Statute. Thus, the preamble of the Rome Statute acknowledges 'that it is the duty of every State to exercise its criminal jurisdiction over those responsible for international crimes'. This statement is codified in Article 1 of the Rome Statute, holding that the ICC 'shall have the power to exercise its jurisdiction over persons for the most serious crimes of international concern, as referred to in this Statute, and shall be complementary to national criminal jurisdictions'. Similarly, the ICTY and ICTR Statutes hold the tribunals were established to 'prosecute persons responsible for serious violations of international humanitarian law',[63] with respective national courts trying lesser war criminals.

The ICC has therefore attempted to be an institution of last resort, with the primary purpose to ensure domestic prosecution. Somewhat similarly, the ICTY and ICTR sought to prosecute only the most serious offenders, whilst assisting domestic courts to prosecute lesser war criminals. In both cases, emphasis is placed on ensuring domestic prosecution of alleged war criminals.

While international courts and tribunals are imperfect, so too are national courts. Arguably, prosecutions by the state, as opposed to an international forum, will have the biggest impact in ensuring compliance with IHL. This is one of the chief reasons the principle of complementarity

62 Guido Acquaviva, 'International Criminal Courts and Tribunals as Actors of General Deterrence? Perceptions and Misperceptions' (2014) 96(895/896) *International Review of the Red Cross* 775, 786.
63 SC Res 827, above n 8, Art. 1; SC Res 955, above n 10, Art. 1.

at the ICC exists. States are encouraged to try war criminals, but if they are unable or unwilling to do so, the ICC can step in and prosecute the alleged offenders.

In a seminal study by the ICRC, *The Roots of Behaviour in War*,[64] it was found that the most important way to promote compliance with IHL was not to persuade combatants or win them over personally, 'but rather to influence the people who have an ascendancy over them'.[65] Consequently, on this view more attention needs to be paid to the national level and the relationship to be fostered between the ICC and domestic jurisdictions through the complementarity principle.

It has been argued that when 'justice is handled locally by credible national or regional institutions, the local population may more easily accept judgments and the accountability process, which can further assist in peacebuilding'.[66] This, in turn, can have the effect of ensuring compliance. If individual offenders are held to account by their own credible judiciary, they – and others – will be compelled to comply with IHL.

B *Before prosecution: effective military training to ensure compliance*

Though the prosecution of war crimes through national or international forums may be one mechanism used to ensure compliance and deterrence, the duty to disseminate IHL 'as widely as possible' also persists.[67] The duty to disseminate IHL has long been held to include military training, where norms are internalised 'through attitudinal change, discourse and repetition', yet it has been acknowledged that national training alone is 'insufficient to ensure compliance with the law'.[68]

---

64 Jean-Jacques Frésard, *The Roots of Behaviour in War: A Survey of the Literature* (International Committee of the Red Cross, 2004).

65 Daniel Muñoz-Rojas and Jean-Jacques Frésard, 'The Roots of Behaviour in War: Understanding and Preventing IHL Violations' (2004) 86(853) *International Review of the Red Cross*, 189, 204.

66 Brammertz, above n 55, 22.

67 GC I, above n 2, Art. 47; GC II, above n 2, Art. 48; GC III, above n 2, Art. 127; GC IV, above n 2, Art. 144; AP I, above n 3, Arts 83, 87(2); *Hague Convention for the Protection of Cultural Property in the Event of Armed Conflict*, 14 May 1954, 249 UNTS 240 (entered into force 7 August 1956) Art. 25; *Convention on Prohibitions or Restrictions on the Use of Certain Conventional Weapons Which May Be Deemed to Be Excessively Injurious or to Have Indiscriminate Effects*, 10 October 1980, 1342 UNTS 137 (entered into force 2 December 1983) Art. 6; *Second Protocol to the Hague Convention of 1954 for the Protection of Cultural Property in the Event of Armed Conflict*, 26 March 1999, 2253 UNTS 212 (entered into force 9 March 2004) Art. 30.

68 Elizabeth Stubbins Bates, 'Towards Effective Military Training in International Humanitarian Law' (2014) 96(895/896) *International Review of the Red Cross* 795, 797.

Recently the ICRC and Government of Switzerland took steps to establish a major consultative project entitled *Strengthening Compliance with International Humanitarian Law*. This project was established, *inter alia*, for the purpose of 'enhancing and ensuring the effectiveness of mechanisms of compliance with international humanitarian law, with a view to strengthening legal protection for all victims of armed conflict'.[69] This initiative began in 2011 and culminated in its presentation at the ICRC's 32nd International Conference in 2015.

The result of this project was a recommendation to establish, *inter alia*, an annual non-politicised forum for states to share best practices and technical expertise.[70] After presenting its findings of the project, states at the ICRC's 32nd International Conference were unable to agree on the new mechanism to strengthen compliance with IHL. Despite the four years of consultations, states agreed to 'launch an inter-governmental process to find ways to enhance the implementation of IHL',[71] to culminate in another four years when it can be presented to the ICRC's 36th International Conference. This has resulted in a consultative process being undertaken by the ICRC through engagement with states, NGOs and academics to identify innovative ways to address perceptions of the law and shape strategies that are less doctrinaire and more effective in ensuring respect for IHL.[72]

The ICRC continues to play a central role in dissemination, but in an accessible manner that seeks to integrate IHL compliance with armed forces and non-state actors within existing command and control processes. This new perspective sees a holistic integration of IHL, as opposed to simple training, at the core of IHL compliance, with combatants needing to be taught the same behaviour for both international and non-international armed conflict.[73] Integration of IHL sees a deepened understanding within the individual as IHL is included in all aspects of 'doctrine, education, training and equipment, plus the crucial role that sanctions play',[74] and with relevance for decision-making and communication within the military command structure.[75]

---

69 International Committee of the Red Cross, *31st International Conference of the Red Cross and Red Crescent* (2011) 25.

70 International Committee of the Red Cross, *No Agreement by States on Mechanism to Strengthen Compliance with Rules of War* (10 December 2015) <www.icrc.org/en/document/no-agreement-states-mechanism-strengthen-compliance-rules-war>.

71 Ibid.

72 One such symposium was conducted at the University of Tasmania by ICRC representatives in October, 2016.

73 Stubbins Bates, above n 68, 801, stating that increasing outreach to non-state armed groups by non-governmental organisations demonstrates dissemination and compliance are more becoming more widespread in non-international armed conflicts.

74 International Committee of the Red Cross, *Integrating the Law* (2007) 2, 17, 19; International Committee of the Red Cross, *Violence and the Use of Force* (2015) 56.

75 Stubbins Bates, above n 68, 798.

Although the principle of integration is yet untested in terms of effectiveness, it represents a novel approach to ensuring compliance with IHL. As the ICTR has closed and moved its residual functions to the Mechanism for International Criminal Tribunals, with the ICTY to soon follow suit, the future lies with the ICC. The ICC's principles will dominate the contours of the jurisprudence of this area, and while ICL will always be relevant, the ICC acts as a last resort. As Stubbins-Bates rightly held, '[i]nstead of simply acknowledging that IHL training is necessary (if insufficient) for compliance with the law, it is time to test its effectiveness, and to build mechanisms that facilitate best practice'.[76] Efforts to integrate IHL and ensure compliance are vital, as not only do they pursue the goal of disseminating IHL, but also they have the potential to reduce IHL violations, the unnecessary loss of life and the activation of elaborate ICL procedures (nationally and/or internationally).

VII Conclusion

The foundational jurisprudence of the ICTY and ICTR has served to strengthen our understanding of what constitutes a war crime. Cases like *Tadić*, which set out a guide for what may constitute a war crime where there is no relevant treaty or rule of customary international law, and *Akayesu*, which explained the requirement of a nexus with armed conflict, have made clear the differences between 'ordinary' crimes and war crimes. Where distinguishing between IAC and NIAC was once deemed vital to determining commission and accountability, these tribunals have held that it is no longer a salient issue; serious violations of IHL, whether committed in IAC or NIAC, are war crimes. With contemporary warfare increasingly occurring in non-international armed conflicts, this means individuals can no longer engage in hostilities with the assumption of impunity in international criminal law.

However, when the trial chambers of these tribunals have attempted to provide calculable tests against the principles of IHL, they have been overturned. The result is that military forces and armed groups are forced to conduct military actions in a grey area of 'reasonableness'. Yet with the ICC developing its own corpus of international legal standards when trying alleged war criminals, those involved in armed conflict must still look to the jurisprudence of the *ad hoc* tribunals for guidance on the tests and limits of IHL and associated tests for criminal liability under ICL. The depth of this grey area deepens with the ongoing development of fully autonomous weapons. Questions are raised concerning the ability of weapons without any human control to comply with principles of distinction and proportionality,

76 Ibid 816.

and if they do commit a war crime, who is to be held responsible? What is obvious from this debate is that our traditional concepts of accountability may need to evolve to address accountability questions posed by the use of fully autonomous weapons.

The evolution of the international criminal justice system has created a multitude of expectations: general or specific deterrence, compliance, peace, and restorative, punitive, or transitional justice. Increasingly, there are expectations of ICL to deliver measurable deterrence and compliance in armed conflict. It is clear that the ICC was created as a system of last resort, through its principle of complementarity to act when states are unable or unwilling to do so. Despite its specific mandate, the ICC has necessarily given rise to expectations concerning the future direction of ICL, which includes the unavoidable interest of fostering and facilitating national mechanisms of accountability. The responsibility then partly falls to the ICC to support states that wish to try their nationals for war crimes, just as the *ad hoc* tribunals have done.

Work continues unabated towards achieving the goal of compliance. The development of novel techniques by the ICRC to ensure compliance with IHL is encouraging. The idea of 'integration', as opposed to the traditional dissemination of IHL, demonstrates an attempt to deepen comprehension of IHL for those engaged in armed conflict. Although integration remains untested, the goal of establishing a non-politicised forum for states to share best practices and technical expertise may result in future adequate integration of IHL for state militaries and private armed groups. Hence it is not solely the role of the international criminal courts and tribunals to deliver deterrence and compliance – the responsibility rests with states and non-governmental bodies.

The topic of war crimes is expansive, with its scholarship reaching beyond the confines of this chapter. This chapter has, however, provided a foundational understanding of what is a war crime, explained future problems for international criminal law in a world of war without human control, and discussed expectations of the international criminal justice system. It is evident that although bodies such as the *ad hoc* tribunals and the ICC may do an imperfect job of interpreting IHL, their very existence demonstrates the seriousness with which the international community regards the commission of war crimes and the perennial goal of ensuring a measure of international legal accountability.

Further reading

Arkin, Ronald C, 'The Case for Ethical Autonomy in Unmanned Systems' (2010) 9(4) *Journal of Military Ethics* 332.

Bates, Elizabeth Stubbins, 'Towards Effective Military Training in International Humanitarian Law' (2014) 96(895/896) *International Review of the Red Cross* 795.

Dancy, Geoff and Florencia Montal, 'Unintended Positive Complementarity: Why International Criminal Court Investigations Increase Domestic Human Rights Prosecutions' (Paper presented at the American Society of International Law Conference, Chicago, November 2014).

Human Rights Watch and International Human Rights Clinic, *Losing Humanity: The Case against Killer Robots* (2012).

Human Rights Watch and International Human Rights Clinic, *Mind the Gap: The Lack of Accountability for Killer Robots* (2015).

Kennedy, David, *Of War and Law* (Princeton University Press, 2006).

Meron, Theodor, *War Crimes Law Comes of Age* (Oxford University Press, 1998).

Schmitt, Michael N and Jeffrey S Thurnher, '"Out of the Loop": Autonomous Weapon Systems and the Law of Armed Conflict' (2013) 4 *Harvard National Security Journal* 231.

7

SEXUAL AND GENDER-BASED CRIMES

Rosemary Grey

I Introduction

Today, sexual and gender-based crimes are widely regarded as crimes of the most serious concern to the international community as a whole. One need not look far for evidence of this view. It is borne out in the juris-prudence of the International Criminal Tribunal for the former Yugoslavia (ICTY) and International Criminal Tribunal for Rwanda (ITCR), which affirms that sexual and gender-based crimes constitute crimes under inter-national law.[1] It is reflected in the Rome Statute of the International Criminal Court (ICC), which recognises a wider range of sexual and gen-der-based crimes than any previous instrument of international criminal law (ICL).[2] Further evidence can be found in texts by leading scholars of ICL,[3] publications by high-profile human rights organisations,[4] and policies

---

1 Kelly Askin, 'Prosecuting Wartime Rape and Other Gender Related Crimes: Extraordinary Advances, Enduring Obstacles' (2003) 21(2) *Berkeley Journal of International Law* 288, 317-346; Helen Brady, 'The Power of Precedents: Using the Case Law of the Ad Hoc International Criminal Tribunals and Hybrid Courts in Adjudicating Sexual and Gender-Based Crimes at the ICC' (2012) 18(2) *Australian Journal of Human Rights* 75; Serge Brammertz and Michelle Jarvis, *Prosecuting Conflict-Related Sexual Violence Crimes at the ICTY* (Oxford University Press, 2016).

2 *Rome Statute of the International Criminal Court,* opened for signature 17 July 1998, 2187 UNTS 90 (entered into force 1 July 2002) Arts 7(1)(g), 7(1)(h), 8(2)(b)(xxii), 8(2)(e)(vi).

3 Eg, Robert Cryer *et al, An Introduction to International Criminal Law and Procedure* (Cambridge University Press, 3rd ed, 2014) 287-289; Christine Chinkin, 'Gender-related Violence and International Criminal Justice' in Antonio Cassese (ed), *The Oxford Companion to International Criminal Justice* (Oxford University Press, 2009) 75.

4 Eg, Women's Initiatives for Gender Justice, *2014 Gender Report Card on the International Criminal Court* (December 2014) <http://iccwomen.org/documents/Gender-Report-Card-on-the-ICC-2014.pdf>; Human Rights Watch, *Courting History: The Landmark International*

and manuals developed by international prosecutors,[5] which recognise the importance of prosecuting sexual and gender-based crimes.

Perhaps most tellingly, sexual and gender-based crimes are now regularly prosecuted in international and internationalised courts. For example in March 2016, the ICC convicted Jean-Pierre Bemba Gombo, a politician from the Democratic Republic of Congo (DRC), for war crimes and crimes against humanity committed by his troops in the Central African Republic, including the rape of civilian men, women, and children.[6] Days later, the ICTY convicted former Bosnian Serb leader Radovan Karadžić for war crimes, crimes against humanity, and genocide committed in the former Yugoslavia, including rape and other gender-based crimes, such as the killing of over 7,000 Bosnian Muslim men and boys in Srebrenica.[7] Two months later, the Extraordinary African Chamber convicted Chad's former dictator Hissène Habré for war crimes and crimes against humanity committed in Chad from 1982 to 1990, including rape and sexual violence crimes.[8]

Prosecuting sexual and gender-based crimes in international and internationalised courts such as these serves several goals. First, it is a powerful expression of the international community's values: it signals that sexual and gender-based violence is unacceptable, and is as serious as other offences, such as murder and pillage, which have long been recognised as crimes under international law.[9] Second, the prosecution of sexual and gender-based crimes may deliver restorative justice benefits to the victims, including recognition

---

Criminal Court's First Years (July 2008) 32, 171, 231 <www.hrw.org/sites/default/files/reports/icc0708webwcover.pdf>.

5 See, eg, Office of the Prosecutor, International Criminal Court, *Policy Paper on Sexual and Gender-Based Crimes* (June 2014) <www.icc-cpi.int/iccdocs/otp/OTP-Policy-Paper-on-Sexual-and-Gender-Based-Crimes--June-2014.pdf>; Office of the Prosecutor, International Criminal Court, *Policy Paper on Case Selection and Prioritisation* (15 September 2016) [46] <www.icc-cpi.int/itemsDocuments/20160915_OTP-Policy_Case-Selection_Eng.pdf>; Michelle Jarvis and Najwa Nabti, 'Policies and Strategies for Successful Sexual Violence Prosecutions' in Brammertz and Jarvis, above n 1, 73; Office of the Prosecutor, International Criminal Tribunal for the former Yugoslavia, *Best Practices Manual for the Investigation and Prosecution of Sexual Violence Crimes in Post-Conflict Regions* (30 January 2014) <http://w.unictr.org/sites/unictr.org/files/legal-library/140130_prosecution_of_sexual_violence.pdf>.

6 *Prosecutor v Bemba (Judgment pursuant to Article 74 of the Statute)* (International Criminal Court, Trial Chamber III, Case No ICC-01/05-01/08-3343, 21 March 2016).

7 *Prosecutor v Karadžić (Public Redacted Version of Judgment Issued on 24 March 2016)* (International Criminal Tribunal for the former Yugoslavia, Trial Chamber, Case No IT-95-5/18-T, 24 March 2016).

8 *Ministère Public v Habré (Judgement)* (Extraordinary African Chambers, 30 May 2016).

9 Margaret deGuzman, 'An Expressive Rationale for the Prosecution of Sex Crimes' in Morten Bergsmo (ed), *Thematic Prosecution of International Sex Crimes* (Opsahl Academic EPublisher, 2012) 11; Cryer *et al*, above n 3, 36-37.

of harm suffered, participation in the trial, and (in some courts, including the ICC) reparations following a conviction.[10] Third, proceedings in international and internationalised courts play a key role in shaping popular understandings of the conflict in question. As such, it is important that they prosecute a representative range of crimes, including sexual and gender-based crimes, in order to produce an accurate historical record.[11] In addition, the prosecution of sexual and gender-based crimes is important from a gender discrimination perspective. This is because while some victims of sexual and gender-based crimes are men and boys, the majority are women and girls. Accordingly, the prosecution of these crimes at both the international and national level is a crucial component of 'gender justice'.[12]

Despite these considerations, sexual and gender-based crimes have only recently become a focus in ICL. Until the 1990s, these crimes were not expressly recognised in instruments of ICL, and were rarely prosecuted in international courts. This chapter explains how this pattern of impunity began to shift, and considers the ongoing challenges for prosecuting sexual and gender-based crimes under international law.

The chapter begins by defining the term 'sexual and gender-based crimes' and by explaining the political significance of this term. Next, it explains how sexual and gender-based crimes moved from the margins to the centre of ICL, due largely to the efforts of gender-sensitive prosecutors and judges in international and internationalised courts, along with women's rights activists and feminist legal scholars who called for greater attention to these crimes. Finally, the chapter discusses some long-standing gender biases and gaps in the legal framework that continue to inhibit the prosecution of sexual and gender-based crimes under international law. The chapter concludes that although sexual and gender-based crimes are now widely recognised as among the most serious crimes of concern to the international community as a whole, the 'end of impunity' for these crimes under international law is still a long way off.

II From 'sexual violence' to 'sexual and gender-based crimes'

Terms such as 'gender-based crimes' and 'gender-based violence' have been widely used in the feminist literature on ICL since the 1990s.[13] While scholars

---

10 Regarding the concept of 'restorative justice', see Benjamin Schiff, *Building the International Criminal Court* (Cambridge University Press, 2008) 10, 33-34.
11 Regarding the role of international courts in shaping the 'historical record', see Cryer *et al*, above n 3, 38-40.
12 See Louise Chappell, *The Politics of Gender Justice at the International Criminal Court: Legacies and Legitimacy* (Oxford University Press, 2016).
13 Eg, Barbara Bedont and Katherine Hall-Martinez, 'Ending Impunity for Gender Crimes under the International Criminal Court' (1999) 6(1) *Brown Journal of World Affairs* 65;

do not always define these terms, the examples they discuss generally include crimes involving sexual violence (such as rape), reproductive violence (such as forced pregnancy), and other forms of violence directed at people due (at least in part) to their gender (such as sex-selective killings). Describing these seemingly unrelated acts as 'gender-based crimes' serves an important purpose: it recognises the way that these acts of violence against individual victims often reflect and reinforce broader gender norms.[14] For example, in conflict settings, women are often raped because they are seen as 'war booty', reflecting widely held beliefs in men's entitlement to women's bodies.[15] Men are also raped in conflict settings, although usually for different reasons, such as to humiliate the victim by making him appear 'emasculated', and therefore weak, in the eyes of his community.[16]

Reflecting this argument, the term 'sexual and gender-based crimes' is increasingly used in the field of ICL to describe crimes which reflect and reinforce socially constructed gender norms, including (but not limited to) sexual violence crimes.[17] A group that helped to popularise this term was the Women's Caucus for Gender Justice, a coalition of women's rights activists and feminist scholars who joined the Rome Statute negotiations in 1997 with the goal of 'ensur[ing] the incorporation of a gender

Rhonda Copelon, 'Gender Crimes as War Crimes: Integrating Crimes against Women into International Criminal Law' (2000) 46(1) *McGill Law Journal* 217; Niamh Hayes, '*La Lutte Continue:* Investigating and Prosecuting Sexual Violence at the ICC' in Carsten Stahn (ed), *The Law and Practice of the International Criminal Court* (Oxford University Press, 2015) 801; Susana SáCouto and Katherine Cleary, 'The Importance of Effective Investigation of Sexual Violence and Gender Based Crimes at the International Criminal Court' (2009) 17(2) *American University Journal of Gender, Social Policy & the Law* 337; Valerie Oosterveld and Patricia Viseur Sellers, 'Issues of Sexual and Gender-Based Violence at the ECCC' in Simon M Meisenberg and Ignaz Stegmiller (eds), *The Extraordinary Chambers in the Courts of Cambodia: Assessing their Contribution to International Criminal Law* (Springer, 2016) 321; Solange Mouthaan, 'The Prosecution of Gender-based Crimes at the ICC: Challenges and Opportunities' (2011) 11 *International Criminal Law Review* 775; Cate Steains, 'Gender Issues' in Roy S Lee (ed), *The International Criminal Court: The Making of the Rome Statute* (Kluwer Law International, 1999) 357.

14 Catharine MacKinnon, 'Creating International Law: Gender as Leading Edge' (2013) 36(1) *Harvard Journal of Law & Gender* 105.

15 See Copelon, above n 13, 223; Mouthaan, above n 13, 777.

16 Sandesh Sivakumaran, 'Sexual Violence against Men in Armed Conflict' (2007) 18 *European Journal of International Law* 253; MacKinnon, above n 14, 106.

17 Michelle Jarvis, 'Overview: The Challenge of Accountability for Conflict-related Sexual Violence Crimes' in Brammertz and Jarvis, above n 1, 1, 10. See, eg, Dianne Luping, 'Investigation and Prosecution of Sexual and Gender-Based Crimes before the International Criminal Court' (2009) 17(2) *American University Journal of Gender, Social Policy & the Law* 431; Catharine MacKinnon, 'The International Criminal Court and Gender Crimes' (Speech delivered at the Consultative Conference on International Criminal Justice, New York, 11 September 2009).

perspective throughout the statute'.[18] Together with like-minded States, the Women's Caucus argued that the ICC should have jurisdiction to prosecute a wide range of crimes involving 'sexual and gender violence'[19] – a term they intended to capture any crimes (sexual violence or otherwise) directed at people *because of* their gender.[20] For example, the Canadian delegation suggested that 'gender violence' would describe a situation in which men from one side of a conflict were being rounded up and killed by the adversary, because due to their gender, they were seen as capable of waging war.[21] The Women's Caucus and their supporters also campaigned for several other references to 'gender' in the Rome Statute, including a new crime against humanity of persecution on 'gender' grounds.[22]

These proposals met fierce opposition from several majority Catholic and Muslim States whose primary concern was that the term 'gender' would be interpreted to include sexual orientation.[23] After much debate, the references to 'gender violence' and 'gender persecution' were included in the Statute, with a caveat stating that the term 'gender' means 'the two sexes, male and female, within the context of society'.[24] This definition was sufficiently ambiguous to appease both sides of the debate, because while it does not refer expressly to sexual orientation, it enabled the Court to consider the socially-constructed aspects of gender and could potentially be interpreted to include violence directed at homosexual men and women as punishment for failing to conform to 'normal' sexual practices for persons of their sex.[25]

A more recent development that helped to popularise the term 'sexual and gender-based crimes' was the release of the ICC Office of the Prosecutor's *Policy Paper on Sexual and Gender-Based Crimes* in June 2014. The Policy Paper states that '"gender-based crimes" are those committed against persons, whether male or female, because of their sex and/or socially constructed gender roles'[26] and notes that these crimes 'may include *non-sexual* attacks on

---

18 Women's Caucus for Gender Justice, *Gender Justice and the ICC (Submission to the Rome Conference)*, 1998, Introduction (on file with the author).
19 Ibid ii, 5, 13; Steains, above n 13, 386-388.
20 Ibid 388.
21 Ibid n 99. See also Women's Caucus for Gender Justice, above n 18, 18.
22 Steains, above n 13, 370-371.
23 Ibid 372; Valerie Oosterveld, 'The Definition of "Gender" in the Rome Statute of the International Criminal Court: A Step Forward or Back for International Criminal Justice?' (2005) 18 *Harvard Human Rights Journal* 55, 63.
24 *Rome Statute*, Art. 7(3).
25 Oosterveld, above n 23, 76-79; MacKinnon, above n 14, 110. For a similar view, see United Nations High Commissioner for Human Rights, *Discriminatory laws and practices and acts of violence against individuals based on their sexual orientation and gender identity*, UN Doc A/HRC/19/41 (11 November 2011) [20] ('Homophobic and transphobic violence has been recorded in all regions . . . These attacks constitute a form of gender-based violence, driven by a desire to punish those seen as defying gender norms').
26 Office of the Prosecutor (2014), above n 5, 3.

women and girls, and men and boys, because of their gender'.[27] In line with this definition, the ICC Office of the Prosecutor regularly refers to 'gender-based crimes' in its policy papers,[28] legal filings,[29] and public statements.[30] In addition to using this term, the Office is also increasingly articulating the links between sexual violence and gender norms in cases before the Court. In the *Bemba* case, for example, the prosecution described sexual violence crimes as 'gender crimes', explaining: '[w]omen were raped systematically to assert dominance and to shatter their resistance. Men were raped in public to destroy their capacity to lead and protect'.[31]

The judiciary, by contrast, has been relatively slow to embrace the concept of 'gender-based crimes'. While judges in international and internationalised tribunals have used the term 'sexual violence' to describe acts such as rape, sexual slavery, and forced nudity since the 1990s,[32] the term 'gender-based crimes' has seldom been used in the jurisprudence of the ICTY,[33] ICTR,[34] Special Court for Sierra Leone (SCLS),[35] or Extraordinary Chambers in the Courts of Cambodia (ECCC),[36] and has only recently begun to appear in the jurisprudence of the ICC.[37] The ICC's adoption of this term can be seen as a positive development: it helps to 'surface' the links between sexual

---

27 Ibid (emphasis added).
28 Eg, Office of the Prosecutor (2016), above n 5, [39], [40], [46].
29 Eg, *Prosecutor v Ongwen (Document Containing the Charges)* (International Criminal Court, Pre-Trial Chamber II, Case No ICC-02/04-01/15-375-AnxA, 22 December 2015) Part 9.
30 Eg, International Criminal Court, Office of the Prosecutor, *Statement of the Prosecutor of the International Criminal Court, Fatou Bensouda, regarding the conviction of Mr Jean-Pierre Bemba: "This case has highlighted the critical need to eradicate sexual and gender-based crimes as weapons in conflict"* (21 March 2016) <www.icc-cpi.int/Pages/item.aspx?name=otp-stat-bemba-21-03-2016>.
31 *Prosecutor v Bemba (Transcript)* (International Criminal Court, Trial Chamber II, Case No ICC-01/05-01/08-T-364-ENG, 12 November 2014) 21.
32 Eg, *Prosecutor v Akayesu (Judgment)* (International Criminal Tribunal for Rwanda, Trial Chamber I, Case No ICTR-96-4-T, 2 September 1998) (*'Akayesu Trial Judgment'*) [10A].
33 Eg, *Prosecutor v Karadžić* (International Criminal Tribunal for the former Yugoslavia, Trial Chamber, Case No IT-95-5/18-T, 24 March 2016).
34 Eg, *Prosecutor v Akayesu* (International Criminal Tribunal for Rwanda, Trial Chamber I, Case No ICTR-96-4-T, 2 September 1998).
35 Eg, *Prosecutor v Brima, Kamara and Kanu (Appeal Judgment)* (Special Court for Sierra Leone, Appeals Chamber, Case No SCSL-2004-16-A, 22 February 2008) (*'AFRC Appeal Judgment'*).
36 Eg, *Prosecutor v Nuon Chea et al (Closing Order)* (Extraordinary Chambers in the Courts of Cambodia, Office of Co-Investigating Judges, Case No 002/19-09-2007-ECCC-OCIJ, 15 September 2010) (*'Case 002 Closing Order'*).
37 Eg, *Prosecutor v Lubanga (Judgment on the appeals against the "Decision establishing the principles and procedures to be applied to reparations" of 7 August 2012)* (International Criminal Court, Appeals Chamber, Case No ICC-01/04-01/06-3129, 3 March 2015) [192]–[199], [249]; *Prosecutor v Ongwen (Decision on the confirmation of charges)* (International Criminal Court, Pre-Trial Chamber II, Case No ICC-02/04-01/15-422-Red, 23 March 2016) Part H.

violence and socially constructed gender norms,[38] and counteract what Chiseche Salome Mibenge describes as 'the erasure of gender from the war narrative'.[39] For those same reasons, the term 'sexual and gender-based crimes' is used throughout this chapter.

III Sexual and gender-based crimes in ICL: past and present approaches

Sexual and gender-based crimes have long been a feature of armed conflict. In particular, the rape and sexual enslavement of women and girls has long been considered one of the spoils of war,[40] and is even portrayed as a justification for war in some early texts on the laws of war.[41] The harms caused by these crimes can be severe. They can include serious damage to physical and mental health, social stigmatisation, exposure to sexually transmitted diseases, and (for women and girls) pregnancy, childbirth, motherhood and/or unsafe abortion, and related costs and health complications. Yet, despite their prevalence and gravity, sexual and gender-based crimes were almost entirely overlooked in ICL until the 1990s.[42] There has been increasing recognition of these crimes in the last twenty years, as detailed below, but the progress has not been steady or smooth.

A *Development of ICL: setting the tone*

The 1899 and 1907 Hague Conventions, the first international treaties setting out the laws of war, devoted almost no attention to sexual and gender-based crimes. As Kelly Askin observes, 'in the entirety of the Hague Conventions and Regulations, one single Article (IV, art. 46) vaguely and indirectly prohibits sexual violence as a violation of "family honour"'.[43]

The charter of the International Military Tribunal at Nuremberg, adopted in 1945, was completely silent on sexual and gender-based crimes, although it expressly recognised other common wartime offences such as murder and

---

38 Rhonda Copelon, 'Surfacing Gender: Re-engraving Crimes against Women in Humanitarian Law' (1994) 5 *Hastings Women's Law Journal* 243. See also Oosterveld and Sellers, above n 13, 11.

39 Chiseche Salome Mibenge, *Sex and International Tribunal: The Erasure of Gender from the War Narrative* (University of Pennsylvania Press, 2013).

40 See Kelly Askin, *War Crimes against Women: Prosecution in International War Crimes Tribunals* (Martinus Nijhoff, 1997) Ch. 1.

41 Emer de Vattell, *The Law of Nations Or, Principles of the Law of Nature, Applied to the Conduct and Affairs of Nations and Sovereigns* (G. G. and J. Robinson, 1797) §122.

42 Askin, above n 1, 294-305; Bedont and Hall-Martinez, above n 13, 70-73; Chappell, above n 12, 37-39; Copelon, above n 13, 220-228; Hilary Charlesworth and Christine Chinkin, *The Boundaries of International Criminal Law* (Manchester University Press, 2000) 313-321.

43 Askin, above n 1, 295.

deportation. Reinforcing this silence, sexual and gender-based crimes received little attention in the proceedings before the Tribunal. In fact, the Tribunal's judgment makes no mention of sexual violence,[44] although the prosecutors presented evidence that women were raped and subjected to sexualised torture by German forces and German guards.[45] Legally speaking, certain gender-based crimes could have been expressly recognised at Nuremberg. For example, it is clear that rape constituted a war crime under international law by the start of World War II, and could therefore have been expressly enumerated in the Tribunal's charter and its final judgment.[46] However, as a political matter, it seems that expressly recognising and denouncing this crime was not a priority at the time.

In addition to failing to refer to rape in its final judgment, the Tribunal did not recognise the broader concept of *gender-based* violence. As Catherine Niarchos observes:

> It may be anachronistic to expect the Nuremberg tribunals to have grasped this concept [of gender-based violence]; after all, it is still considered novel today. By analogy, however, it now would be unthinkable to cast the Holocaust as persecution of civilians, without taking into account the ethnic and religious aspects of the crime.[47]

The International Military Tribunal at Tokyo, by contrast, expressly prosecuted the rape of women by Japanese forces in Nanking using its general war crime provision.[48] However, while this was relatively progressive for the time, the Tribunal's record in prosecuting sexual and gender-based crimes had some serious flaws. For example, the Tribunal prosecutors did not produce a shred of evidence regarding the sexual enslavement of an estimated 80,000 to 200,000 women in 'comfort stations' established by the Japanese military.[49] Research into military archives indicates that the Allies were aware of this system.[50] However, no efforts were made to prosecute this conduct in the Tokyo Tribunal, a fact which, to quote the late Rhonda

44 Judgment of the International Military Tribunal (1 October 1946), reprinted in (1947) 41(1) *American Journal of International Law* 172.
45 Catharine Niarchos, 'Women, War, and Rape: Challenges Facing The International Tribunal for the Former Yugoslavia' (1995) 17 *Human Rights Quarterly* 649, 663-665.
46 Askin, above n 40, 42-43; Patricia Viseur Sellers, 'Gender Strategy Is Not a Luxury for International Courts' (2009) 17(2) *American University Journal of Gender, Social Policy & the Law* 301, 304.
47 Niarchos, above n 45, 679.
48 Judgment of the International Military Tribunal for the Far East (12 November 1948), reprinted in John Pritchard and Sonia M Zaide (eds), *The Tokyo War Crimes Trial, Vol. 22* (Garland, 1981) 49, 604-649.
49 Niarchos, above n 47, 666.
50 Copelon, above n 13, 222.

Copelon, suggests that 'the notion of women and the "booty" of war and the entitlement of fighting men was never in question'.[51]

Sexual and gender-based crimes were also sidelined in the 1949 Geneva Conventions, certain 'grave breaches' of which constitute war crimes under international law.[52] The 'grave breaches' provisions do not refer to any sexual or gender-based crimes, although other serious crimes such as murder and torture are listed as 'grave breaches' in their own right. The only reference to sexual and gender-based violence in the 1949 Geneva Conventions is in Article 27 of Convention IV (on the protection of civilians), which states that 'women shall be especially protected against any attack on their honour, in particular against rape, enforced prostitution, or any form of indecent assault'. As many commentators have observed, this language underestimates the gravity of sexual violence crimes by referring to them as attacks on the victims' 'honour' and by failing to describe this conduct as a 'grave breach', while saying nothing of the physical or psychological damage to the victim or the possibility of sexual violence against girls, boys, and men.[53] Likewise, the 1977 Additional Protocols to the Geneva Convention describe rape, enforced prostitution and any form of indecent assault as 'outrages on personal dignity', rather than as examples of 'violence to the life, health and physical or mental well-being'.[54]

B *Ending impunity for sexual and gender-based crimes: progress and setbacks*

The practices of overlooking and trivialising sexual gender violence crimes began to change in the 1990s, as a result of the efforts of women's rights activists, feminist legal scholars, and forward-thinking prosecutors and judges in the ICTY and ICTR. However, even in this era, sexual and gender-based crimes remained at risk of being overlooked and de-prioritised in investigations and indictments. For example in the first cases before the ICTY and ICTR, *Tadić* and *Akayesu,* there were initially no charges for sexual and

---

51 Ibid 223.

52 *Geneva Convention (I) for the Amelioration of the Condition of the Wounded and Sick in Armed Forces in the Field*, opened for signature 12 August 1949, 75 UNTS 31 (entered into force 21 October 1950); *Geneva Convention (II) for the Amelioration of the Condition of Wounded, Sick and Shipwrecked Members of Armed Forces at Sea*, opened for signature 2 August 1949, 75 UNTS 85 (entered into force 21 October 1950); *Geneva Convention (III) relative to the Treatment of Prisoners of War*, opened for signature 12 August 1949, 75 UNTS 135 (entered into force 21 October 1950); *Geneva Convention (IV) relative to the Protection of Civilian Persons in Time of War*, opened for signature 12 August 2012, 75 UNTS 287 (entered into force 21 October 1950).

53 Askin, above n 1, 304; Bedont and Hall-Martinez, above n 13, 70-71; Chappell, above n 12, 38; Copelon, above n 13, 221; Niarchos, above n 45, 674-675.

54 *Protocol Additional to the Geneva Conventions of 12 August 1949, and relating to the Protection of Victims of Non-International Armed Conflicts (Protocol II)*, opened for signature 8 June 1977, 1125 UNTS 609 (entered into force 7 December 1978).

gender-based crimes against women, despite numerous reports of such crimes. Such charges were later added in both cases, but only after considerable pressure from civil society and interventions from the Bench.[55]

The *Akayesu* case clearly illustrates this point. The case focused on Jean-Paul Akayesu, the mayor of a commune where sexual violence crimes had reportedly been committed during the Rwandan genocide. He was not initially charged with any sexual and gender-based crimes, in part because the ICTR prosecutors assumed that the victims would be unwilling to speak about their experiences of rape,[56] although many of their accounts were documented in a report published by Human Rights Watch and FIDH in 1996.[57] That same report referred to a 'widespread perception among the Tribunal investigators that rape is somehow a "lesser" or "incidental" crime',[58] indicating that these attitudes continued to influence prosecutorial practices as late as the 1990s.

Thus, Akayesu was not charged with any sexual and gender-based crimes. However, once the trial began, one of the prosecution witnesses revealed that her daughter had been raped during the genocide, and another told the tribunal about her own experience of rape. The Trial Chamber responded by asking these witnesses and other prosecution witnesses about sexual violence during the Rwandan genocide, leading to further evidence of these crimes.[59] Seeking to ensure that these crimes were properly prosecuted, a coalition of human rights activists and feminist legal scholars filed an *amicus curiae* brief, calling on the Prosecutor to add charges for sexual and gender-based crimes in the *Akayesu* case. They argued:

> The absence of charges of rape [...] not only fails to redress the harms done to women raped under Akayesu's ostensible control but also fails to normatively establish that rape is egregious and unacceptable conduct.[60]

Shortly after this brief was filed, the Prosecutor added sexual violence charges to Akayesu's indictment and called additional witnesses to testify about these

---

55 Regarding the *Tadić* case, see Copelon, above n 13, 229-230; Michelle Jarvis and Kate Vigneswaren, 'Challenges to Successful Outcomes in Prosecution Cases' in Brammertz and Jarvis, above n 1, 33, 56-57.

56 Binaifer Nowrojee, *Shattered Lives: Sexual Violence during the Rwandan Genocide and its Aftermath* (Human Rights Watch and FIDH, 1996) 91-93.

57 Ibid.

58 Ibid.

59 See Beth Van Schaack, 'Engendering Genocide: The Akayesu Case before the International Criminal Tribunal for Rwanda' (2008) *Santa Clara Law Digital Commons* <http://digital commons.law.scu.edu/cgi/viewcontent.cgi?article=1626&context=facpubs>

60 Coalition for Women's Human Rights in Conflict Situations, *Amicus Brief Respecting Amendment of the Indictment and Supplementation of the Evidence to Ensure the Prosecution of Rape and Other Sexual Violence within the Competence of the Tribunal* (undated) <www. essex.ac.uk/armedcon/story_id/000053.pdf>.

crimes.[61] The Trial Chamber subsequently convicted Akayesu for rape and other sexual violence crimes, and confirmed that sexual violence could constitute an act of genocide when committed with intent to destroy, in whole or in part, a group protected under the Genocide Convention.[62] This interpretation of the crime of genocide was seen by some scholars as a display of 'sentimentalism and high-handedness'.[63] However, it was soon widely accepted as a valid interpretation of the law. Accordingly, a provision stating that sexual violence could be an act of genocide was inserted into the ICC Elements of Crimes,[64] and this interpretation of the crime was followed in subsequent cases before the ICTR and other tribunals.[65] Looking back at this landmark case, Mariana Pena and Gaelle Carayon observe: 'Had it not been for the attitude of vigilant judges and for intense pressure from human rights organizations, crimes of sexual violence suffered by victims in that case would have been sidelined'.[66]

Yet in other cases, sexual and gender-based crimes continued to go unprosecuted, despite interventions by civil society. An example was the *Ntagerura et al* case, where the coalition that appeared as *amicus curiae* in the *Akayesu* case once again challenged the ICTR Prosecutor's decision not to include charges for sexual and gender-based crimes. Unlike in *Akayesu*, however, the Trial Chamber denied the coalition leave to appear as *amicus curiae*, and the Prosecutor declined to add charges for sexual and gender-based crimes despite previous assurances that she would file a separate indictment with respect to those crimes.[67] Thus, in this case, there was no accountability for sexual and gender-based crimes.

Yet despite such setbacks, the ICTY and ICTR made considerable progress in prosecuting sexual and gender-based crimes. The ICTY in particular

61 Copelon, above n 13, 225-226.
62 *Prosecutor v Akayesu* (International Criminal Tribunal for Rwanda, Trial Chamber I, Case No ICTR-96-4-T, 2 September 1998), [731]–[734].
63 See Chappell, above n 12, 93.
64 See Copelon, above n 13, n 57.
65 Eg, *Prosecutor v Seromba (Appeals Judgment)* (International Criminal Tribunal for Rwanda, Appeals Chamber, Case No ICTR-2001-66-A, 12 March 2008) [46]; *Prosecutor v Karadžić* (International Criminal Tribunal for the former Yugoslavia, Trial Chamber, Case No IT-95-5/18-T, 24 March 2016) [545]; *Situation in Darfur (Public Redacted Version of the Prosecutor's Application under Article 58)* (International Criminal Court, Pre-Trial Chamber I, Case No ICC-02/05-157-AnxA, 14 July 2008) [130].
66 Mariana Pena and Gaelle Carayon, 'Is the ICC Making the Most of Victim Participation?' (2013) 7(3) *International Journal of Transitional Justice* 518, 521.
67 Beth Van Schaack, 'Obstacles on the Road to Gender Justice: the International Criminal Tribunal for Rwanda as Object Lesson' (2009) 17(2) *American University Journal of Gender, Social Policy & the Law* 361, 372-374; *Prosecutor v Ntagerura et al (Decision on the Coalition for Women's Human Rights in Conflict Situation's [sic] Motion for Reconsideration of the Decision on the Application to File an Amicus Curiae Brief)* (International Criminal Tribunal for Rwanda, Trial Chamber III, Case No ICTR-99-46-T, 24 September 2016) [8].

developed a strong track record in this respect.[68] This was a difficult feat for many reasons, including the fact that the Tribunal Statutes did not expressly recognise a wide range of sexual and gender-based crimes. Accordingly, such crimes were often prosecuted under other provisions, such as torture, enslavement, and inhumane acts.[69] This charging strategy was often controversial, including among the tribunal prosecutors. For example, there was initially disagreement within the ICTY Office of the Prosecutor about whether to charge rape as a form of torture and enslavement. However, the Office ultimately agreed to pursue this charging strategy, leading to some groundbreaking decisions on sexual violence as an international crime.[70]

The negotiations for the Rome Statute, the founding statute of the ICC, provided further opportunities for the recognition of sexual and gender-based crimes. The Women's Caucus for Gender Justice played a key role in this regard. Seeking to challenge the historical silence on sexual and gender-based crimes in ICL, and to reinforce the progress made in the ICTY and ICTR, the Caucus argued that the Rome Statute should expressly recognise a wide range of sexual and gender-based crimes. As a result of their efforts, and the support of like-minded States, the Rome Statute expressly enumerates rape, sexual slavery, enforced prostitution, forced pregnancy, enforced sterilisation, and 'any other form of sexual violence of a comparable gravity' as war crimes and crimes against humanity, and also recognises persecution on 'gender' grounds as a crime against humanity for the first time in ICL.

Most of these crimes were included in the Rome Statute with little opposition, as most were already regarded as crimes under customary international law.[71] However, as noted above, the proposal to recognise persecution on 'gender' grounds as a crime against humanity faced strong opposition from certain States. These same States were also reluctant to recognise the crime of 'forced pregnancy', because they were concerned that if this crime was included in the Rome Statute, they would be forced to remove restrictions on abortion under domestic law.[72] To placate those States, the delegates agreed to insert a caveat in the Rome Statute stating:

'Forced pregnancy' means the unlawful confinement of a woman forcibly made pregnant, with the intent of affecting the ethnic composition of any population or carrying out other grave violations of international law. *This definition shall not in any way be interpreted as affecting national laws relating to pregnancy.*[73]

68 Brammertz and Jarvis, above n 1; Van Schaack, above n 67.
69 See Askin, above n 2, 317-346; Brady, above n 2; Brammertz and Jarvis, above n 1.
70 Jarvis and Nabti, above n 5, 91; Jarvis and Vigneswaren, above n 55, 38.
71 Steains, above n 13, 365.
72 Chappell, above n 12, 95-96; Steains above n 13, 365-369.
73 *Rome Statute*, Art. 7(2)(f) (emphasis added).

In addition to recognising a wide range of sexual and gender-based crimes, the Rome Statute seeks to address gender discrimination in international criminal justice more broadly. For example, it includes provisions aimed at supporting victims and witnesses of sexual and gender-based crimes,[74] requires the ICC Prosecutor to appoint an advisor with expertise in 'sexual and gender violence',[75] and directs the Court to interpret and apply the law without 'adverse distinction' on the grounds of 'gender'.[76] Yet despite these innovations in its legal framework, the ICC's early record in prosecuting sexual and gender-based crimes was patchy. In particular, the first case tried before the ICC, the *Lubanga* case, presented concerns in this regard.[77]

The case focused on Thomas Lubanga Dyilo, leader of an armed group involved in the 2002-2003 conflict in Ituri, DRC. He was charged by the (then) ICC Prosecutor, Luis Moreno Ocampo, with the war crimes of 'conscripting or enlisting children under the age of fifteen years into armed forces or groups or using them to participate actively in hostilities'.[78] After Lubanga was brought before the ICC, Prosecutor Ocampo decided to 'temporarily suspend' further investigations into further charges.[79] This decision was widely criticised, because Lubanga's troops were reportedly responsible for a wide range of crimes in Ituri, including sexual and gender-based crimes.[80] In an open letter to the Prosecutor, a coalition of human rights groups expressed their disappointment in the Prosecutor's decision to suspend the investigation. They urged the Prosecutor to 'send a clear signal to the victims in Ituri and the people of the DRC that those who perpetrate crimes such as rape, torture and summary executions will be held to account'.[81] One of the groups which signed this letter, the Women's Initiatives for Gender Justice, sent the Prosecutor a second letter containing detailed evidence of sexual violence

---

74 Ibid Arts 54(1)(b), 68(1).
75 Ibid Art. 42(9).
76 Ibid Art. 21(3).
77 Chappell, above n 12, 110-117; Niamh Hayes, 'Sisyphus Wept: Prosecuting Sexual Violence at the International Criminal Court' in William Schabas, Yvonne McDermott and Niamh Hayes (eds), *The Ashgate Research Companion to International Criminal Law* (Routledge, 2013) 7, 10-25.
78 *Situation in the Democratic Republic of Congo (Decision on the Prosecutor's Application for Warrants of Arrest, Article 58)* (International Criminal Court, Pre-Trial Chamber I, Case No ICC-01/04-02/06-20-Anx2, 10 February 2006.)
79 *Prosecutor v Lubanga (Prosecutor's information on further investigation)* (International Criminal Court, Pre-Trial Chamber I, Case No 01/04-01/06-170, 28 June 2007) [7]–[8].
80 United Nations Security Council, *Letter dated 16 July 2004 from the Secretary-General addressed to the President of the Security Council*, UN Doc s/2004/573 (6 July 2004) [151-153]; Human Rights Watch, *Seeking Justice: The Prosecution of Sexual Violence in the Congo War* (March 2005) 19-20 <www.hrw.org/sites/default/files/reports/drc0305.pdf>.
81 Avocats Sans Frontières *et al*, *DR Congo: ICC Charges Raise Concern: Joint letter to the Chief Prosecutor of the International Criminal Court* (31 June 2006) <www.hrw.org/news/2006/07/31/dr-congo-icc-charges-raise-concern>.

crimes committed by Lubanga's troops, including against female children who had been recruited into his armed group.[82]

Despite this pressure from civil society, the Prosecutor did not add any further charges in the Lubanga case. However, once the charges were confirmed and the case proceeded to trial, the prosecution broadened its case. It alleged that girls in Lubanga's armed group were sexually abused by their commanders, and argued that this sexual violence was captured by the existing charges of 'conscripting', 'enlisting', and 'using' children under fifteen.[83] This belated attempt to address sexual and gender-based violence did not succeed. In a dissenting judgment, Judge Odio Benito accepted that the alleged sexual violence was 'encoded' in the charges against Lubanga.[84] However, the Majority of the Trial Chamber refused to determine Lubanga's culpability for the sexual violence crimes, because the evidence supporting these crimes was introduced too late in the proceedings.[85]

The factors that led to impunity for sexual and gender-based crimes in this case, most notably a failure to properly investigate sexual and gender-based crimes at the outset, suggests that the tradition of sidelining and deprioritising these crimes continued in the ICC's initial years.[86] But while the pressure from civil society did not overcome this problem in the *Lubanga* case, it appears to have contributed to a greater focus on sexual and gender-based crimes in subsequent cases before the ICC. As the current ICC Prosecutor, Fatou Bensouda, has stated:

> In the ICC's first trial, against Thomas Lubanga Dyilo, the Prosecution explained the gender dimension of the crime of enlisting and conscripting children under the age of 15. It took note, however, of the reaction of civil society's preference for these aspects to be explicitly charged. Sexual and gender crimes were included directly in the charges in *Katanga*, *Ngudjolo*, *Mbarushimana* and *Mudacumura* cases, as well as in the additional charges presented against Bosco Ntaganda.[87]

---

82 Women's Initiatives for Gender Justice, *Public redacted version of confidential letter to ICC Prosecutor* (August 2006) <www.iccwomen.org/news/docs/Prosecutor_Letter_August_2006_Redacted.pdf>.

83 *Prosecutor v Lubanga (Prosecution's Closing Brief)* (International Criminal Court, Trial Chamber I, Case No ICC-01/04-01/06-2748-Red, 20 July 2011) [139]–[143].

84 *Prosecutor v Lubanga (Judgment pursuant to Article 74 of the Statute: Separate and Dissenting Opinion of Judge Odio Benito)* (International Criminal Court, Trial Chamber I, Case No ICC-01/04-01/06-2842, 14 March 2012) [21].

85 *Prosecutor v Lubanga (Judgment pursuant to Article 74 of the Statute)* (International Criminal Court, Trial Chamber I, Case No ICC-01/04-01/06-2842, 14 March 2012) [629]–[631].

86 See Katy Glassborrow, *ICC Investigative Strategy Under Fire*, Institute for War and Peace Reporting (27 October 2008) <https://iwpr.net/global-voices/icc-investigative-strategy-under-fire>.

87 Fatou Bensouda, 'Gender Justice and the ICC: Progress and Reflections' (2014) 16(4) *International Journal of Feminist Politics* 538, 540.

Indeed, in the majority of cases after *Lubanga*, the ICC Prosecutor has explicitly included charges for sexual and gender-based violence crimes such as rape, while also prosecuting this violence using seemingly gender-neutral crimes, such as torture.[88] The types of sexual and gender-based violence charged before the ICC include a wide range of acts including rape, sexual slavery, mutilation of sexual organs, forcing people to have sex with one another, forcing people to watch the rape of their family members, cutting open the bellies of pregnant women, sex-selective killings, and electric shocks to the genitals.[89]

The victims of these crimes include men and boys, indicating that concerns about the under-recognition of male experiences of sexual violence are less pertinent to the ICC than they may have been in other international courts.[90] One case in which this critique might apply, however, is the *Lubanga* case, in which the prosecution alleged that boys in Lubanga's armed group were forced to rape civilian women, and procure girls for their commanders. However, these allegations of gender-based violence received relatively little attention in the prosecution's case.[91]

In recent years, the ICC Office of the Prosecutor has also made progress by developing innovative strategies for charging sexual and gender-based crimes. For example, in the *Ntaganda* case, Prosecutor Bensouda charged the accused with the war crimes of rape and sexual slavery, based on evidence that female child soldiers in his armed group were sexually abused by their commanders.[92] This is the first case in any international court, past or present, to include distinct charges for the war crimes of rape and sexual slavery against child soldiers by their commanders. The defence challenged these charges on the basis that the concept of a 'war crime' excludes violence towards members of one's 'own' military force. However, the Appeals Chamber rejected this argument,[93] and confirmed that the ICC has jurisdiction to prosecute such conduct using the war crimes of rape and sexual slavery under Article 8(2)(e)(vi).

More recently, in the *Ongwen* case, the Prosecutor charged Lord's Resistance Army commander Dominic Ongwen for war crimes and crimes against

88 See Rosemary Grey, *Prosecuting Sexual and Gender Violence Crimes in the International Criminal Court: Historical Legacies and New Opportunities* (PhD Thesis, University of New South Wales, 2015) Ch. 4.

89 Ibid.

90 See, eg, Sivakumaran, above n 16, 253; Dustin Lewis, 'Unrecognized Victims: Sexual Violence against Men in Conflict Settings under International Law' (2009) 27(1) *Wisconsin International Law Journal* 1.

91 Grey, above n 88, 123-124.

92 *Prosecutor v Ntaganda (Decision Pursuant to Article 61(7)(a) and (b) of the Rome Statute on the Charges of the Prosecutor against Bosco Ntaganda)* (International Criminal Court, Pre-Trial Chamber II, Case No ICC-01/04-02/06-309, 9 June 2014) Counts 6 and 9.

93 *Prosecutor v Ntaganda (Judgment on the appeal of Mr Ntaganda against the "Second decision on the Defence's challenge to the jurisdiction of the Court in respect of Counts 6 and 9")* (International Criminal Court, Appeals Chamber, Case No ICC-01/04-02/06-1962, 15 June 2017).

humanity allegedly committed in Uganda, including a wide range of sexual and gender-based crimes.[94] The charges include the crime of 'forced pregnancy', which has never before been prosecuted in an international or internationalised court, as well as the crime of 'forced marriage' (as an inhumane act), which has never before been prosecuted in the ICC, but has previously been recognised by the SCSL[95] and ECCC.[96]

In short, after *Lubanga*, the ICC Office of the Prosecutor has become increasingly focused on charging sexual and gender-based crimes.[97] Initially, this shift in charging practices was not sufficient to secure accountability for sexual and gender-based crimes: overall, the prosecution was less effective at substantiating these crimes than other crimes at both the pre-trial and trial phase.[98] Weaknesses in the prosecution's evidence continued to pose a problem, particularly in relation to establishing the criminal responsibility for the accused.[99] However, since 2014, the Office of the Prosecutor has developed a stronger track record in prosecuting sexual and gender-based crimes, as evinced by the conviction for rape in the *Bemba* case, and the confirmation of charges for sexual and gender-based crimes in the *Ntaganda, Gbagbo & Blé Goudé* and *Ongwen* cases. It seems that the Office of the Prosecutor now has both the will and the skills to prosecute sexual and gender-based crimes, and is making use of the wealth of jurisprudence developed by other internationalised and international courts in this respect.

IV Ongoing gender biases and gaps in ICL

As discussed above, since the 1990s, sexual and gender-based crimes have increasingly been recognised as crimes under international law. There are, however, continuing challenges to the prosecution of these crimes.

One challenge is that historic gender biases in ICL continue to create obstacles to accountability for sexual and gender-based crimes. For example, there is a historical tendency to view conflict-related sexual violence crimes as 'private' or 'opportunistic' crimes, which are unrelated to the war.[100]

---

94 *Prosecutor v Ongwen (Decision on the confirmation of charges against Dominic Ongwen)* (International Criminal Court, Pre-Trial Chamber II, Case No ICC-02/04-01/15-422-Red, 23 March 2016).

95 *Prosecutor v Brima, Kamara and Kanu* (Special Court for Sierra Leone, Appeals Chamber, Case No SCSL-2004-16-A, 22 February 2008) [181]–[203]; *Prosecutor v Sesay, Kallon and Gbao (Appeal Judgment)* (Special Court for Sierra Leone, Appeals Chamber, Case No SCSL-04-15-A, 26 October 2009) [735]–[736].

96 *Case 002 Closing Order* (Extraordinary Chambers in the Courts of Cambodia, Office of Co-Investigating Judges, Case No 002/19-09-2007-ECCC-OCIJ, 15 September 2010) [1443].

97 See Jarvis, above n 17, 9.

98 Grey, above n 88, 228-229.

99 Ibid 229-236.

100 Van Schaack, above n 67, 376.

Due to this perception, prosecutors in the ICTY and ICTR at times struggled to persuade judges that indirect perpetrators, such as senior military commanders, were responsible for the sexual and gender-based crimes carried out by their troops. By contrast, the argument that senior military commanders are criminally responsible for unlawful killings, pillage, or destruction of property carried out by their troops was more readily accepted in the tribunals.[101]

This double standard was also seen in the ICC Trial Chamber's judgment in the *Katanga* case, issued in 2014. The accused in that case, Germain Katanga, was allegedly the leader of one of the two militias that attacked the village of Bogoro, DRC, during the 2002-2003 Ituri conflict. He was convicted by the majority of the Trial Chamber for the crimes of murder, directing attacks against the civilian population, destruction of property, and pillage committed during the attack. The Chamber reasoned that these crimes were part of the 'common purpose' of the group that Katanga supplied with weapons, namely to obliterate the village. By contrast, it acquitted Katanga on the charges of rape and sexual slavery, reasoning that these crimes were not necessarily part of the 'common purpose' of the group.[102] For many commentators, this decision echoed the historic presumption that sexual and gender-based crimes, unlike other offences such as murder and pillage, are necessarily private or opportunistic crimes.[103]

In addition, the historical under-prosecution of sexual and gender-based crimes has had ongoing consequences for the prosecution of these crimes today. An example can be seen in the 2012 decision by the ECCC appellate chamber, which found that the crime against humanity of rape did not exist under international law in 1975-1979.[104] One of the factors that the Chamber relied on to make this finding was that although rape was listed as a crime against humanity in Control Council Law No 10 (the law used by the Allied Powers to prosecute German war criminals after the Nuremberg Tribunal), none of the defendants tried under this instrument, or in the Nuremberg Tribunal itself, were charged with rape.[105] In other words, the Chamber used a historical gender bias in the *enforcement* of ICL to justify a finding about the *content* of ICL at the relevant time. This logic is highly problematic. As Patricia Sellers and Valerie Oosterveld argue,

---

101 SáCouto and Cleary, above n 13, 352-358; Kelly Askin, 'Katanga Judgment Underlines Need for Stronger ICC Focus on Sexual Violence' (11 March 2014) <www.opensocietyfoundations.org/voices/katanga-judgment-underlines-need-stronger-icc-focus-sexual-violence>.

102 *Prosecutor v Katanga (Judgment pursuant to Article 74 of the Statute)* (International Criminal Court, Trial Chamber II, Case No ICC-01/04-01/07-3436-tENG, 7 March 2014) [1663]–[1664].

103 Eg, Askin, above n 101; Chappell, above n 12, 119-120; Brigid Inder, 'Prosecuting Sexual Violence in Conflict -- Challenges and Lessons Learned: A Critique of the Katanga Judgment' (Speech delivered at Global Summit to End Sexual Violence in Conflict, London, 11 June 2014).

104 *Prosecutor v Duch (Appeal Judgment)* (Extraordinary Chambers in the Courts of Cambodia, Supreme Court Chamber, 001/18-07-2007-ECCC/SC, 3 February 2013) [174]–[180].

105 Ibid [176].

The absence of numerous direct prosecutions for the crime against humanity of rape [prior to 1975] illustrates that prosecutors and courts paid inadequate attention to this and all forms of sexual violence ... However, it does not necessarily logically follow that rape was not a distinct crime against humanity at the time: impunity does not prove that a law does not exist.[106]

Historic gender biases are not the only impediment to prosecuting sexual and gender-based crimes before international courts today.[107] There can also be significant challenges in gathering evidence, although experienced investigators have emphasised that these challenges can often be overcome.[108] In addition, there continue to be gaps and silences in the legal framework which make it difficult, if not impossible, to prosecute some of the most serious and most ubiquitous forms of sexual and gender-based violence in the world today. A key example is domestic violence, which continues to pose a major risk to women's lives in all parts of the world, but has not yet been recognised as an international crime.[109] Another example is persecution on the grounds of sexual orientation and gender identity, an issue that has already received considerable attention in international human rights law[110] and refugee law,[111] but is yet to be expressly or impliedly prosecuted as a crime under international law.

Broader still is the concern that ICL is not 'transformative', meaning it does not fundamentally alter the social, political, and economic forces that contribute to sexual and gender-based crimes and to violence against women and girls more broadly.[112] Reflecting on this point in 2000, Hilary Charlesworth and Christine Chinkin predicted that the increasing recognition of sexual and gender-based crimes under ICL, while important, 'would not lead to a restructuring of the international legal system that would address the continued subordination'.[113] This critique of ICL remains relevant twenty years on:

106 Oosterveld and Sellers, above n 13, 341. See also Sarah Williams and Emma Palmer, 'The Extraordinary Chambers in the Courts of Cambodia: Developing the Law on Sexual Violence?' (2015) 15 *International Criminal Law Review* 452, 459-463.
107 For further examples of the ongoing effects of historical gender biases in ICL, see Chappell, above n 12, 4; Louise Chappell, 'Conflicting Institutions and the Search for Gender Justice at the International Criminal Court' (2014) 67(1) *Political Research Quarterly* 183.
108 Eg, Luping, above n 17; Jarvis and Nabti, above n 5, 82-90.
109 See Copelon, above n 13, 239-240; Catharine MacKinnon, *Are Women Human?* (Belknap Press, 2007) Ch. 25. For current statistics, see UN Statistics Division, *The World's Women 2015: Trends and Statistics* (United Nations 2015) 139-161.
110 See United Nations High Commissioner for Human Rights, above n 25, 1-7.
111 See Valerie Oosterveld, 'Gender, Persecution, and the International Criminal Court: Refugee Law's Relevance to the Crime against Humanity of Gender-Based Persecution' (2006) 17(1) *Duke Journal of Comparative & International Law* 49.
112 See Chappell, above n 12, 8; Copelon, above n 13, 240.
113 Charlesworth and Chinkin, above n 42, 335.

while there have been some important jurisprudential developments during this period, the boundaries of ICL remain unchanged.

V Conclusion

The prosecution of sexual and gender-based crimes in international and internationalised courts sends a powerful message. It signals that sexual and gender-based crimes, a category of crimes committed primarily against women and girls, are among the most serious crimes of concern to the international community as a whole.

The clear and emphatic communication of this message matters because these crimes have historically received little attention in ICL. Over the last thirty years, however, this pattern has begun to change. The issue of 'sexual and gender-based crimes' has emerged as a key concern for ICL. Feminist scholars and women's rights activists have insisted that these crimes be recognised as crimes under international law; States have increasingly thrown their weight behind the codification of these crimes; prosecutors in international and internationalised courts have (for the most part) demonstrated a commitment to prosecuting these crimes; and there have also been some important interventions from judges in these courts.

Even so, there remain gaps and limitations in the legal framework, and historic gender biases continue to present challenges for the prosecution of these crimes in international and internationalised courts. The 'end of impunity' for sexual and gender-based crimes under international law, while drawing closer, is still a long way off.

Further reading

Brammertz, Serge and Michelle Jarvis, *Prosecuting Conflict-Related Sexual Violence Crimes at the ICTY* (Oxford University Press, 2016).

Chappell, Louise, *The Politics of Gender Justice at the International Criminal Court: Legacies and Legitimacy* (Oxford University Press, 2016).

Copelon, Rhonda, 'Gender Crimes as War Crimes: Integrating Crimes against Women into International Criminal Law' (2000) 46(1) *McGill Law Journal* 217.

Mibenge, Chiseche Salome, *Sex and International Tribunal: The Erasure of Gender from the War Narrative* (University of Pennsylvania Press, 2013).

Oosterveld, Valerie, 'The Definition of "Gender" in the Rome Statute of the International Criminal Court: A Step Forward or Back for International Criminal Justice?' (2005) 18 *Harvard Human Rights Journal* 55.

8

THE CRIME OF AGGRESSION

Shifting authority for international peace?

Sean Richmond[1]

I Introduction

The modern crime of aggression is, in essence, the planning or executing by an individual in one state of a use of force against another state in manifest violation of the United Nations Charter. It applies to persons who are in positions to effectively control or direct the political or military action of a country. As such, aggression is a leadership crime involving the conduct of high government officials. To this extent, it is potentially linked to questions of politics and, as I will suggest below, authority more than other international crimes. For example, although the crime of aggression was important in the Allied trials of German and Japanese individuals following the Second World War, it was not included in the work of the *ad hoc* tribunals created in the 1990s. Moreover, to ensure agreement at the Rome Conference of the International Criminal Court (ICC) in 1998, aggression was listed but not included in the Court's jurisdiction. At that time, delegates disagreed on the definition of the crime, and the conditions under which the ICC would exercise jurisdiction over it. One key reason for this disagreement was that countries had different views on what role the UN Security Council should play in the Court's exercise of jurisdiction over aggression.

Under Article 24 of the Charter, the Security Council has primary responsibility for the maintenance of international peace and security.[2] To help meet this responsibility, Article 39 states in part that the Council shall

1 The author would like to thank Philipp Kastner for organizing this handbook, and for his helpful comments on earlier drafts of the chapter. He would also like to thank Lily Hands for her excellent research assistance. The chapter reflects the author's academic research, and is not related to his work for Global Affairs Canada.
2 *Charter of the United Nations*, Art. 24.

determine the existence of any threat to the peace or act of aggression.[3] In practice, the Council has exercised its responsibility for maintaining peace more in the past 25 years than in any other time, and this has led some observers to suggest that the Council's power and authority have increased accordingly.[4] Downplaying these legal and empirical observations, other perspectives, such as realist international relations (IR) theory, emphasize that states, and not international institutions, have primary responsibility for maintaining their individual and collective security in world affairs.[5]

The negotiations behind the 2010 Review Conference of the ICC in Kampala, however, appear to challenge the legal, empirical and theoretical viewpoints above.[6] In these negotiations, states parties to the Rome Statute[7] amended that treaty to define the crime of aggression and the conditions for the exercise of jurisdiction over this crime.[8] A key principle affirmed was that – unlike war crimes, crimes against humanity, or genocide – a state must commit an act of aggression before an individual can commit a crime of aggression. States parties also resolved that jurisdiction will be triggered through referrals by the Security Council, states parties or the ICC Prosecutor, and outlined related 'filter' mechanisms to achieve such referrals.[9] This means that, if the current delay on the exercise of jurisdiction is lifted in 2017, an international criminal judicial body, and not just the Security Council or countries themselves, will be empowered to determine whether an act of aggression by a state has occurred in international affairs.[10]

---

3 Ibid Art. 39.

4 See, eg, the conceptual observations and empirical studies in Bruce Cronin and Ian Hurd (eds), *The UN Security Council and the Politics of International Authority* (Routledge, 2008).

5 See, eg, John Mearsheimer, 'The False Promise of International Institutions' (1994-1995) 19(3) *International Security* 5.

6 For accounts of these negotiations, see Carrie McDougall, *The Crime of Aggression under the Rome Statute of the International Criminal Court* (Cambridge University Press, 2013); Stefan Barriga and Claus Kreß (eds), *The Travaux Préparatoires of the Crime of Aggression* (Cambridge University Press, 2012); Jennifer Trahan, 'The Rome Statute's Amendments on the Crime of Aggression' (2011) 11 *International Criminal Law Review* 49; and Beth Van Schaack, 'Negotiating at the Interface of Power and Law: the Crime of Aggression' (2011) 49 *Columbia Journal of Transnational Law* 505.

7 *Rome Statute of the International Criminal Court*, opened for signature 17 July 1998, 2187 UNTS 90 (entered into force 1 July 2002).

8 For the full amendments, see *2010 Resolution on the Crime of Aggression* in Barriga and Kreß, above n 6, 101–107.

9 Trahan, above n 6, 49.

10 See Art. 15 *bis* (4) (the ICC may exercise jurisdiction over a crime of aggression, arising from an act of aggression committed by a State Party, unless that State Party has previously declared that it does not accept such jurisdiction); and Art. 15 *bis* (8) (if after six months of notification the Security Council has not determined that an act of aggression has occurred, the Prosecutor may proceed with the investigation if the Pre-Trial Division has authorized this in accordance with Article 15, and the Council has not decided otherwise under Article 16).

This possibility sparks the following question: to what extent has authority for international peace and security changed or shifted from the Security Council to the ICC, or from states to the Court? This chapter aims to help interested scholars and graduate students think about why such interdisciplinary questions are relevant to important theoretical debates within and outside existing international criminal law (ICL) research, and how we can address such queries in an analytically reflective and methodologically rigorous manner. With these specific aims in mind, the chapter thus also seeks to help contribute to this handbook's broader objectives of exploring ICL's relationship to IR and international law (IL) more generally, and the changes that have possibly occurred in these fields regarding criminal law.

To these ends, the chapter begins by outlining some relevant theoretical and methodological perspectives on the topic of international authority, the ICC and the UN Security Council. In this section, I first consider two potentially relevant views – realist IR theory and formal IL theory – and the insights and limits of each. As an alternative, I discuss a third approach in the interdisciplinary literature, namely studying the distinct influence of authoritative institutions in international law and world politics. One key revelation of this approach, I suggest to legal researchers who may be less familiar with social science perspectives, is that questions (such as the one addressed by this chapter) that are *conceptually* significant are often *methodologically* difficult to answer.

Drawing on the sociological insights of the third approach, I argue that for purposes of understanding the complex links between the Security Council, the ICC and states regarding aggression, authority is best thought of as a social relationship between actors who recognize that the right and power to decide is shared but contested. And one way to study whether and how international authority for peace and security is shifting or changing from the Security Council to the ICC, or from states to the Court, is to analyse the conduct and beliefs of states – particularly under-studied countries – leading up to and during the 2010 Kampala Conference.

With this theoretical argument and methodological focus in mind, I then briefly discuss why such a focus is justified in light of the chapter's research question. I also posit some observable implications that can be used to empirically evaluate the state conduct and beliefs noted above, and to critically analyse which of the three foregoing perspectives best explains the aggression negotiations. Employing observable implications, legal scholars may further note, is common among IR researchers but is less known among IL scholars.

The chapter then applies the above theoretical and methodological thinking to empirically investigate important aspects of the four 'post-Rome' phases of negotiations on the crime of aggression: phase one from 1999 to 2002, which involved the Preparatory Commission; phase two from 2002 to 2009, which involved the Special Working Group on the Crime of Aggression; phase three from February 2009 to May 2010, which involved the Assembly of States Parties to the Rome Statute; and phase four from 31 May to 11 June 2010, which involved the Review Conference. This assessment, I should stress, is aimed to provide some initial empirical analysis, and to encourage and guide future related research.

There is evidence, I argue, that before and during the Review Conference, several states aimed to reaffirm the primary responsibility of the Security Council in maintaining international peace and responding to aggression, but an even greater number sought to protect the viability and independence of the ICC. Moreover, many states wanted to break the Council's perceived monopoly on determining whether an act of aggression has occurred, and empower the ICC to decide this issue for itself in situations within its jurisdiction. In order to secure these two aims, though, the principles of state consent and, by implication, state sovereignty were also reaffirmed. In this way, the negotiations on aggression indicate that a growing number of states appear to believe that international courts such as the ICC – and not just the Security Council or states themselves – have a role to play in maintaining international peace and security.

II International authority: theory and method

The concept of authority is central to political and legal philosophy, and the practice of politics and law. This is in part because the idea of authority is linked to many of the fundamental questions such philosophy and practice seek to address, such as who has power over whom, and why should the latter comply. Despite or perhaps because of its centrality, Richard Friedman notes that authority is 'an elusive concept'.[11] There is, Friedman usefully observes, 'no single view of authority that can serve as the model for understanding all the different uses to which it is put'.[12] Alongside this diversity of potential views on authority in political and legal philosophy, it is also important to note that the concept has received comparatively less attention in the fields of IL and IR.[13] To this extent, efforts to theorize and study *international* authority in these areas are relatively new and admittedly still evolving.[14]

---

11 Richard B Friedman, 'On the Concept of Authority in Political Philosophy' reprinted in Joseph Raz (ed), *Authority* (Basil Blackwell, 1990) 57.

12 Ibid.

13 Ian Hurd, 'Theories and Tests of International Authority' in Bruce Cronin and Ian Hurd (eds), *The UN Security Council and the Politics of International Authority* (Routledge, 2008) 24.

14 See, eg, ibid; Tomer Broude and Yuval Shany (eds), *The Shifting Allocation of Authority in International Law* (Hart, 2008); Michael Zurn, Martin Binder and Matthias Ecker-Ehrhardt, 'International Authority and its Politicization' (2012) 4(1) *International Theory* 69; Andrei Marmor, 'An Institutional Conception of Authority' (2011) 39(3) *Philosophy &*

A *Realist IR theory and formal IL theory*

With the above caveats in mind, two potentially relevant perspectives are realist IR theory and formal IL theory. If conceptions of international authority exist on a spectrum, and insofar as 'power and right' are the key aspects of authority, realist approaches arguably represent the 'power' end of this spectrum, while formal views represent the 'right' end.[15] Interestingly, though, adopting either approach would likely lead one to conclude *a priori* that – whatever may or may not have occurred in the negotiations on aggression – authority for international peace and security has not changed or shifted from the Security Council to the ICC, or from states to the Court.

This would likely be a realist conclusion because, according to this perspective, international affairs are anarchic in that there is no true supranational authority able to protect states or control their conduct when disputes arise.[16] By implication, therefore, authority for peace and security cannot have changed or shifted from the Security Council to the ICC, or from states to the Court. Realist views usefully highlight the large power disparities that underlie the formal structure of sovereign equality in international institutions like the UN and the ICC, and the important role played by the strongest members of such institutions.[17] As will be seen later below, there is evidence of such power disparities and the disproportionate role played by the permanent five (P5) members of the Security Council leading up to and during the Kampala Conference.

However, realist approaches provide less help in understanding why great powers often have trouble getting what they want out of international institutions.[18] As will also be seen below, during the aggression negotiations, members of the P5 tried but were unable to convince a majority of other states to (a) affirm the Security Council's exclusive authority to determine an act of aggression, or (b) expand the Council's control over ICC prosecutions of this crime. More fundamentally, by focusing on the anarchy side of the 'anarchy/authority' dichotomy, realist views risk *assuming* that authority is absent in international affairs rather than demonstrating

Public Affairs 238; and the special issue edited by Karen J Alter *et al*, 'How Context Shapes the Authority of International Courts' (2016) 79(1) *Law and Contemporary Problems* 1.

15 One definition of authority in *The Oxford English Dictionary* is the 'Power or right to enforce obedience'.

16 See, eg, Kenneth Waltz's argument that 'National politics is the realm of authority', while 'international politics is the realm of power, of struggle'. Kenneth Waltz, 'Anarchic Orders and Balances of Power' in Robert Keohane (ed), *Neorealism and its Critics* (Columbia University Press, 1986) 111.

17 Michael Barnett and Martha Finnemore, 'Political Approaches' in Thomas G Weiss and Sam Daws (eds), *The Oxford Handbook on the United Nations* (Oxford University Press, 2008) 44.

18 Ibid 45.

this empirically.[19] And this means that realist approaches ultimately have less to tell us about a concept that other perspectives, and states themselves, appear to think is important in order to understand contemporary world politics and international law.

In contrast to realism, formal views would likely accept that international authority for particular issues exists because the right to decide has been delegated by states to international institutions through consensual legal processes such as the creation and amendment of treaties.[20] From this perspective, the question of whether the aggression negotiations indicate that authority for international peace and security is changing or shifting would turn mainly on the degree to which member states have consented to such changes or shifts in accordance with the relevant provisions of the Rome Statute and, perhaps, the UN Charter.

Formal views usefully highlight that authority for particular issues might be shared among different international actors, and that such authority can change among these actors over time through relevant processes of creation and delegation. For example, authority for international criminal law has arguably been shared by, and evolved from, the Nuremberg and Tokyo Trials created by the Allies after World War II, the UN Security Council's establishment of the International Criminal Tribunal for the Former Yugoslavia in 1993 and the International Criminal Tribunal for Rwanda in 1994, and the creation of the world's first permanent International Criminal Court in 2002 by states acting outside the UN system.

Formal perspectives also remind us of the important role played by state consent in the creation and development of international institutions like the ICC. As we will see later below, in order to break the Security Council's perceived monopoly on determining whether an act of aggression has occurred, and to empower the ICC to decide this issue for itself in situations within its jurisdiction, the principles of state consent and state sovereignty were ultimately reaffirmed at the Kampala Conference. As will also be seen, however, there is evidence that countries were divided on this issue, and that half of the participating states parties initially favoured no requirement of state consent for jurisdiction to be initiated through the state party and ICC Prosecutor referral mechanisms.

As the latter observation suggests, formal approaches also have limits. First, they cannot adequately explain the potential role and influence of states

---

19 See, eg, Helen Milner, 'The Assumption of Anarchy in International Relations Theory: A Critique' (1991) 17(1) *Review of International Studies* 67.

20 For studies that resonate with this perspective see, eg, Danesh Sarooshi, *The United Nations and the Development of Collective Security* (Oxford University Press, 2000); Michael Barnett, 'Authority, Intervention, and the Outer Limits of International Relations Theory' in Thomas M Callaghy *et al* (eds), *Intervention and Transnationalism in Africa* (Cambridge University Press, 2001) 47.

which are not parties to an international institution like the ICC but which nonetheless actively participate in such institutions. Relatedly, formalism cannot adequately account for the potential impact of such institutions on non-states parties.

Most importantly, by explaining delegations of authority primarily through state consent, and by locating an institution's right to decide mainly in its treaty provisions, formalism may miss other interactive social processes through which authority is contested and changed.[21] For example, insofar as states parties to the Rome Statute have delayed the possibility of the ICC exercising jurisdiction over the crime of aggression until at least 2017, then they have not yet consented to any changes or shifts in international authority in a formal sense. And yet, ending our inquiry with this conclusion would tell us little about: (a) the *variety* of state views leading up to and during the Kampala negotiations; (b) the *reasons* states gave for these views; (c) the *disagreements* and *debates* about how jurisdiction for aggression should be balanced between states and institutions such as the Security Council and ICC; and (d) the ways prior shared legal understandings of aggression may have *structured* these debates and shaped what could be agreed to at Kampala. Focusing on such questions is arguably relevant to understanding whether and how the negotiations on aggression indicate that states think authority for international peace and security is changing or shifting.

B *Third interdisciplinary approach: distinct influence of authoritative institutions*

In response to the limits of realist and formal perspectives regarding international authority, one interdisciplinary alternative in the fields of IR and IL is to focus on the distinct *influence* authoritative institutions have in world politics and international law. There are different versions of this view, but a common assumption is that authoritative institutions are recognized by relevant actors as impacting conduct and beliefs in ways that are different from, for example, coercion or instrumental calculations of self-interest.[22]

One challenge of this conceptual assumption is that it is methodologically difficult to determine *why* complex actors such as states do what they do and think what they think.[23] For example, as legal scholars will note, establishing whether a customary international legal rule exists requires analysing state practice and *opinio juris*, but the latter is often inferred from the former because it is difficult to assess. Another challenge of the view that authoritative institutions have distinct effects is that actors such as states likely do

---

21 For a related theory of how international law is created and operates, see Jutta Brunnée and Stephen Toope, *Legitimacy and Legality in International Law* (Cambridge University Press, 2010).

22 See, eg, Hurd, above n 13, 25; Friedman, above n 11, 59; Alter *et al*, above n 14.

23 For an elaboration of this point, see Hurd, above n 13, 32–36.

what they do and believe what they believe for a variety of reasons. These may include, among other things, coercion, self-interest and the impact of institutions.

In light of the above challenges, it must be acknowledged that examining the presence, influence or change of international authority will always be an indirect estimation based on the evidence that is available. For present purposes, this evidence includes public statements and draft proposals from states parties and observer countries regarding the aggression negotiations, the voting behaviour of states in this process, the reflections of key people involved in the talks, and relevant preparatory documents that guided these discussions.

One example of work that focuses on the distinct effects of authoritative institutions is a 2016 special issue of *Law and Contemporary Problems* on international courts edited by Karen Alter *et al.* In this research, the authors note that they are interested in when 'formal legal authority', namely the powers that states have delegated to a court, evolves into 'authority in fact', as indicated by recognizing an obligation to comply with court rulings, and engaging in meaningful action toward giving effect to those rulings.[24]

This approach reminds us that authoritative institutions are seen by relevant actors as impacting both conduct *and* beliefs in world politics and international law. It also reiterates the important point that, although authority is often viewed as a hierarchical relationship where a superior has ultimate power or the 'final word' over a subordinate,[25] international courts operate within a context of international complexity that features 'nested, partially overlapping, and parallel international regimes that are not hierarchically ordered'.[26]

Despite these insights, however, Alter *et al*'s framework also has limits for this study. By their conception, for example, we cannot properly assess the 'factual authority' of the ICC regarding aggression until the current jurisdictional delay for this crime is lifted, and the Court issues relevant rulings against which state reaction can then be assessed.

As such, another potentially relevant example is the work of Ian Hurd. Like Alter *et al*, Hurd argues that when theorizing and studying international authority, one important issue is the *effects* such authority has in world

---

24 Alter *et al*, above n 14, 1, 3, 7.
25 See, eg, Hurd, above n 13, 24–25.
26 Karen J Alter and Sophie Meunier, 'The Politics of International Regime Complexity' (2009) 7(1) *Perspectives on Politics* 13. In the context of international courts, Alter *et al*, above n 14, note at p. 5 that the lack of a clearly established hierarchy arises because states often create new treaties and institutions without specifying their relationship to pre-existing ones, and many treaties give national governments discretion to decide how to implement international obligations. The result, they argue, is that multiple actors within nested and parallel regimes can plausibly claim supremacy over overlapping legal domains.

politics and international law.[27] Unlike Alter *et al*, though, Hurd focuses on how these effects stem from legitimated power. As he explains:

> Authority is a social relation that exists between actors and the structures that make up their social setting. It exists when actors believe that the structures embody legitimated power and they act in ways that reinforce it. Studying possible relations of authority between states and international organizations requires that we pay attention to both how states are affected by the existence of legitimated structures and how those international organizations are affected by the behaviour of states.[28]

In order to study 'possible relations of authority' between states and international organizations, Hurd suggests two approaches that are relevant to this chapter.

First, if an organization like the ICC has international authority, then we should see evidence that other actors, such as states, feel a need to justify their behaviour to it. Second, if these other actors must, whether they want to or not, include the ICC and its effects on the world as part of their strategic thinking about international affairs, then this may also constitute evidence that they, or some subset of them, view the Court as authoritative.

C *Theoretical argument and methodological justification*

Building from Hurd's ideas and my earlier observations above, I argue that for purposes of understanding the complex links between the Security Council, the ICC and states regarding aggression, authority is best thought of as a social relationship between actors who recognize that the right and power to decide is shared but contested. And one way to study whether and how international authority for peace and security is shifting or changing from the Security Council to the ICC, or from states to the Court, is to analyse the conduct and beliefs of states – particularly less-examined countries – leading up to and during the Kampala Conference on aggression.

With this theoretical argument and methodological focus in mind, a few related points should be made about why such a focus is justified in light of this chapter's research question. Interested interdisciplinary scholars and graduate students may note here that IL researchers do not always justify their case selection and methodological approach, although IR scholars are often expected to explain these decisions in advance. In principle, such explanations help contextualize one's work in the broader literature, and clarify its contributions and limits.

Regarding this chapter, analysing the behaviour and beliefs of states regarding aggression is illuminating for at least three reasons. First, 116 states

---

27 Hurd, above n 13, 26.
28 Ibid 25–26.

reportedly attended the Kampala negotiations: 84 of 111 then states parties to the Rome Statute (including Britain, France, Germany and Japan); 31 observer countries (including the United States of America, Russia, China, Iran, India, Pakistan, Israel and Egypt); and one of 21 invited states (Laos).[29] Thus, as a general matter, studying state views of aggression at the Review Conference is a helpful way of estimating the positions of: (a) a majority of countries in the world (60%, or 116 of about 192 possible states); (b) most states parties to the ICC (76%, or 84 of 111); and (c) a significant number of observer countries (38%, or 31 of about 81 possible states), including the world's most militarily and economically powerful states.

Second, reviewing – as this chapter has – the available public interventions made during the General Debate of the Conference reveals the views of countries which are not permanent members of the Security Council (non-P5).[30] These views have been under-documented and under-studied in the existing literature on the crime of aggression.[31]

Finally, if, as IR and IL scholars often emphasize, state conduct and beliefs are the primary phenomena in world politics and the main source of obligation in international law, then analysing the actions and positions of P5 *and* non-P5 states leading up to and during the Review Conference will help increase our understanding of whether and how these important international actors believe that authority for peace and security is changing or shifting.

D *Observable implications*

In light of the above argument and methodological justification, the following observable implications guide this chapter's brief empirical analysis, and could be used to encourage and assist future related research. These implications are meant to act as useful analytical references, and it should be acknowledged that the complex reality of the aggression negotiations – like other important topics of interest to ICL researchers – may not correspond

---

29 *Delegations to the Review Conference of the Rome Statute of the International Criminal Court*, 31 May–11 June 2010, RC/INF.1 (26 August 2010).

30 Over 80% of participating states parties and about half of the observer countries spoke during the General Debate. However, six of these statements are not available as submitted interventions, and some statements may have differed slightly from the interventions that states submitted. Research for this chapter reviewed the approximately 75 state interventions that are available in English or French, but not the seven state interventions that are only available in Spanish or Arabic. See 'ICC – General Debate – Review Conference' <https://asp.icc-cpi.int/en_menus/asp/reviewconference/Pages/review%20conference.aspx>.

31 Existing work, such as Barriga and Kreß (above n 6, 811–817), tends to include only a few direct statements of positions by countries after the amendments were passed at Kampala, or to focus on the views of the P5.

exactly with them. Nonetheless, positing such references in advance helps in interpreting the evidence discussed below, and in critically assessing the theoretical ideas outlined above.

First, if, as Articles 24 and 39 of the Charter might imply, the Security Council has exclusive authority for determining whether an act of aggression by a state has occurred, then we should see evidence that states parties and observer countries leading up to and during the Kampala negotiations believe that this body has the only power and right to make such decisions. We should see, for example, countries speak or act in ways that reinforce this view of the Council, and minimizes any potential role for the ICC regarding aggression.

Second, if, as realist perspectives might suggest, states have exclusive authority for determining acts of aggression, then we should see evidence that states parties and observer countries leading up to and during the Kampala negotiations believe that they have the only power and right to make such decisions. We should see, for instance, countries speak or act in ways that reinforce this view of themselves, and minimize any potential role for international institutions regarding aggression.

Third, if, as this chapter assumes, authority regarding aggression is likely shared among different international actors, then a number of possibilities arise depending on the way this authority is shared. I suggest three possibilities here, but other outcomes could also be imagined. One possibility is that, in light of Article 24 of the Charter granting the Security Council primary responsibility for maintaining international peace, and of the potential influence of P5 states at Kampala, the Council will have a role for the crime of aggression that is broader than the role it has for the other three crimes of the Rome Statute – i.e. war crimes, crimes against humanity and genocide. By implication, the ICC will have a role for aggression that is narrower than the role it has for these other three crimes. We should thus see, for example, states leading up to and during the Kampala negotiations speak or act in ways that reinforce this unequal distribution of roles.

Alternatively, if states view aggression as similar to the other three crimes of the ICC, or if they prioritize the Court's independence over other goals, a second possibility is that the Security Council and ICC will have roles for aggression that are the same as the roles they have for the other three crimes. We should thus see countries speak or act in ways that reinforce this equal distribution of roles.

Finally, if states view other international institutions as relevant for determining whether an act of aggression has occurred, a third possibility is that the UN General Assembly or the International Court of Justice will have a role to play in such determinations. Where there is disagreement, for example, between the Security Council and the ICC about a particular determination, we should thus see countries speak and act in ways that reinforce the power and the right of the General Assembly or the ICJ to help resolve such disagreements.

III The four phases of negotiation on the crime of aggression

Keeping the above theoretical and methodological thinking in mind, the rest of the chapter applies this thinking to briefly assess important aspects of the four recent phases of negotiation on the crime of aggression. There is evidence, I argue, that before and during the Review Conference, several states aimed to reaffirm the primary responsibility of the Security Council in maintaining international peace and responding to aggression, but an even greater number sought to protect the viability and independence of the ICC. Moreover, many states wanted to break the Council's perceived monopoly on determining whether an act of aggression has occurred, and empower the ICC to decide this issue for itself in situations within its jurisdiction. In order to secure these two aims, though, the principles of state consent and, by implication, state sovereignty were also reaffirmed. In this way, the negotiations on aggression indicate that a growing number of states appear to believe that international courts such as the ICC – and not just the Security Council or countries themselves – have a role to play in maintaining international peace and security.

A *The winding road to Kampala*

Under Article 39 of the UN Charter, recall, the Security Council shall determine the existence of any threat to the peace or act of aggression. In light of such wording, Article 5(2) of the Rome Statute states in part that any future provision on aggression in that treaty 'shall be consistent with the relevant provisions of the [UN] Charter'. This implies, at first blush, that participating states parties at the Kampala Conference think that the amendments made there regarding aggression are consistent with the relevant provisions of the Charter.

The road to the historic Kampala amendments, however, was not straightforward. Following the disagreement over aggression at the Rome Conference, recall that four broad phases of negotiation occurred: phase one from 1999 to 2002, which involved the Preparatory Commission (PrepCom); phase two from 2002 to 2009, which involved the Special Working Group; phase three from February 2009 to May 2010, which involved the Assembly of States Parties; and phase four from 31 May to 11 June 2010, which involved the Review Conference in Kampala.[32] During the first and second phases, note that both states parties and observer countries were allowed to

---

32 Stefan Barriga, 'Negotiating the Amendments on the Crime of Aggression' in Barriga and Kreß, above n 6, 3–57.

participate on 'an equal footing' – i.e. both could vote or call for a vote on the issues being discussed.[33] In the third and fourth phases, observer countries lost their voting rights, but retained the ability to participate fully in the formal and informal consultations associated with these phases.

B First phase: Preparatory Commission from 1999 to 2002

During the initial negotiating phase, a key point on which PrepCom participants developed agreement was that a state must commit an act of aggression before an individual can commit a crime of aggression.[34] Thus, discussion papers from 2002 and 2007 noted that a precondition to the ICC exercising jurisdiction over the crime of aggression is that 'an appropriate organ' has determined the existence of the act of aggression.[35] These papers did not define 'appropriate organ'. Instead, they prioritized the Security Council and left open the issue of how to proceed if that body is unable or unwilling to act.[36]

This issue was not ultimately resolved until the Kampala Conference in 2010. In the negotiating phases beforehand, five potential responses were identified.[37] For present purposes, note that these options envisioned three additional international institutions – the ICC, the UN General Assembly, and the International Court of Justice (ICJ) – as potentially 'appropriate organs' with authority to determine whether a state has committed aggression. Moreover, by envisioning these institutions in this way, four of the five options implied that the Security Council does not have exclusive authority to make such determinations. However, the options involving the General Assembly and ICJ enjoyed only limited support, and most states favoured either the Security Council or ICC options.[38]

Therefore, at a conceptual level, the identification and reception of these five options in some ways suggest an *expansion* of authority for international peace – i.e. an international court, and not just the Security Council or states themselves, was seen as an 'appropriate organ' to determine whether an act of aggression has occurred. At the same time, the identification and reception of these options also indicate a *narrowing* of such authority in other respects – i.e. two UN institutions, the General Assembly and ICJ, which might otherwise be thought of as appropriate actors were viewed less favourably than the Security Council and the ICC regarding this issue.

---

33 Ibid 14, 42.
34 Mauro Politi and Giuseppe Nesi (eds), *The International Criminal Court and the Crime of Aggression* (Ashgate, 2004) 49.
35 See *Chairman's Paper* from January 2007, and similar wording in *Coordinator's Paper* from July 2002, in Barriga and Kreß, above n 6, 12, 527–528.
36 Ibid.
37 Barriga, above n 32, 12–13, 33–36.
38 Ibid 36, and the discussion in the text later below.

Option one was to have the ICC dismiss a case if the Security Council has not determined that an act of aggression has occurred. Stefan Barriga, a key legal adviser and expert in charge of the proposals and reports drafted in the negotiations of 2003-10, recalls that this 'was obviously the preferred option of the [P5]'.[39] Alongside the P5, though, some non-P5 states also appeared to think, at least initially, that consistency between the Rome Statute and the UN Charter means the Council must first determine that aggression has occurred. For example, a German proposal in 1999 and Cameroonian proposal in 1998 required the Council to determine such an act before the ICC could proceed with a case.[40]

Option one is conceptually noteworthy because it implies that, for legal and/or policy reasons, the Security Council has or should have exclusive authority to determine whether an act of aggression has been committed by a state. Absent such a determination, the ICC cannot proceed. Legally, support for this option could stress that the UN Charter specifically assigns the function of determining aggression to the Security Council under Article 39, and does not attribute this function to any other body.[41] From a policy viewpoint, insofar as most conflicts are now internal and states disagree about what constitutes aggression, the Council's political discretion and power realities can be seen as advantages in making such decisions.

If states at the Kampala Conference ultimately supported option one, this arguably *would* suggest that, at least regarding aggression, the relationship between the Council and the ICC is hierarchical and the former, as superior, has ultimate power or the 'final word' over the latter, as subordinate. And this, in turn, would challenge a theoretical premise noted earlier – i.e. that international courts operate within a context of global complexity that features nested, overlapping, and parallel regimes that are not hierarchically ordered.

In contrast to the first option, a second possibility identified in PrepCom negotiations was that a case should proceed at the ICC even if the Security Council has not determined that aggression has occurred. In support of this option, Barriga recalls that 'some delegations argued that the crime of aggression should not be treated differently than the other three core crimes in the [Rome] Statute'.[42] Prosecution of these three crimes by the ICC, recall, does not require that the Council has first determined that the relevant acts have been committed. Notwithstanding such potential similarity between aggression and the other ICC crimes, however, most delegations thought an

---

39 Barriga, above n 32, 13. See, eg, *1999 Proposal by the Russian Federation*, UN Doc PCNICC/1999/DP.12, in Barriga and Kreß, above n 6, 339.

40 *1999 Proposal by Germany*, UN Doc PCNICC/1999/DP.13; and *1998 Proposal by Cameroon*, UN Doc A/CONF.183/C.1/L.39, in Barriga and Kreß, above n 6, 340, 274–276.

41 See, eg, Paula Escarameia, 'The ICC and the Security Council on Aggression: Overlapping Competencies?' in Politi and Nesi, above n 34, 140-141.

42 Barriga, above n 32, 13.

additional jurisdictional 'filter' should be used for the former.[43] Further details of this perspective will be seen later below.

Option two is conceptually noteworthy because it implies that, for legal and/or policy reasons, the Security Council does not or should not have exclusive authority to determine whether a state has committed aggression. If the Council is unwilling or unable to respond – for instance because of the threat or use of the veto by a P5 member – the ICC can and should proceed with a case. Legal support for this option could stress relevant state practice, such as the Uniting for Peace resolution described below, and ICJ jurisprudence that the Council's responsibility for maintaining international peace is primary but not exclusive.[44] From a policy viewpoint, the Council's historical reluctance to formally describe prior uses of force as aggression suggests it may be unlikely to make such determinations in future conflicts.[45]

If states at the Kampala Conference ultimately favoured option two, this would indicate that, at least regarding aggression, the relationship between the Council and the ICC is not hierarchical and the former does not have ultimate power or the 'final word' over the latter. And this, in turn, would support the theoretical premise noted above about the non-hierarchical order of international courts.

The third, fourth and fifth options identified in PrepCom meetings envisioned the UN General Assembly or the ICJ determining whether an act of aggression has occurred. Under option three, if the Security Council is unable to act, the ICC could request the General Assembly to make a determination. This option was inspired by the US-led Uniting for Peace Resolution passed by the Assembly in November 1950.[46] This instrument provides that if the Council fails to exercise its primary responsibility for maintaining international peace, the Assembly shall consider the matter and recommend appropriate collective measures.[47] For present purposes, note that this initiative can be seen as one of the most important attempts by the US and its allies to change the institutional balance of power between the Security Council and the General Assembly regarding matters of peace and security.[48] Since its passing, the Uniting for Peace framework has also been used by countries in the Non-Aligned Movement to raise issues of importance in the General Assembly, such as decolonization.

43 Ibid 35.
44 See, eg, *Certain Expenses of the United Nations (Advisory Opinion)* [1962] ICJ Rep 151, 163.
45 See, eg, Nico Krisch, 'Article 39' in Bruno Simma *et al* (eds), *The Charter of the United Nations: A Commentary* (Oxford University Press, 3rd ed, 2012) 1272–1296.
46 Barriga, above n 32, 13.
47 *GA Res 377 (V) of 3 Nov 1950*, cited in Dominik Zaum, 'The Security Council, the General Assembly, and War: the Uniting for Peace Resolution' in Vaughan Lowe *et al* (eds), *The United Nations Security Council and War* (Oxford University Press, 2010) 157.
48 Ibid 155.

Thus, if states in the Kampala talks ultimately decided that the ICC could request the General Assembly to determine an act of aggression where the Security Council is unable to respond, this would further suggest a potential shift in the balance of authority between the two UN bodies, and the continued potential use of the Assembly by Non-Aligned countries.

The fourth option identified in PrepCom discussions was that the ICC could ask the General Assembly to request an advisory opinion from the ICJ on whether an act of aggression has occurred. This option was based on a 2001 proposal by Bosnia and Herzegovina, New Zealand and Romania.[49] Another version of this option proposed that the Security Council could request an advisory opinion through a (veto-immune) procedural vote. This was suggested by the Netherlands in 2002.

The fifth and final possibility was that the ICC could proceed with a case if the ICJ determines in contentious proceedings that an act of aggression has occurred. This option was also based on the 2001 three-state proposal noted above.

Options four and five are conceptually noteworthy because the ICJ has addressed the use of force by states and related issues of international responsibility in cases such as *Nicaragua*, *Lockerbie*, *Yugoslavia v. NATO*, and *Congo v. Uganda*. As Paula Escarameia observes, the

> ICJ has never refused a case that involved the determination of the use of force based on arguments of inadmissibility of a political question and on the competencies of the Security Council, having considered that its judgments, even when they went against [Council] determinations, prevailed, as legal determinations, over political ones.[50]

In light of this prior practice and legal legitimacy, if states at Kampala ultimately decided that the ICC could seek a determination from the ICJ that an act of aggression has occurred, this would arguably indicate an affirmation of, or increase in, the perceived authority of the ICJ regarding issues of international peace and security.

C Second phase: Special Working Group on the Crime of Aggression from 2002 to 2009

The second phase of negotiations, recall, was the Special Working Group (SWG) from 2002 to 2009. For present purposes, two highlights from this period should be emphasized. First, in discussing what definition should be adopted for the crime of aggression in the Rome Statute, countries involved in SWG talks were in some ways debating the nature and role of the Security

---

49 Barriga, above n 32, 13.
50 Escarameia, above n 41, 140.

Council, General Assembly and ICC regarding matters of international peace, and the relationship between these institutions with respect to such matters.

For example, the fact that most states supported a definition of aggression that would be based on the 1974 definition and acts listed in General Assembly Resolution 3314 indicates that these countries saw the prior practice of this organization as relevant to shaping what could be agreed to in the SWG negotiations, and to guiding the future work of the ICC.[51] This instrument provides in part that the Assembly: (a) is convinced that adopting a definition of aggression will contribute to the strengthening of international peace and security; (b) calls on states to refrain from acts of aggression and other uses of force contrary to the UN Charter and the Assembly's earlier Declaration on Friendly Relations; and (c) recommends that the Security Council consider the resolution's definition in determining future acts of aggression.[52] Like the Uniting for Peace framework noted earlier, using Resolution 3314 to help define aggression for the ICC thus further implies an acknowledgement among states that the Assembly has some responsibility for international peace, and that it can ask the Council to consider its views when responding to a perceived breach of the peace.

Broad support for a definition based on Resolution 3314, however, was only achieved by adding a 'threshold clause' that limited the ICC's jurisdiction to acts of aggression which by their character, gravity and scale constitute manifest violations of the UN Charter.[53] Countries in favour of this clause argued the ICC should only take up the most serious crimes of concern to the world community, and avoid borderline cases. This implies that other institutions, such as the Security Council, are better suited to address such borderline cases.

The second highlight from the SWG talks is the modest progress that was made regarding jurisdictional issues, and what this says about how states view the role and relationship of the Security Council and the ICC regarding aggression. As with the PrepCom meetings, SWG negotiations did not resolve the ultimate question of whether, absent a Council determination that aggression has occurred, the ICC could proceed with a case. However, agreement was reached on some important related issues.

First, it was agreed that a Council determination of an act of aggression should be procedurally relevant, but not substantively binding on the ICC. To safeguard the rights of defendants accused of aggression, a strong majority of delegations argued that a determination by the Council or another organ could not legally bind the Court, although it would suggest that such an act had

---

51 For a discussion of this support, and the drafting challenges it posed, see Barriga, above n 32, 25–28.

52 For the full definition and acts, see *1974 GA Resolution 3314*, in Barriga and Kreß, above n 6, 179–183.

53 Support for the threshold clause grew over time. However, a few Non-Aligned Movement states, including Egypt and Iran, continued to express concern until the conclusion of the SWG (Barriga, above n 32, 29).

occurred.[54] In response to this view, Barriga recalls that 'some delegations that argued for a strong role for the Security Council were uneasy about the prospect of the Court reviewing and possibly disagreeing with a Council determination of aggression, but the due-process argument was simply too compelling'.[55]

This discussion also sparked debate about how a future definition of aggression in the Rome Statute would affect the Security Council in determining acts of aggression. 'Delegations', Barriga notes, 'agreed that the Council would not be bound by these provisions, just as the Court would not be bound by a determination of aggression by the Council'.[56] As a 2007 SWG report observed, each institution had 'autonomous, but complementary roles'.[57] A provision was thus drafted that reflected these understandings, and this was ultimately adopted in Kampala.[58]

Another jurisdictional issue on which agreement was reached at the SWG talks was that the Security Council should not be the exclusive 'trigger' for initiating an investigation of an alleged crime of aggression. Instead, the two other triggers relevant to other ICC crimes under Article 13 of the Rome Statute – state referrals and Prosecutor-initiated investigations – should also apply to aggression. Reflecting this view, a draft provision from 2007 proposed that 'The Court may exercise jurisdiction over the crime of aggression in accordance with Article 13'.[59] And the substance of this provision was ultimately adopted in Kampala.

For present purposes, note that what made clarification of this issue possible was the context provided by the Rome Statute itself.[60] From a negotiating perspective, Barriga recalls that this progress:

> [R]epresented a significant concession by those arguing for the Security Council's exclusive competence to determine an act of aggression. It made clear at a relatively early stage in the negotiations that the initiative for an investigation into a crime of aggression could also come from the Prosecutor or a State Party ... [It] also confirmed that the main outstanding question regarding the ... Council was about its possible role as a jurisdictional *filter*, not the trigger.[61]

54 Barriga, above n 32, 30. There were also concerns that new evidence might appear after such a determination.
55 Ibid.
56 Ibid 31.
57 *2007 SWGCA Report (December)* [24], in Barriga and Kreß, above n 6, 589.
58 The final provision, listed in Articles 15 *bis* and 15 *ter*, states that 'A determination of an act of aggression by an organ outside the Court shall be without prejudice to the Court's own findings under this Statute'.
59 *2007 Chairman's Non-Paper on the Exercise of Jurisdiction*, in Barriga and Kreß, above n 6, 555.
60 Barriga, above n 32, 32.
61 Ibid.

Resonating with some of the theoretical ideas posited earlier, these reflections support the observation that realism cannot adequately explain why powerful states, in this case members of the P5, often have trouble getting what they want out of international institutions. The reflections also support the idea that prior shared legal understandings of the relevant provisions of the Rome Statute helped structure the SWG talks, and shape what could be ultimately agreed to at Kampala. Finally, they suggest that most countries involved in the SWG process wanted to empower the ICC to be able to initiate investigations, and not have to rely solely on the Security Council or states to start such investigations.

D *Third phase: Assembly of States Parties from February 2009 to May 2010*

Following the SWG process, a third shorter phase of discussions occurred among the Assembly of States Parties leading up to the Kampala conference. Two highlights from this phase are relevant for present purposes. First, support grew among delegations for an additional consent-based filter for the crime of aggression, thus suggesting the broader perceived significance of state sovereignty in the final negotiations. Where an investigation would be initiated through a state referral or the ICC Prosecutor, for example, approximately half of the delegations now thought the accused aggressor state needed to consent to such jurisdiction beforehand (a) through an 'opt-in' declaration, or (b) by not 'opting-out'.[62]

Second, after an eight-year absence, the United States returned to the negotiations as an active observer, and had an important impact on the talks. For example, the US raised concerns about the draft definition of the crime of aggression, and the political risk of the Court acquiring jurisdiction over this crime. Some delegations responded by expressing support for the hard-won agreements that had been made up to that point. But the US continued to engage with states parties, and eventually had its concerns addressed by the Review Conference, notably in the form of interpretive understandings which aimed in part at narrowing the definition of aggression.[63] This reminds us that, reflecting a realist idea noted earlier, power disparities can underlie the formal equality of institutions like the ICC, and strong countries, including non-members, can unequally influence such institutions.

On the other hand, while the US and some other states wanted the Security Council to be the exclusive filter for an aggression investigation to proceed, the great majority of delegations wanted the Council to be the primary but

---

62 Ibid 43.
63 McDougall, above n 6, 24–25.

not exclusive filter, thus allowing the Court to proceed if the Council failed to act.[64] Within this majority, very few states supported the UN General Assembly or ICJ having a filtering role, and most wanted the ICC's Pre-Trial Division to be given this role. This preference, it is worth emphasizing, was ultimately part of the amendments adopted at Kampala.

E *Fourth phase: Review Conference in Kampala from 31 May to 11 June 2010*

In the twelve days of conference debate and negotiations leading up to the amendments, states expressed views not just on aggression but on the broader relationship between themselves, the Security Council and the ICC. During the opening statements, for instance, several countries – such as Austria, the Czech Republic and Suriname – reaffirmed the Council's primary responsibility for maintaining international peace.[65] But an even greater number of states expressed concern with protecting the viability and independence of the ICC. [66] Indeed, this goal was almost universally acknowledged during the negotiations, including by the P5. Reflecting this goal, members of the Non-Aligned Movement stressed that the ICC is a judicial body which should not become an object of political manipulation.[67]

Notably, many Latin American states, the African Group and a few European and smaller states parties went so far as to push for a Security Council role that would be similar to the one it plays regarding the other three crimes of the Rome Statute.[68] But in the end, this view was not included in the final amendments, and additional jurisdictional filters for aggression were endorsed. Recalling the observable possibilities hypothesized earlier, this outcome and the other evidence reviewed above suggest that international authority for aggression may be increasingly shared among different international actors, but the ICC has a narrower role for this crime than it does for the other crimes under its jurisdiction.

---

64 Barriga, above n 32, 35, 46.
65 See, eg, *Statement by the Austrian Delegation*, Review Conference of the Rome Statute of the ICC, General Debate, 1 June 2010, above n 30.
66 The following countries expressly highlighted the viability and independence of the Court as a goal: Austria, Belgium, Brazil, Bulgaria, Canada, Ecuador (on behalf of the Union of South American Nations), Finland, Germany, Ghana, Iran, Lesotho, Mauritius, Namibia, New Zealand, Nigeria, the Non-Aligned Movement, Peru, Poland, Romania, Senegal, Slovenia, South Africa, Switzerland, Trinidad and Tobago, and Venezuela.
67 *Statement by Mahmoud Samy, Ambassador of Egypt to The Hague (on behalf of the Non-Aligned Movement)*, Review Conference, 1 June 2010, above n 30.
68 Van Schaack, above n 6, 514.

IV Conclusion

This chapter aimed to help interested scholars think about why interdisciplinary topics like aggression and authority are relevant to important theoretical debates within and outside existing international criminal law research, and how we can address such topics in an analytically reflective and methodologically rigorous manner. With these particular aims in mind, the chapter thus also sought to help contribute to this handbook's broader objectives of exploring ICL's relationship to international relations and international law more generally, and the changes that have possibly occurred in these fields regarding criminal law.

Because this collection is a research handbook, let me conclude briefly with two suggestions about how future work could build on this chapter's findings. First, while part of this chapter considered important aspects of the four phases of aggression negotiations described above, future research could assess upcoming discussions on the topic. For instance, at the December 2017 meeting of the Assembly of States Parties, delegates are scheduled to discuss activating the ICC's jurisdiction over aggression.[69]

Second, the evidence analysed by this chapter focused on key public statements and draft proposals from state parties and observer countries regarding the aggression negotiations. Future work could examine other sources by interviewing state officials and legal advisors who participated in the negotiating process. For example, the views of such individuals could help shed more light on what happened during the informal, bilateral talks that followed the General Debate at Kampala from June 2 to 10, 2010. There is limited evidence currently available about the details of these talks.

Further reading

Barriga, Stefan and Claus Kreß (eds), *The Travaux Préparatoires of the Crime of Aggression* (Cambridge University Press, 2012).

McDougall, Carrie, *The Crime of Aggression under the Rome Statute of the International Criminal Court* (Cambridge University Press, 2013).

Raz, Joseph (ed.), *Authority* (Basil Blackwell, 1990).

---

69 See Assembly of States Parties to the Rome Statute, 'Provisional Agenda', ICC-ASP/16/1 (6 March 2017) <https://asp.icc-cpi.int/iccdocs/asp_docs/ASP16/ICC-ASP-16-1-ENG. pdf>.

9

RETHINKING LIBERAL LEGALITY THROUGH THE AFRICAN COURT OF JUSTICE AND HUMAN RIGHTS

Re-situating economic crimes and other enablers of violence

Kamari Maxine Clarke

I Introduction

In the influential text, *The Justice Cascade: How Human Rights Prosecutions Are Changing World Politics,* Harvard professor Kathryn Sikkink argues that the enactment of international, foreign, and domestic prosecutions across the globe constitutes a new trend in world politics toward holding state officials criminally accountable for human rights violations.[1] By examining the way that prosecutorial justice is establishing a new basis for morality, she celebrates the increasing demands for judicial prosecutions and argues that they reflect a radical change in which social demands for accountability through prosecutions are becoming the new norm. This development is reflective of the prevailing trends in liberal legal thought and mirrors what Sikkink calls *justice cascades.*

From the Nuremberg and Tokyo trials to the prosecutions of former presidents Pinochet and Milosevic through various ad hoc tribunals and the coming into force of the International Criminal Court (ICC), Sikkink insists that the popularity of international prosecutorial solutions has spread and concretised a popular new norm toward individual accountability as an equal manifestation of justice. As she argues,

> Norms are 'inter-subjective,' that is, they are held by groups of people. But norms start as ideas held by a handful of individuals. These individuals try to turn their favoured ideas into norms. ... When these norm entrepreneurs succeed, norms spread rapidly, leading to a norms cascade'.[2]

---

1 See Kathryn Sikkink's *The Justice Cascade: How Human Rights Prosecutions Are Changing World Politics* (Norton & Company, 2011).
2 Ibid 11.

Sikkink is thus concerned with the emergence of new moral values in relation to the popularisation of justice as legal accountability for crimes.

While it is empirically true that we have seen the increased growth of legal mechanisms,[3] there are many ways to account for the rise in new judicial institutions that involve larger global governance developments. However, to suggest that the contemporary development and cascading of new international courts reflect a widespread acceptance of new norms around ending impunity is to miss the significance of a range of other developments in shaping what we understand to be contemporary justice. For Sikkink, the expansion of the demands for accountability and the spread of new norms are widespread. But what she overlooks is how the application of international law in contemporary legal circuits is not only perceived by large numbers of constituencies as unequal but is also seen as not necessarily productive of justice.

The reality is that there is an equally sobering destabilisation of the justice cascades metaphor that points to the actual retraction or rethinking of the nature of various prosecutorial trends especially from the Global North to the South. We are seeing contrary prosecutorial norm developments underway in the form of 'push-backs' to not only international justice institutions but also to the conduct being criminalised. Examples include the announcements of withdrawals from the Rome Statute and the Inter-American Court, the failures of the Southern African Development Community (SADC) court in which its first case resulted in Zimbabwe challenging the legitimacy of the court and eventually led to its 2012 dissolution, the push back against the European Court of Human Rights, and the most recent expansion of the criminal jurisdiction of the African Court of Justice and Human Rights which re-activates 'immunity for heads of state'.[4] These responses reflect something more ominous about what justice looks like and calls for further analysis of how the adjudication of mass atrocity core crimes within the jurisdiction of the ICC, namely genocide, crimes against humanity, war crimes and aggression, exclude other forms of conduct, such as various economic and corporate crimes. They also exclude other forms of oppression that are enablers of mass atrocity violence, such as those issues related to land, or ethnic and/or class inequalities. In this light, the chapter highlights the way that the exclusion of other forms of conduct demand significant attention and points to new responses underway through which categories of culpability are being re-attributed. An examination of the establishment of the African Court of Justice and Human Rights, with its three chambers, including a criminal

---

3 See the emergence of international judicial tribunals as outlined in ibid. See also Matiangai Sirleaf, 'The African Justice Cascade and the Malabo Protocol' (2017) 11(1) *International Journal of Transitional Justice* 71.

4 *Malabo Protocol*, 23rd Ordinary Session, AU Doc Assembly/AU/Dec.529 (XXIII) (30 June 2014), Art. 46(A). See also Kamari Maxine Clarke, *Affective Justice* (Duke University Press, forthcoming 2018).

chamber of international and transnational crimes, is an example of the re-attribution of culpability by Pan-African stakeholders engaged in rethinking the types of crimes of greatest threat in Africa. By exploring the formation of the African Court of Justice and Human Rights and the type of crimes being presented as crimes that an international court ought to be addressing in Africa, I show that the move toward international criminal prosecutions or what Sikkink refers to as 'justice cascades' is not arbitrary or objective. Nor is it a reflection of the natural progression and cascading of prosecutorial justice in the contemporary period, as Sikkink suggests.[5]

The new pro-legal accountability demands (otherwise known as anti-impunity demands) represent the contemporary manifestation around which legality functions. But they also reflect particular processes of selectivity as well as the historical conditions of extraction and debilitation that are part of African postcolonial histories. The result is that the prosecution of particular crimes in particular regions highlights the limits of international criminal legality in producing the terms of a universal form of justice. What we see through the African Court example, therefore, is that the principles of ICL are being utilised by domestic African governments/judicial institutions as a means of determining the line between transnational and international criminality as an alternative to pre-existing judicial means that are born of their colonial pasts. As such, the institutionalisation of regionally relevant judicial criminal mechanisms can be seen to reflect the aspirations of African policymakers attempting to use international legal tools to reconceptualise the terms by which the crimes of greatest concern to Africans are elevated. What we see through this example are attempts to introduce crimes that are economic and transnational in scope, as well as attempts to rethink modes of criminal responsibility for crimes. This form of re-attribution forces us to take seriously various affective push-backs to ICC principles that offer a contrary view to the management of violence in Africa. The contrary position suggests that the root causes of African violence are not being addressed through conceptualisations of guilt that focus on individual criminal responsibility – that is the re-attribution of collective guilt for mass atrocity violence onto a handful of leaders or commanders. Instead, this position features questions about the particularities of the crime, the historical and structural conditions under which they contribute to Africa's violence, and the realisation that justice is not meaningful if it does not address root causes of violence – especially economically driven violence or violence enabled through corporate greed.

Despite the frequently quoted passage in the preamble of the Statute of the ICC that the 'most serious crimes of concern to the international

---

5 Ibid.

community as a whole must not go unpunished',[6] the foregoing highlights the reality that the increasing use of prosecutorial justice modalities is unfolding within a hierarchy of crimes that are not cascading widely. Rather, they exist within controversial geo-political fields. This chapter reflects on how other forms of conduct are being introduced into the Africa ICL framework and are used to counteract the ICC movement by foregrounding other crimes of grave concern to the African continent. For example, the crime of Unconstitutional Change of Government (UCG) was driven by the unconstitutional takeovers of African governments and their direct impact on peace and stability of African countries. The crime of UCG was incorporated as a crime in the 2014 Malabo Protocol (discussed in more detail below) to promote greater respect for the rule of law and to induce a concomitant reduction in the prevalence of armed conflicts.[7] Yet, the acts constituting UCG, listed under Article 23 of the 2003 African Charter on Democracy, Elections and Governance (ACDEG) – military coups d'état, the rigging of elections, and so on – have consistently and for a long time been rejected by the majority of African states. As evidenced by myriad treaties and declarations adopted over several decades to outlaw them, the ACDEG is a codification of what had become a quintessential custom in Africa: the rejection of UCG.[8] Thus, in order for the African regional court to prosecute the crime of UCG, the AU drafters and negotiators felt that the crime should be legislated by the AU's Malabo Protocol and, in doing so, it should be regarded as a 'serious' international crime. The treatment of the UCG is hence one of the few norms in Africa that gradually evolved through custom, culminating in its codification by the ACDEG.[9]

By not accounting for the way that these growing international judicial horizons are delimited and the way that they are emerging as protests against judicial institutions unable to address the violence they were meant to end, Sikkink misses the way that discourses surrounding international justice cascades actually crowd out other justice cosmologies. While it is clear that people everywhere feel comforted by the existence of judicial mechanisms that reflect their values – harmful and violent actions should be prevented

---

6 This relates to the preamble of the International Criminal Court which states, 'Affirming that the most serious crimes of concern to the international community as a whole must not go unpunished and that their effective prosecution must be ensured by taking measures at the national level and by enhancing international cooperation'. *Rome Statute of the International Criminal Court*, opened for signature 17 July 1998, 2187 UNTS 90 (entered into force 1 July 2002).

7 *Malabo Protocol*, above n 4, Art. 28E.

8 Ademola Abass, 'The Proposed International Criminal Jurisdiction for the African Court: Some Problematical Aspects' (2013) 60 *Netherlands International Law Review* 27, 29.

9 Ibid.

or punished, for example – the reality is that justice cosmologies that are seen as producing contrary effects are called into question. Of late, and in relation to ICC decisions, the effects have led to various announcements of state withdrawals from relevant treaties, retractions, protests, or attempts to re-attribute culpability. Such re-attributions are the focus of this chapter.

I end by suggesting that what scholars like Katherine Sikkink identify as a changing public value is actually complicated by protests against the perception of inequality in the application of the jurisdictional reach of international (read: Global North) interests and the debunking of other justice aspirations. Ultimately, perceptions of inequality in the international criminal law domain have led to calls for a withdrawal of African states from the ICC and the development of a new African Court of Justice and Human Rights in which new approaches to justice in Africa have led to the introduction of new international crimes of particular significance to Africa. This provides an opportunity for rethinking the crimes that should be punished and who should be held accountable for mass atrocity crimes.[10]

Despite the controversies surrounding the development of an African Court with criminal jurisdiction, the newly proposed court would be the first of its kind operating at the regional level with the objective of addressing both human rights and international criminal law.[11] These developments call into question the current trends and emphasise the need to think critically about the particularities of new judicial formations underway and what categories of crime are needed to re-attribute culpability for mass violence – especially in Africa.

II The African Criminal Court as a response to perceived inequalities in international justice

In the first decades of its formation, the ICC has been riddled with disagreement and struggles over its perceived legitimacy and institutional power. The 34 African states that ratified the Rome Statute in 1998 initially embraced the rule of law movement as an extension of their commitments

---

10 See Tefera Degu Addis, 'Some reflections on the current Africa's project on the establishment of African Court of Justice and Human Rights (ACJHR)' on *AfricLaw* (29 June 2015) <https://africlaw.com/2015/06/29/some-reflections-on-the-current-africas-project-on-the-establishment-of-african-court-of-justice-and-human-right-acjhr/>; Vincent Nmehielle, '"Saddling" the New Regional Human Rights Court with International Criminal Jurisdiction: Innovative, Obstructive, Expedient?' (2014) 7(1) *African Journal of Legal Studies* 7, 29; Sirleaf, above n 3; Kristen Rau, 'Jurisprudential Innovation or Accountability Avoidance? The International Criminal Court and Proposed Expansion of the African Court of Justice and Human Rights' (2012) 97(2) *Minnesota Law Review* 669, 678-79, 681-82, 685.
11 Addis, above n 10.

to Africa's emancipatory future. The violence that unfolded in Africa in the 1980s and 1990s played an important role in compelling their moral conscience to act. It instigated feelings of indignity and anger that were tied to the inaction of the international community during the Rwandan genocide, the injustice of South African apartheid, and the results of the long anti-colonial struggles against European imperialism. With these realities in mind, the various leaders in these states initially saw the ICC as a beacon of emancipation – a solution for their continent's injustices. However, since the entry into force of its Statute in 2002 until December 2016, the ICC had pursued 22 cases in nine situations across several African states: the Central African Republic (CAR), the Democratic Republic of the Congo (DRC), the Ivory Coast, Sudan, Uganda, Kenya, the Republic of Mali, Burundi, and Libya. Overall, the court has ten situations and another ten cases are under preliminary investigation.[12]

In prosecuting the above cases the ICC has indicted 39 individuals. From the cases of alleged African warlords to the indictments of African leaders – including President Uhuru Kenyatta and Deputy President William Ruto of Kenya, Presidents Omar al-Bashir of Sudan and Laurent Gbagbo of the Ivory Coast – all of the cases involved African subjects and hardly addressed the forms of economic culpability that surrounded the violence being adjudicated.

The passage of the African Court Malabo Protocol unfolded on the heels of these ICC indictments of African leaders. At its July 2011 Summit, the AU Assembly held that the ICC arrest warrants for African leaders seriously complicated efforts aimed at finding a negotiated political solution to the crisis in Libya and decided 'that Member States shall not cooperate in the execution of the arrest warrant' against Gaddafi.[13] At subsequent Heads of State and Government (HOSG) summits, the Assembly decisions involved the call for solidarity among AU member states in their opposition to the proceedings launched against Al Bashir. This involved the call for the UN Security Council to defer the ICC's prosecutions against Al Bashir, Kenyatta, and Ruto under Article 16 of the Rome Statute.[14] At the October 2013 Summit in Addis Ababa, some AU member states called on all signatory African states to withdraw their membership of the Rome Statute.[15] The Assembly also formally decided that

12 For the current list of situations under investigation, see <www.icc-cpi.int/pages/situations. aspx>.
13 Assembly of the African Union, *Seventeenth Ordinary Session Decisions, Declarations and Resolutions* Assembly/AU/Dec.366(XVII), 17th Ordinary sess, (30 June–1 July 2011), Malabo, Equatorial Guinea <http://au.int/web/sites/default/files/decisions/9647-assembly_au_dec_363-390_xvii_e.pdf> 9.
14 Ibid.
15 Assembly of the African Union, *Decision on Africa's Relationship with the International Criminal Court,* Extraordinary Session, Decision No Ext/Assembly/AU/Dec. 1 (12 October 2013).

'no charges shall be commenced or continued before any International Court or Tribunal against any serving AU Head of State or Government or anybody acting or entitled to act in such capacity during their term of office'.[16] These initiatives propelled the expansion of the ACHPR's mandate to try international crimes, leading to the adoption of the Malabo Protocol in June 2014.[17]

Yet, the Malabo Protocol also represents the culmination of a process that began in 1981 with the adoption of the African Charter on Human and Peoples' Rights by the Organisation of African Unity (OAU), the AU's predecessor.[18] This charter entered into force in 1986 and enabled the 1987 establishment of the African Commission on Human and Peoples' Rights, the quasi-judicial oversight body tasked with interpreting the charter and hearing complaints.[19] In 1998, a Protocol to the charter was adopted that created the African Court on Human and Peoples' Rights (ACHPR). That Protocol entered into force on January 25, 2005 and currently 27 of 54 possible states are party to it.[20] The ACHPR sits in Arusha, Tanzania and may hear applications relating to human rights violations brought before it by the AU Commission, as well as African inter-governmental organisations and member states.[21] Since 2008, 23 applications have been brought before the ACHPR with only two judgments being delivered.[22]

In 2001, a second inter-state court structure was included in the AU's Constitutive Act and was further developed in the 2003 Protocol of the Court of Justice of the AU, becoming known as the African Court of Justice (ACJ).[23] The ACJ was intended to be the principal judicial organ of the AU, with authority to rule on disputes over the interpretation of AU treaties.[24] Although this Protocol entered into force in 2010, the ACJ was in effect stillborn and superseded by the Protocol on the Statute of the African Court of Justice and Human Rights (the Merger Protocol).[25] At its 2008 summit meeting in Sharm El-Sheikh, the AU adopted a Merger Protocol, thus confirming the joining of the ACHPR and the ACJ into a 'Merged Court'

---

16 Ibid [10].
17 Ibid.
18 Organisation of African Unity (OAU), *African Charter on Human and Peoples' Rights* ('Banjul Charter'), 27 June 1981, CAB/LEG/67/3 rev. 5, 21 ILM 58 (1982) <www.achpr. org/instruments/achpr/>.
19 Ibid.
20 Organisation of African Unity (OAU), *Protocol to the African Charter on Human and Peoples' Rights on the Establishment of an African Court on Human and Peoples' Rights* (10 June 1998) <www.achpr.org/instruments/court-establishment/>.
21 Ibid.
22 See Open Society Justice Initiative, *Case Digest: Decisions of the African Commission on Human and Peoples' Rights, 2010-2014* (September 2015) Open Society Foundations <www.opensocietyfoundations.org/sites/default/files/case-digests-achpr-20151014.pdf>.
23 African Union, *Protocol of the Court of Justice of the African Union* (11 July 2003) <www. au.int/en/treaties/protocol-court-justice-african-union>.
24 Ibid.
25 Ibid.

meant to have two jurisdictional chambers: a general chamber to consider inter-state issues and labour matters affecting employees of the AU (which was the original jurisdiction of the ACJ) and a human and peoples' rights chamber with the same powers as the ACHPR. The Merger Protocol is to enter into force after 15 ratifications. To date, only five states have ratified it.[26]

In 2009, the AU Commission requested the Pan African Lawyers Union (PALU) to prepare recommendations and a draft amendment to the Merger Protocol to allow the Court to try international crimes such as genocide, crimes against humanity, and war crimes.[27] Based on the draft submitted by PALU, the HOSG Assembly of the AU adopted in June 2014 a Protocol on Amendments to the Protocol on the Statute of the African Court of Justice and Human Rights (the 'Malabo Protocol'), which proposed the addition of a third section to the proposed African Court of Justice and Human Rights (ACJHR), which would have jurisdiction over 14 international crimes.[28] In all, it would be composed of three chambers: a General Affairs Section, a Human Rights Section, and an International Criminal Law Section.[29]

The Malabo Protocol hence extended the jurisdiction of the ACJHR to cover individual criminal liability for serious crimes committed in violation of international law. It also expanded the terrain of punishable crimes to new transnational offenses. Thus, one of the most innovative aspects of the African Court is that it joins the existing three core international crimes (i.e. crimes against humanity, genocide, and war crimes) together with nine new crimes that have never been part of an international criminal justice mechanism.[30] The new Criminal Law Section would have jurisdiction over the following crimes: (1) Genocide (2) Crimes against Humanity (3) War Crimes (4) The Crime of Unconstitutional Change of Government (5) Piracy (6) Terrorism (7) Mercenarism (8) Corruption (9) Money Laundering (10) Trafficking in Persons (1) Trafficking in Drugs (12) Trafficking in Hazardous Wastes (13) Illicit Exploitation of Natural Resources, and (14) The Crime of Aggression.[31] The inclusion of these crimes has implications for the development of a framework that goes beyond ICC crimes, often seen as insufficient for addressing criminal responsibility for violence in Africa.

---

26 Ibid.
27 Ibid.
28 Garth Abraham, 'Africa's Evolving Continental Court Structures: At the Crossroads?' (Occasional Paper No 209, South African Institute of International Affairs, January 2015) <www.saiia.org.za/occasional-papers/africas-evolving-continental-court-structures-at-the-crossroads> 7.
29 *Malabo Protocol*, above n 4, Art. 6/16.
30 See Abraham, above n 28, 11; Firew Kebede Tiba, 'Regional International Criminal Courts: An Idea Whose Time Has Come?' (2016) 17 *Cardozo Journal of Conflict Resolution* 521. It should be noted that the Special Tribunal for Lebanon is an exception, as it has jurisdiction over terrorism (Special Tribunal for Lebanon, 'Unique Features' <www.stl-tsl.org/en/about-the-tl/unique-features>).
31 *Malabo Protocol*, above n 4, Art. 14/28A.

The ratification of the Malabo Protocol and the subsequent operationalisation of the court would also open an alternative avenue for justice to be delivered on the African continent, echoing the motto of 'African Solutions to African Problems'. Yet, many concerns have been raised about the broad jurisdictional reach of the proposed court.[32] Max du Plessis called the scope of the court's jurisdictional reach 'breathtaking', noting that even before the addition of the International Criminal Law Section, the African Court would have had an extensive caseload related to its general affairs and human rights jurisdictions.[33] Even under its original jurisdiction, experts worry that the court would suffer from an overextension of responsibilities. However, as I will argue below, although various African leaders have been associated with the new court as a mechanism for evading justice, the Protocol to expand the criminal jurisdiction of the African Court should be seen, not through this exception but through the spirit of its innovation, as a Pan-African project born of inequalities tied to Africa's place in the world but conceptualised in relation to the realities of political and economic violence in African landscapes. It represents the rectification of concessions made during the negotiations of the Rome Statute for the ICC to eliminate those crimes that were seen as too controversial to include yet for many were key to addressing Africa's violence.[34] Various AU peace and security representatives also point to the growing disillusionment with the efficacy of the global security architecture and the ICC. In this vein others have written that '[i]t is not entirely un-coincidental that the two places where we have seen the most development of regional options – Europe and Africa – have also been the site of the UN's greatest failures in the 1990s . . .'.[35]

---

32 See Abass, above n 8, 29, 32; Max du Plessis, 'A New Regional International Criminal Court for Africa?'(2012) 25 *South African Journal of Criminal Justice* 286; Max du Plessis, 'Implications of the AU Decision to Give the African Court Jurisdiction over International Crimes' (Research Paper No 235, Institute for Security Studies, 28 June 2012) <www.issafrica.org/publications/papers/implications-of-the-au-decision-to-give-the-african-court-jurisdiction-over-international-crimes>; Max du Plessis, Tiyanjana Maluwa and Annie O'Reilly, 'Africa and the International Criminal Court (Programme Paper, Chatham House, 1 July 2013) <www.chathamhouse.org/sites/files/chathamhouse/public/Research/International%20Law/0713pp_iccafrica.pdf>; Rau, above n 10, 679; Manuel J Ventura and Amelia J Bleeker, 'Universal Jurisdiction, African Perceptions of the International Criminal Court and the New AU Protocol on Amendments to the Protocol on the Statute of the African Court of Justice and Human Rights' in Evelyn A Ankumah (ed), *The International Criminal Court and Africa: One Decade On* (Intersentia, 2016) 441.
33 Du Plessis, 'Implications of the AU Decision', above n 32, 289.
34 See generally Kamari Maxine Clarke, *Fictions of Justice: The International Criminal Court and the Challenge of Legal Pluralism in Sub-Saharan Africa* (Cambridge University Press, 2009). See also Kamari Maxine Clarke, 'The Rule of Law through Its Economies of Appearances: The Making of the African Warlord' (2011) 18(1) *Indiana Journal of Global Legal Studies* 7.
35 Bruce Jones and Feryal Cherif, 'Evolving Models of Peacekeeping: Policy Implications and Responses' (United Nations Peacekeeping and Center on International Cooperation, NYU) <www.operationspaix.net/DATA/DOCUMENT/5880~v~Evolving_Models_of_Peacekeeping__Policy_Implications_and_Responses.pdf >.

As such, the passage of the Malabo Protocol and its related extension of the criminal jurisdiction of the African Court are seen as addressing the gap between those crimes seen as politically motivated crimes, such as genocide and crimes against humanity, and those crimes that reflect enabling economic crimes, such as toxic dumping, corruption, and drug trafficking. From being focused on adding these substantive enabling crimes and ensuring that too much political power was not given to the prosecutor, the actual process by which it unfolded precluded open, public deliberations. Rather, the Malabo Protocol was expedited following the indictments of President Al-Bashir and Kenyatta/Ruto. Unlike Sikkink's argument that prosecutorial justice is at large, what we are seeing is a modified formation of criminal justice in which an alternative sense of justice is being reconceived through a widespread questioning of liberal prosecutorial institutionalism, the expansion of crimes, and the creation of new modalities for conceptualising the criminal basis upon which culpability is shaped.

It is not just the rise in prosecutorial institutions that is relevant to the establishment of such institutions, but various perceptions of the ICC's injustices have contributed to the perception of inequality by which justice in Africa is being reconceived. This points to the reality that through this formation, it is clear that prosecutions are not seen as the only solution to such mass atrocity developments. Political action through diplomacy and sequencing as well as deferrals of prosecution are also strategies being used. This includes the use of the Malabo Protocol's Immunity Provision – 46A *bis*[36] as a sequencing modality. In this light, the next section locates the expansion of international crimes within particular political contexts to understand the expansion of the criminal jurisdiction of the African Court and to determine what these dynamics may tell us about the ways that various African stakeholders are engaged in the expansion of categories of crimes relevant to African ecologies.

The attempt to establish an African Court with criminal jurisdiction to adjudicate cases currently pursued by the ICC represents the insistence of locating Africa as a site for the management of violence. As we shall see, attempts to make sense of new AU justice formations require that we understand the way that legal landscapes work together with re-conceptualisations of crimes of concern to humanity, especially in relation to international criminal justice in Africa. These invocations of African justice reflect particular commitments to adjudicating violence that address structures of inequality – economic, political, social – that are important to recognise. This is especially the case when thinking about the way that invocations of 'African solutions to African problems' locate Africa and its new regional institutions in the globalising world and as a player in the rectification of

---

36 *Malabo Protocol*, above n 4, Art. 46A.

the legacy of Africa's structural inequalities. Here we can see the proactive engagement in the formation of an African court as a way to re-attribute what justice means through the deployment and application of international crimes in new judicial spaces.

III African solutions to African problems: innovating international crimes in African ecologies

Some of the crimes under the Malabo Protocol are not international crimes in the strict sense of the word.[37] Some are defined in existing AU instruments, some are from more general instruments, and some are *sui generis*. The treaties that define some of these actions merely create obligations on states to enact criminal offences in their domestic law.[38] To qualify as a crime for prosecution by an international tribunal, it is important that the crime concerned is recognised as 'international' and 'serious' enough by customary international law for the majority of the states designating it as such and/or is a subject of a treaty in force for those states. Legal scholars such as Ademola Abass explain that the twin criteria of 'international' and 'seriousness' are indispensable to establishing jurisdiction over international crime since international criminal tribunals are, by their very nature, reserved for the most serious international crimes.[39] However, what is important to highlight is that the legitimacy of including these crimes in the jurisdiction of the African Court should not be measured by their non-inclusion in the Rome Statute and a related assumption that they are not 'serious' enough to warrant international prosecution.[40] Rather, as I have outlined elsewhere,[41] the process of determining which crimes were to be included in the Rome Statute was a product of political negotiations and compromise.

In addition to these crimes being new to international criminal law, scholars also note that the crimes enable the prosecution of those acts that are of particular significance violence in Africa.[42] Also, because the Statute lists the crimes, defines them, and expressly provides that the Court shall have the power to try them, as well as includes a provision – Article 46B(1) – which provides that 'a person who commits an offence under this Statute shall be held individually responsible for this crime', it suggests that (a) the Statute itself creates these crimes, and (b) that given individual responsibility is being applied, the crime is by definition no longer just a transnational crime but is, at

---

37 Abass, above n 8, 34.
38 Ibid.
39 Ibid.
40 Ibid. See also Addis, above n 10.
41 See Clarke, *Fictions of Justice*, above n 34 and Clarke, 'The Rule of Law', above n 34.
42 See Abass, above n 8, 36; Nmehielle, above n 10, 30; Sirleaf, above n 3; Tiba, above n 30, 544.

least within Africa, a regional international crime (i.e. a supranational crime in the region, rather than just a crime in the domestic law of AU member states).

Some of the prohibited acts have a uniquely African relevance, and some people generalise and argue that the rule of law and human rights are not respected and that governments are routinely overthrown, etc.[43] As Tiba points out, 'Africa has been watching itself helplessly as numerous governments were unconstitutionally overthrown, its human and material resources looted, became a dumping ground for hazardous wastes and its waters infested by pirates'.[44] Similarly, Matiangai Sirleaf observes that African borders are notoriously non-natural and porous, rendering them more susceptible to transnational crimes such as drug and arms trades and terrorist attacks.[45] The frequency and pervasiveness of such crimes ultimately compromises the security and stability of many African states; the particular grouping of quotidian crimes under the Malabo Protocol involves responding to such common security threats.[46] Because many of the conflicts or common security threats in Africa tend to diffuse or have a contagion effect, a regional tribunal may be the best-placed institution to adequately address the many different groups of crimes.[47] Ultimately, the Malabo Protocol recognises both the background and foreground of international criminal law violations, with massive atrocity not taking place in a vacuum, but instead being embedded in systems of criminality.[48] As such, the particular grouping of crimes under the Malabo Protocol can be seen as an innovative approach to tackling both everyday security threats as well as structural violence that is unique to the African context.

It is also worth mentioning that none of the crimes falling within the jurisdiction of the African Court shall be subject to any statutes of limitation.[49] Moreover, this is the first time that white-collar crimes, such as corruption and money laundering, etc. are treated en par with those acts seen as the most egregious crimes.[50] The importance of Article 28(A)(2), which provides that 'The Assembly may extend upon consensus of the States Parties the jurisdiction of the Court to incorporate additional crimes to reflect the developments of international law', points to the existence of an awareness that both criminal conduct and international law are seen as evolving and that the jurisdiction of the Court might be expanded at some point.[51] The AU's

43 Tiba, above n 30, 544.
44 Ibid.
45 Sirleaf, above n 3.
46 Ibid.
47 Ibid.
48 Ibid.
49 *Malabo Protocol*, above n 4, Art. 28A(3).
50 Tiba, above n 30, 544.
51 *Malabo Protocol*, above n 4, Art. 28A(2); Abass, above n 8, 36.

incorporation of economic crimes into the AC Malabo Protocol can hence be seen as statements about the need to reconsider the centrality of the ICC's core crimes.

IV Re-conceptualising the crimes of greatest concern to Africa as enabling economic crimes

A *The crime of trafficking in hazardous waste*

There is a range of reasons why such economically driven crimes have been included in the Malabo Protocol. From the role of cross-border drug trafficking in enabling and funding the means for armed attacks to the significance of criminalising corporations that dump toxic waste on African shores and simply pay fines to avoid individual criminal liability, the Malabo Protocol highlights particular developments that are worth noting. One example is the trafficking in hazardous waste seen through Trafigura, a multinational company that dumped toxic waste in Abidjan, Ivory Coast in 2006 and that made over 100,000 people seek medical assistance. The incident spurred litigation in multiple countries yet led to only one criminal judgment.[52]

The waste in question had originally been brought to The Netherlands, but Trafigura decided not to have the waste treated there, considering it too expensive. The company was found guilty in a Dutch court of illegally exporting the waste. However, no judgment was reached holding Trafigura liable for the dumping itself. The problem with such crimes is that there is a significant risk that hazardous, even radioactive materials could be transported and left undetected until local residents begin to suffer severe negative health consequences. In an attempt to operationalise international instruments that address trafficking of hazardous waste, the drafters of the Malabo Protocol incorporated provisions that would criminalise trafficking in hazardous wastes.

Though not novel in its substantive structure (as there are existing international and regional conventions on such forms of trafficking),[53] the Article is innovative insofar as it creates a transnational criminal forum

---

52 See Trafigura Beheer BV that offloaded toxic waste to Ivorian company. See *Probo Koala: the cargo and journey of the Trafigura-chartered supertanker – Le Scandale du Probo Koala* <https://probo-koala.org/probo-koala-the-cargo-and-journey-of-the-trafigura-chartered-supertanker/?lang=en>.

53 See the *Basel Convention on the Control of Transboundary Movements of Hazardous Wastes and Their Disposal*, opened for signature 22 March 1989, 1673 UNTS 57 (entered into force 5 May 1992) and the *Bamako Convention on the Ban of the Import to Africa and the Control of Transboundary Movement and Management of Hazardous Wastes Within Africa*, opened for signature 30 January 1991, 2101 UNTS 177 (entered into force 22 April 1998).

for its enforcement. However, the court's ability to exercise effectively its jurisdiction over alleged offenders will often be difficult. There is a high likelihood that violators importing waste will come from states that are not parties to the Statute. Hazardous waste tends to be moved from the Global North to the South – to Africa, Latin American, and South East Asia. Therefore, putting in place an international mechanism for pursuing offenders, rather than only a regional institution, is seen as helping with the jurisdictional difficulties related to making offenders accountable.

B *The crime of illicit exploitation of natural resources*

Like the trafficking of hazardous waste, another economically driven crime is the exploitation of natural resources. It is seen as causing problems across borders, creating a need for some regional institution to help regulate those consequences. Pollution of the air and water, deforestation, and diverting of fresh water can cause negative effects across borders. In response, Article 28L *bis* criminalises the exploitation of natural resources through any of the following acts if they are of a serious nature affecting the stability of a state, region, or the African Union (AU):

(a) Concluding an agreement to exploit resources, in violation of the principle of peoples' sovereignty over their natural resources;

(b) Concluding with State authorities an agreement to exploit natural resources, in violation of the legal and regulatory procedures of the State concerned;

(c) Concluding an agreement to exploit natural resources through corrupt practices;

(d) Concluding an agreement to exploit natural resources that is clearly one-sided;

(e) Exploiting natural resources without any agreement with the State concerned;

(f) Exploiting natural resources without complying with norms relating to the protection of the environment and the security of the people and the staff; and

(g) Violating the norms and standards established by the relevant natural resource certification mechanism.

As we see, the requirement of acts being criminalised are those classified as being 'of a serious nature' and, as such, create a high bar for African Court jurisdiction. Article 28L *bis* (a) criminalises the act of 'concluding an agreement to exploit resources, in violation of the principle of peoples' sovereignty over their natural resources'. The 'principles of peoples' sovereignty' highlights the basis by which particular acts are seen as being relevant to the constitutional orbit of the state. Article 28L *bis* (b) criminalises the act of '[c]oncluding with state authorities an agreement to exploit natural resources, in violation of the legal and regulatory procedures of the State concerned'. Here, we see an interest in enacting a supra-state mechanism that is intended to hold defendants criminally liable for colluding with state authorities that are acting ultra vires, circumventing the rules of the sovereign.

Many acts of natural resource exploitation cause serious damage to the environment and deprive local communities of the benefit of those resources without actually threatening the stability of a state, region, or the AU. Nevertheless, what we see is the formation of a regime of complementarity with the national state in which states are expected to address acts that impoverish local communities, degrade the environment, violate property rights, and focus its jurisdiction to acts of exploitation.

A survey of state constitutions reveal that protection of natural resources involves many underlying social values and interests beyond just state and regional stability. Yet, the use and misuse of natural resources affect important property rights that are state-specific and highlight the logic for national determinations for relevant constitutionally driven actions. For example, the Constitution of Liberia guarantees the right of private property.[54] It further provides that only Liberian citizens may own real property. The exploitation of crops and timber, for example, may violate Liberian citizens' right to private property. The public welfare and revenue is another key interest underlying the regulation of natural resource extraction. Although the Liberian constitution gives citizens the right to own real property, the state and not private citizens have a property right in any mineral resources within its territorial jurisdiction and those resources are to be used 'by and for the entire Republic'.[55]

Similarly, Angola's constitution provides that the natural resources within its territorial jurisdiction belong to the state, and use of those resources is to be determined pursuant to law.[56] This constitution also guarantees that the state will take measures to 'protect the environment and species of flora and fauna through the national territory, maintain ecological balance, ensure the correct location of economic activities and the rational development and use of all natural resources'.[57] Yet, it is worth noting that Article 28L *bis* would allow exploitation of natural resources causing severe degradation of the environment and public health, provided that the exploitation did not affect state or regional stability.

The constitution of DRC provides that all Congolese have a right to enjoy the national wealth, which the state has a duty to distribute equitably

---

54 See the *Liberian Constitution* <www.liberianlegal.com/constitution1986.htm>.
55 Ibid Art. 22(b).
56 See the *Angolan Constitution* <www.servat.unibe.ch/icl/ao00000_.html>, Art. 16.
57 Ibid Art. 39.

(Article 58). Article 28L *bis* would cover exploitation such as the mineral trade in the DRC and the diamond trade in Sierra Leone, insofar as those activities have fuelled armed conflict. For while national constitutions offer great leverage and diversity for managing national resources, the inclusion of Article 28L *bis* was motivated by the goal of internationally regulating the exploitation of natural resources through the protection of the environment and the supranational enforcement of the Article's principles.

C *Mercenarism*

Another crime included in the Malabo Protocol is that of mercenarism. Its roots derive from Article 3 of the 1989 International Convention against the Recruitment, Use, Financing and Training of Mercenaries which, however, imposes legal obligations on states to take action under their domestic law and no international jurisdiction is provided for it.[58] In its drafting, Article 28H was structured along the lines of Articles 1 and 2 of the 1989 Convention, itself incorporating the provisions of Article 47 of Additional Protocol I of 1977 to the Geneva Conventions.[59]

Like the 1989 Convention, Article 28H has two definitions of mercenarism. Paragraph 1(a) describes a mercenary as any person who:

    i. Is specially recruited locally or abroad in order to fight in an armed conflict;

    ii. Is motivated to take part in the hostilities essentially by the desire for private gain and, in fact, is promised, by or on behalf of a party to the conflict, material compensation;

    iii. Is neither a national of a party to the conflict nor a resident of territory controlled by a party to the conflict;

    iv. Is not a member of the armed forces of a party to the conflict; and

    v. Has not been sent by a State which is not a party to the conflict on official duty as a member of its armed forces.

Paragraph 1 (b) describes a mercenary as any person who, in any other situation:

    i. Is specially recruited locally or abroad for the purpose of participating in a concerted act of violence aimed at:

---

58 *International Convention against the Recruitment, Use, Financing and Training of Mercenaries*, opened for signature 4 December 1989, 2163 UNTS 7789 (entered into force 20 October 2001).

59 Ibid. Note that these provisions are also contained in the *OAU Convention for the Elimination of Mercenarism in Africa*, signed 3 July 1977, OAU CM/817 (entered into force 22 April 1985) Art. 3; the Convention has been ratified by 31 out of 54 Member States of the African Union.

   1. Overthrowing a legitimate Government or otherwise under-
      mining the constitutional order of a State;
   2. Assisting a Government to maintain power;
   3. Assisting a group of persons to obtain power; or
   4. Undermining the territorial integrity of a State;

   ii. Is motivated to take part therein essentially by the desire for private
       gain and is prompted by the promise or payment of material com-
       pensation;
  iii. Is neither a national nor a resident of the State against which such
       an act is directed;
   iv. Has not been sent by a State on official duty; and
    v. Is not a member of the armed forces of the State on whose territory
       the act is undertaken.

The first definition – Definition (a) – refers to 'armed conflict'; the second –
Definition (b) – refers to 'a concerted act of violence'. Under each definition, a
person is a mercenary if the person satisfies five requirements. What is interesting
in relation to the two definitions of mercenaries is that rather than insisting that to
be deemed a mercenary, a person must *know or intend* that they are participating
in a 'concerted act of violence', instead definition (b) contains a broad definition: to be deemed a mercenary, a person must be essentially motivated by the
desire for private gain – as made explicit in subsection ii. And though proving
a person's essential motivation is difficult, the inclusion of it suggests that
because of the vast consequences of violence in African situations, the drafters
were less concerned with whether the offender must have acted knowingly or
purposefully. Rather, what we see is a concern with the persons, their status,
and their purposes, and not their mental state. The reality of these definitions
suggest that some of the problems related to proving the existing conditions of
hostilities contributed to by foreign fighters have led to the desire to pursue the
culpability of foreign fighters specially recruited to engage in violent hostilities.
The inclusion of mercenaries as an international crime in the Protocol reflects an
attempt to insist on the relevance of such economically driven acts as detrimental
contributors to Africa's violence.

V Corporate criminal responsibility

One of the most ground-breaking aspects of the Malabo Protocol that
many scholars point to is the inclusion of corporate criminal liability
under Article 46C.[60] Vincent Nmehielle, international law scholar and

---

60 Matasi W Martin and Jürgen Brohmer, 'The Proposed International Criminal Chamber
   Section of the African Court of Justice and Human Rights: A Legal Analysis' (2012) 37(1)
   South African Yearbook of International Law 248; Sirleaf, above n 3; Tiba, above n 30, 544.
   Article 46C of the *Malabo Protocol* reads:

Legal Counsel for the AU from 2013 to 2016, argued that including the principle of corporate criminal responsibility in the Malabo Protocol is significant in light of corporate entities having fuelled many of the conflicts that have plagued African states.[61] He observes that many of these conflicts are over natural resources such as oil, diamonds, gold, etc., for which a number of multinational and national corporations compete, and that some of these entities would do anything to obtain concessions over those resources, even if it means fuelling wars in Africa.[62] He concludes that extending criminal responsibility to corporate entities may be Africa's way of putting an end to 'business as usual', whereby corporate players that aid and abet, or that are complicit in gross violations of human rights and the commission of other serious egregious crimes, escape prospective liability because of traditional international criminal law's reluctance to extend criminal responsibility to the principals of such entities.[63]

Western philosophical and legal thought focuses on the individual. This focus has shaped criminal law. Guilt, moral responsibility, and therefore liability in criminal law have been conventionally perceived as resting on the individual, as it is the individual who is generally regarded as being endowed with the natural capacity to rationalise his or her actions and the autonomy to causally control them.[64]

Article 46C provides that 'Corporate intention to commit an offence may be established by proof that it was the policy of the corporation to do the act which constituted the offence'. It further provides that '[c]orporate knowledge of the commission of an offence may be established by proof that the actual or constructive knowledge of the relevant information was possessed within the corporation'.

1. For the purpose of this Statute, the Court shall have jurisdiction over legal persons, with the exception of States.
2. Corporate intention to commit an offence may be established by proof that it was the policy of the corporation to do the act which constituted the offence.
3. A policy may be attributed to a corporation where it provides the most reasonable explanation of the conduct of that corporation.
4. Corporate knowledge of the commission of an offence may be established by proof that the actual or constructive knowledge of the relevant information was possessed within the corporation.
5. Knowledge may be possessed within a corporation even though the relevant information is divided between corporate personnel.
6. The criminal responsibility of legal persons shall not exclude the criminal responsibility of natural persons who are perpetrators or accomplices in the same crimes.

61 Nmehielle, above n 10, 30.
62 Ibid.
63 Ibid.
64 Desislava Stoitchkova, *Towards Corporate Liability in International Criminal Law* (Intersentia, 2010) 29 (referring to Michael S Moore, 'The Moral and Metaphysical Sources of the Criminal Law' in Ronald Pennock and John Chapman (eds), *Criminal Justice* (New York University Press, 1985) 23).

The Article borrows from the broad agency model, including the idea of collective knowledge insofar as the Article provides that '[k]nowledge may be possessed within a corporation even though the relevant information is divided between corporate personnel'.[65] The broad agency model locates each employee as an agent of the employer corporation. A corporation may be held criminally liable for the acts of any of its agents if an agent commits a crime within the scope of his or her employment and with intent to benefit the corporation. In contrast with the 'identification' model, the position of the agent within the corporation is not important since the corporation is presumed to have 'collective knowledge'. Collective knowledge is based on the idea that information known in part to multiple actors within the corporation but not known fully to one actor be aggregated and imputed to the corporation.

The predominant model that has shaped the development of the AU's criminal corporate liability approach is the Holistic Model of corporate responsibility. Under this model, courts look to corporate culture. 'Corporate culture' can be found in an attitude, policy, rule, course of conduct, or practice within the corporate body generally or in the part of the body corporate where the offence occurred. These Articles locate criminal intent and knowledge within the corporate culture and corporate policy, rather than individual employees or officers of the corporation. Evidence may include that the company's unwritten rules tacitly authorised non-compliance or failed to create a culture of compliance.[66] And it is this culture that can give rise to liability.[67] But the problem is that such a holistic approach can also fail to impose liability where the *absence* of a policy leads to criminal behaviour by a corporation's employees. The issues that may unfold with the operationalisation of the court remain to be seen. But the most pressing remains the viability of pursuing corporate criminal liability on an international level. For the same challenges that are present in international criminal litigation against natural persons will be present in cases against corporations, except the challenges will likely be greater. And one of the challenges that the African Court must face is finding a way to enforce its criminal judgments effectively. Some states have been unwilling to fulfil various obligations under international law to impose sanctions or arrest natural persons accused of international crimes and it is likely that the same issues will unfold with corporations.

Despite these pending challenges, today the inclusion of Article 46C is not surprising given the increasing global convergence toward corporate criminal liability in domestic systems.[68] Before the 1990s, many states within the

---

65 *Malabo Protocol*, above n 4, Art. 46C(4).
66 Ibid.
67 Celia Wells, *Corporations and Criminal Responsibility* (Clarendon Press, 1993).
68 Joanna Kyriakakis, 'Article 46C: Corporate Criminal Liability at the African Criminal Court' in Charles C Jalloh and Kamari M Clarke (eds), *The African Court of Justice and Human and Peoples' Rights* (forthcoming).

civil law tradition opposed the concept of corporate criminal capacity, but as of 2013, only Greece, Germany, and Latvia remain without some kind of corporate criminal liability in Europe.[69] The significant question has been how should traditional notions of criminal law, based as it is on the idea of a natural person capable of moral and immoral actions, be applied to corporations? And in the context of Africa, the question involves how to rethink criminal responsibility for violence using parameters that extend well beyond traditional ICC crimes.

VI Immunity provision – Article 46A *bis*

One of the most controversial and widely discussed issues in the literature relates to the issue of immunity for heads of state.[70] The relevant provision in the Malabo Protocol reads as follows:

> No charges shall be commenced or continued before the Court against any serving African Union Head of State of Government, or anybody acting or entitled to act in such capacity, or other senior state officials based on their functions, during their tenure of office.[71]

The exact scope of the provision has been one of the many issues under debate since the Amended Protocol was released in June 2014. Without precise definitions for terms such as 'African Union Head of State or Government', 'anybody acting or entitled to act in such capacity', and 'senior state officials', many scholars have raised concern that it remains unclear who exactly benefits from such immunity.[72] According to Max du Plessis, the phrase 'African Union Head of State or Government' presumably refers to people occupying such an office in a state which is party to the AU Constitutive Act; however, the circumstances in which someone might be 'acting or entitled to act' in

---

69 Ibid.
70 See, eg, Max du Plessis, 'Shambolic, Shameful and Symbolic: Implications of the African Union's Immunity for African Leaders' (Research Paper No 278, Institute for Security Studies, 6 November 2014) <www.issafrica.org/uploads/Paper278.pdf>; Max du Plessis and Nicole Fritz, 'A (New) New Regional International Criminal Court for Africa?' on Wayne Jordash, *iLawyer: A Blog on International Justice* (1 October 2014) <http://ilawyerblog.com/new-new-regional-international-criminal-court-africa/>; Chacha Bhoke Murungu, 'Towards a Criminal Chamber in the African Court of Justice and Human Rights' (2011) 9 *Journal of International Criminal Justice* 1067; Dire Tladi, 'The Immunity Provision in the AU Amendment Protocol and the Entrenchment of the Hero-Villain Trend' (2015) 13 *Journal of International Criminal Justice* 3, 5; Beth Van Schaack, 'Immunity Before the African Court of Justice & Human & Peoples Rights – The Potential Outlier' on *Just Security* (10 July 2014) <www.justsecurity.org/12732/immunity-african-court-justice-human-peoples-rights-the-potential-outlier/>.
71 *Malabo Protocol*, above n 4, Art. 46A *bis*.
72 Du Plessis, above n 32, 8; Van Schaak, above n 70; Tladi, above n 70, 5.

the capacity of a head of state remain unclear.[73] A broad interpretation could result in the inclusion of all ministers and even all members of parliament in some states, while a narrow one could confine the definition to a deputy head of state or government.[74] Van Schaack and du Plessis both note that the term 'senior officials' is not defined, with the former suggesting that the records of the deliberations on the Protocol indicate that it has been left to the new court to determine the reach of the term.[75] There is also a lack of clarity on what exact 'functions' are likely to result in the granting of immunity.[76]

A second ambiguity with regard to scope is whether Article 46A *bis* aims to provide both immunity *ratione personae* and immunity *ratione materiae*, or only one.[77] Article 46A *bis* supports two separate categories, with the first category, immunity *ratione personae*, applicable to 'Heads of State or Government' and 'anybody acting or entitled to act in such capacity'.[78] The second category, approximating immunity *ratione materiae*, would apply to 'other senior officials based on their functions'.[79] The phrase 'based on their functions' appears to only qualify 'other senior officials' and not 'Heads of State or Government, or anybody acting or entitled to act in such capacity'.[80] Assuming the 'two types of immunity' interpretation is correct, Tladi notes that this would mean that immunity *ratione personae* under the Statute of the African Court would not be extended to Ministers for Foreign Affairs, contrary to the finding of the International Court of Justice (ICJ) decision in the *Arrest Warrant* case.[81] An alternative interpretation of Article 46A *bis*, according to Tladi, is that it establishes only immunity *ratione personae*.[82] Under such an interpretation, the qualifier 'based on their functions' does not qualify the extent of immunity but rather forms part of the description of the senior officials (i.e. senior officials, defined in terms of their functions, enjoy the same type of immunity of heads of state or governments and anyone acting or entitled in that capacity).[83] Some argue that this second interpretation is more convincing as the phrase 'based on their functions' appears to have been drawn from the ICJ's reasoning for extending immunity *ratione personae* to Ministers for Foreign Affairs in the *Arrest Warrant* case and that this second alternative would resolve the inconsistency between the first interpretation

73 Du Plessis, above n 32, 8;
74 Tladi, above n 70, 6.
75 Du Plessis, above n 32, 8; Van Schaak, above n 70.
76 Ibid.
77 Tladi, above n 70, 7.
78 Ibid.
79 Ibid.
80 Ibid.
81 Ibid; See *Arrest Warrant of 11 April 2000 (Democratic Republic of the Congo v Belgium) (Judgment)* [2002] ICJ Rep 3, [54].
82 Tladi, above n 70, 8.
83 See *Arrest Warrant* case, above n 81.

and the ICJ decision relating to Ministers for Foreign Affairs.[84] Other officials whose functions do not exhibit the characteristics identified by the Court in the *Arrest Warrant* case as indicating immunity *ratione personae* would hence not have immunity before the African Court's criminal law section.[85]

This interpretation is supported mainly by the fact that in its earlier decisions leading to the adoption of Article 46A *bis*, the AU never made a distinction between the immunities of heads of state and those of other senior state officials.[86] Assuming the immunity *ratione personae* interpretation is the one intended by the drafters, it is important to note that this type of immunity is temporary and may be relied upon only while the individual in question holds the relevant office.

Article 46A *bis* has also received extensive criticism from civil society groups in Africa and around the globe, which similarly argue that such a provision is a setback in the fight against impunity for international human rights abuses.[87] In May 2014, more than 30 civil society and international NGOs appealed to a meeting of African ministers of justice and attorneys general not to include Article 46A *bis* in its draft of the Malabo Protocol.[88] In addition, organisations, including Human Rights Watch, the International Bar Association, FIDH, Amnesty International, the South African Litigation Centre, and the New York City Bar Association, released statements sharply criticising the provision as retrogressive and inconsistent with ensuring that perpetrators are held to account.[89]

---

84 Tladi, above n 70, 5.
85 Ibid.
86 Ibid.
87 See 'Article 46A bis: Implications for Peace, Justice, and Reconciliation in Africa' on The Social Science Research Council, *Kujenga Amani* (21 October 2014) <http://forums.ssrc.org/kujenga-amani/2014/10/21/article-46a-bis-implications-for-peace-justice-and-reconciliation-in-africa/#.VkptHd-rSRt>.
88 See Action of Christian Activists for Human Rights in Shabunda *et al*, *Joint Letter to the Justice Ministers and Attorneys General of the African States Parties to the International Criminal Court Regarding the Proposed Expansion of the Jurisdiction of the African Court of Justice and Human Rights* (3 May 2012) <www.hrw.org/news/2012/05/03/joint-letter-justice-ministers-and-attorneys-general-african-states-parties>; Abraham, above n 28, 14.
89 See Action of Christian Activists for Human Rights in Shabunda *et al*, above n 88; Human Rights Watch, *Statement Regarding Immunity for Sitting Officials Before the Expanded African Court of Justice and Human Rights* (13 November 2014) <www.hrw.org/news/2014/11/13/statement-regarding-immunity-sitting-officials-expanded-african-court-justice-and>; FIDH, 'Immunity of Heads of State and Government for International Crimes? The African Union must act with coherence and political courage' (Press Release, 20 June 2014) <www.fidh.org/International-Federation-for-Human-Rights/15601-immunity-of-heads-of-state-and-government-for-international-crimes-the>; Amnesty International, *AU Summit decision a backward step for international justice* (1 July 2014) <www.amnesty.org/en/latest/news/2014/07/au-summit-decision-backward-step-international-justice/>; International Bar Association, *IBA and SALC express alarm at AU's endorsement of immunity for heads of state* (9 July 2014); <www.ibanet.org/Article/Detail.aspx?ArticleUid=f0c41e45-693d-4712-98c8-3da28c2b949d>.

An additional source of criticism has stemmed from the fact that the draft Protocol presents contradictions to the AU's Constitutive Act. At Article 4(h), the Act obliges parties to 'intervene in a member state ... in respect of grave circumstances', which, according to Ebobrah, when strictly applied 'compels the AU to intervene even during an official's incumbency and makes prosecution after incumbency a significantly lesser evil that African leaders would embrace'.[90] Others have pointed out further contradictions with specific Articles, including Article 4(o), which obliges member states to respect the sanctity of human life, and condemn and reject impunity.[91] Accordingly,

> this internal inconsistency will not only make it difficult for the AU to carry out its task of providing political, technical, and material support to member states engaged in prosecuting perpetrators of international crimes before the regional court; it will also make it difficult to render justice to the victims of these crimes.[92]

Furthermore, some argue that in circumstances where immunity attaches to an office holder, it can create an incentive for that person to remain in office to avoid prosecution.[93] It has been maintained that with this immunity provision, 'we can expect the creation of an atmosphere of impunity for perpetrators of human right violations who will hold onto power'.[94] Yet, the AU has defended the need for the immunity provision from a doctrinal perspective on the grounds that immunities provided for by international law apply not only to proceedings in foreign domestic courts but also to international tribunals and that states cannot circumvent such obligations by establishing an international tribunal.[95] With regard to the ICC Statute, for example, the

---

90 Solomon Ebobrah, 'Article 46A Bis: Implications for Peace, Justice, and Reconciliation in Africa' on The Social Science Research Council, *Kujenga Amani* (21 October 2014) <http://forums.ssrc.org/kujenga-amani/2014/10/21/article-46a-bis-implications-for-peace-justice-and-reconciliation-in-africa/#.WMMCavkrKUk>.

91 Idayat Hassan, 'Article 46A Bis: Implications for Peace, Justice, and Reconciliation in Africa' on The Social Science Research Council, *Kujenga Amani* (21 October 2014) <http://forums.ssrc.org/kujenga-amani/2014/10/21/article-46a-bis-implications-for-peace-justice-and-reconciliation-in-africa/#.WMMCavkrKUk>.

92 Anne Kubai, 'Article 46A Bis: Implications for Peace, Justice, and Reconciliation in Africa' on The Social Science Research Council, *Kujenga Amani* (21 October 2014) <http://forums.ssrc.org/kujenga-amani/2014/10/21/article-46a-bis-implications-for-peace-justice-and-reconciliation-in-africa/#.WMMCavkrKUk>.

93 Chino Obiagwu, 'Article 46A Bis: Implications for Peace, Justice, and Reconciliation in Africa' on The Social Science Research Council, *Kujenga Amani* (21 October 2014) <http://forums.ssrc.org/kujenga-amani/2014/10/21/article-46a-bis-implications-for-peace-justice-and-reconciliation-in-africa/#.WMMCavkrKUk>.

94 Hassan, above n 91.

95 Tladi, above n 70, 10. See also the press release cited in Tladi above n 70, fn 32. Dapo Akande has remarked that 'what the AU wants is an opinion [from the ICJ] that would clarify the immunity (or otherwise) of State officials from prosecution by the ICC and

AU approaches Article 27 as a treaty rule applicable only to state parties and that for non-state parties, the rules of customary international law relating to immunities remain intact.[96] In response to the decisions of the ICC on noncooperation, Malawi and Chad reiterated their position that a treaty may not deprive non-Party States of rights that they ordinarily possess. According to Tladi, this position

> essentially presents Article 27 of the ICC Statute, and similar provisions in the statutes of other international tribunals, as exceptions to the rules of customary international law relating to immunities and applying only as between parties to the constitutive treaties. The immunities provision in the Amendment Protocol is, from this perspective, seen not only as acceptable but as reflecting customary international law.[97]

In evaluating the AU's argument on immunity, many argue that this position ignores the ICJ decision in *Arrest Warrant*, which held that state officials may be prosecuted before international courts under certain circumstances.[98] Accordingly, a more fundamental problem with the AU's postulation is that the immunity of state officials, whether *ratione personae* or *ratione materiae*, under customary international law means, in essence, the immunity of state officials from the jurisdiction of courts of *foreign* states.[99] This immunity is seen as an extension of the immunity of the state from the jurisdiction of other states based on the principle of sovereign equality of states.[100] Since international tribunals such as the ICC and the African Court are not foreign *states*, the rationale for immunity of states and its officials (i.e. the sovereign equality of states) does not apply.[101] Tladi concludes that 'the AU argument that the insertion of Article 46A *bis* is not only consistent with, but is reflective of, customary international law is doctrinally flawed'.[102]

from enforcement action taken by States acting at the request of the ICC'. Dapo Akande, 'The African Union's Response to the ICC's Decisions on Bashir's Immunity: Will the ICJ Get Another Immunity Case?' on *EJIL: Talk!* (8 February 2012) <www.ejiltalk.org/the-african-unions-response-to-the-iccs-decisions-on-bashirs-immunity-will-the-icj-get-another-immunity-case/>.
96 Tladi, above n 70, 11.
97 Ibid. This has been the legal basis of the AU's call for non-cooperation with the ICC's call for the arrest and surrender of Al Bashir. According to the AU, Article 27 leaves intact customary international law on immunities and the waiver of immunities implied by Article 27 applies only between states parties to the ICC Statute. Thus, while there may be a duty on states parties to the ICC to cooperate in the arrest and surrender of a head of a state party, no such duty exists in relation to the arrest and surrender of a head of non-state party.
98 Tladi, above n 70, 12.
99 Ibid.
100 Ibid.
101 Ibid 12-13.
102 Ibid 13.

Despite such positions and their relevance to the perceived legitimacy of the crimes under the Malabo Protocol, the key to my analysis is not concerning whether the interpretation is flawed. Rather, the targeting of African leaders can also be seen as exacerbating conflict in Africa.[103] In real world situations, the temporary granting of immunity to sitting heads of state may not necessarily be antithetical to human rights. And given that no statute of limitations exists for war crimes and crimes against humanity and the other crimes within the jurisdiction of the African Court, the eventual prosecution of those held most responsible for mass atrocity crimes is a viable prospect. Viewing the judicial process as part of a larger political process and sequencing it in this way could potentially protect more Africans from repression and violence than their targeting for international prosecution could ever hope to achieve.[104]

VII Conclusion

While it is clear that justice cascades have resulted from the emergence of the pro-legal accountability movement, the more important arguments that shape how norms unfold are tied to the vociferously debated questions around what should be criminalised, who or what should be held accountable, what the spaces of justice are, and what form it should take. Asking these various questions redirects us from quantifying the expansion of international trials as the measure of new justice formations. It allows us to recast the way that norms are shaped as products of affective commitments that reflect particular historical taxonomies through which subjectivities and practices are constituted. This is important because attention to how legal forms are brought into being and become institutionalised is critical for making sense of the limits and possibilities of justice itself.

However, unlike Sikkink's assumptions about justice, these articulations of justice do not spread through evenly articulated norms and histories. They spread within sites of inequality and attempts to rectify formations that have arisen in an effort to counter the spread of a Nuremberg justice model that does not quite reflect the particularities of the roots of political violence in Africa. This reality not only highlights the problem with the ICC's failure to universalise its forms of judicial justice, but what we see is that law operates within horizons that shape its norms and authority. Highlighting the fissures around the nature of contemporary judicial commitments allows us to make sense of the contested terrain within which prosecutorial justice is actually unfolding. It is the meaning of judicial prosecutions and the socio-political

103 Ibid.
104 Ibid.

sentiments that accompany them that are key to how and why the demand for prosecutorial accountability is unfolding.

Through particular ways of organising subjects and erasing the conditions of their making, liberal legalist discourses shape notions of justice using particular constructions of crime. Yet, those engaged in the instrumentalisation of legal articulations do not necessarily recognise the role of the socio-political dependencies that shape their work. Instead, the opposite relationship to international law's existence is at play. Liberal legality reflects constructions of predictability and objectivity – all central to the ICC's anti-impunity discourse and carried over to the making of the African Court but substantively invigorated to address the nature of inequality in the classification of crimes and their relevance in ending impunity. But in ICC anti-impunity domains, the place of politics in lawmaking is often disavowed because of its overt forms of subjectivity. For it is seen as contrary to law's principles of objectivity that are reflective of the nature of such justice-making projects.

The reality is that the formation of new regional institutions reflect an embodied push-back against the internationalising trend and in many cases reflect attempts to re-attribute the individualisation of criminal responsibility without addressing other forms of responsibility. The African system and African realities being imagined by those engaged in the making of the Malabo Protocol – the lawyers and leaders, civil society members and everyday people – is an Africa to which longstanding and deep patronage commitments lie but for which the application of legal instruments are seen as needing to address various structural and economic concerns. This requires that its stakeholders engage in re-attributing culpability and re-assigning for economic and political action those matters that are of grave concern to the African continent.

Regarding the types of crimes, liberal legalism focuses on the crimes that are the *result* of political processes that produce its subject matter jurisdiction, such as the inclusion of political crimes like genocide and crimes against humanity, but not those outside of its jurisdiction that actually enable such forms of violence, like mercenarism, money laundering, illicit exploitation of natural resources, and the trafficking in hazardous waste. This conundrum has led to new Pan-African initiatives through which the nature of conduct to be criminalised has been interrogated. For questions about which crimes, when, why, who, and under what conditions to extradite or not are not simply the legal questions that require that we take seriously the complexities of politics of decisions that actually shape prosecutorial justice. These questions involve examining the socio-economic and political conditions through which justice is both celebrated and re-attributed through new ways of rethinking the contours of culpability by which violations should be handled, in this case inquiring into which actions should be criminalised and which bodies (political, legal, etc.) should handle them.

Further reading

Boister, Neil, *An Introduction to Transnational Criminal Law* (Oxford University Press, 2012).

Clarke, Kamari Maxine, *Fictions of Justice: The International Criminal Court and the Challenge of Legal Pluralism in Sub-Saharan Africa* (Cambridge University Press, 2009).

Sirleaf, Matiangai, 'The African Justice Cascade and the Malabo Protocol' (2017) 11(1) *International Journal of Transitional Justice* 71.

Tiba, Firew Kebede, 'Regional International Criminal Courts: An Idea Whose Time Has Come?' (2016) 17 *Cardozo Journal of Conflict Resolution* 521.

Tladi, Dire, 'The Immunity Provision in the AU Amendment Protocol and the Entrenchment of the Hero-Villain Trend' (2015) 13 *Journal of International Criminal Justice* 3.

PART III

The implementation of international criminal law

10

THE AD HOC TRIBUNALS

Image, origins, pathways, legacies

Timothy William Waters

I Image: looking at the tribunals, looking at themselves

There is so much to read in this world, that really, one must not only make choices, but take shortcuts. If one were to ask oneself, for example, what we should make of the two ad hoc tribunals, well, where to begin – and where to end? The ink spilled might almost equal the blood splashed out on the killing fields of Yugoslavia and Rwanda, though it would be obscene to actually make the measurement.

Certainly, these two courts – these great twin projects of the late human rights era – loom large in the construction of the post-Cold War world, with its reflexive, almost genuflective turn to law and institutions and its exhilarating, exasperating admixture of optimism and decadence. They take up an inordinate amount of conceptual space, and though they have long since ceded priority and attention to the International Criminal Court (ICC), such is the backwards-looking nature of the international criminal law (ICL) project – which, after all, seeks to build a future by prosecuting the past – that these institutions continue to exercise a gravitational influence, and long will. They matter, and thus the bewildering, smothering text-fall about them does too. So let us begin with the websites.

The websites of the ad hoc tribunals are instructive about a great many things: accomplishments, and therefore claims about what was to be accomplished, what success might look like; differences, because everything from the substance to the design of the two sites reflects the very different trajectories of the two tribunals; and image, both self- and projected.

And of course, the websites have the singular advantage, and defect, of being partisan. They are the tribunals' own claims about themselves: puffery, self-aggrandizement and self-justification are to be expected. But this is quite valuable, because it means that for most things we can trust that this is the very best foot forward, the most positive story that might be true. (For most things: sometimes outsiders see things insiders miss, or that insiders simply cannot say publicly. For example, the tribunals may or may not be the anvil on which a new world order is to forged,[1] but we can be sure they won't be making that claim themselves.) This is especially true for things we might view critically: a claim the tribunals make about themselves may be true; but if we find fault, failing and shortcomings even when the tribunals themselves are making the case, we can be fairly sure the truth is no better.

So, what do the tribunals say they are? What do they say they have done? As with so much on its website, and in the institution generally, the International Criminal Tribunal for the former Yugoslavia (ICTY) has a clearer, more organized line; it notes the following accomplishments:

- holding leaders accountable,
- bringing justice to victims and giving them a voice,
- establishing the facts,
- developing international law, and
- strengthening the rule of law.[2]

The International Criminal Tribunal for Rwanda (ICTR) website, now grandfathered into the Mechanism for International Criminal Tribunals (MICT) since its closure in December 2015, is less schematic, but we can extract similar claims:

- 'played a pioneering role in the establishment of a credible international criminal justice system, producing a substantial body of jurisprudence',[3]
- establishing facts – especially 'genocide beyond dispute',[4]
- laying the foundations for a new era of international criminal justice, and
- other implicitly similar goals – transferring cases implies strengthening rule of law; bringing justice to victims; holding leaders accountable.

For the ICTY, by far the longest section is 'Establishing the facts', a catalogue of highlights from major cases. 'The ICTY has established crucial facts about

---

1 See John Laughland, *Travesty: The Trial of Slobodan Milosevic and the Corruption of International Justice* (Pluto Press, 2007) 5: 'Such trials are anvils upon which a new political order is supposed to be forged . . . to emphasize the dawn of a New World Order . . .' Laughland thinks this is a bad thing, but it follows from his thesis that those doing the hammering are entirely satisfied with the new order they're making; but if so, you won't find them admitting it in Laughland's terms on their websites.

2 ICTY, *Achievements* <www.icty.org/en/about/tribunal/achievements>. The ICTY's statute lays out somewhat different goals; see the next section.

3 United Nations Mechanism for International Criminal Tribunals (MICT), *The ICTR in Brief* <http://unictr.unmict.org/en/tribunal>.

4 MICT, *ICTR Milestones* <http://unictr.unmict.org/en/ictr-milestones>.

crimes, once subject to dispute, beyond a reasonable doubt'.[5] (In an earlier iteration, 'developing international law' received the greatest attention, followed by 'strengthening the rule of law', and these sections are still quite substantial.) The ICTR's distribution of accomplishment is similar.

So this is what the tribunals themselves believe they have done. Appropriately or ironically, there is no page entitled 'failures and omissions', so we shall have to consider, even construct, the negative case as we go along. The remainder of this chapter discusses, first, the origins of the two tribunals; then their jurisprudence and processes, and the politics surrounding their development; and finally, it returns to the tribunals' accomplishments and failings – to their legacies.

II Origins

Few would have predicted the tribunals just a few years before they were established; ICL had been a perpetually deferred project, Nuremberg's legacy an increasingly distant monument. In the event, they were created in reaction to great crises, though ones that raised as many questions as they answered: Why exactly those crises, why exactly then? Because it was not as if there hadn't been other occasions in the preceding 40 years when the guns had come out and the bodies started floating downriver.

A *The ICTY*

So it was perhaps fortuitous – from the point of view of ICL, that is – that one of those crises broke out in Europe. The Yugoslav crisis brought Europe's first real war in two generations, a jarring counterpoint to the optimism of post-Cold War rapprochement on a continent whole and free. And the images – emaciated white men behind barbed wire – invited ready comparisons to the last European conflagration, and therefore to the response. So, in May 1993, a year and a half into the violent dissolution of Yugoslavia, the Security Council established the first international criminal court since Nuremberg and Tokyo – the first truly international tribunal, since neither of the Second World War courts was quite that. But even so, the willingness to intervene was half-hearted, slouching – and in certain respects, this helped to bring the tribunal about: making a court was as much about avoiding greater involvement as committing to international justice. As with most things, the motives were complex.

The tribunal was preceded by a Commission of Experts mandated to report on atrocities in this new European war. In retrospect, this looks like a step towards creating a tribunal – and most subsequent tribunals have followed a

5 ICTY, above n 2.

similar sequence – but at the time, it was a compromise between those who wanted more and those who wanted nothing, and it was not certain it would lead to a court. In the end, when the decision to establish the tribunal was taken, the Commission had not yet issued its final report, which the ICTY's prosecution later made little use of – an ambiguous legacy.

The foot-dragging did not end with Resolution 827 establishing the ICTY. It took an additional 15 months to appoint a prosecutor who actually took office (the first withdrew after seven moribund months), and the first indictments were not issued until November 1994, some three years into the wars. And so the court was created *in medias res.* For those who hoped the tribunal would deter, it was an imperfect experiment, too late to tell. For those who hoped it would promote reconciliation, the wars were still going on, so that lay in the future. If not necessarily a promising beginning, it was at least a beginning with which one could promise much.

B *The ICTR*

And the pattern was now established, an expectation which, precisely because it was untested, retained its full attractive power. That same November, the Security Council voted to establish a second ad hoc tribunal, with jurisdiction over the events in Rwanda earlier that year. It followed a similar pathway: a commission, a series of resolutions, a report by the Secretary General defining the statute, Council approval. Its path was faster, marked out and smoothed by convergence on the same model for Yugoslavia just the year before, and by post-colonial sentiments, difficult to counter once raised, that such shocking slaughter in Africa merited as good a response as the much smaller crisis in Europe.

Post-colonialism only went so far, though: the thoroughly internationalist project of ICL had its own momentum. Some Yugoslav successor states had opposed a tribunal, but marginal as they were, they were ignored. By contrast, Resolution 955 notes that Rwanda requested a tribunal, though that is only half true: Rwanda, which at the time had a seat on the Security Council, had called for a tribunal, but by the time of the vote opposed it. Rwanda's new government objected to several things: the tribunal's limited temporal jurisdiction, which only covered 1994 (thus leaving out earlier massacres and preparations for the events of that year); its lack of complete autonomy from The Hague; the exclusion of capital punishment, which would result in the anomalous spectacle of low-level perpetrators being executed in Rwanda while the most senior leadership escaped the ultimate punishment; and the decision to locate the tribunal outside Rwanda. Thus, although heralded as an advance for international justice, the Rwandan tribunal was born in an atmosphere of tension and embarrassment, a premonition of the difficulties that would lie ahead.

The Rwandan genocide was palpably more terrible in important ways, even taking into account the notorious calculus of how much more suffering in Africa is needed to gain the world's attention: a death toll four to eight times greater than all the Yugoslav wars combined, in just four months, much of it done with machetes. But the Yugoslav crisis had come first, and so it had shaped the debates that the struggles over a judicial response to the later Rwandan crisis followed in large measure.

The tribunals' statutes were remarkably similar, because they were largely copied one from the other. The greater conceptual battles were fought over the ICTY; the following year, the decision to create the ICTR was an exercise in reciprocity, transcontinental equity and boiler-plating. After all, the ICTY was still not operational by the time the Rwandan tribunal was approved, so there was no practice to draw upon in refining the model – a two-fold exercise in abstraction and wishful thinking. The Rwanda tribunal received a statute fitted to another continent's conflict and crimes; but then, if one accepts the universalizing ideology of the ICL project, homogeneity is a virtue, its very uniformity expressing the immutable, non-negotiable principles of a single, shared vision of justice.

And the differences that made it in are instructive about the rapidly changing expectations and aspirations for the newly revived project of ICL. Thus, where the Council has asserted that the ICTY would 'contribute to the restoration and maintenance of peace',[6] for Rwanda, the Council affirmed an additional purpose: 'Convinced that in the particular circumstances of Rwanda, the prosecution of persons responsible. . . would contribute to the process of national reconciliation and to the restoration and maintenance of peace'.[7]

The wording is the same save for the added reference to national reconciliation. And few could doubt that, although the Yugoslav tribunal's statute didn't say so explicitly, it harboured similar ambitions. Yet their 'particular circumstances' could hardly have been more different: in Rwanda, a one-sided slaughter ended by the total victory of the rebel Rwandan Patriotic Front (RPF), led by ethnic Tutsis from the same group as the principal victims of the genocide; in Yugoslavia, a multi-sided conflict that was still ongoing but had already produced several sovereign states.[8] The two tribunals would have very different interlocutors, who cooperated with and contested the tribunal's work in very different ways.

---

6 SC Res 827, UN SCOR, 47th sess, 3217th mtg, UN Doc S/RES/827 (25 May 1993).

7 SC Res 955, UN SCOR, 48th sess, 3453rd mtg, UN Doc S/RES/955 (8 November 1994) (emphasis original).

8 The Rwandan crisis was also complex. Indeed, one defect of the ICTR was its inability to deal with the broader, regional aspects of the genocide, which was embedded in a series of interlocking conflicts across the Great Lakes region. See Mahmoud Mamdani, *When Victims Become Killers: Colonialism, Nativism and Genocide in Rwanda* (Princeton University Press, 2002). One-sided does not mean only the Hutu government and its supporters committed crimes: the RPF committed atrocities too, whose scale only looks small compared to the genocide.

But on many issues, even when there was controversy, the outlines laid down for the Yugoslav tribunal determined the path of the Rwandan. For example, the ICTY's exclusion of the death penalty – uncontroversial in the European context – was adopted for the ICTR as well, even though Rwanda strenuously opposed this and abolition was not the norm in Africa or required by international law.[9] But other states on the Council, such as New Zealand, were adamant that they would not support a court that included the death penalty. And the path had already been laid by the ICTY: this African court was marked in ways large and small by its European origins and a globalized justice project's sensibilities.

Being second – and African – also came with another price: a kind of subordination. The Rwandan tribunal was institutionally bound to its older sister in The Hague in order 'to ensure a unity of legal approach, as well as economy and efficiency of resources'.[10] A homogeneous vision of global justice was therefore advanced, not only intentionally, but as a matter of economy and convenience. In practice, that unity – a single prosecution service with a deputy in Arusha, and a common appellate instance in The Hague – tended to subordinate the interests of the ICTR.

But at least it was a separate court: the Commission of Experts had originally recommended simply amending the ICTY's statute to include Rwanda, a proposal rejected for fear it might 'gradually take on the characteristic of a permanent judicial institution'.[11] In December 1995, just over a year after its establishment on paper, a year and a half after the events that precipitated it, the ICTR issued its first indictment.

C Courts of the Council

Both tribunals were established by the Security Council under Chapter VII. This allowed for greater speed and flexibility in starting up – slow as the process was, it was far faster than a treaty would have been – and also ensured jurisdiction over the warring parties, who could not have been compelled to

---

9 A similar pathway appeared a few years later, when the ICTR's judges amended their rules of procedure concerning referral of cases. They adopted the same rule as the ICTY, including prohibition on referrals to countries with the death penalty, without any discussion, even though such a limitation looked radically different in Africa, where many countries retained the death penalty. (Confidential conversation with a judge of the ICTR.)

10 *Report of the Secretary General pursuant to paragraph 5 of SC Res 955 (1994)*, UN Doc S/1995/134 (13 February 1995) [9] <www.un.org/en/ga/search/view_doc.asp?symbol=S/1995/134>.

11 Payam Akhavan, 'The International Criminal Tribunal for Rwanda: The Politics and Pragmatics of Punishment' (1996) 90 *American Journal of International Law* 501, 502. The recommendation is appended to *Letter Dated 1 October 1994 from the Secretary-General Addressed to the President of the Security Council*, UN Doc S/1994/1125 (4 October 1994) [152].

sign a treaty. It also raised important questions about legitimacy, purpose and authority.

Was the creation of a court a proper exercise of the Security Council's powers to maintain international peace and security? In the *Tadić* interlocutory appeal, the chamber found that it was – one of the least surprising conclusions in the history of law – but its decision offered the intriguing possibility that the Council's actions might in theory be subject to judicial review.[12] It was not a possibility the tribunal ever seriously exercised.

The use of Chapter VII – for the maintenance of international peace and security – suggested a more directive purpose for these courts, concerned not only with abstract justice but with its concrete effects on war and peace. For some, this was to bring the tribunals into tension with the forensic imperatives of trial and the procedural norms of the criminal law; but for others, it was a welcome convergence of law's authority with the programmatic morality of human rights – a kind of empowered, purposive justice. Regardless of one's view, Chapter VII gave the tribunals considerable formal authority, obliging all UN member states to cooperate with them – creating, at a stroke, courts with global reach. In this, the statutes were an early example of the Security Council's turn to legislation, which only increased after 9-11.

III Pathways: jurisprudence, procedure, politics, immortality

Similar as they were, the two tribunals did have significant differences, with further changes over time – some of which might reflect correction or a rapid learning curve, but others obscure enough to suggest the Brownian motions of a metastasizing enterprise thrown together on the fly.

A *Jurisprudence: establishing facts and producing law*

At the beginning, the International Criminal Tribunals (ICTs) were compelled to look outside themselves for authority. When the field was established at Nuremberg, there was no real human rights movement; indeed, Nuremberg helped establish it. But by the time the tribunals were created, human rights were firmly established, and their principles and perspectives shaped ICL's revival – really, its refounding. The human rights world view has proved a troubling fit with the norms of the criminal law: in the domestic sphere, activists have long been concerned with defendants' rights, but in ICL, they remade themselves as advocates for

---

12 *Prosecutor v Tadić (Decision on the Defence Motion for Interlocutory Appeal on Jurisdiction)* (International Criminal Tribunal for the Former Yugoslavia, Appeals Chamber, Case No IT-94-1-AR72, 2 October 1995) [9]–[48].

victims' rights, and for justice, by means of trial and conviction. Human rights' teleological bent has contributed to institutions uncomfortably focused on purposes and effects outside of the courtroom – though for their advocates, this is precisely what gives the endeavour meaning.[13]

Over time, the tribunals began to rely less on national courts and international human rights bodies, and more on their own jurisprudence – an understandable turn, if also an inward one, relying on a reserve of legitimacy that may never have been as deep as was needed.

At the ICTY, *Tadić* figures as the *Ur*-case, the defining *milliarium* from which all other cases are measured, even in their departures. Its centrality is a function of timing – it was the tribunal's first full case – but otherwise it is a curious choice, a better exemplar for the muddling, haphazard pathways of ICL. Dušan Tadić was no one in particular, a camp official of shocking cruelty but limited consequence, whose principal qualification for trial was his availability, having gotten himself arrested in Germany, from where the ICTY arranged to transfer the case. Tadić's trial and appellate judgments, and the interlocutory appeal challenging the tribunal's jurisdiction, established patterns for both tribunals. Almost all cases at the ICTY point back to *Tadić* in significant ways. The *Krstić* judgment, for example – about a senior general at Srebrenica – largely forwent a history section, citing *Tadić's* extensive primer.[14]

At the ICTR, *Akayesu* played a similar role: procedurally less decisive, the case's significance lay more in its definitions of substantive law.[15] Jean-Paul Akayesu, mayor of a town in Rwanda, was a tragic figure who at first resisted the slaughter but then went over to the genocidal camp. His case brought the first conviction for genocide, in 1998, as well as significant expansions in the definition of sexual violence, which subsequent cases limited or refined but took their bearings from.[16]

The law applied: The tribunals were only supposed to apply existing law. In theory, the drafters of the statutes had adopted a conservative standard, only including definitions drawn from widely recognized conventions that were also unquestionably customary law binding on all states – the Genocide Convention, parts of the Geneva and Hague Conventions. But this conservative

---

13 See Darryl Robinson, 'The Two Liberalisms of International Criminal Law' in Carsten Stahn and Larissa van den Herik (eds), *Future Perspectives on International Criminal Justice* (T.M.C. Asser, 2010) 115.

14 *Prosecutor v Krstić (Judgement)* (International Criminal Tribunal for the Former Yugoslavia, Trial Chamber, Case No IT-98-33-T, 2 August 2001) [6] (referring, at n 4, to a 53-paragraph section of the *Tadić* judgment).

15 *Prosecutor v Akayesu (Judgement)* (International Criminal Tribunal for Rwanda, Trial Chamber I, Case No ICTR-96-4-T, 2 September 1998).

16 See Catharine A MacKinnon, 'The ICTR's Legacy on Sexual Violence' (2008) 14 *New England Journal of International and Comparative Law* 101.

approach was in tension with the very purpose of the tribunals, informed by the logic of human rights, to bring justice to and transform torn societies, and with the need to respond to the novel forms of violence these conflicts had produced. These were, by their nature, progressive institutions, and, without ever quite admitting to it, their jurisprudence came to reflect that.

The ICTY statute required a nexus to armed conflict for crimes against humanity. The ICTR did not, and thus was spared considerable expenditure of time, effort and jurisprudential arabesques proving an element not strictly required by the state of the law. Similarly, the ICTY did not expressly incorporate common Article 3 of the Geneva Conventions, governing internal conflicts. The ICTR – sitting in judgment of an internal conflict – did. But already in *Tadić*, most of the internal provisions of Geneva were incorporated at the ICTY too, under the logic that they reflected the laws and customs of war.

On the other hand, the ICTR mysteriously required a discriminatory element for *all* crimes against humanity, which the ICTY had not; the addition of this more restrictive element – not required by the state of the law[17] – created make-work in Arusha. In neither place was this particularly hard to prove, of course – in Rwanda, the idea that there might be discrimination accompanying crimes against humanity that were also genocidal could have gone without saying, if this had not been a court. The attention lavished on these distinctions simply reminds us how much of a lawyers' paradise the whole enterprise has become.

Indeed, one of the strongest impressions one gets from the broad arc of the tribunals' jurisprudence is just how plastic the categories have proven and, in this, how valid the concerns of those parties who sought to limit the new ICC's ability to innovate were, as well as how fruitless those efforts are likely to prove. Statutory differences do not necessarily hold up a homogenizing project of global justice.

Sexual violence: The treatment of sexual violence highlights the discipline's progressive, legislative, programmatic instincts. Both tribunals – and the Special Court for Sierra Leone – undertook to systematically expand the jurisprudence, ensuring that sexual violence would be expressly criminalized as war crimes, crimes against humanity and genocide, and would feature prominently in indictments. For example, the *Foča* trial, beginning in 2000, against several Serbs for acts against Bosnian Muslim women, focused on charges of a sexual nature, including enslavement as a crime

17 The language of the Article on crimes against humanity in the Arusha statute at certain points is almost technically incomprehensible if read literally, since its chapeau requires discrimination for all underlying crimes but also separately as an element of persecution – a nonsensical redundancy. SC Res 955, UN SCOR, 49th sess, 3453rd mtg, UN Doc S/RES/955 (8 November 1994) annex (*'Statute of the International Tribunal for Rwanda'*) Art. 3.

against humanity, while in *Akayesu*, the ICTR identified rape as a means of perpetrating genocide.[18]

In part, this focus reflected the gruesome course of the conflicts, in which rape played a significant role as tactic and weapon. In part too it reflected the broader coalition of interests for whom these were not tribunals ad hoc for these conflicts alone, but instruments of a global movement expressing and advancing its values. Women were often marginalized victims in the Yugoslav and Rwandan conflicts; but in that curious way, in these latter days, that victimhood can confer power, the international advocates of those dead and defiled women deployed that marginal status to steer these institutions and define their jurisprudence.

Genocide: If there is a conservative counterpoint to the progressive jurisprudence on sexual violence, it is the treatment of the supreme crime. Genocide prosecutions at Arusha, including *Akayesu*, the *Media* trial, *Kambanda* and *Karemera*, produced a robust jurisprudence, comprehensive and authoritative enough that after 2006, the tribunal took judicial notice of the genocide as an indisputable fact – a move of considerable economy as well as good sense.[19] And for this same reason, in some respects the Rwandan cases were less 'interesting' for defining genocide; the slaughter so over-performed the requirements of the category that there was little question, and therefore less learned.

It was otherwise in The Hague, where many prosecutions have failed, and – unless something extraordinary happens in the last cases – the jurisprudence will settle on a theory of 'the little genocide': only Srebrenica, but nowhere else in Bosnia, and any link to the Belgrade leadership severed. In one case, the defendant, Goran Jelisić – who styled himself 'the Serbian Adolf' – pled guilty to numerous counts of crimes against humanity and war crimes, but contested the genocide charge. That charge was thrown out at the midpoint; on appeal, the chamber said this had been done in error, but declined to order a retrial.[20] More than any other case, *Jelisić* marks the line between what is genocide and what is not – at least for securing a conviction; it certainly shows up the real challenges of prosecuting genocide, and that is not something everyone would have predicted before these tribunals began their work.

---

18 *Prosecutor v Kunarac et al* (*"Foča"*) (International Criminal Tribunal for the former Yugoslavia, Case No IT-96-23-T & IT-96-23/1-T); *Prosecutor v Akayesu* (*Judgement*) (International Criminal Tribunal for Rwanda, Trial Chamber I, Case No ICTR-96-4-T, 2 September 1998) [731]–[734].

19 *Prosecutor v Nahimana et al* (*Judgement and Sentence*) (International Criminal Tribunal for Rwanda, Trial Chamber I, Case No ICTR-99-52, 3 December 2003) ("Media Case"); *Prosecutor v Kambanda* (International Criminal Tribunal for Rwanda, Case No ICTR-97-23); *Prosecutor v Karemera et al* (International Criminal Tribunal for Rwanda, Case No ICTR-98-44).

20 *Prosecutor v Jelisić* (*Judgement*) (International Criminal Tribunal for the Former Yugoslavia, Appeals Chamber, Case No IT-95-10-A, 5 July 2001) [II. 53-77], [IV. 4].

B *Procedure and purpose*

One of the greatest challenges facing the tribunals was creating their institutions and procedures out of whole cloth, often no cloth at all. There had been no comparable court in half a century, and in the absence of actual trials, the procedural and institutional aspects of the discipline were chimerical. So, did these new institutions create their own intentional pathways, or did they react to events in an improvisational, even muddled way?

The tribunals adopted a hybrid procedure, mixing elements from civil and common law. The initial influence of the adversarial model was clear – a strong American hand. Over time, the rules of procedure were frequently modified, becoming more inflected with civil law sensibilities, although this was hardly uniform – early on the tribunals did not allow plea bargaining, but later moved towards it – and adopted innovations not derived from either model, such that we could speak of an entirely new, international procedure. That new model could be haphazard: the editors of one book discussing the ICTY's legacy describe the procedural 'favela' that arose around self-represented defendants, one of the most challenging areas in these highly public and publicized trials.[21]

The admixture produced obvious dysfunctions. For example, ICTY Rule 98*bis* provides for what is known in the common law as 'no case to answer', requiring the judge to throw charges out after the prosecution's case if no reasonable trier of fact could convict.[22] This is a provision designed to protect defendants against ill-informed juries, but it works entirely differently – one could say, not at all – when the trier of fact is the judge himself. The tribunals have no juries, so judges try both facts and the law: Rule 98*bis* therefore asks the judges to protect a defendant against themselves. A judge who is personally convinced that there are insufficient grounds for conviction would nonetheless compel himself to continue a case if some other notional judge might convict, perhaps adding years to a trial whose outcome is already clear. This interpretation of the rule is a nonsense that arose solely due to the mashup of two magisterially distinct legal systems.

But these were the teething pains of institutions inventing themselves on the fly. Indeed, it is one of the set-piece questions about these tribunals, and ICL: are these problems of immaturity, or are they endemic diseases of the discipline? The optimist and activist will point to signs of change, course correction, institutional entrenchment and expansion, and conclude that this is a dynamic process. The skeptic will see path-dependency, logics of weakness

21 Bert Swart, Alexander Zahar and Göran Sluiter (eds), *The Legacy of the International Criminal Tribunal for the Former Yugoslavia* (Oxford University Press, 2011) 1.
22 This was the basis for throwing out the genocide charge in the *Jelisić* trial: *Prosecutor v Jelisić (Judgement)* (International Criminal Tribunal for the Former Yugoslavia, Trial Chamber, Case No IT-95-10-T, 14 December 1999) [16], [99]–[108], [138].

and accommodation, marks of ad hockery even at the permanent ICC, and conclude that this is what we are likely to have.

C Politics – cooperation, competition, cooptation

Part of the muddle was not of the tribunals' own making – indeed, it could hardly have been otherwise, since they were born into a world of politics. The ICTs' early years were precarious, with insufficient funding and, for the ICTY, the threat that the institution might be bargained away in a Balkan peace deal. But from 1997 or so, its trajectory improved, its budget and staff expanded; the North Atlantic Treaty Organization (NATO), with substantial forces in Bosnia, began actively working to arrest indictees rather than ignoring them as they drove through checkpoints. Cooperation with Croatia and Serbia was fraught and seriously hampered the prosecution's work, but the occasional threat of Security Council intervention and, later, the more consistent pressure of conditionality – the willingness of the European Union to calibrate accession to cooperation with the tribunal – ensured a more pliant relationship.

By contrast, the ICTR, though it also had tremendous difficulties starting up, entered its greatest period of crisis around 2000. When it appeared the prosecution, responding to criticism that it was focused only on Hutus, began seriously investigating RPF crimes, Rwanda suspended most cooperation. This brought investigations and trials to an effective halt, and demonstrated the intense degree to which the tribunal was dependent on a single state – as well as showing that the formal obligation to cooperate was meaningless unless the Security Council enforced it. The crisis was resolved in Rwanda's favour: the prosecution was split, with a separate, autonomous prosecutor now sitting in Arusha. Only the appellate instance remained unified, still in The Hague. And there never was any indictment touching the RPF. Crisis was averted through capitulation, a convergence between the project of ICL and the policy of Rwandan elites to replace the ethnic dichotomy of Hutu and Tutsi with an official narrative of perpetrators and victims.[23] In time, the prosecution and the Rwandan state became close collaborators.

Bias. Accusations of bias were an endemic part of the tribunals' jurisprudence and the context in which they operated. Rwanda successfully mobilized the enormous reserves of guilt surrounding the events of 1994 to ensure that the ICTR was only deployed against its enemies. The ICTR was criticized for never indicting any RPF actors, but the ICTY was criticized both for bias

---

23 See Victor A Peskin, *International Justice in Rwanda and the Balkans: Virtual Trials and the Struggle for State Cooperation* (Cambridge University Press, 2008) 170.

against Serbs and for indicting actors from all the warring parties. Two-thirds of the ICTY's indictees were Serbs, a fact that either reflected Serbophobia or the distribution of criminality in wars in which Serbs were long the dominant actors. Whichever the truth – whatever the subjective mindset of the prosecution – many Serbs came to believe the claim of bias. Interestingly, other groups were inclined to see the tribunal as biased against them too, focusing not on the gross numbers but specific cases injurious to their own cause and worldview: Bosnian Muslims incensed by the prosecution of Nasser Orić, defender of Srebrenica; Kosovar Albanians aggrieved by prosecution of leading members of the Kosovo Liberation Army; Croats offended by cases against Generals Blaškić and Gotovina, heroes of the Homeland War.

And the accusations of bias were not merely about ethnic animus, but servitude to the great powers of the earth. Unlike the ICTR, the ICTY had an open-ended temporal jurisdiction, beginning in 1991 and only ending when the Security Council terminated it. Thus, when, after several years of peace, the Kosovo conflict broke out, there was little question that the ICTY had jurisdiction. That war resulted in the first indictment of a sitting head of state, Slobodan Milošević, and extensive prosecutions of the Belgrade leadership, but also a curiously public, 50-page 'inquiry' explaining why the prosecution would not be investigating any incident in NATO's air war against Serbia. More than any outsiders' accusations of cooptation, this document, in the prosecution's own hand, makes a strong case that direct control of the tribunal was unnecessary, because it had so thoroughly absorbed a worldview consistent with that of its principal supporters.[24]

But the accusations of bias were only that – claims, not truth – and therefore more telling, surely, about the problem of perception and the politics of the enterprise: the futility of imagining that such an institution would rise above, or escape, its context, even as it was trying to affect that context as an agent of reconciliation. The real bias was the hubris of the founders, who seemed wilfully to forget that there is no pleasing everyone, and sometimes no pleasing anyone, and that while it's hard to get people to agree on the truth, most people can agree that they don't like to be told what the truth is by a bunch of outsiders. The depressing lesson is that while there may be neutral, professional standards for investigation and indictment, there are none for the politics surrounding that process. The tribunals did not ever operate effectively as courts outside of politics, but we have yet to find a model of politically engaged courts with which we are comfortable, or which their undisciplined subjects will submit to as we think they should.

---

24 See Timothy William Waters, 'Unexploded Bomb: Voice, Silence, and Consequence at the Hague Tribunals: A Legal and Rhetorical Critique' (2003) 35 *New York University Journal of International Law and Politics* 1015.

D *Death and immortality: closing down and continuing*

As ad hoc institutions, the tribunals were never supposed to become permanent – indeed, fears of permanent entrenchment were part of the opposition to their creation, and considering how long they survived, it was not an unreasonable concern. The tribunals had barely begun to function effectively when the first calls came for them to begin shutting down.

In late 2003, the Security Council instructed the tribunals to begin reporting on their completion strategies, which originally called for the courts to complete trials by 2008 and appeals by 2010.[25] The ICTY issued its final indictments in 2004 – a total of 161 persons; the ICTR indicted 93 persons. All ICTY indictees have been accounted for – arrested, convicted, acquitted, charges dropped or died. There are still eight fugitives from ICTR indictments.

Investigations were completed on schedule, but the other goals, finishing trials and appeals by 2010, were not met – in the case of the ICTY, '[d]ue to the late arrest of the remaining fugitives. . . and the sheer complexity of certain cases, initial estimates had to be revised to ensure the highest standards of procedural fairness'.[26] Indeed, more than seven years late, those trials continue at the ICTY, while the ICTR has transferred its docket to the new Mechanism or to Rwanda (see below). Judges regularly denied that the completion strategy in any way influenced their decisions, and observers regularly speculated that it did. The late reversals in important cases – the acquittals on appeal of Generals Gotovina and Perišić, which cut back on expanded doctrines of liability for military commanders – were seen as blows to the accomplishments of the ICTY and the entrenchment of a robust ICL. Even its supporters were hard pressed to defend an optimistic interpretation of those late acquittals, which simply raises the even more difficult question: what kind of court's legacy is dependent on conviction?

The very existence of a completion strategy demonstrates one of the principal differences between the ad hocs and the permanent ICC. At the same time, the pressures and the politics that drove completion – the desire to control costs and to constrain judicial expansion – are not factors that disappear with the declaration of permanence. The tribunals' experience will prove instructive to the ICC, because when there is no termination date, there may instead be a kind of permanent pressure. And, as we shall shortly see, the tribunals are not truly gone.

25 SC Res 1503, 57th sess, 4817th mtg, UN Doc S/RES/1503 (28 August 2003). See also SC Res 1534, 58th sess, 4935th mtg, UN Doc S/RES/1534 (26 March 2004), clarifying the completion process; ICTY, *Completion Strategy* <www.icty.org/sid/10016>, and MICT, *Completion Strategy Reports* <http://unictr.unmict.org/en/documents/completion-strategy-reports>.

26 Ibid (emphasis removed), noting also that 'developments related to the health of detainees can sometimes cause delays to the Tribunal's work'.

Referrals: Neither tribunal was able to try more than a fraction of the participants in the conflicts they adjudicated. It was always going to be necessary to make choices, and to find other mechanisms for processing lower- and middle-ranking participants. In Rwanda, this was a combination of national trials and the *gacaca* courts; in the successor states of the former Yugoslavia, a clunky system for the ICTY to vet local prosecutions, known as the Rules of the Road,[27] and the slow establishment of specialized chambers. In addition, third states have tried cases from these conflicts, sometimes on their own initiative, sometimes referred from the tribunals.

Both tribunals have primary and concurrent jurisdiction: states can hold their own trials, but must defer to the tribunal if it requires. So, when Colonel Théoneste Bagosora was arrested in Cameroon in 1996, and both Belgium and Rwanda sought his extradition, the ICTR was able to require his transfer to Arusha; this was also the mechanism by which the ICTY acquired Tadić from a cooperative Germany. In the early years, this power was used to bring cases to the tribunals, but with the increased focus on closing down, it equally allowed their redistribution back to states. The ICTY transferred cases against 13 individuals back to courts in the former Yugoslavia. Most of these were lower-level accused, early indictments which notionally should have helped build cases against higher-ranking accused but ultimately were orphaned.

The first case the ICTR tried to refer was *Bagaragaza*,[28] and it proved instructive about the values, and the blind spots, of the broader project. Rwanda opposed the referral, arguing that it was the appropriate forum for trying Michel Bagaragaza, but at the time Rwanda retained the death penalty and did not meet the procedural standards for fair trial the tribunal required. The prosecution had another interest: Bagaragaza had struck a deal with the prosecution to testify in other cases in exchange for his case being transferred to a jurisdiction outside of Africa – as well as generous provisions for relocation of his family, plastic surgery and other benefits. But attempts to refer the case to Norway and the Netherlands failed, and eventually Bagaragaza was returned to Arusha, where he pled guilty to complicity in genocide and served a short sentence in Sweden. By that time Rwanda had abolished the death penalty, and the tribunal began assisting Rwanda in procedural reforms and supported referrals there.

The Mechanism: The tribunals have lasted far longer than was originally anticipated – a testimony both to human beings' inability to predict the consequences of their own actions and their capacity to sustain institutions and

---

27 *Rome Implementation Agreement* (18 February 1996) Art. 5 (Cooperation on War Crimes and Respect for Human Rights), in (The Implementation Force) IFOR, *Agreed Measures* <www.nato.int/ifor/general/d960218b.htm>.

28 *Prosecutor v Bagaragaza* (International Criminal Tribunal for Rwanda, Case No ICTR-065-86).

bureaucracies. (I myself once explained the bloated nature of the institutions by predicting that the *Karadžić* trial might last 'probably more than two years from start to finish'.[29] While technically true, this fell rather short of the nearly eight it actually took, not counting appeal.) The seemingly endless life of these institutions has created its own set of issues that have to be addressed. Institutions may live forever, but men do not, and the tribunals have seen a surprising number of defendants perish before judgment – including, at the ICTY, Goran Hadžić, one of those indictees whose late arrest justified the tribunal's delayed closing.

But even with their longevity, the tribunals have run their course before exhausting their dockets, and have therefore given birth to a successor: the Mechanism for International Criminal Tribunals or MICT. From 2013, MICT began progressively taking over responsibilities, such as supervising sentences and maintaining archives. The MICT is responsible for remaining appeals and retrials as well as trials for three ICTR fugitives if they are captured. It also has responsibility for ancillary cases, such as contempt trials, which in the latter days of the tribunals came to be their own cottage industry – a powerful indication both of the institutions' entrenchment and their inward orientation.

With branches in The Hague and Arusha, it is not entirely clear why the MICT is not simply a streamlined continuation of the tribunals. And even that reduced form is contingent: the Mechanism will experience the same pressures and incentives to ramp up again if the few outstanding trials do materialize: After all, what would justify providing lower levels of process, protection and service for a late arriving defendant, not to mention for the interests of international justice?

The very fact that the MICT exists, nearly a quarter century after the ICTs were created, suggests their closing is merely the opening of another chapter – a continuing future for two courts trying the events of an increasingly distant past. Soon I will be teaching my seminar on the Yugoslav crisis to students not even born when the last victims died – that's already true for Rwanda – but the tribunals, in some form, will still be there.

IV Legacies

A *The casual attraction of causality*

When we speak of the tribunals' legacy, it is tempting to imagine we know what it is. Peace has been maintained in Yugoslavia since 2001, and in Rwanda since 1994 – is that owing to the tribunals? One can certainly find people saying so, but how would we know? Surely the repressive and controlling

---

29 'Karadzic on Trial', *New York Times* (New York), 24 July 2008.

government under President Paul Kagame has something to do with it too, as do Rwanda's measures to push the conflict into eastern Congo; in the Balkans, the involvement of outside forces – and the simple fact that the territory has been politically divided – surely had much to do with it. It is entirely possible that the tribunals have not contributed to peace at all; again, how would we know?

In thinking about causality, the inevitable foil is Germany and Nuremberg. Germans' initial resistance to the trials gave way to acceptance, and now the Nuremberg legacy forms one of the moral foundations of the German state and society's humane policies. But what is the true relationship? Did Nuremberg cause this shift, or did the shift happen, and then seek out its own origin myth? One thing we can say for sure: the Nuremberg effect, if it happened, began some 20 years after the trials ended. If that is our benchmark, we should be looking at Yugoslavia and Rwanda today, with an eye on the clock.

So we should be careful. But we can nonetheless say some things about the tribunals' legacy.

B *An inward, international gaze*

If anything, the likeliest truth is that the tribunals have been feckless. Here we can return to those websites, and notice how little they really say about transformation in attitudes, provable claims of creating peaceful conditions, or reconciliation. So much of their legacy is inward-gazing, inside the discipline: institutions, precedents, building ICL – things that only matter if they in turn contribute to something else, unless one simply likes the idea of international law for its own sake.

And even that story depends on how one tells it. The ICTY website includes a timeline. A late entry notes that Stanišić and Simatović, prominent Serb operatives in Bosnia who had been acquitted, will be retried by the MICT. But the highly controversial acquittals on appeal of prominent indictees like Perišić and Gotovina are nowhere to be found. Similarly, one entry entitled 'First genocide conviction' notes the judgment in 2001 against General Radislav Krstić for crimes at Srebrenica, and then artfully mentions that the 'Appeals Chamber will unanimously find that "genocide was committed in Srebrenica" and will find Krstić guilty of "aiding and abetting genocide"'.[30] True, though anyone familiar with the whole sequence understands that this was a step down from the earlier conviction for perpetration – a defeat for the prosecution. None of that appears here. And indeed, not a single entry in the timeline focuses on acquittal, of which there were several, or dropped

---

30 ICTY, *ICTY Timeline* <www.icty.org/en/in-focus/timeline>, entry 'August 2, 2001: First genocide conviction'.

charges, or anything of the kind. The single discordant entry is 'Termination of proceedings against Slobodan Milošević', following his death from natural causes – an unavoidable medical event.

The timeline is a catalogue of triumphant institutional moments: indictments, trials commenced, convictions. But triumphs with a particular inflection: The idea that acquittal might also be a victory is not available. It is a hagiographic document, an act of interpretation and omission that produces the appearance of a progress narrative, a march towards justice defined as a project of conviction, and the entrenchment of an institution. That such a text was produced by the neutral registry simply demonstrates the deep institutional orientation towards the project of international justice for its own sake.[31]

And so with the broader field: too much study of the tribunals' legacy is focused on the tribunals themselves – on the fact of them and their institutional accomplishments. We have undeniably built two courts, assembled vast archives, developed rules and procedures, held trials in which points of law were discovered and clarified. All true. And to what effect? Too often, this question is left unanswered in the fascinated gaze at the things we have built, rather than the shattered places and wounded people they were built for.

So much of the tribunals' legacies is measured against the perspectives, interests and attention of an abstract international community, whose most concise identity is Not-There: not Rwanda, not the former Yugoslavia. When the Rwandan prosecution proposed its first referral to Norway, despite the objections of Rwanda that it was the natural judge and the home of the victims, one of its arguments was the importance of educating Norwegians about the Rwandan genocide. The advocates of ICL have embraced their own creed: that these are crimes against humanity, against all of us, sometimes even to the point of prioritizing 'all of us' over the actual victims.

C No reconciliation

In part this inward and international attention has arisen because of the awkward fact that there is less to see in the target states than one might have wished. The fantasy that courts were going to produce national reconciliation has been discredited – at least, it is less often argued that reconciliation has happened in the places these tribunals have sought to heal. 'And what of healing and national reconciliation? Alas, that is not a job that can be undertaken by an international court or tribunal—for healing and national reconciliation cannot come into being with the stroke of a pen'.[32]

---

31 The ICTR timeline tells the same story: heavy on institutional accomplishments, arrests and convictions; no mention of acquittal or failure. MICT, above n 4.
32 Leila Nadya Sadat, 'The Legacy of the International Criminal Tribunal for Rwanda' (Paper presented at Whitney R. Harris World Law Institute Occasional Papers, Washington

The tribunals still claim reconciliation as a goal and accomplishment, but in more muted tones, defeated by the lack of evidence that anything like it has happened. Despite confident claims that '[c]rimes across the region can no longer be denied',[33] crimes *are* denied across the region – particularly in the region. There is ample polling evidence from the former Yugoslavia that knowledge and acceptance of crimes track closely with ethnicity. And in Rwanda the shift from ethnic identity to an official culture of victims and perpetrators is a rather uglier and more coercive process than might first appear.

Attention towards the actual post-conflict communities is often mediated through outreach programmes – themselves a somewhat belated effort, with the ICTY only establishing its in 1999 – 'dedicated to making the work of the Tribunal more accessible and understandable to the communities of the former Yugoslavia'.[34] With such a goal – and limited opportunities for people actually to affect the workings of an autonomous, professional court – it is unsurprising that analysis and policy recommendations often revolve around messaging and perception, rather than the substance of the tribunals' work.

The reason is not hard to find. It was always a dubious proposition that a foreign court – for international or not, the tribunals are foreign to the societies they sit in judgment over – was going to have the legitimacy and capacity to speak with real authority. Or more, that any court could: even domestic courts operating in stable societies are rarely tasked with such an ambitious goal, but the tribunals, by design, sat in judgment over societies that had ceased to have a common matrix of identity and values. In such a context, how could judgment ever be anything other than a deracinated forensic exercise, or an impossibly politicized one? Instead, the tribunals' judgments became ideological weapons, deployed by each side to prove its point, accepted when consistent, repudiated when not: a proxy for the conflict itself. '[T]ribunal truth is ultimately less important for reconciliation than the everyday events and developments taking place within individual communities', leading to the 'the problem of *rejected truth*'.[35]

But the nails will not stay in the coffin. The abstract logic that lasting peace requires justice – meaning the criminal law – is an attractive claim, though not necessarily a true one. Indeed, claims about reconciliation simply reconfirm the weirdly myopic, abstract, inward-outward-anywhere-but-there focus of ICL, whose audience is often the very communities most convinced of

University School of Law, 3 July 2012) <https://law.wustl.edu/harris/documents/ICTRLecture-LegacyAd%20HocTribunals9.12.12.pdf>.

33 ICTY, *About the ICTY* <www.icty.org/en/about>.

34 ICTY, *ICTY Timeline* <www.icty.org/en/in-focus/timeline>.

35 Janine Natalya Clark, 'The Impact Question: The ICTY and the Restoration and Maintenance of Peace' in Bert Swart, Alexander Zahar and Göran Sluiter (eds), *The Legacy of the International Criminal Tribunal for the Former Yugoslavia* (Oxford University Press, 2011) 73 (emphasis in original).

the rightness of the institutional cause, rather than those being adjudicated. But like many abstractions, it has a special power, impervious to testing and falsifiability – and the less one knows of a place, the easier it is to maintain. It is an almost structural part of the discourse of ICL that it must promise more. For who will fund the next great project, if it is presented with sufficient modesty to be accurate?

D *Effects on the ICC and ICL*

One effect we can see: ICL is now the default norm, the assumption about what we should and will do after great violence. Twenty-five years ago, there were no international courts; now there are several, and every new conflict – Syria, ISIS[36] – brings almost reflexive calls for trial, whether at the ICC, new hybrid courts or domestic courts applying international principles.

So the principal legacy of the ICTs is ICL itself, both its institutions and the project as a part of international politics. It is almost certainly true that the ICTs made the ICC a real possibility, and with it a number of other courts – for Sierra Leone, Cambodia, East Timor, Lebanon. Some of these might have come into existence anyway – after all, the moment that created the ICTs could have been realized somewhere else, and if it is true that they are all part of a great enthusiastic expansion after the Cold War, then it is likely they would have appeared in some form, like a discovery in physics made in several places at once. But the tribunals' particular experiences shaped the pathways these other courts followed. Sometimes this was literal and mechanical, as when the Special Court for Sierra Leone (SCSL) statute expressly required it to follow the procedure, sentencing practice and appellate decisions of the ICTR, or when new courts copy the innovations of the tribunals. But surely it happened at deeper, conceptual levels as well – what we see as possible, what necessary.

And in smaller but more concrete ways, the tribunals have been the expression and enabler of that great driver of human politics: people with projects. The tribunals have been a training ground. When the tribunals began, there were almost no people with direct experience in ICL, and those with experience had it almost exclusively in national jurisdictions. Now, there are thousands of individuals working in ministries, universities, NGOs and courts whose view of the field and the world is shaped by their experience at the tribunals.

Many are intensely, reflexively committed to a justice project that is expressly criminal and legal in orientation, even as there is a counterchord – found in the broader transitional justice movement – from observers critical of ICL's hegemony, of how it drives out the diverse responses to conflict we might deploy. But that dominance, for good or ill, is real: ICL is the default,

---

36 Islamic State of Iraq and the Levant, or Daesh.

the response to conflict and violence that we deploy or explain away, but no longer ignore. And that shift, if not the literal legacy of the ICTs, has come about through the experience of these two courts and their conflicts – their particular circumstances.

That particular, intense focus should make us ask how likely we are to repeat a thing like it. The conflicts the ad hocs adjudicated were not uniquely large or grotesque – certainly nothing like the violence that birthed Nuremberg. The Rwandan genocide was a singular horror, but hardly the only great slaughter on that continent; and its entire course ran in one small country in a few months. The Yugoslav conflicts were just one set of nasty civil wars – UN Secretary General Boutros-Ghali notoriously told the residents of Sarajevo that he could name ten conflicts worse than theirs, and while it was a bit callous to point that out, he wasn't necessarily wrong. Indeed, if not for the tribunals, we would think much less about these two conflicts today – and that is both a testament to their legacy and a reminder that they have drawn our attention away from other things. So we should ask ourselves where our gaze is likely to linger, in the world they leave behind.

The tribunals were expensive. The ICTR indicted 93 persons, convicted 61 of them, with 14 acquittals. At a cost of roughly two billion dollars, it was enormously expensive compared to domestic jurisdictions or the *gacaca* system in Rwanda, which processed over one million people at a fraction of the price, albeit under much more relaxed procedural standards. Even the more efficient ICTY was a costly undertaking.[37]

But even if we think they have been worth it in material terms, the ICTs' level of investment and coverage will not easily be sustained. With a whole world's crises to adjudicate (at least that portion over which it has jurisdiction), the ICC cannot possibly try as many cases or go into as much depth – however defectively – as the tribunals did. It will inevitably be limited to a tiny number of cases for any situation. And so far, this is how things have gone: one or two cases, and on to the next crisis in Africa.

Of course, a few cases might be enough. If the true audience for ICL is the international community, not the target society, then a small number of trials might be the right number. After all, who really can keep track of all those Rwandan genocidaires or Yugoslav killers? A single trial might do to educate the world – and, more cynically, if it's true that the many trials at the ICTY and ICTR have not created reconciliation, why over-invest?

Paradoxically, all this suggests the ICTs may have a larger legacy than at first might appear. Despite having a permanent court, we are likely to find

---

37 But see Stuart Ford, 'Complexity and Efficiency at International Criminal Courts' (2014) 29 *Emory International Law Review* 1, arguing that the ICTY's trials are roughly as efficient as US murder trials when one accounts for the complex work they involve – overseas investigations, translations, and the like.

more occasions for ad hockery – for regional courts, single-conflict courts. The institutional constraints and the politics that make states favour one-off solutions and disfavour a permanent, plenary court did not end when the Rome Statute was signed or when the ICTs closed. Things will continue, projects will proliferate: it will be called a glorious florescence of plural models of justice, or a ghastly, complicated, dysfunctional mess. It will be called both.

Oh, and there is one more reason their legacy is likely to be larger, longer and more ambiguous: the things they sat in judgment of will continue too. The tribunals, their trials and the broadening network of courts that have followed them have not deterred our nature, nor made us better. So whether they in fact achieve anything, we will feel the same need for what they do, well or badly, because of what we are.

Further reading

Cruvelier, Thierry, *Court of Remorse: Inside the International Criminal Tribunal for Rwanda* (University of Wisconsin Press, 2010).

Elias-Bursać, Ellen, *Translating Evidence and Interpreting Testimony at a War Crimes Tribunal: Working in a Tug-of-War* (Palgrave Macmillan, 2015).

ICTY, *Publications* <www.icty.org/en/documents/publications>.

Mettraux, Guénaël, *International Crimes and the* ad hoc *Tribunals* (Oxford University Press, 2005).

Organization for Security and Cooperation in Europe, *Supporting the Transition Process: Lessons Learned and Best Practices in Knowledge Transfer: Final Report* (Warsaw, The Hague, Turin: OSCE-ODIHR, 2009).

Peskin, Victor A, *International Justice in Rwanda and the Balkans: Virtual Trials and the Struggle for State Cooperation* (Cambridge University Press, 2008).

Steinberg, Richard H (ed), *Assessing the Legacy of the ICTY* (Brill, 2011).

Swart, Bert, Alexander Zahar and Göran Sluiter (eds), *The Legacy of the International Criminal Tribunal for the Former Yugoslavia* (Oxford University Press, 2011).

United Nations, *ICTR Special Bibliography: 2015* (United Nations, 2016).

11

HYBRID TRIBUNALS

Institutional experiments and the potential for creativity within international criminal law

Philipp Kastner

I Introduction

The hybrid criminal tribunals, sometimes also called internationalised or mixed tribunals, discussed in this chapter present themselves as unusual institutional experiments that take different forms. They combine aspects of international criminal tribunals, like the *ad hoc* tribunals (discussed in the previous chapter), with domestic institutions administering international criminal law (to be discussed in chapter 13). Most of them have their seat in the state where the crimes in question were committed, but they are typically staffed by both international and national judges, prosecutors and other personnel. Moreover, they often apply a mix of international and national criminal law.

It was hoped that these tribunals, which have been established *inter alia* in Sierra Leone, Cambodia, Kosovo, Timor Leste, Bosnia and Herzegovina and Lebanon from the early 2000s onwards, would deliver international criminal justice more effectively, and with a smaller price tag, than the *ad hoc* tribunals. These hybrid tribunals were also supposed to be inherently more legitimate and to facilitate national capacity-building and the penetration of international norms.[1] However, as the practice of these tribunals has shown, the imperative to punish only certain high-level offenders both as swiftly and inexpensively as possible has meant that the hybrid tribunals have not lived up to their promises and have not been able to contribute

---

1 For a critique of such expectations, see Pádraig McAuliffe, 'Hybrid Tribunals at Ten: How International Criminal Justice's Golden Child Became an Orphan' (2011) 7 *Journal of International Law and International Relations* 1.

significantly to such broader objectives as capacity-building, reconciliation and peace-building.[2]

This chapter considers some of the lessons learnt from the hybrid tribunals that have already been established, but it argues that we should try to resist the common impulse to draw any final conclusions on these experiments. Instead, the hybrid tribunals should be considered as an ongoing manifestation of the potential for institutional creativity within international criminal law (ICL). Hybrid tribunals also allow us to consider in a particular light a number of conceptual issues related to ICL, such as the multifaceted relationship between international and national criminal law and the legitimacy of the respective institutions. In fact, although the hybrid tribunals, as institutional experiments, were supposed to combine the best aspects of the international and national spheres, they have perhaps unveiled even more complexities in the field of ICL than they managed to circumvent.

II An uncompleted institutional experiment

It became clear in the 1990s – at the height of the accountability bubble spearheaded by the international criminal tribunals for the former Yugoslavia (ICTY) and Rwanda (ICTR) – that purely international *ad hoc* institutions have important shortcomings. And although international crimes can be prosecuted before national courts, the international criminal legal community – if one can speak of such a community – was clearly not ready to renounce its claim to institutional enforcement of international crimes before special tribunals. The idea matured in the late 1990s that even when the national justice system concerned does not have sufficient capacity or expertise to deal with international crimes by itself, seeking justice for international crimes does not necessitate the establishment of a fully fledged international tribunal.[3] The international community hence sought to actively support national endeavours and became involved in the establishment and operation of special tribunals. Yet these tribunals would remain closely connected to the national system, even if to different degrees.

If one considers the institutionalisation of ICL in a chronological order, the establishment of hybrid tribunals can be seen as a wave that started to surface in the late 1990s, i.e. after the establishment of the ICTY and ICTR, and that ebbed away in the mid-2000s, when a genuine international institutional framework consolidated itself – at least seemingly or provisionally – with the

2 Pádraig McAuliffe, 'Hybrid Courts in Retrospect: Of Lost Legacies and Modest Futures' in William Schabas, Yvonne McDermott and Niamh Hayes (eds), *Ashgate Research Companion to International Criminal Law: Critical Perspectives* (Ashgate, 2013) 453, 453.
3 On this lesson learned from the *ad hoc* tribunals, see Harold Hongju Koh, 'International Criminal Justice 5.0' (2013) 38(2) *Yale Journal of International Law* 525, 531-533.

operationalisation of the ICC. Therefore, tribunals like the Special Court for Sierra Leone (SCSL), the Extraordinary Chambers in the Courts of Cambodia (ECCC), the Special Panels for Serious Crimes in the Dili District Court and the Special Tribunal for Lebanon (STL) are often presented as constituting the third institutional phase in ICL – or 'ICL 3.0' – with the Nuremberg and Tokyo tribunals being phase 1, the *ad hoc* tribunals phase 2, and the ICC phase 4.[4] In light of these developments, it has been argued that 'we have come to an end of the software- and hardware-building phase . . . of modern international criminal justice'.[5] One might wonder whether assuming such a presumably linear development is helpful and, in fact, accurate: in their extreme, such narratives presume that the experimental phase has been completed, that the ICL toolbox is pretty much full and that, when pursuing justice for international crimes in the future, one could open one of the drawers containing the different institutions and graft it – perhaps in modified form – onto a new situation. However, as it is argued here, this is not necessarily the case.

A *The Special Court for Sierra Leone*

The SCSL, one of the first hybrid tribunals, was established in 2002 through an agreement concluded between the United Nations and the Sierra Leonean government. The SCSL was mandated to deal with the crimes committed during the brutal decade-long civil war that took place in Sierra Leone in the 1990s, more specifically with crimes against humanity, war crimes committed in a non-international armed conflict and certain domestic crimes of particular relevance in this context, such as offences relating to the abuse of girls.[6]

Interestingly, neither the agreement between the United Nations and the Sierra Leonean government establishing the court nor the court's Statute, annexed to this agreement, reveal much about the objectives of the SCSL. The agreement recalls a resolution from 2000, in which the Security Council was 'deeply concerned at the very serious crimes committed within the territory of Sierra Leone against the people of Sierra Leone and United Nations and associated personnel and at the prevailing situation of impunity',[7] whereas Article 1 of the Statute gives the court 'the power to prosecute persons who bear the greatest responsibility for serious violations of international humanitarian law and Sierra Leonean law committed

---

4 Ibid 531.
5 Ibid 539.
6 *Agreement between the United Nations and the Government of Sierra Leone on the Establishment of a Special Court for Sierra Leone*, signed 16 January 2002, 2178 UNTS 137 (entered into force 12 April 2002) annex (*'Statute of the Special Court for Sierra Leone'*) Arts 2-5.
7 SC Res 1315, UN SCOR, 55th sess, 4186th mtg, UN Doc S/RES/1315 (14 August 2000) preamble.

in the territory of Sierra Leone since 30 November 1996'.[8] Therefore, a textual analysis of these foundational documents shows that the SCSL was not only given a narrow jurisdictional mandate but was established to pursue one main objective: ending impunity by bringing to justice those who bear the greatest responsibility for the atrocity crimes committed during the Sierra Leonean civil law. What these documents do not reveal is that the SCSL was set up to pursue a number of additional objectives. A contextual analysis shows that this court – just like the subsequently established hybrid tribunals – was also supposed to contribute to domestic law reform and capacity-building of the national justice system.[9] Moreover, when compared to the international tribunals, the SCSL was also expected to be less costly and more efficient, especially regarding the collection of evidence. Finally, being located in Freetown and staffed by both internationals and Sierra Leoneans, the SCSL promised to be closer to the communities most immediately concerned than were the ICTY and the ICTR. It was hence hoped that there would be greater local ownership over this *internationalised* and not purely *international* institution. These objectives have only partially been met: by way of example, empirical research conducted several years after the establishment of the SCSL has found 'a pervading sense of disconnect with the Court, which seemed removed and irrelevant to the issues now facing Sierra Leone'.[10]

Four trials against a total of ten accused were held before the SCSL, including against a former head of state, the former Liberian President Charles Taylor. He was convicted of aiding and abetting as well as planning crimes against humanity and war crimes, notably by providing assistance, encouragement or moral support to the armed groups Revolutionary United Front/Armed Forces Revolutionary Council and their widespread commission of serious crimes during the conflict in Sierra Leone. The sentence of 50 years imprisonment was upheld on appeal in 2013.[11]

---

8 *Statute of the Special Court for Sierra Leone*, above n 6.

9 For the various expectations of the establishment of the SCSL, see, eg, Alison Smith, 'The Expectations and Role of International and National Civil and the SCSL' in Charles Chernor Jalloh (ed), *The Sierra Leone Special Court and its Legacy* (Cambridge University Press, 2014) 46 and Peter Penfold, 'International Community Expectations of the Sierra Leone Special Court' in Charles Chernor Jalloh (ed), *The Sierra Leone Special Court and its Legacy* (Cambridge University Press, 2014) 60. For a more general analysis of the 'promise' of hybrid tribunals, written when the first ones were being established, see Laura Dickinson, 'The Promise of Hybrid Courts' (2003) 97 *American Journal of International Law* 295.

10 Rachel Kerr and Jessica Lincoln, *The Special Court for Sierra Leone: Outreach, Legacy and Impact* (King's College London, Department of War Studies, February 2008) 20.

11 *Prosecutor v Taylor (Judgment)* (Special Court for Sierra Leone, Appeals Chamber, Case No SCSL-03-01-A, 26 September 2013).

B *The Extraordinary Chambers in the Courts of Cambodia*

Similarly established as the SCSL, the ECCC were created through an agreement adopted in 2003 between the United Nations and the Cambodian government.[12] The inherent characteristic of both international and internationalised justice being highly selective is also visible in the case of the ECCC, which have charged only a very small number of individuals. Aside from these similarities, however, the two tribunals are very different. Among others, the ECCC were set up to examine crimes that were committed several decades ago, namely during the 1975-1979 rule of the Khmer Rouge. The first case before the ECCC was against Kaing Guek Eav (also known as Duch), who had been responsible for a notorious security centre where numerous opponents of the ruling Communist Party of Kampuchea had been interrogated and executed. Duch was convicted in 2012, *inter alia*, of the crimes against humanity of persecution, enslavement, imprisonment and torture, and sentenced to life imprisonment.[13] Four further defendants were charged in the second case. Since one of them passed away and one was found unfit to stand trial (given that the ECCC deal with crimes committed in the 1970s, all the defendants are of very advanced age), a final judgment – also life imprisonment for various crimes against humanity – could be reached only against two of them, in 2016.[14]

While these first two cases were not immune to criticism, the attempt to open additional cases plainly exposed some of the weaknesses in the structure of this tribunal and especially the possibility of undue political interference given that the Cambodian government actively tried to prevent the opening of two further cases. In fact, already the establishment of the ECCC themselves was only possible after arduous negotiations, with the Cambodian government attempting to control the tribunal and the United Nations seeking to avoid too much domestic influence.[15] In the end, it was concluded, among others, that nationally appointed judges would constitute the majority in each chamber, but that decisions could only be made through a qualified majority of the judges, which can quite obviously result in serious deadlocks.

---

12 GA Res 57/228 B, UN GAOR, 57th sess, 85th plen mtg, UN Doc A/RES/57/228 B (22 May 2003).

13 *Kaing Guek Eav alias 'Duch' (Appeal Judgment)* (Extraordinary Chambers in the Courts of Cambodia, Supreme Court Chamber, Case No 001/18-07-2007-ECCC/SC, 3 February 2012).

14 *Khieu Samphân and Nuon Chea (Appeal Judgment)* (Extraordinary Chambers in the Courts of Cambodia, Supreme Court Chamber, Case No 002/19-09-2007-ECCC/SC, 23 November 2016).

15 For a succinct overview of the history of the negotiations, see Sarah Williams, 'The Cambodian Extraordinary Chambers – A Dangerous Precedent for International Justice?' (2004) 53 *International & Comparative Law Quarterly* 227, 228-230.

Despite such efforts to carefully balance the demands of the respective con-stituencies, the ECCC have been severely criticised for the substantial degree of political interference,[16] and the United Nations have been accused of 'acting too much like a technical assistance provider and not enough like a founding partner'.[17]

C Timor Leste, Kosovo, Bosnia and Herzegovina

Other hybrid tribunals, which are perhaps more accurately described as domestic courts with international elements, were established by interna-tional authorities to deal with post-conflict situations. The United Nations Transitional Administration in Timor Leste, which had been established by the Security Council in 1999, created the so-called Special Panels for Serious Crimes in the Dili District Court.[18] These Special Panels had jurisdiction over the international crimes of genocide, crimes against humanity and war crimes as well as certain domestic crimes, such as murder and sexual offences.

Quite similarly, in Kosovo, the United Nations administration that had been established in 1999 issued regulations allowing international judges to participate in locally held trials.[19] This approach did not create a tribunal in any comprehensive manner but has been described as 'gradual, ad hoc and responsive'.[20] More recently, in 2015, the systematically internationalised Kosovo Specialist Chambers and Specialist Prosecutor's Office were created under the auspices of the European Union, with the objective of finally bring-ing to justice certain senior leaders of the Kosovo Liberation Army allegedly responsible for grave crimes committed during the 1998-2000 conflict.[21]

In Bosnia and Herzegovina, a War Crimes Chamber, which began its work in 2005, was established within the national system but with strong

16 Tomas Hamilton and Michael Ramsden, 'The Politicisation of Hybrid Courts: Observations from the Extraordinary Chambers in the Courts of Cambodia' (2014) 14(1) *International Criminal Law Review* 115.

17 Anne Heindel and John D Ciorciari, *Hybrid Justice: The Extraordinary Chambers in the Courts of Cambodia* (University of Michigan Press, 2014) 201.

18 UNTAET Regulation 2000/11, UN Doc UNTAET/REG/2000/11 (6 March 2000) (amended by subsequent UNTAET regulations).

19 On the appointment of international judges and prosecutors, see in particular UNMIK Regulation 2000/6, UN Doc UNMIK/REG/2000/6 (15 February 2000) and UNMIK Regulation 2000/34, UN Doc UNMIK/REG/2000/34 (27 May 2000).

20 Sarah Williams, 'The Specialist Chambers of Kosovo' (2016) 14(1) *Journal of International Criminal Justice* 25, 31. Of note, the appointment of international judges and prosecu-tors was taken over from the United Nations mission by the European Union Rule of Law Mission in Kosovo (EULEX) in 2008.

21 See, for instance, the 2016 issue 14(1) of the *Journal of International Criminal Justice* on a symposium on the Specialist Chambers of Kosovo.

international support.[22] The main objectives in this case were to give the national system the capacity to hold trials according to international standards involving international crimes committed during the 1992–1995 conflict and to facilitate the ICTY's completion strategy.

D *The Special Tribunal for Lebanon*

The STL, a quite peculiar institution in this list, was created in 2007 to try those allegedly responsible for the assassination of the former prime minister of Lebanon, Rafiq Hariri, in 2005. While initially negotiated between the United Nations and the Lebanese government, the agreement was not ratified by Lebanon because of a stalemate in the parliament, and the STL was, in the end, established unilaterally through a Security Council resolution.[23] The STL is, indeed, quite 'special' and distinguishes itself from the other hybrid tribunals for a number of reasons, of which the most important will be mentioned here. First, the STL was created to deal essentially with one specific attack, namely the assassination of Hariri (and, as is often forgotten, 22 others who were also killed in the attack).[24] Second, it applies Lebanese law (with minor modifications) and has jurisdiction over the crime of terrorism, another important novelty for an international or internationalised tribunal.[25] Third, it is not located in the country primarily concerned but in The Hague, a situation that can be explained by the important security concerns related to the volatile political context in Lebanon. Finally, unlike any another international or internationalised tribunal, the STL may hold trials *in absentia*.[26] As a matter of fact, the main

22 The establishment of the War Crimes Chamber was initially agreed upon by the ICTY and the Office of the High Representative, an international institution created under the Dayton Peace Agreement. For some context and an assessment of war crimes trials in Bosnia and Herzegovina, see OSCE Mission to Bosnia and Herzegovina, *Delivering Justice in Bosnia and Herzegovina: An Overview of War Crimes Processing from 2005 to 2010* (May 2011).

23 SC Res 1757, UN SCOR 62nd sess, 5685th mtg, UN Doc S/RES/1757 (30 May 2007). For a discussion of the establishment of the STL as an apparent emancipation of ICL from international peace and security, see Frédéric Mégret, 'A Special Tribunal for Lebanon' (2008) 21(2) *Leiden Journal of International Law* 485.

24 For some context on the creation of the STL, see Nicolas Michel, 'The Creation of the Tribunal in its Context' in Amal Alamuddin, Nidal Nabil Jurdi and David Tolbert (eds), *The Special Tribunal for Lebanon: Law and Practice* (Oxford University Press, 2014) 10.

25 On the highly controversial decision of the Appeals Chamber's decision that transnational terrorism constituted a crime under customary international law, see Ben Saul, 'The Special Tribunal for Lebanon and Terrorism as an International Crime: Reflections on the Judicial Function' in William Schabas, Yvonne McDermott and Niamh Hayes (eds), *Ashgate Research Companion to International Criminal Law: Critical Perspectives* (Ashgate, 2013) 79.

26 For a discussion of trials *in absentia* in the context of the STL, see Paola Gaeta, 'Trials in Absentia before the Special Tribunal for Lebanon' (2007) 5(5) *Journal of International Criminal Justice* 1165.

case before the STL, against *Ayyash et al*, started in January 2014, without the accused being present.[27]

E *The Extraordinary African Chambers in the Senegalese Courts – regionalising hybrid justice*

Another quite unique internationalised tribunal, the Extraordinary African Chambers in the Senegalese Courts, was established in 2013 to try the former Chadian president Hissein Habré. Here, it was not the United Nations but a regional organisation, the African Union, that concluded an agreement with the host nation Senegal to try those most responsible for the serious crimes committed in Chad during Habré's dictatorial rule in the 1980s. In reality, only Habré has been indicted, which is consistent with the primary purpose of the tribunal and a result of the significant international campaign headed by the non-governmental organisations Human Rights Watch and Amnesty International and by certain states, in particular Belgium, to bring Habré to justice.[28] The trial started in 2013, and Habré was convicted in 2016 for crimes against humanity, war crimes and torture and sentenced to life imprisonment.[29]

The international elements – comparatively few in number for a hybrid tribunal – consist in a mixed bench of mostly Senegalese judges and only a small number of judges of another African nationality appointed by the African Union.[30] The African Union hence remains involved to some extent in the operation of the Chambers after their joint establishment with Senegal. Another international element consists in the fact that the Chambers are financed primarily by international donors. Therefore, the Extraordinary African Chambers are to be considered a primarily domestic tribunal exercising jurisdiction under the universality principle and not, as has otherwise been the case for hybrid tribunals, under the principle of territoriality. This jurisdictional basis could have rendered the proceedings more complicated. However, Chad, as the state on whose territory the crimes had been committed

---

27 *Ayyash et al* (Special Tribunal for Lebanon, Case No STL-11-01).
28 For more information on the background of the Extraordinary African Chambers and an early analysis, see Sarah Williams, 'The Extraordinary African Chambers in the Senegalese Courts: An African Solution to an African Problem?' (2013) 11 *Journal of International Criminal Justice* 1139.
29 *Ministère Public c. Hissein Habré (Jugement)* (Chambre Africaine Extraordinaire d'Assises, 30 May 2016). The sentence was confirmed on appeal in April 2017.
30 *Statut des Chambres africaines extraordinaires au sein des juridictions sénégalaises pour la poursuite des crimes internationaux commis au Tchad durant la période du 7 juin 1982 au 1er décembre 1980, Annexe to the Accord entre le gouvernement de la République du Sénégal et l'Union africaine sur la création de chambres africaines extraordinaires au sein des juridictions sénégalaises* (22 August 2012) Art. 11.

and also as the state of Habré's nationality, did not challenge the jurisdiction of the Chambers. Moreover, the precondition for the exercise of universal jurisdiction, namely the existence of crimes against humanity, war crimes and torture under treaty or customary international law at the relevant time, was not doubted by the chamber rendering the trial judgment. In sum, the Extraordinary African Chambers present themselves as yet another quite creative form that internationalised criminal justice can take.

F *The Iraqi High Tribunal and further definitional aspects of 'hybridity'*

The Iraqi High Tribunal, which, among others, tried and condemned Saddam Hussein, is sometimes added to the list of hybrid tribunals. In 2004, it was even introduced by one commentator as 'the latest experiment in international criminal justice'.[31] This tribunal, with jurisdiction over genocide, crimes against humanity, war crimes (closely following the ICTY statute in this respect) and violations of certain Iraqi laws, was first established in 2003 as the Iraqi Special Tribunal by the Iraqi Interim Governing Council and authorised by the occupying powers' Coalition Provisional Authority. It initially received significant international support, including with respect to funding and training, and although no international judges or prosecutors were appointed, many international advisors worked in the tribunal at the beginning. However, it quickly fell into disgrace because of serious flaws in the proceedings, in particular regarding judicial independence and the application of the death penalty.[32]

The Iraqi High Tribunal exemplifies that not every court with some kind of international element or involvement may usefully be described as a hybrid or internationalised tribunal. The focus and scope of the analysis obviously depends on our definition of 'hybridity' or 'internationalisation'. In other words, when is a tribunal really a 'hybrid'? And to what extent does the international community need to be involved to make a tribunal 'internationalised'? Several criteria, or rather common features, of hybrid or internationalised tribunals have usefully been articulated, which include: establishment on an *ad hoc* basis; a mixed bench of international

---

31 Ilias Bantekas, 'The Iraqi Special Tribunal for Crimes Against Humanity' 54 (2004) *International & Comparative Law Quarterly* 237, 237.

32 For early critiques of the tribunal, see Yuval Shany, 'Does One Size Fit All? Reading the Jurisdictional Provisions of the New Iraqi Special Tribunal in the Light of the Statutes of the International Criminal Tribunals' (2004) 2(2) *Journal of International Criminal Justice* 338 and Michael P Scharf, 'Is It International Enough? A Critique of the Iraqi Special Tribunal in Light of the Goals of International Justice' (2004) 2(2) *Journal of International Criminal Justice* 330.

and domestic judges; funding, often to an important extent, from the international community; and applicability, in addition to international criminal law, of national laws.[33] Based on an assessment in 2006, another commentator argued that it was a mixed bench of international and local judges that stands out as 'the only defining common feature of the current hybrid courts'.[34]

Despite such useful criteria, hybridity seems to defy definitions, and recent developments challenge even the seemingly low common denominator of a mixed bench: the Kosovo Specialist Chambers mentioned above are staffed entirely by international judges and are hence clearly not just a domestic tribunal. Moreover, since they apply domestic law and not international law, they could hardly count as a genuinely international tribunal either. They are thus a hybrid tribunal of yet another nature, which shows that the institutional enforcement of ICL through hybrid tribunals is not a homogeneous endeavour. Nor is it one whose experimental phase has been completed, as the classification of hybrid tribunals as 'ICL 3.0' might suggest.

It is true that until a few years ago, the experiment of hybridising international criminal justice seemed to have come to a standstill, with a number of additional hybrid tribunals, such as special courts for Darfur and for Kenya, only being envisaged but not actually being established. However, the establishment of a hybrid court following the more traditional model of a mixed bench, but applying domestic law, is underway in the Central African Republic. This Special Criminal Court would be mandated to deal with serious crimes committed in the Central African Republic since 2003 and would complement ICC jurisdiction (the ICC opened investigations in 2007 following a referral to the Office of the Prosecutor by the government of the Central African Republic). A memorandum of understanding with the United Nations peacekeeping mission on the establishment of a hybrid tribunal was signed in 2014, the interim parliament adopted a law establishing such a court in 2015, and a further agreement on the operationalisation of the court was signed in 2016.[35]

---

33 Sarah Williams, *Hybrid and Internationalised Criminal Tribunals: Selected Jurisdictional Issues* (Hart, 2012) 249.

34 Sarah MH Nouwen, 'Hybrid Courts: The Hybrid Category of a New Type of International Crimes Courts' (2006) 2(2) *Utrecht Law Review* 190, 213.

35 MINUSCA, *Signature d'un accord relatif à l'opérationnalisation de la cour pénale spéciale de la RCA* (26 August 2006) <http://minusca.unmissions.org/signature-d%E2%80%99un-accord-relatif-%C3%A0-l'op%C3%A9rationnalisation-de-la-cour-p%C3%A9nale-sp%C3%A9ciale-de-la-rca>. A hybrid court, to be established by the African Union, is also foreseen in the 2015 peace agreement for South Sudan: *Agreement on the Resolution of the Conflict in the Republic of South Sudan* (17 August 2015) <https://unmiss.unmissions.org/sites/default/files/final_proposed_compromise_agreement_for_south_sudan_conflict.pdf> Ch. V.3. On the delays in the establishment of the court, see Patryk I Labuda, 'The Hybrid Court for South Sudan? Looking for a Way Forward (Part 1)' on Mark Kersten, *Justice in*

Yet even aside from the recent developments in places like Kosovo, Senegal and the Central African Republic, the common narrative of closure appears simple and short-sighted, as if institutions were given only one opportunity to succeed (and if they fail according to some test, they are part of history). It is true that just as the shortcomings and costliness of the ICTY and the ICTR generated an impulse to design different institutions, the hybrid tribunals have often been seen as not living up to their promises.[36] Nevertheless, the model is not dead, the institutional experiments continue, and creative thinking is still needed. Moreover, the hybrid tribunals that have already closed down have had a significant influence on the development of ICL, and they have encouraged crucial thinking about the very *raison d'être* of ICL and the form that institutional enforcement of ICL can or should take. In other words, while 'a time for reflection'[37] may have come to evaluate the experiences of the respective hybrid tribunals, it is clearly too early to draw any final conclusions or to assume that the experimental phase is over.

III Hybrid tribunals as insightful reflectors of the field

In addition to challenging a grand linear narrative of institutional experiments in ICL, hybrid tribunals also allow us to consider in a particular light a number of conceptual issues, such as the multifaceted relationship between international and national criminal law and the legitimacy of the respective institutions.

A *Bridging and fragmenting*

Hybrid tribunals can be imagined as bridges between the international and the national spheres. Indeed, whether one leans more towards the monist or dualist perspective on the relationship between international and national law, the traditional institutional set-up administering ICL appears essentially dualist in nature, with international and national institutions operating in relative isolation. Hybrid tribunals transcend this divide; in this sense, they are an embodiment of the monist postulation that international law and domestic law can interact and are, in fact, part of the same normative framework, while remaining two different spheres within this

---

Conflict (23 February 2017) <https://justiceinconflict.org/2017/02/23/the-hybrid-court-for-south-sudan-looking-for-a-way-forward-part-1/#more-7281>.

36 See, eg, Parinaz Kermani Mendez, 'The New Wave of Hybrid Tribunals: A Sophisticated Approach to Enforcing International Humanitarian Law or an Idealistic Solution with Empty Promises?' (2009) 20 *Criminal Law Forum* 53; McAuliffe, above n 2.

37 Sarah Williams, 'Hybrid Tribunals: A Time for Reflection (Book Review)' (2016) 10(3) *International Journal of Transitional Justice* 538.

framework. The word 'hybrid' itself illustrates this nicely: it comes from the Latin word 'hybrida', commonly translated as 'mongrel' and now used to describe anything derived from heterogeneous sources. Hybrid tribunals hence exemplify the dynamic legal processes that interconnect international law with regional and domestic processes.[38] They show that ICL, as it has been argued with respect to international law more generally, is 'full of human choice and rich in individual and group participation'.[39] The tribunals discussed above show that innovative institutions, each with different features and applying a different mix of laws, may be created through the input of a potentially greater variety of actors than in the context of purely international or national institutions.

From a realist perspective, some political will to work towards such hybridity must, of course, be present. The state primarily concerned needs to be open to the establishment of such a tribunal and also to the involvement of the international community, or rather of a few key states driving decisions of international organisations like the United Nations or the African Union. These states, in turn, must be sufficiently concerned – because of the particular gravity of the crimes, or because of geopolitical interests – to become involved and, typically, to fund the tribunal. As for the national justice system, it must be considered deficient in some way in order to require international involvement, but it must not be completely unwilling or unable to host the proceedings.[40] These conditions alone explain why only a small number of hybrid tribunals have been established so far, and why it is unlikely that many more will be established in the future.

Too many actors, and too many bridges, might also render the path to justice more devious. Indeed, from an orthodox international legal perspective, every additional legal institution applying international law augments the risk of fragmenting it. Without one single authoritative interpreter at the top, institutions like the hybrid tribunals – which are not even truly international tribunals – may apply and interpret international law quite differently. The initial sentencing decision of the SCSL in the case against the Civil Defence Forces (CDF), which supported the elected government against rebel groups and were by many Sierra Leoneans considered to be national heroes, is a good example. In short, the trial chamber held that fighting for a legitimate

---

38 For a discussion of these processes, see Jordan J Paust, 'Basic Forms of International Law and Monist, Dualist, and Realist Perspectives' in Marko Novakovic (ed), *Basic Concepts of Public International Law: Monism & Dualism* (University of Belgrade, 2013) 244, 248.

39 Ibid.

40 Antonio Cassese, 'The Role of Internationalized Courts and Tribunals in the Fight Against International Criminality' in Cesare PR Romano, André Nollkaemper and Jann K Kleffner (eds), *Internationalized Criminal Courts and Tribunals: Sierra Leone, East Timor, Kosovo, and Cambodia* (Oxford University Press, 2004) 1, 5.

cause can be a mitigating factor.[41] What sent an important signal to the local constituency – i.e. it was held that the CDF did commit serious crimes, but they were, nevertheless, fighting for a just cause – was widely seen by international commentators as a dangerous precedent for ICL and a muddling of *jus in bello* and *jus ad bellum*. In the end, the Appeals Chamber held, from an orthodox perspective correctly, that the motive of the CDF should not be taken into account as a mitigating factor.[42]

While this debate on fragmentation is not new,[43] it remains alive and is a continuous concern for international law more generally and for ICL more specifically. Hybrid tribunals, among others because of the involvement of national judges and prosecutors who may view international law differently than international judges (more on this below), may even be seen as questioning the normative autonomy and integrity of ICL as a body of law, regarding both its substantive and procedural aspects. In other words, while hybrid tribunals draw on and also ground their legitimacy in the international criminal legal order, certain features of this presumably autonomous order may be contested, precisely as a result of the establishment of such tribunals. Such critiques and challenges are not necessarily a bad thing. Rather, as it is suggested here, they invite the actors involved, from international criminal law practitioners and governments to non-governmental organisations and academics, to constantly and critically evaluate the operation, objectives and impact of ICL's institutions.

B *Legitimacy and authority: the non-hybrid judge*

Hybrid tribunals – in particular thanks to their mixed bench of 'international' and 'local' judges – also invite us to consider more carefully who can speak authoritatively on ICL: on the one hand, the international judge, who is often viewed, rather naïvely, as an inherently neutral and perfectly unbiased expert; on the other hand, the local judge, who may have in-depth knowledge about the conflict situation but who is always suspected of bias and, especially when compared to the international 'expert', of incompetence.[44] While the reality is, of course, more complex than suggested by this presumed dichotomy, such considerations are directly related to a tribunal's legitimacy, or perceptions thereof. As it has been argued,

---

41 *Prosecutor v Fofana and Kondewa (Sentencing Judgment)* (Special Court for Sierra Leone, Trial Chamber I, Case No SCSL-04-14-T-296, 9 October 2007) [83].

42 *Prosecutor v Fofana and Kondewa (Judgment)* (Special Court for Sierra Leone, Appeals Chamber, Case No SCSL-04-14-A-829, 28 May 2008) [530]–[534].

43 See, eg, Martti Koskenniemi and Päivi Leino, 'Fragmentation of International Law? Postmodern Anxieties' (2002) 15(3) *Leiden Journal of International Law* 553.

44 Harry Hobbs, 'Hybrid Tribunals and the Composition of the Court: In Search of Sociological Legitimacy' (2016) 16(2) *Chicago Journal of International Law* 482, 487.

> [h]ybrid courts may unconsciously reinforce this model by tacitly supporting an unstated assumption that the role of the international judge is to impart her wisdom on lesser local counterparts ... [which] directly results in lower public support for the hybrid tribunal as an institution.[45]

Given that the question of legitimacy lies at the heart of the establishment, operation and legacy of all institutions enforcing ICL, one may wonder whether hybrid tribunals can avert at least certain criticisms that have plagued other institutions. In fact, while ICL has encountered the critique of imperialism from its inception – from victors' justice delivered through the Nuremberg and Tokyo tribunals to the somewhat arrogant and selective imposition of *ad hoc* tribunals by the Security Council – this critique has intensified over recent years, and especially since the operationalisation of the ICC and its almost exclusive focus on African situations.[46] In this light, hybrid tribunals appear, by design, more consensual and collaborative, and less imperialist and neo-colonial. With respect to the background of key officials more specifically, any tribunal will be considered more legitimate by those in whose name justice is meted out if they can relate to the tribunal and its officials; typically, this hinges on whether judges are reflective of a tribunal's constituencies. Since hybrid tribunals speak and are accountable to both the local communities most immediately affected by the crimes committed as well as the so-called international community as a whole, a mixed bench of international and local judges can, in principle, meet these concerns.

ICL has historically not paid much attention to this concern. No judges from the affected states sat on the benches of the Nuremberg and Tokyo tribunals or on those of the ICTY and ICTR. As for the ICC, it is possible, but not guaranteed, that a judge holding the same nationality as the accused sits on the bench (this happened, for instance, in proceedings against Joseph Kony in the Ugandan situation). Hybrid tribunals hence offer themselves quite uniquely as institutions where the composition of the bench can be customised and adapted to the likely concerns of the main constituencies of the respective tribunal. It may, for instance, be more important to have a higher ratio of national judges in some situations than in others; as was seen in the case of the ECCC, without this concession made to the Cambodian government, the tribunal would not have been established. Local judges may indeed be more attuned to local traditions and preferences; yet appointments according to unavoidably oversimplified categorisations, like the ethnic, religious or cultural background of a particular judge, would be difficult at best and counterproductive at worst.[47] Instead of conveying an image of impartial

---

45 Ibid 519.
46 For a summary of such critiques, see chapter 9 in this book.
47 On very practical concerns of appointing international judges to sit on tribunals located in states emerging from violent conflict, see Hobbs, above n 44, 514.

justice, appointments made on such bases would risk entrenching the very fault lines that caused or fuelled the conflict in question and led to the perpetration of serious crimes. As an alternative, it would be useful to appoint international judges who are knowledgeable of local legal traditions and possibly speak the local language (or languages).[48]

It is worth recalling that internationally and domestically appointed judges do not, respectively, *represent* the international community or the affected state. They do not act for these constituencies; rather, they are appointed to act impartially, and in the interests of justice.[49] If judges, however, are *reflective* of society, there is an increased likelihood that their decisions will be perceived as legitimate by the different communities making up this society.[50] Indeed, the symbolic value of fair representation – potentially resulting in more favourable perceptions of the tribunal by the affected communities – seems to be more important than the argument that a mixed bench, thanks to the diverse expertise of its members and higher level of argument, necessarily produces better judgments.

C Deconstructing the inter/national dichotomy

As argued above, hybrid tribunals attempt to bring together, to bridge, the spheres of the international and the national. They do so not only symbolically but in a very tangible, real way, among others by making internationally appointed and nationally appointed officials work together. What is important to remember in the context of hybrid tribunals, and of ICL more generally, is that 'the international' and 'the local' are far from homogeneous entities. In fact, both sides are complex, speak with an endless number of voices, and may have blended or highly diverse interests and objectives. Moreover, each actor, including 'the international judge' and 'the local judge', needs to be further particularised. For instance, nationally appointed judges are normally part of national elites, with close ties to international elites. They may even have been educated or trained abroad, and may therefore be seen as speaking, at least in part, to and in the name of international constituencies.

More fundamentally, however, is the fact that behind the appointment of international judges and the associated, very common discourse of an international community lies the imagination of a cosmopolitan community.[51] Through 'we-talk', this community asserts that 'we' are concerned with

---

48 Ibid 498.

49 Ibid 496.

50 On a discussion of the principle of fair reflection in this context, see ibid 495-498. In particular, as Hobbs concludes, 'the presence of local judges *can* enhance the sociological legitimacy of the court'. Ibid 492.

51 Immi Tallgren, 'The Voice of the International: Who is Speaking?' (2015) 13(1) *Journal of International Criminal Justice* 135, 137.

international crimes committed against 'our shared humanity',[52] which is why 'we' need to become involved in the establishment of international and internationalised tribunals. Although this common 'we' in ICL discourses may often appear natural and obvious,[53] reflecting one of the great achievements of modernity, it is problematic and needs to be examined more carefully. Once again, this is of course not only relevant in the context of hybrid tribunals, but the ways in which the 'international' is imagined and opposed to the 'local' play a particularly salient role here. As Immi Tallgren has usefully noted, there is 'the "we" of societies prone to "savage" or "natural" violence, ignorant or non-respectful of international law, constantly requiring the involvement and investment of the "we in charge", masters of the law and order'.[54] This shows that hybrid tribunals, and the body of ICL more generally, are not built on an effective, inclusive 'we-union'. Rather, in light of the dominant discourses in ICL, it seems that the 'most audible "we" . . . occupies privileged positions outside and above the violence and suffering ICL addresses'.[55] From the international, humanitarian intervener's perspective, the two 'we' are actually constructed as a 'we' and a 'them', with the latter having little agency.[56]

It could be argued that in the context of hybrid tribunals, 'they' are, in fact, given a lot of agency; depending on the tribunal's structure, the international may indeed play only a slightly dominant role or, as in the case of the ECCC, an even lesser one. But what is key here is that the persisting image of two opposing poles is highly influential, and that the relationship between the international criminal legal order and national legal systems is typically construed as being unidirectional: the international, seen as inherently more developed, as better, is supposed to help national systems rise to the bar. It has been said that hybrid tribunals embody this promise by representing 'unique opportunities for capacity-building in all areas', including with respect to training court officials and to introducing best practices regarding case management, thus being a model for the local legal system.[57] This reasoning is, of course, not necessarily flawed: hybrid tribunals, just like the ICTY and the ICTR, were established precisely because the national systems were seen as unwilling or unable to deal adequately with the crimes committed, which is why the so-called international community, in the form of ICL and

---

52 For a discussion of the 'we' of international community and the 'we' of humanity, see ibid 144-149.

53 Ibid 138.

54 Ibid 143.

55 Ibid 152.

56 Ibid 151.

57 David Cohen, '"Hybrid" Justice in East Timor, Sierra Leone, and Cambodia: "Lessons Learned" and Prospects for the Future' (2007) 43 *Stanford Journal of International Law* 1, 36-37.

specifically established institutions, stepped in. However, the association of knowledge with the international community and the view that this knowledge is to be imparted through a solely unidirectional influence, for example through the teaching of procedural fairness and related fundamental principles like the respect of the rights of the accused, entrenches this unhelpful dichotomy. It also precludes an appreciation of different kinds of knowledges and different understandings of justice and truth as well as of the many ways in which various actors, including in the context of hybrid tribunals, can – or could – influence the international.

Therefore, we – and by this 'we' I have in mind the community of people involved in the establishment and operation as well as the critique of international and internationalised tribunals – we need to interrogate ourselves for whom we actually speak. Do we at least attempt to understand those who may be our partners but who are often considered to be 'the others'? As in the case of the relationship between international and local judges, ICL and local legal traditions ought to be ready to learn from each other. This, in turn, leads to a call for more critical self-awareness, modesty and openness: self-awareness, because we need to know who we are, where we come from and how we conceptualise the world; modesty, because ICL as a field needs to recognise its shortcomings and limitations; and openness, because ICL must be open to dialogue and to change if it wants to have a positive impact in the long run.

IV Conclusion

It is trite to say that high expectations often result in great disappointment, but this seems particularly true for the hybrid tribunals. None of them has contributed, to any significant extent, to capacity-building and law reform. In hindsight, the hope that the best aspects of both the international and the national spheres could be combined turned out to be an illusion. Yet the hybrid tribunals have perhaps been judged too harshly and not on the basis of what they can actually achieve. In fact, all ICL institutions have, in many instances, not been assessed based on their primary institutional mandate, which usually consists in contributing to the fight against impunity for serious crimes, but on other concerns that could perhaps be achieved as a corollary, such as ending armed conflicts or bringing about reconciliation within war-torn societies.[58] In our rapidly moving world, it is indeed the immediate, measurable political impact that we are typically interested in.

---

58 See, eg, Philipp Kastner, 'Armed Conflicts and Referrals to the International Criminal Court: From Measuring Impact to Emerging Legal Obligations' (2014) 12(3) *Journal of International Criminal Justice* 471, 480-482.

International actors – both politicians and donor communities – need to justify their involvement and require almost instant success stories. The result is that the long-term vision is often lost. In other words, although too much was expected of the hybrid tribunals established in the early years of the twenty-first century, and although it is unlikely that this model will be used very frequently in the future, the underlying ideas and principal structural features of these tribunals might not be flawed and still hold important promises.

This chapter has not attempted to envisage any new institutional arrangements. However, it seems that, as a minimum, the possibility of radically different institutions must be considered. Together with primarily international approaches (and also national and regional ones), hybrid tribunals have already demonstrated that, with some creativity, new paths may be taken with respect to the institutional enforcement of ICL. Future institutions may require even more creativity, and they may be challenging or even disruptive for the existing international criminal legal order and its now fairly well-established institutions. In fact, given the important shortcomings of all official institutions delivering international criminal justice, perhaps unofficial, non-state-based institutions like peoples' tribunals[59] will end up playing a more significant role in the fight against impunity for serious crimes. Indeed, while the widespread ratification of the Rome Statute suggested that the newly established, truly international criminal court might be able to deal with all serious crimes committed anywhere in the world, we are clearly not witnessing such an end of history, where one international court with global jurisdictional reach enforces ICL. Rather, the ICL project remains highly contested, fragmented, pluralistic and in flux.

The first hybrid tribunals might not have lived up to their promises, but they have allowed exploring novel institutional options, which demonstrates, in turn, that the enforcement of ICL does not depend on a pre-determined, specifically designed institution (or set of institutions). In this sense, it can be argued with Lon Fuller that ICL and the establishment and operation of institutions meant to enforce ICL is not 'a one-way projection of authority'.[60] Rather, it is a process itself that is continuously negotiated by legal actors, both international and domestic ones (and those that are both or neither). These actors, as critical legal pluralists claim, 'possess a transformative capacity that enables them to produce legal knowledge and to fashion the very structures of law that contribute to constituting their legal subjectivity'.[61] Hybrid tribunals, despite all their shortcomings, embody the promise of a continued

---

59 See, eg, Andrew Byrnes and Gabrielle Simm, 'Peoples' Tribunals, International Law and the Use of Force' (2013) 36(2) *University of New South Wales Law Journal* 711.

60 Lon L Fuller, *The Morality of Law* (Yale University Press, rev ed, 1969) 192.

61 Martha-Marie Kleinhans and Roderick A Macdonald, 'What is a Critical Legal Pluralism?' (1997) 12 *Canadian Journal of Law and Society* 25, 38.

conversation that allows different actors and communities to engage with and interact within the ICL framework, while considering and possibly transforming this very framework. Hybridity may create a more productive space than the purely international and, to a large extent, top-down-driven *ad hoc* tribunals and the ICC. And it can be argued that the hybrid tribunals have already made us think more carefully about ICL's constituencies: for whom is justice, in fact, delivered? Should we pay substantial attention to local needs and concerns, or should they only be considered if and when ICL principles are not affected? In other words, can – or should – the international criminal legal order be flexible and open-minded?

Further reading

Alamuddin, Amal, Nidal Nabil Jurdi and David Tolbert (eds), *The Special Tribunal for Lebanon: Law and Practice* (Oxford University Press, 2014).

Heindel, Anne and John D Ciorciari, *Hybrid Justice: The Extraordinary Chambers in the Courts of Cambodia* (University of Michigan Press, 2014).

Hobbs, Harry, 'Hybrid Tribunals and the Composition of the Court: In Search of Sociological Legitimacy' (2016) 16(2) *Chicago Journal of International Law* 482.

Jalloh, Charles Chernor (ed), *The Sierra Leone Special Court and its Legacy* (Cambridge University Press, 2014).

McAuliffe, Pádraig, 'Hybrid Tribunals at Ten: How International Criminal Justice's Golden Child Became an Orphan' (2011) 7 *Journal of International Law and International Relations* 1.

Williams, Sarah, *Hybrid and Internationalised Criminal Tribunals: Selected Jurisdictional Issues* (Hart, 2012).

12

THE INTERNATIONAL CRIMINAL COURT

Between law and politics

Christian M. De Vos

Introduction

On a crisp fall morning in October 2014, Kenyan President Uhuru Kenyatta became the first sitting head of state to appear before the International Criminal Court (ICC). Kenyatta had taken office in April of the previous year: he had been elected despite (or perhaps because of) the ICC Prosecutor having charged him with crimes against humanity for his alleged role in the post-election violence that gripped Kenya in late 2007. Kenyatta's attendance was unusual for a pre-trial 'status conference', but in this case the ICC judges had ordered he appear in light of persistent accusations that the government had failed to cooperate, and indeed actively obstructed, the Prosecutor's investigation. Furthermore, in an extraordinary act of political theatre, Kenyatta had days before temporarily transferred his powers to Deputy President William Ruto – himself another ICC accused – so that he would appear before the Court, in his view, as a private citizen. In his words, it was an act to 'protect the sovereignty of the Kenyan Republic'.[1]

Kenyatta later appeared on the ICC's steps with dozens of MPs who had flown with him to The Hague, and with supporters who had gathered in front of the Court to protest the proceedings. Their celebrations continued when by early 2016 all charges against the remaining accused were withdrawn or dismissed in their entirety. In his end-of-year address on Jamhuri Day – meant to commemorate the country's independence from colonial rule – Kenyatta reflected on Kenya's experience with the ICC:

---

1 Tom Maliti, 'President Kenyatta Temporarily Lays Down Powers to Attend ICC' *International Justice Monitor* (6 October 2014) <www.ijmonitor.org/2014/10/president-kenyatta-temporarily-lays-down-powers-to-attend-icc/>.

In our pursuit of a more stable and just order, we are champions of global institutions grounded in fairness and respect for national sovereignty. The Kenyan cases at the ICC have ended but the experience has given us cause to observe that this institution has become a tool of global power politics and not the justice it was built to dispense. We are not the world's richest or most powerful nation, but we are entitled to an equal share of respect for our nationhood, our sovereignty, and our laws.[2]

Kenyatta concluded that Kenya would 'need to give serious thought' to its continued membership in the Court.

The ICC's Kenyan experience (in which a legal hearing was transformed into a quasi-political rally) and Kenya's ICC experience (in which a trial became a verdict on sovereignty itself) illustrate the extent to which the Court, as both an institution and a project, is situated between law and politics. Its interventions and the effects they produce are a form of juridified politics, or what Gerry Simpson has elsewhere called juridified diplomacy: 'the phenomenon by which conflict about the purpose and shape of international political life (as well as specific disputes in this realm) is translated into legal doctrine or resolved in legal institutions'.[3] With its emergence at the turn of the century as the world's first permanent criminal court, the ICC arguably represents the culmination of this phenomenon. It marks the institutional realization of what has been termed a 'justice cascade': the emergence of a 'dramatic new trend in world politics toward holding individual state officials, including heads of state, criminally accountable for human rights violations'.[4]

This chapter addresses the ICC's place as part of this dramatic trend. It suggests that while the Court continues this growing juridification of international politics, its structural design – wherein it is intended to supplement, not supplant, national jurisdictions – also represents a departure from predecessor courts and tribunals. Commonly referred to as complementarity, this principle has become not only a legal concept (an organizing principle for the regulation of concurrent jurisdiction), but also the political cornerstone of the Court: it represents the very future of international criminal justice. In the words of one leading transitional justice NGO, 'How the complementarity principle is put into practice will be the key to the fight

2 Uhuru Kenyatta, 'Speech during 53rd Jamhuri Day celebrations' *The Star* (12 December 2016) <www.the-star.co.ke/news/2016/12/12/read-president-uhuru-kenyattas-speech-during-53rd-jamhuri-day_c1472055>.

3 Gerry Simpson, *Law, War and Crime: War Crimes Trial and The Reinvention of International Law* (Polity Press, 2007) 1.

4 Kathryn Sikkink, *The Justice Cascade: How Human Rights Prosecutions Are Changing World Politics* (W.W. Norton & Company, 2011) 5.

against impunity and thus the future of international justice will largely turn on these efforts'.[5]

In considering how the ICC has fared in these efforts, the chapter is structured in four parts. Part one outlines the Court's historical origins and key aspects of the negotiations that led first to the drafting of the Rome Statute and, four short years later, to the establishment of the Court itself. Part two provides a broad overview of the ICC's juridical and institutional architecture, paying particular attention to the principle of complementarity and to the Office of the Prosecutor (OTP), given its central role in shaping the Court's engagements around the world. Part three provides a select overview of the Court's operations to date – its preliminary examinations, investigations, and cases – with a particular focus on how the complementarity regime has thus far been interpreted and defined by ICC judges. Finally, part four reflects on some critical flash points and tensions that have arisen in the Court's work to date, as it seeks to navigate between law and politics.

I Negotiating a new Court

Unlike its *ad hoc* predecessors in Rwanda and the former Yugoslavia (both of which were established under the UN Security Council's authority), the ICC is a treaty-based institution. In the Rome Statute, signed in 1998, the idea for such a court re-emerged as a global project on the wave of a post-Cold War renaissance in international institutions and the rule of law.[6] Trinidad and Tobago first requested that the UN General Assembly consider the question of a permanent court in 1989. While this initial request ostensibly focused on a court with narrower subject matter jurisdiction (drug trafficking), the General Assembly subsequently requested that the UN International Law Commission (ILC) prioritize drafting a proposed statute for an international court with more expansive jurisdiction.

The ILC, in turn, 'seized enthusiastically' upon the mandate. As one commentator has noted, 'The Draft Code of Crimes which it had been working on for many years had been a largely academic exercise, but now there was a chance to develop an implementation mechanism that might actually punish perpetrators of these crimes'.[7] Subsequent atrocities in Yugoslavia and the Rwandan genocide – as well as the establishment of their attendant tribunals – accelerated the process. By 1994, and 'at lightning speed by its own standards', the ILC had finished its work and presented a first draft

---

5 International Center for Transitional Justice, *The Future of International Justice: National Courts Supported by International Expertise* (22 April 2011) <www.ictj.org/news/future-international-justice-national-courts-supported-international-expertise>.

6 See, eg, Ruti G Teitel, *Transitional Justice* (Oxford University Press, 2000).

7 Marlies Glasius, *The International Criminal Court: A Global Civil Society Achievement* (Routledge, 2006) 11.

statute for an ICC.[8] Over the course of the next four years, 'the original 43-page 1994 ILC draft Statute expanded into a draft Statute of 173 pages replete with bracketed options, alternative phrasing, and footnotes for consideration at the Rome Conference'.[9]

In the final text that emerged, the court's subject matter jurisdiction included the 'core' international crimes of genocide, war crimes, and crimes against humanity (but not the much-debated crime of aggression[10]). While the definitions of both genocide and war crimes were largely borrowed from the Yugoslavia and Rwandan tribunals (themselves modeled on the definitions contained in the Genocide Convention and Geneva Conventions), the Statute is notable, in part, for its enumerations of crimes against humanity, many of which – the recruitment of child soldiers, apartheid, rape, and sexual violence – were defined for the first time in unparalleled detail. Reflecting a gradual erosion in the distinction between crimes committed in the context of international and non-international armed conflicts, the Statute also explicitly addresses crimes committed in both.[11] Consistent with the consent-based nature of treaties, the Statute further provides that the ICC may exercise territorial jurisdiction over a crime if the 'State on the territory of which the conduct in question occurred' is a party to the Statute or has accepted the Court's jurisdiction by a declaration.[12] An alternative precondition for jurisdiction is nationality: the Court may exercise its jurisdiction when an accused is a national of an ICC member state.[13]

From a temporal perspective, the ICC only has jurisdiction over events that occurred after the entry into force of the Rome Statute on July 1, 2002, following its 60th ratification (currently, 124 countries have ratified the Statute).[14] For states that became (or become) a party after this date, the Court may exercise its jurisdiction with respect to crimes committed on their territory after the Statute's entry into force for that particular state, unless it makes a declaration accepting the Court's jurisdiction retroactive to 2002.[15]

Provided these jurisdictional preconditions are met, the ICC may become seized of a matter in one of three ways. First, member states may either refer

---

8 Ibid 13.

9 Benjamin N Schiff, *Building the International Criminal Court* (Cambridge University Press, 2008) 70.

10 An agreeable definition of that crime was not reached until the ICC's first Review Conference in Kampala, Uganda in 2010, but it has yet to receive sufficient ratification for the Court to exercise jurisdiction. See also the discussion in Chapter 8 in this book.

11 See, eg, *Rome Statute of the International Criminal Court*, opened for signature 17 July 1998, 2187 UNTS 90 (entered into force 1 July 2002) ('*Rome Statute*') Art. 8.

12 Ibid Arts 12(2)(a) and 12(3).

13 Ibid Art. 12(2)(b).

14 Of the 124 states, 34 are African, 19 are from the Asia-Pacific region, 18 are from Eastern Europe, 28 are from Latin America/the Caribbean, and 25 are from Western Europe.

15 *Rome Statute*, Art. 11.

their own situations to the Court (so-called 'self referrals'), or those of another contracting state.[16] Second, after much debate, it was also agreed that the ICC Prosecutor could, subject to judicial approval, seek to open an investigation into a member state under her *proprio motu* authority.[17] Finally, inserted into the structure of the Statute is a form of exceptional jurisdiction: Article 13(2) grants the UN Security Council the power to also refer situations to the ICC Prosecutor, even where the state concerned has not ratified the Statute.[18] Further, under Article 16, the Council is empowered to prevent situations from being dealt with by the Court.

The Court's broad ambitions are marked by other novelties, notably the Statute's provisions for a complex regime of victim participation and reparations in ICC proceedings.[19] In this sense, the Court 'seeks to incorporate restorative dimensions that bring it more explicitly into a relationship with the field of transitional justice'.[20] The network of actors it engages is similarly wide-ranging, including not only political entities like the UN Security Council and the Assembly of States Parties (ASP, i.e., the Court's governing body of member states), but a dense, interconnected web of non-state actors as well: international and domestic NGOs working in conflict and post-conflict contexts, human rights advocates, academics, and philanthropic foundations. Many of these same non-state actors were also integral to the Court's establishment and exercised a degree of influence in the negotiations that was largely unprecedented in previous international treaty negotiations.

II Juridical and institutional architecture

The ICC's architecture extends inwards, in terms of its own institutional structures, and outwards, in terms of its relationship to other national

---

16 Ibid Art. 14. A number of states to date have self-referred their situations to the ICC: Uganda, Democratic Republic of Congo, Central African Republic, Mali. This practice has generated a significant literature amongst commentators who contend that such referrals are unsupported by the Statute and the intention of the drafters. See, eg, William Schabas, 'Prosecutorial Discretion v. Judicial Activism' (2008) 6 *Journal of International Criminal Justice* 731. Darryl Robinson, however, has persuasively contested this view, noting that Art. 14 expressly provides for state party referrals, and that they were a 'recurring and explicit topic of deliberation throughout the negotiations'. Darryl Robinson, 'The Controversy over Territorial State Referrals and Reflections on ICL Discourse' (2011) 9 *Journal of International Criminal Justice* 364.

17 *Rome Statute*, Art. 15(1).

18 Libya and Sudan, discussed further below, are the ICC's only Security Council referrals to date.

19 On the ICC's victim participation regime, see also the discussion in Chapter 16 in this book.

20 Christian De Vos, Sara Kendall and Carsten Stahn, 'Introduction' in Christian De Vos, Sara Kendall and Carsten Stahn (eds), *Contested Justice: The Politics and Practice of International Criminal Court Interventions* (Cambridge University Press, 2015) 1, 4.

jurisdictions. While the ICC's *ad hoc* predecessors enjoyed primacy over national jurisdictions, a defining feature of the Court is that it is meant to complement domestic investigations and prosecutions. The ILC had presaged much of the debate around complementarity by noting early on that the main question to resolve in establishing a permanent international court was whether it was intended to 'replace, compete with or complement national jurisdictions'.[21] Ultimately, the ILC's draft endorsed the third option: the court should be 'complementary to national criminal justice systems in cases where . . . trial procedures may not be available or may be ineffective'.[22] The Commission further proposed a regime according to which jurisdiction would be allocated based on a determination of the admissibility of a case (not a 'situation' in general).[23] The ILC report thus reflected the 'classical' conception of complementarity as a limiting jurisdictional principle. In Carsten Stahn's words, it was a 'concept to regulate potential conflicts as between the (primary) jurisdiction of national courts and the residual jurisdiction of the ICC'.[24]

Article 17 of the Rome Statute sets out the substantive criteria for determining the admissibility of a case, while Article 19 grants the right to challenge admissibility to an accused, as well as to a state that could claim jurisdiction over the case. Article 17 states that 'a case is inadmissible where . . . [it] is being investigated or prosecuted by a State which has jurisdiction over it, unless the State is *unwilling or unable* genuinely to carry out the investigation or prosecution'.[25] The Statute thus sets forth a two-step test: first, whether a state is investigating or prosecuting the case (or has done so) and, if so, whether it is 'unwilling or unable' to do so genuinely. Notably, this latter question involves a more subjective assessment of the standards by which such proceedings should be judged, although commentators and Court documents alike have noted that, 'complementarity does not require an assessment of [a] state's overall justice system . . . merely that it is

---

21 Mohamed El Zeidy, 'The Genesis of Complementarity' in Carsten Stahn and Mohamed M El Zeidy (eds), *The International Criminal Court and Complementarity* (Cambridge University Press, 2011) 111.
22 *ILC Draft Statute*, Preamble.
23 Ibid Art. 35 ('Issues of Admissibility'). The Rome Statute retains this provision: admissibility assessments are case-specific. Cases 'comprise specific incidents during which one or more crimes within the jurisdiction of the Court seem to have been committed by one more identified suspects, [and] entail proceedings that take place after the issuance of a warrant of arrest or a summons to appear'. Situations, by contrast, are 'generally defined in terms of temporal, territorial and in some cases personal parameters'. *Situation in the Democratic Republic of Congo (Decision on the Applications for Participation in the Proceedings of VPRS 1, VPRS 2, VPRS 3, VPRS 4, VPRS 5 and VPRS 6)* (International Criminal Court, Pre-Trial Camber I, Case No ICC-01/04-101, 17 January 2006) [65].
24 Carsten Stahn, 'Complementarity: A Tale of Two Notions' (2008) 19 *Criminal Law Forum* 90.
25 *Rome Statute*, Art. 17 (emphasis added).

capable of conducting genuine proceedings in the particular case'.[26] While the condition of that system can undoubtedly influence the ability to investigate or prosecute a particular case, it is not a determinative basis for admissibility.

But while technically understood as a legal principle, complementarity has also increasingly become an instrument of policy. This policy, often referred to as 'positive' complementarity, envisions a far more ambitious relationship between the ICC and national forums, wherein the Court itself – either through the threat of prosecution, or through support to and cooperation with domestic jurisdictions – seeks to actively encourage criminal proceedings. As stated by former Prosecutor Luis Moreno-Ocampo in a speech to the ICC's Assembly of States Parties, one of his office's 'core policies' would be to pursue a 'positive approach to cooperation and to the principle of complementarity'. This meant, in his words, 'encouraging genuine national proceedings where possible, relying on national and international networks, and participating in a system of international cooperation'.[27] In this conception, complementarity is no longer merely a constraint on the Court; it is a way to magnify its effects.

As a matter of institutional architecture, the ICC is divided into four organs: the Registry, the Presidency, the Office of the Prosecutor, and its three judicial divisions. While the Registry conducts 'non-judicial' activities – overseeing such vital tasks as ensuring victim and witness protection, establishing the ICC's 'field offices', and providing support to defense counsel and victims' lawyers – the Presidency coordinates the Court's internal judicial matters (e.g. allocating judges, situations, and cases to various divisions) and conducts external relations with states. The Court's 18 judges are organized into three divisions: Pre-Trial, Trial, and Appeals Division. They are assigned to divisions according to their qualifications and experience, sitting in panels of three for all pre-trial and trial proceedings, and as a panel of five for appellate proceedings.

The OTP, however, is perhaps the most closely watched of the Court's organs. Situated between the ICC's institutional center in The Hague and the various country contexts in which it operates, the Office's choices – through the exercise of prosecutorial discretion, as well as its access to and reliance upon local actors working on the ground – affect not only the overall work of the Court, but can also have a significant influence on the contours of domestic accountability efforts. Led by Prosecutor Fatou Bensouda since 2012,

---

26 Sarah MH Nouwen, *Complementarity in the Line of Fire: The Catalysing Effect of the International Criminal Court in Uganda and Sudan* (Cambridge University Press, 2013) 74, 106.

27 Third Session of the Assembly of States Parties to the Rome Statute of the International Criminal Court, *Address by Prosecutor Luis Moreno-Ocampo* (6 September 2004) 2 <www.icc-cpi.int/iccdocs/asp_docs/library/asp/LMO_20040906_En.pdf>.

the Office is made up of three divisions: Jurisdiction, Complementarity, and Cooperation (JCCD); Investigations; and Prosecutions.[28]

Of the three, the JCCD has significant influence on the Office's policy decisions, and it is here that the Prosecutor's selective choices originate.[29] Its Situation Analysis Section is primarily responsible for conducting preliminary examinations (discussed further below), which includes evaluating information the Office receives and making recommendations as to whether an investigation has a sufficient basis to proceed. Its International Cooperation Section is regarded as the Office's 'diplomatic' arm: it carries out external relations activities, including negotiating cooperation agreements, providing legal advice on complementarity and cooperation, and 'liais[ing] with external actors to implement the complementarity policy'.[30] By contrast, the OTP's Investigations Division is responsible for 'the provision of factual crime analysis and the analysis of information and evidence, in support of preliminary examinations and evaluations, investigations and prosecutions'.[31] The following section addresses these three aspects of the ICC's work in turn.

III Sites of intervention: examinations, investigations, cases

A Preliminary examinations

Preliminary examinations comprise a unique pre-investigative stage within the ICC's statutory framework. While the scope and length of the examination falls within the discretion of the Prosecutor, Article 15 of the Rome Statute mandates the Prosecutor to first determine, regardless of the manner in which a situation comes before the Court, whether there is a 'reasonable basis to proceed' with an investigation.[32] 'Reasonable basis' is the lowest evidentiary standard in the Statute; as compared to evidence gathered during the investigation stage, it is neither 'comprehensive' nor 'conclusive'.[33]

---

28 *Regulations of the Office of the Prosecutor ('OTP Regulations')*, ICC-BD/05-01-09 (23 April 2009) Regulations 7-9.

29 Ignaz Stegmiller, *The Pre-Investigation Stage of the ICC* (Duncker and Humblot, 2011) 457.

30 Gregory Townsend, 'Structure and Management' in Luc Reydams, Jan Wouters and Cedric Ryngaert (eds), *International Prosecutors* (Oxford University Press, 2012) 289 (citing ICC OTP Operations Manual (February 2011)).

31 The Division is additionally responsible for 'the preparation of the necessary security plans and protection policies for each case to ensure the safety and well-being of victims, witnesses, Office staff, and persons at risk on account of their interaction with the Court', in 'cooperation and coordination' with the Registrar; providing investigative expertise and support; and preparing and coordinating the field deployment of Office staff. See *OTP Regulations*, Reg. 8.

32 *Rome Statute*, Art. 15.

33 *Situation in the Republic of Kenya (Decision pursuant to Article 15 of the Rome Statute on the Authorization of an Investigation into the Situation in the Republic of Kenya)* (International Criminal Court, Pre-Trial Chamber II, Case No ICC-01/09-19, 31 March 2010) [27].

Of those it has made public, the Court currently lists ten active examinations in various stages of review: Afghanistan, Burundi, Colombia, Gabon, Guinea, Iraq (for alleged war crimes committed by United Kingdom nationals in the context of the Iraq conflict), Nigeria, and Ukraine. Two additional examinations broadly pertain to the Israel/Palestine conflict: one for Palestine proper (following Palestine's June 2014 declaration accepting ICC jurisdiction); the other for Israel's 2010 raid on the *Mavi Marmara*, which was part of a humanitarian aid flotilla bound for the Gaza strip.[34]

In a policy paper on preliminary examinations (first published in 2010, later updated in 2013), the OTP subsequently divided the process into four phases.[35] Each phase entails a progressively more detailed review of the situation, including a 'thorough factual and legal assessment' of the crimes allegedly committed (phase 2); 'the scale, nature, manner of commission of the crimes, and their impact' (phase 3); and whether any 'interests of justice' should apply to the Prosecutor's determination to initiate, or not to initiate, a formal investigation (phase 4).[36]

Unlike investigations, where the Prosecutor must obtain the authorization of the Pre-Trial Chamber to proceed, judicial oversight of preliminary examinations is limited, nor are Article 17's admissibility requirements applicable at this stage. Furthermore, in the Office's view, 'there is no obligation under the Statute or the Rules' to set a time period for the length of examinations, although this view has been increasingly criticized by certain member states.[37] Also attracting criticism has been the OTP's adoption of a progressively more public approach to examinations. For instance, the Office now often publicizes when it initiates an examination and provides periodic updates of its activities.[38] It may also 'disseminate statistics on information on alleged crimes under Article 15' and 'publicize events, such as OTP high-level visits to the concerned countries'.[39] Collectively, these measures seek to bring greater transparency to the examination process but also greater scrutiny to those states under review.

---

34 The latter situation was referred to the OTP by the Comoros, on the basis that the vessel had been registered there. See 'Referral under Articles 14 and 12(2)(a) of the Rome Statute arising from the 31 May 2010, Gaza Freedom Flotilla situation' (14 May 2013) <https://www.icc-cpi.int/iccdocs/otp/Referral-from-Comoros.pdf>.

35 Office of the Prosecutor, 'Policy Paper on Preliminary Examinations' (November 2013).

36 For the Office's interpretation and approach to applying criteria with respect to the 'interests of justice', see 'Policy Paper on the Interests of Justice' (September 2007).

37 See *Situation in the Central African Republic (Prosecution's Report Pursuant to Pre-Trial Chamber III's 30 November 2006 Decision Requesting Information on the Status of the Preliminary Examination of the Situation in the Central African Republic)* (International Criminal Court, Pre-Trial Camber III, Case No ICC-01/05-06, 30 November 2006).

38 These measures include publishing, as of 2011, an annual summary of activities performed during the course of the year. These reports are available online at the OTP's website.

39 Office of the Prosecutor, 'Prosecutorial Strategy 2009-2012' (1 February 2010) [38]–[39]; see also 'Policy Paper on Preliminary Examinations' [89]–[90].

The OTP's investment in the preliminary examinations stage has expanded under Prosecutor Bensouda's leadership. As noted in her assessment of the Office's current strategic plan:

> As one of the three core activities of the Office, stronger emphasis is now placed on the Office's preliminary examinations activities. Through its preliminary examinations work, the Office is committed to contributing to two overarching goals: the ending of impunity, by encouraging genuine national proceedings through its positive approach to complementarity, and the prevention of crimes.[40]

The Prosecutor has likewise drawn a direct link between the potential of preliminary examinations and complementarity to serve as both a deterrent and a catalyst for national accountability efforts. Writing in 2012, she noted that the phrase 'gives the States concerned the possibility of intervening to put an end to crimes before the Office of the Prosecutor initiates an investigation', enabling the latter 'to act as a catalyst for national proceedings'.[41]

B *Investigations*

Investigations mark the point where the OTP is not only engaged in a 'situation', but also gathering evidence that can lead to the identification of specific individuals against whom a 'case' may be built. While the Rome Statute is silent as to how such evidence collection is to be carried out, the OTP adopted early on a policy of 'focused investigations', wherein it would seek to carry out investigations in a 'few months, involving as few witnesses and incidents as possible'.[42] Related to this approach has been the Office's use of small teams of rotating investigators to carry out its investigations. Unfortunately, the pursuit of this strategy has meant that ICC investigators spend relatively little time in the field: in practice, they are Hague-based and travel 'on mission'.[43] This approach is also a result of the ICC's limited resources and financing, as many member states have continually insisted upon a 'zero growth' budget for the Court, notwithstanding its growing number of situations. At present, the ICC maintains investigations in ten situations. None have been closed to date,

---

40 Fatou Bensouda, 'Foreword' in Carsten Stahn (ed), *The Law and Practice of the International Criminal Court* (Oxford University Press, 2015).
41 Fatou Bensuoda, 'Reflections from the International Criminal Court Prosecutor' (2012) 45(1-2) *Case Western Reserve Journal of International Law* 505, 508.
42 Katy Glassborow, 'ICC Investigative Strategy on Sexual Violence Crimes Under Fire' *Institute for War & Peace Reporting* (27 October 2008). Glassborow quotes Beatrice Le Fraper du Hellen, who headed the JCCD from 2006 to 2010.
43 See Christian M De Vos, 'Investigating from Afar: The ICC's Evidence Problem' (2013) 26(4) *Leiden Journal of International Law* 1009.

although Prosecutor Bensouda announced in December 2014 that she was 'hibernating' the Office's activities in Darfur due to persistent non-cooperation of the Sudanese government with the Court's outstanding warrants.[44]

This approach to investigations has led to notable criticism of the Court by states and affected communities alike. For one, the limited charges brought against some early accused – notably that of Thomas Lubanga in the Democratic Republic of Congo (DRC), who was charged with conscripting and enlisting child soldiers – resulted in dissatisfaction on the part of those who contend that the OTP favoured expediency over thorough investigations, with sexual and gender-based crimes, in particular, receiving insufficient attention. Another concern is the Office's reliance on, and failure to adequately protect, so-called 'intermediaries'. These locally situated individuals (and organizations) often assist the Prosecutor in identifying witnesses, assisting victims, as well as providing a variety of vital services in support of the Court's core functions; however, they have also led to concerns about witness tampering and credibility.[45]

More directly, such methods have also imperiled the ICC's credibility; indeed, while the withdrawal of charges against Kenyatta and other Kenyan accused was undoubtedly the most damaging for the OTP, to date nearly one-third of those individuals brought before the Court have had the charges against them dismissed by the pre-trial chamber or later withdrawn. One report has noted that this is 'a substantially higher rate of dismissal than the acquittal rate seen at other international criminal bodies following a full trial, even though the standard at trial – beyond a reasonable doubt – is higher than the burden at the confirmation stage'.[46] These statistics, in turn, have a further bearing on complementarity: the ICC's ability to function as a credible threat depends on the quality of its investigations and prosecutions.

In response to such criticisms, the Office's 2012-2015 strategic plan announced a departure from the policy of 'focused investigations' in favour of a principle of 'in-depth, open-ended investigations', and explicitly committed the Office to ensuring that its 'cases at the confirmation hearings . . . are as trial-ready as possible', an approach that the Office's 2016-2018 strategic

44 Thomas Weatherall, 'The Evolution of "Hibernation" at the International Criminal Court: How the World Misunderstood Prosecutor Bensouda's Darfur Announcement' 20(10) *ASIL Insights* (13 May 2016) <www.asil.org/insights/volume/20/issue/10/evolution-hibernation-international-criminal-court-how-world>.

45 See, eg, Christian M De Vos, '"Someone Who Comes Between One Person and Another": *Lubanga*, Local Cooperation and the Right to a Fair Trial' (2011) 12 *Melbourne Journal of International Law* 217.

46 War Crimes Research Office, *Investigative Management, Strategies, and Techniques of the International Criminal Court's Office of the Prosecutor* (2012) 9. The burden of proof during the ICC confirmation of charges stage is 'substantial grounds to believe'. See *Rome Statute*, Art. 61(7).

plan maintains.[47] Perhaps drawing on the lessons of the Kenyan experience, the Office also announced a departure from its previously stated policy of prosecuting only those 'most responsible' for crimes in favor of a strategy of 'gradually building upwards', wherein it 'first investigates and prosecutes a limited number of mid-and high-level perpetrators in order to ultimately have a reasonable prospect of conviction for those most responsible'.[48]

C Cases

ICC cases are divided into multiple stages: pre-trial, trial, appeals, and reparations. Cases are considered 'closed once a conviction/sentence or an acquittal becomes final, or where charges are withdrawn or dismissed either due to a lack of evidence or because the charges were not confirmed. The latter process – known as the confirmation of charges stage – is one of two key stages that comprise the pre-trial phase of ICC proceedings; the other is admissibility. As noted, the admissibility regime is a function of the ICC's complementary role to national prosecutions. Much of the Court's early jurisprudence in this regard has unfolded in the context of individual defendants who raised challenges following the referral of situations to the Court by the state itself, as in Uganda and the DRC. More recent decisions have been triggered at the behest of states, notably in Kenya and Libya.

Interestingly, the more expansive notion of 'positive' complementarity developed by the Court's non-judicial actors and supporters has been at odds with much of the ICC's admissibility jurisprudence (to date, only one admissibility challenge has been successful).[49] Given the desire to use complementarity to catalyze accountability efforts at the national level, it might be expected that the Court would seek to grant states a relatively wide margin of discretion over the contours of their criminal proceedings; however, rather than encouraging such flexibility, a series of relatively strict tests have instead characterized the ICC's Article 17 jurisprudence. Most notable amongst these is an emphasis on whether proceedings initiated by the OTP and a state that would seek to successfully challenge admissibility are sufficiently similar – if not identical – such that they concern the same person, conduct, and possibly even the same factual incidents. As described by the Appeals

---

47 Office of the Prosecutor, 'Strategic Plan', June 2012-2015 <www.icc-cpi.int/iccdocs/otp/ OTP-Strategic-Plan-2013.pdf>; see also OTP 'Strategic Plan', 2016-2018 (6 July 2015) <www.icc-cpi.int/iccdocs/otp/070715-otp_strategic_plan_2016-2018.pdf>.

48 Ibid.

49 The successful challenge, which has also been much criticized, was filed by Libya on behalf of its former chief of intelligence, Abdullah al-Senussi. *Prosecutor v Saif Al-Islam Gaddafi and Abdullah Al-Senussi (Decision on the admissibility of the case against Abdullah Al-Senussi)* (International Criminal Court, Pre-Trial Chamber I, Case No ICC-01/11-01/11, 11 October 2013).

Chamber, 'What is required is a judicial assessment of whether the case that the State is investigating sufficiently mirrors the one that the Prosecutor is investigating'.[50]

Furthermore, when faced with competing claims about domestic proceedings (particularly challenges brought by an individual accused) ICC judges have undertaken a relatively superficial review, while setting a high evidentiary threshold for challengers to satisfy. The Appeals Chamber's treatment of Kenya's admissibility challenge is noteworthy here, as it noted that to 'discharge' its burden of proof to show that a case is inadmissible, the state would have to submit concrete evidence that pointed to 'specific investigative steps', including, *inter alia*, 'interviewing witnesses or suspects, collecting documentary evidence, or carrying out forensic analyses'.[51] The Court has also applied substantial procedural limitations to admissibility challenges, for instance by restricting the timing of such challenges and the scope of the pre-trial chambers' review.[52] For these reasons, some commentators have suggested that the ICC should fundamentally rethink its relationship to national criminal justice systems such that, 'as long as a state is making a genuine effort to bring a suspect to justice, the ICC should find his or her case inadmissible regardless of the conduct the state investigates or the prosecutorial strategy the state pursues'.[53]

---

50 *Prosecutor v Saif Al-Islam Gaddafi and Abdullah Al-Senussi (Judgment on the appeal of Libya against the decision of Pre-Trial Chamber I of 21 May 2013 entitled 'Decision on the admissibility of the case against Saif Al-Islam Gaddafi')* (International Criminal Court, Appeals Chamber, Case No ICC-01/11-01/11 OA 4, 21 May 2014) ('Gaddafi Admissibility Appeals Judgment') [73]; see also *Prosecutor v. Saif Al-Islam Gaddafi and Abdullah Al-Senussi (Judgment on the appeal of Mr. Abdullah Al-Senussi against the decision of Pre-Trial Chamber I of 11 October 2013 entitled 'Decision on the admissibility of the case against Abdullah Al-Senussi')* (International Criminal Court, Appeals Chamber, Case No ICC-01/11-01/11 OA 6, 24 July 2014) [119].

51 See *Prosecutor v Francis Kirimi Muthaura, Uhuru Muigai Kenyatta and Mohammed Hussein Ali (Judgment on the appeal of the Republic of Kenya against the decision of Pre-Trial Chamber II of 30 May 2011 entitled 'Decision on the Application by the Government of Kenya Challenging the Admissibility of the Case Pursuant to Article 19(2)(b) of the Statute')* (International Criminal Court, Appeals Chambers, Case No ICC-01/09-02/11 OA, 30 August 2011) [40], [61].

52 See, eg, *Prosecutor v Germain Katanga and Mathieu Ngudjolo Chui (Judgment on the Appeal of Mr. Germain Katanga Against the Oral Decision of Trial Chamber II of 12 June 2009 on the Admissibility of the Case)* (International Criminal Court, Appeals Chambers, Case No ICC-01/04-01/07-OA8, 25 September 2009) [81]. In *Katanga*, the Court held that the DRC met the 'inactivity' prong of Art. 17 because it had closed its proceedings against Katanga upon his transfer to The Hague, but failed to note that he had no prior notice of his transfer. In a further limitation, the Appeals Chamber left unchallenged the Trial Chamber's determination that admissibility challenges must be filed prior to the commencement of trial, which it defined as the moment of the Chamber's constitution, rather than the actual proceedings.

53 Kevin Jon Heller, 'Radical Complementarity' (2016) 14(3) *Journal of International Criminal Justice* 637, 640. For a forceful rejoinder to Heller, see Rod Rastan, 'What is 'Substantially the Same Conduct'? Unpacking the ICC's 'First Limb' Complementarity Jurisprudence' (2017) 15(1) *Journal of International Criminal Justice* 1.

But perhaps the biggest criticism of the ICC thus far (not unlike those leveled at other international courts) has been the length and cost of its trials. Of those cases that have been deemed admissible, the ICC has thus far only completed five trials, four of which touch or concern the conflict in the DRC, the site of one of the world's bloodiest and longest-running conflicts. One of these trials resulted in an acquittal.[54] In what has since proved to be a landmark case, another conviction concerned the actions of Al Faqi Al Mahdi (the member of an Islamist militia that seized control of Timbuktu, in Mali, in 2012), who pled guilty to one count of directing an attack against buildings dedicated to religion and historic monuments.[55]

At the time of writing, three more trials are underway: against former Ugandan child soldier and Lord's Resistance Army commander, Dominic Ongwen; against Laurent Gbagbo, the former President of Côte d'Ivoire, and Charles Blé Goudé, the leader of a pro-Gbagbo militia group; and against former rebel commander Bosco Ntaganda, for crimes allegedly committed in 2002-2003 in the Ituri district of the DRC. But the length and paucity of trials has frustrated states parties (who support the ICC's budget) and affected communities alike. In part, these delays reflect competence issues that have bedevilled the OTP, but they also reflect perennial challenges of securing cooperation from states when the Court itself possesses few enforcement mechanisms.

IV The ICC and juridified politics

Returning to the concept of juridified politics, the myriad ways in which political objectives, negotiations, and decisions are stitched into the ICC's architecture come more clearly into focus. This section considers three broad areas in which politics have mediated the Court's operations to date.

A *Selectivity and bias*

As its docket illustrates, the ICC, since its inception, has been a court almost exclusively concerned with Africa: nine of its ten current investigations involve situations on the continent. Growing criticism that the ICC was targeting African states exploded with the issuance of the 2009 warrant against the Sudanese President Omar al-Bashir and, later, the summonses against Kenyatta and other Kenyan leaders. Moreover, in Sudan and Libya, the Court targeted heads of state following referrals by the UN Security

---

54 *Prosecutor v. Mathieu Ngudjolo (Judgment Pursuant to Article 74 of the Statute)* (International Criminal Court, Trial Chamber II, Case No ICC-01/04-02/12, 18 December 2012).
55 *Prosecutor v. Ahmad Al Faqi Al Mahdi (Judgment and Sentence)* (International Criminal Court, Trial Chamber VIII, Case No ICC-01/12-01/15, 27 September 2016).

254 Christian M. De Vos

Council, an institution whose permanent, veto-wielding members include three states (the United States, Russia, and China) that have not ratified the Rome Statute.

These developments effectively brought the ICC into the center of the African Union's politics, forcefully pushed on by the Kenyan government and culminating by late 2016 in a series of announced withdrawals from the Court by three other African states: The Gambia, South Africa, and Burundi.[56] Indeed, when announcing its withdrawal, The Gambia's former information minister denounced the ICC in explicitly racial terms, as an 'International Caucasian Court for the persecution and humiliation of people of color'.[57] Critical legal scholars have leveled similar charges, arguing that the ICC's apparent bias is itself a function of the Court's role as an institutional vessel to control and maintain the political and economic interests of Western states. As Simpson argues, 'humanity and hegemony are conjoined', with the enduring interests of 'Great Power states' continuing to maintain control over how and where the Court intervenes.[58]

And yet, while the ICC's near exclusive interventions on the African continent – notwithstanding the many situations elsewhere in the world of greater or comparable gravity – reflect the inequalities of the international political order, African states and leaders have also used the cover of ICC intervention to protect or further their own political interests. For instance, where states have 'self-referred' their situations to the ICC, the cases that have ensued have been almost entirely directed at non-state actors who have threatened the government's own claim to power. In Uganda, the OTP has still only charged members of the rebel Lord's Resistance Army, notwithstanding serious allegations of atrocities committed by the Ugandan People's Defense Force; in the DRC, charges have only been brought against armed groups active in the country's long-running civil war;

---

56 Notably, at the time of writing, Gambia has since withdrawn its withdrawal following a change of government, while a South African High Court ruled the country's unilateral withdrawal unconstitutional, absent parliamentary approval and repeal of its own domestic ICC statute. The government has also since indicated that, for now, it will not seek legislative approval for withdrawal. See, eg, Norimitsu Onishi, 'South Africa Reverses Withdrawal from International Criminal Court', *New York Times* (New York), 8 March 2017. While an AU 'Withdrawal Strategy', released in early 2017, also set out a series of ambitious goals with respect to the ICC, mass withdrawal is notably not one of them. Rather, the strategy seeks to 'ensure that international justice is conducted in a fair and transparent manner, devoid of any perception of double standards', 'enhance the regionalization of international criminal law', and 'encourage the adoption of African solutions for African problems'. African Union, 'Withdrawal Strategy Document', Version 12.01.2017 (on-file).

57 Siobhan O'Grady, 'Gambia: The ICC Should Be Called the International Caucasian Court' *Foreign Policy* (26 October 2016) <http://foreignpolicy.com/2016/10/26/gambia-the-icc-should-be-called-the-international-caucasian-court/>.

58 Gerry Simpson, 'Punishing Human Rights Violators' in Conor Gearty and Costas Douzinas (eds), *The Cambridge Companion to Human Rights Law* (Cambridge University Press, 2012) 123.

while in Côte d'Ivoire, only pro-Gbagbo forces have thus far been pursued. Of Uganda, Sarah Nouwen and Wouter Werner have further noted:

> [The] Ugandan government used the ICC to transform the LRA from its own enemy into an enemy of mankind. Meanwhile, the government could present its fight against the LRA as a fight for humanity and itself as the upholder of community values. Its cooperation with the ICC led to an impression of friendship with the Court, which boosted its international legitimacy.[59]

Such decisions may have been the political price paid for 'cooperation' with the relevant states, but they cast doubt on the ICC's ability to serve as an impartial arbiter. And even in countries like Kenya, where the Court did pursue accused from dueling political parties, the proceedings against Kenyatta and Ruto allowed the former rivals to forge a successful political alliance built on vilifying the ICC.[60] Nor is there reason to think that debates about the Court's selective geographies – even if a non-African investigation is begun – are likely to abate.[61] Faced with a deeply unequal international political order, finite resources, and a potentially infinite number of crimes, the OTP must make hard choices not only about when, but also where and how it chooses to intervene. Wherever the Court chooses to acts (or not to act), politics are implicated.

B *Effects and constituencies*

For whom, and in whose name, does the ICC act? This question animates another dimension of the Court's inherent politics, underscoring tensions between and among the ICC's competing stakeholders. As Frédéric Mégret asks, '[W]ho is being imagined as being the symbolic authority behind the [ICC's] work?'[62] In one sense, it may be the states of the ASP, who have ratified the Rome Statute and fund the Court's work; in another, it may be victims and affected communities. Kendall and Nouwen note, for instance, that actors both within and outside the ICC have invoked victims' interests as a 'telos of the work of the ICC – sometimes together with other ends such as

---

59 Sarah MH Nouwen and Wouter G Werner, 'Doing Justice to the Political: The International Criminal Court in Uganda and Sudan' (2010) 21(4) *European Journal of International Law* 962.

60 See, eg, Sara Kendall, '"UhuRuto" and Other Leviathans: the International Criminal Court and the Kenyan Political Order' (2014) 7 *African Journal of Legal Studies* 399.

61 It is possible that several non-African cases will soon come onto the ICC's docket, potentially unsettling this neo-colonial critique. The OTP's current investigation in Georgia, for instance, pits it directly against Russian interests; an investigation into crimes in Afghanistan (which acceded to the Statute in 2003) could encompass the conduct of United States soldiers there.

62 Frédéric Mégret, 'In Whose Name? The ICC and the Search for Constituency' in Christian De Vos, Sara Kendall and Carsten Stahn (eds), *Contested Justice: The Politics and Practice of International Criminal Court Interventions* (Cambridge University Press, 2015) 23.

"the rule of law" or "ending impunity."[63] Or perhaps it is the Court itself, who must demonstrate that the ICC is a relevant and influential force on the international stage.

Numerous examples illustrate these tensions but perhaps most telling is the ICC's intervention in situations of on-going conflict, as well as the effects of its judicial activity on political diplomacy. In Uganda, for instance, the unsealing of the OTP's warrants was touted in part as a necessary precursor to – and condition of – a successful peace negotiation; there could not be peace without justice. Yet, in the end, the Court's intervention did little to contribute to peace-building, caught as it was between the Ugandan government, whose cooperation the OTP required, and the needs of victims (in northern Uganda), many of whom saw the government itself as, at the very least, a co-equal perpetrator in the commission of atrocity crimes. As Adam Branch argues,

> Given the possibility that the ICC's intervention may prolong the conflict and intensify the government's militarism, the ICC, in its quest for effectiveness, may end up not only undermining its legitimacy but also lending support to violent and anti-democratic political forces.[64]

In this sense, there is a risk that the legal processes ICC interventions trigger can calcify politics, rather than challenge or change them.

Elsewhere they can produce backlash, as in the enforcement of ICC arrest warrants. Indeed, the threatened withdrawal of South Africa from the Court was largely triggered by the efforts of South African human rights advocates and NGOs to compel the government to execute the outstanding warrant against President al-Bashir when he entered the country for an African Union Summit in June 2015. While the South African government's formal position has been that the ICC's position on head-of-state immunities puts it at odds with international customary law, its refusal to detain Bashir – in defiance of orders from its own domestic courts to do so – signaled a breaking point in the government's obligations under the Rome Statute and the preferred conduct of its foreign affairs.[65]

63 Sara Kendall and Sarah Nouwen, 'Representational Practices at the International Criminal Court: The Gap Between Juridified and Abstract Victimhood' (2013) 76(3&4) *Law and Contemporary Problems* 239.

64 Adam Branch, 'Uganda's Civil War and the Politics of ICC Intervention' (Summer 2007) 21(2) *Ethics & International Affairs* 189.

65 The issue was litigated all the way to South Africa's Supreme Court, which in March 2016 rejected the state's appeal and ruled that Bashir should indeed have been arrested. Shortly thereafter, the government attempted its notification of withdrawal. Notably, South Africa's courts have also relied on its domestic ICC legislation to insist that the government has a duty to not only cooperate with the Court in the execution of its warrants, but to investigate international crimes perpetrated beyond its borders. One novel decision held that South Africa's National Prosecuting Authority has a duty to investigate credible allegations of torture by members of Robert Mugabe's ZANU-PF party in neighboring Zimbabwe.

Taken together, these examples illustrate the varied, and often unanticipated, effects that ICC interventions can produce, not only by the Court itself but also by the broad network of actors and interests it engages.

C *Complementarity and compliance*

Finally, complementarity's expansion from legal principle to policy tool underscores the way in which political objectives mediate the ICC's work. As noted, a key challenge for the Prosecutor and for the principle of complementarity that underwrites the Court is how she can use the 'shadow' of the ICC to threaten or cajole states into pursuing accountability at the domestic level. This vision was aptly illustrated by Prosecutor Moreno-Ocampo's famous statement, that

> [t]he effectiveness of the International Criminal Court should not be measured by the number of cases that reach the Court. On the contrary, the absence of trials by the ICC, as a consequence of the effective functioning of national systems, would be a major success.[66]

But what should the ICC's influence be on accountability at the domestic level? Given the ambitious goals that animate a policy like 'positive' complementarity, one desirable approach might be to conceive of it as 'primarily a device to accommodate diversity'.[67] Indeed, if the Court is to encourage national investigations and prosecutions, then it will likely have to do so in a way that preserves political discretion and flexibility to states. And yet, as seen above, there is a tension in achieving the goal of greater domestic accountability through judicial fiat. As three commentators have noted,

> [T]he complementarity regime of the Court ... allows for a process of negotiation in which states are able or at least try to protect their interests. It is through this process of negotiation that the complementarity regime has set in place structures of inequality, because some states are simply better equipped to protect their interests in these negotiations than others.[68]

Furthermore, by mandating that states should largely mirror ICC action in the context of admissibility challenges, one key goal of complementarity is

---

66 OTP, 'Paper on some policy issues before the Office of the Prosecutor' (September 2003) 4 <www.icc-cpi.int/nr/rdonlyres/1fa7c4c6-de5f-42b7-8b25-60aa962ed8b6/143594/030905_policy_paper.pdf>.

67 Frédéric Mégret, 'Too Much of a Good Thing? Implementation and the Uses of Complementarity' in Carsten Stahn and Mohamed M El Zeidy (eds), *The International Criminal Court and Complementarity* (Cambridge University Press, 2011) 390.

68 Kamari M Clarke, Abel S Knottnerus and Eefje de Volder (eds), *Africa and the ICC: Perceptions of Justice* (Cambridge University Press, 2016) 11.

arguably inverted: the ICC becomes the center of the accountability process, with domestic systems at the periphery.

While this approach seeks to pull states towards compliance with the Rome Statute framework, it also suggests that the domestic forms and possibilities for post-conflict justice have increasingly been delimited, with attention predominantly paid to criminal prosecution and punishment rather than the plural approaches more commonly associated with transitional justice. As Mark Drumbl has argued, 'Pressures emanating from dominant international norms [can] narrow the diversity of national and local accountability modalities'.[69] The narrowing of such modalities can be seen in several ICC countries, where influential actors have sought to emulate the Court. Sarah Nouwen quotes the first presiding judge of Uganda's International Crimes Division, who 'explained the readiness to copy the ICC model by saying that "[t]he ICC wants us to do everything the way they did it: we must use the same Statute and the same standards."'[70] Such statements raise difficult and enduring questions about the desirability of seeking accountability before international venues like the ICC – at a geographical, political, and cultural distance from where atrocities occur – and its pursuit at in different, possibly non-criminal forms the national or local level.

V Conclusion

The ICC is a pivotal institution in the growing juridification of international politics, but while some have interpreted the Court's establishment as a triumph of law over politics, it is better understood as law mediated through politics, and as politics mediated by law. From Uganda to Kenya to Libya, ICC interventions underscore how, in Simpson's words, 'concepts of the political remain perpetually in play'.[71] In one iteration, the ICC may be humanity's last, best hope to end impunity and deter future atrocity; in another, as President Kenyatta described it, it is 'a tool of global power politics and not the justice it was built to dispense'.[72] Political objectives and calculations will thus always define the ICC's actions – where and when it intervenes, and where and when it does not. Moreover, while the Court may signal the ascendance of a new accountability norm in our international

---

69 Mark A Drumbl, *Atrocity, Punishment, and International Law* (Cambridge University Press, 2007) 121.

70 Sarah MH Nouwen, *Complementarity in the Line of Fire: The Catalysing Effect of the International Criminal Court in Uganda and Sudan* (Cambridge University Press, 2013) 205.

71 Simpson, *Law, War and Crime*, above n 3, 11.

72 Uhuru Kenyatta, 'Speech during 53rd Jamhuri Day celebrations' *The Star* (12 December 2016) <www.the-star.co.ke/news/2016/12/12/read-president-uhuru-kenyattas-speech-during-53rd-jamhuri-day_c1472055>.

political life, it also ushers in a new, evolving chapter about when, how, and who should prosecute the world's worst crimes.

Further reading

Branch, Adam, *Displacing Human Rights: War and Intervention in Northern Uganda* (Oxford University Press, 2011).

Burke-White, William W, 'Proactive Complementarity: The International Criminal Court and National Courts in the Rome System of International Justice' (2008) 49(1) *Harvard International Law Journal* 53.

Clarke, Kamari M, Abel S Knottnerus and Eefje de Volder (eds), *Africa and the ICC: Perceptions of Justice* (Cambridge University Press, 2016).

De Vos, Christian, Sara Kendall and Carsten Stahn, (eds), *Contested Justice: The Politics and Practice of International Criminal Interventions* (Cambridge University Press, 2016).

Heller, Kevin Jon, 'Radical Complementarity' (2016) 14(3) *Journal of International Criminal Justice* 637.

Kersten, Mark, *Justice in Conflict: The Effects of the International Criminal Court's Interventions on Ending Wars and Building Peace* (Oxford University Press, 2016).

Robinson, Darryl, 'Inescapable Dyads: Why the International Criminal Court Cannot Win' (2015) 28(2) *Leiden Journal of International Law* 323.

Stahn, Carsten and Mohamed M El Zeidy, (eds), *The International Criminal Court and Complementarity: From Theory to Practice* (Cambridge University Press, 2011).

13

COMPLEMENTARITY REVISITED

National prosecutions of international crimes and the gaps in international law

Fannie Lafontaine and Sophie Gagné

Introduction

One of the justifications for the creation of international criminal institutions is the traditional failure of States where the crimes occurred, or of which the perpetrator is a national, to undertake investigations and prosecutions in respect of such crimes. Despite this fundamental rationale for the existence of international courts, the International Criminal Court (ICC) has not followed the model of the *ad hoc* Tribunals for the former Yugoslavia and Rwanda (ICTY and ICTR), whose Statutes had recognised 'concurrent jurisdiction', subject to 'primacy over national courts'.[1] The ICC is rather 'complementary to national jurisdictions' and its Statute further affirms in the Preamble that it is 'the duty of every State to exercise its criminal jurisdiction over those responsible for international crimes' and that 'their effective prosecution must be ensured by taking measures at the national level and by enhancing international cooperation'. Complementarity has been hailed as the 'cornerstone' and 'foundational principle' of the ICC Statute.[2]

The ICC is thus based on the hope that post-conflict dynamics may not always prevent domestic war crimes trials. It is also based on the idea that

---

1 SC Res 827, UN SCOR, 48th sess, 3217th mtg, UN Doc S/RES/827 (25 May 1993) as amended by SC Res 1411, UN SCOR, 56th sess, 4535th mtg UN Doc S/Res/1411 (17 May 2002) Art. 9 (*'Statute of the International Criminal Tribunal for the Former Yugoslavia'*); SC Res 955, UN SCOR, 49th sess, 3453rd mtg, UN Doc S/RES/955 (8 November 1994) annex as amended by SC Res 1717, UN SCOR, 61st sess, 5550th mtg, UN Doc S/Res/1717 (13 October 2006), Art. 8 (*'Statute of the International Tribunal for Rwanda'*).
2 *Rome Statute of the International Criminal Court*, opened for signature 17 July 1998, 2187 UNTS 90 (entered into force 1 July 2002); see Sarah MH Nouwen, *Complementarity in the Line of Fire: The Catalysing Effect of the International Criminal Court in Uganda and Sudan* (Cambridge University Press, 2013) 8 and references cited therein.

it forms part of a system of accountability for core international crimes, composed of a web of national jurisdictions able and willing to investigate and prosecute such crimes wherever they were committed. Indeed, the ICC has raised expectations that the principle of complementarity would have a 'catalysing effect' at the domestic level, not only by inciting investigations and prosecutions of international crimes in national courts, but also by spurring reforms of domestic legal norms and justice systems.

Complementarity has thus replaced primacy as the 'leitmotiv' of international criminal justice.[3] It has become trite to say that the promise of the new system of international justice depends on States' capacity and will to put their legal systems to use for the global enterprise. This 'system' of global justice is composed of this vertical interaction between the ICC and its States Parties, but the focus on States also implies a broader – horizontal – relationship between States in cooperating to enforce international criminal law (ICL). The responsibility of States in the prosecution of international crimes is not limited to the obligations they have undertaken in ratifying the ICC Statute, but also emanates from other sources of international law. The development of the principle of universal jurisdiction, for instance, which vests in every member of the international community the right or duty to ensure that so-called atrocity crimes do not go unpunished, is part of the 'tools' in the hands of States to contribute to closing the impunity gap.

Numbers will always be difficult to ascertain, but scholars and organisations count that over 35 countries have been involved in the prosecution of international crimes over the last 15 years, including some 20 where the crimes had taken place. Courts of States where crimes occurred are indeed very busy: the closed and closing *ad hoc* international tribunals have transferred some accused persons to Serbia, Bosnia and Herzegovina and Rwanda,[4] for instance, and national courts there have already tried thousands of perpetrators.[5] Latin American countries have now prosecuted hundreds of suspects of international crimes associated with the brutal dictatorships of the 1970s.[6] A few dozens in 14 States – Argentina, Canada, Denmark, Finland, France, Germany, Netherlands, Norway, Senegal, South Africa, Spain, Sweden, Switzerland, United Kingdom – have also been prosecuted on the

---

3 Payam Akhavan, 'Complementarity Conundrums: The ICC Clock in Transitional Times' (2016) 14 *Journal of International Criminal Justice* 1043, 1045 ('Complementarity Conundrums').

4 Transfers are made pursuant to Article 11*bis* of the Tribunals' respective Rules of Procedure and Evidence and can also be made by the International Residual Mechanism for Criminal Tribunals (Art. 6 of its Statute, contained in UN Doc S/RES/1966 (2010)).

5 Rwanda has prosecuted over 10,000 perpetrators in its criminal courts, and more than 1 million others have been processed through the *gacaca*: see, eg, William Schabas, 'Genocide Trials and *Gacaca* Courts' (2005) 3 *Journal of International Criminal Justice* 879.

6 A March 2015 report of the special section of the Attorney General's office in Argentina highlights that 456 cases are active, with over 500 previous convictions: Procuraduría de Crímenes contra la Humanidad, *Actualización de datos sobre el proceso de justicia por crímenes de lesa humanidad. Datos al 18 de marzo de 2015.*

basis of universal jurisdiction.[7] These numbers are increasing steadily,[8] and the topic features quite highly on international and regional political and judicial agendas.[9]

This chapter discusses two main features of the international normative architecture that concern national prosecutions. The first part looks at what could be called 'vertical complementarity' and focuses on complementarity as a central feature of the ICC. It introduces the legalistic criteria for admissibility of cases and discusses whether the legal embodiment of the norm respects the spirit and objectives of the idea behind complementarity. It also presents complementarity as a broader idea that could spur the creation of a 'system' of international criminal justice that relies primarily on States. The second part looks at what could be called 'horizontal complementarity' and focuses on States' obligations in the prosecution of international crimes that emanate from sources of international law other than the ICC Statute. It presents the relevant legal framework and current gaps in the international system and discusses some of their consequences in relation to States' contribution to the fight against impunity.

I Vertical complementarity: the ICC as a catalyst for domestic proceedings?

The *travaux préparatoires* of the ICC Statute show that States expressly rejected the idea of ICC's primacy over national jurisdictions.[10] The main

---

7 Robert J Currie and Joseph Rikhof, *International and Transnational Criminal Law* (Irwin Law, 2nd ed, 2013) 233, 284-8; Maximo Langer, 'The Diplomacy of Universal Jurisdiction: The Political Branches and the Transnational Prosecution of International Crimes' (2011) 105 *American Journal of International Law* 1; Maximo Langer, 'Universal Jurisdiction Is Not Disappearing: The Shift from "Global Enforcer" to "No Safe Haven" Universal Jurisdiction' (2015) 13 *Journal of International Criminal Justice* 245.

8 TRIAL International *et al*, *Make Way for Justice #3: Universal Jurisdiction Annual Review 2017* <https://trialinternational.org/wp-content/uploads/2017/03/UJAR-MEP_A4_0 12.pdf> 3.

9 As examples, the topic of universal jurisdiction is discussed at the Sixth Committee of the United Nations General Assembly; the closely related concept of the obligation *aut dedere aut judicare* was on the agenda of the International Law Commission; the International Court of Justice in 2012 delivered a judgment on the issue of *aut dedere aut judicare* and universal jurisdiction pursuant to the *Convention against Torture and Other Cruel, Inhuman or Degrading Treatment or Punishment*, opened for signature 10 December 1984, 1465 UNTS 85 (entered into force 26 June 1987) ('*Convention against Torture*'); the Council of the European Union established a 'European Network of contact points in respect of persons responsible for genocide, crimes against humanity and war crimes' to strengthen Member States' capacities in the investigation and prosecution of the core crimes, including on the basis of universal jurisdiction (*Strategy of the EU Genocide Network to combat impunity for the crime of genocide, crimes against humanity and war crimes within the European Union and its Member States* (November 2014) <www.eurojust.europa.eu/doclibrary/genocide-network/genocidenetwork/Strategy%20of%20the%20EU%20Genocide%20Network%20(November%202014)/Strategy-Genocide-Network-2014-11-EN.pdf>); Interpol launched projects to help international courts, but also States, in locating fugitives suspected of atrocity crimes.

10 Bartram S Brown, 'Primacy or Complementarity: Reconciling the Jurisdiction of National Courts and International Criminal Tribunals' (1998) 23 *Yale Law Journal* 383, 385-9.

rationale has to do with respect for States' sovereignty,[11] although it also responds to economic and other pragmatic concerns.[12] One such pragmatic reason is that it would be 'both unrealistic and undesirable' for the ICC to prosecute all suspects of international crimes, which means that justice efforts must be decentralised.[13] The idea that the ICC would be subsidiary to national jurisdictions is also a continuation of the growing understanding 'that international justice is an instrument to strengthen domestic justice efforts'.[14] The transfer of cases to national courts by the *ad hoc* Tribunals according to rule 11*bis*, the discussions on their legacy upon closure, and the expectations associated with the co-existence of internationalised tribunals and national courts for capacity-building are also part of the trend to conceive international justice as a tango between different jurisdictions which share the workload to achieve a common objective, with States taking the lead and carrying most of the weight.

The principle of complementarity underpinning the ICC is first and foremost the rule that gives States priority in prosecuting genocide, crimes against humanity and war crimes. It is a technical admissibility rule that governs whether a national court or the ICC should exercise jurisdiction over a specific case. However, as hinted above, complementarity is also a concept that has broader systemic ramifications, with the ICC incentivising domestic accountability efforts based on the idea of 'positive complementarity'.[15]

These two narratives of complementarity interact to create high expectations for the ICC's role in stimulating, incentivising or pressuring States to use their domestic systems to ensure accountability for international crimes.

A *Complementarity: the strict admissibility criteria*

There is abundant literature on the evolving jurisprudence at the ICC concerning the interpretation and application of the admissibility criteria. This section

---

11 Kevin Jon Heller, 'Radical Complementarity' (2016) 14 *Journal of International Criminal Justice* 637, 639 and references therein ('Radical Complementarity').

12 See Britta Lisa Krings, 'The Principles of "Complementarity" and Universal Jurisdiction in International Criminal Law: Antagonists or Perfect Match?' (2012) 4(3) *Goettingen Journal of International Law* 737, 750.

13 Carsten Stahn, 'Introduction: Bridge over Troubled Waters?' in Carsten Stahn and Mohammed M El Zeidy (eds), *The International Criminal Court and Complementarity: From Theory to Practice* (Cambridge University Press, 2011) 3 ('Bridge over Troubled Waters?'); see also Office of the Prosecutor (OTP), *Policy Paper on Case Selection and Prioritisation* (15 September 2016) <www.icc-cpi.int/itemsDocuments/20160915_OTP-Policy_Case-Selection_Eng.pdf> [5].

14 Stahn, 'Bridge over Troubled Waters?', above n 13, 2.

15 Patryk I Labuda, 'The Special Criminal Court in the Central African Republic: Failure or Vindication of Complementarity?' (2017) 15(1) *Journal of International Criminal Justice* 175, 180-1 (footnotes omitted).

presents a brief overview of some of the issues most critical to the relationship between the Court and national jurisdictions and related critiques.[16]

Article 17 (1) (a) of the ICC Statute provides:

> 1. Having regard to paragraph 10 of the Preamble and Article 1, the Court shall determine that a case is inadmissible where:
>
> (a) The case is being investigated or prosecuted by a State which has jurisdiction over it, unless the State is unwilling or unable genuinely to carry out the investigation or prosecution;
>
> (b) The case has been investigated by a State which has jurisdiction over it and the State has decided not to prosecute the person concerned, unless the decision resulted from the unwillingness or inability of the State genuinely to prosecute;

The Appeals Chamber has held that this Article entails a two-step analysis to determine whether a case is inadmissible:

> in considering whether a case is inadmissible under Article 17 (1) (a) and (b) of the Statute, the initial questions to ask are (1) whether there are ongoing investigations or prosecutions, or (2) whether there have been investigations in the past, and the State having jurisdiction has decided not to prosecute the person concerned. It is only when the answers to these questions are in the affirmative that one has to look to the second halves of sub-paragraphs (a) and (b) and to examine the question of unwillingness and inability. To do otherwise would be to put the cart before the horse.[17]

---

16 For a complete analysis of the admissibility criteria, see the literature cited herein and William A Schabas, *The International Criminal Court: A Commentary on the Rome Statute* (Oxford University Press, 2nd ed, 2016).

17 *Prosecutor v Simone Gbagbo (Decision on Côte d'Ivoire's challenge to the admissibility of the case against Simone Gbagbo)* (International Criminal Court, Appeals Chamber, Case No ICC-02/11-01/12-75-Red 27 May 2015) [27] ('*Gbagbo* Admissibility Decision'); *Prosecutor v Katanga (Judgment on the Appeal of Mr. Germain Katanga against the Oral Decision of Trial Chamber II of 12 June 2009 on the Admissibility of the Case)* (International Criminal Court, Appeals Chamber, Case No ICC-01/04-01/07-1497, 25 September 2009) [78] ('*Katanga* Admissibility Judgment'). See also *Prosecutor v Ruto (Judgment on the appeal of the Republic of Kenya against the decision of Pre-Trial Chamber II of 30 May 2011 entitled 'Decision on the Application by the Government of Kenya Challenging the Admissibility of the Case Pursuant to Article 19(2)(b) of the Statute')* (International Criminal Court, Appeals Chamber, Case No ICC-01/09-01/11-307, 30 August 2011) [41] ('*Ruto* Admissibility Judgment'); *Prosecutor v Kenyatta (Judgment on the appeal of the Republic of Kenya against the decision of Pre-Trial Chamber II of 30 May 2011 entitled 'Decision on the Application by the Government of Kenya Challenging the Admissibility of the Case Pursuant to Article 19(2)(b) of the Statute')* (International Criminal Court, Appeals Chamber, Case No ICC-01/09-02/11-274 30 August 2011) [40] ('*Kenyatta* Admissibility Judgment').

Indeed, 'in case of inaction, the question of unwillingness or inability does not arise; inaction on the part of a State having jurisdiction . . . renders a case admissible before the Court'.[18] Commentators have noted that the first step of the analysis has taken significant importance in ICC jurisprudence, leaving the 'unable or unwilling' part of the analysis almost absent from debates:

> Adjudication of whether a national proceeding is 'genuine' or not is a weighty matter. It puts a national judicial system on trial. It is not surprising that the ICC would prefer to avoid such confrontations by deciding admissibility based on the more technical first step of the two-step test.[19]

This first step of admissibility determination turns on the issue of whether the 'same case' is being investigated: a 'case is only inadmissible before the Court if the *same suspects* are being investigated' by a State 'for *substantially the same conduct*'.[20] States have a high threshold to meet: 'what is required is a judicial assessment of whether the case that the State is investigating sufficiently mirrors the one that the Prosecutor is investigating'.[21]

The strict mirror requirement remains unclear in practice at various levels, but it certainly forces national authorities to follow the ICC Prosecutor to a large extent in the crafting and implementation of their prosecutorial strategies. Such a result has the advantage of inducing States to investigate and prosecute mass atrocities – a 'catalysing effect' of the ICC at the domestic level. But it may also be at odds with more nuanced understandings of the idea behind complementarity, jeopardising local visions of justice, 'considerably constrain[ing] the space of domestic autonomy' and 'pay[ing] limited attention to systemic integration between international and domestic justice, and broader challenges of sustainability'.[22] The 'same person' requirement may also prevent States from pursuing a 'pyramidal' prosecutorial strategy,[23] adopted at the ICTY and recently made part of the ICC Office of the Prosecutor's

---

18 *Katanga* Admissibility Judgment, above n 17, [78].
19 Akhavan, 'Complementarity Conundrums', above n 3, 1046.
20 *Kenyatta* Admissibility Judgment, above n 17, [40]–[42] (emphasis added). The 'substantial' aspect of the test is a judicial creation for which the Appeals Chamber 'failed to explain the origin, meaning, and legal basis of this differentiation': Carsten Stahn, 'Admissibility Challenges before the ICC: From Quasi-Primacy to Qualified Deference?' in Carsten Stahn (ed), *The Law and Practice of the International Criminal Court* (Oxford University Press, 2015) 228, 242 ('Quasi-Primacy'). Heller advances that '[t]he most reasonable interpretation is that it simply believed the "same conduct" requirement made it too difficult for states to challenge admissibility' (Heller, 'Radical Complementarity', above n 11, 647).
21 *Prosecutor v Gaddafi and Al-Senussi (Judgment on the Appeal of Libya against the Decision of Pre-Trial Chamber I)* (International Criminal Court, Appeals Chamber, Case No ICC-01/11-01/11 OA 4, 21 May 2014) [73] ('*Gaddafi* Appeal Judgment').
22 Stahn, 'Quasi-Primacy', above n 20, 240.
23 Heller, 'Radical Complementarity', above n 11, 643.

Prosecutorial Strategy, which consists in building up cases by starting with a few mid- and high-level perpetrators to get to those most responsible in the end.[24]

As for 'substantially the same conduct' criteria, the strict mirror approach puts great emphasis on the incidents investigated in the domestic proceedings. The Appeals Chamber in *Gaddafi* noted that the extent of overlap would depend upon the facts and offered examples on a scale:

> If, and perhaps most straightforwardly, the underlying incidents that the Prosecutor and the State are investigating are identical, the case will be inadmissible before the Court (subject to any finding of unwillingness or inability). At the other end of the scale, the Appeals Chamber finds it hard to envisage a situation in which the Prosecutor and a State can be said to be investigating the same case in circumstances in which they are not investigating any of the same underlying incidents.[25]

It is now clear, however, that 'the assessment of the subject matter of the domestic proceedings must focus on the alleged conduct and not on its legal characterisation'.[26] The absence of domestic legislation criminalising genocide, crimes against humanity or war crimes or significant discrepancies between the domestic and international definitions – a rampant reality as will be discussed below – might therefore not necessarily affect the 'same case' determination.

Though jurisprudence is not entirely settled on the proper interpretation of the 'same conduct' criteria, there have been numerous critiques along the same line of arguments mentioned above: the analysis forces States to defer to the ICC 'OTP's choice of incidents to investigate', interfering with domestic prosecutorial discretion, and effectively turns complementarity into 'primacy'.[27] Cogent calls have been made to 'critically reflect the "mirror" imagery, and to (re-)connect ICC practice more closely to longer-term visions of complementarity', urging that greater attention be paid 'to the idea of "qualified deference" to domestic jurisdictions in complementarity assessments'.[28]

---

24 See OTP, *Strategic Plan 2016–2018* (6 July 2015) <www.icc-cpi.int/iccdocs/otp/070715-OTP_Strategic_Plan_2016-2018.pdf> 16.

25 *Gaddafi* Appeal Judgment, above n 21, [72].

26 *Prosecutor v Gaddafi and Al-Senussi (Decision on the Admissibility of the Case Against Abdullah Al-Senussi)* (International Criminal Court, Pre-Trial Chamber I, Case No ICC-01/11-01/11, 11 October 2013) [66] ('*Al-Senussi* Admissibility Judgment'); confirmed on appeal: *Judgment on the Appeal of Mr. Abdullah Al-Senussi Against the Decision of Pre-Trial Chamber I)* (International Criminal Court, Appeals Chamber, Case No ICC-01/11-01/11 OA 6, 24 July 2014) ('*Al-Senussi* Appeal Judgment').

27 Heller, 'Radical Complementarity', above n 11, 648-9.

28 Stahn, 'Quasi-Primacy', above n 20, 253.

As for the expression 'the case is being investigated' in Article 17 (1) (a) of the Statute, it must be understood as requiring the 'taking of steps' directed at determining whether the person is responsible for the alleged conduct, which may include 'interviewing witnesses or suspects, collecting documentary evidence, or carrying out forensic analyses'.[29] A State has again a high threshold to meet, as it must 'provide the Court with evidence of a sufficient degree of specificity and probative value that demonstrates that it is indeed investigating the case'[30] and provide evidence of 'concrete and progressive investigative steps'.[31] Commentators and a dissenting judge have criticised this requirement, noting that it 'elides[s] the difference between inactivity and unwillingness'[32], requiring a State to show the existence of 'a full-fledged investigation in order to establish that there is no situation of inactivity'.[33]

Furthermore, a decision on the admissibility of the case must be based on the circumstances prevailing at the time of 'the proceedings on the admissibility challenge before the Pre-Trial Chamber'[34], which also creates tensions between the realities of post-conflict justice and the exigencies of The Hague. The situation in Libya provides a stark example. As of the time of writing, the *Al-Senussi* case is the only successful admissibility challenge before the ICC. It was concluded that Libya was carrying out proceedings relative to the *same case* (same person, same conduct), and that the State was not unable or unwilling to genuinely conduct the proceedings, despite fair process concerns.[35] By contrast, the *Gaddafi* case was ruled admissible, although Saif Al-Islam Gaddafi was suspected of the same crimes as Al-Senussi. The temporal factor appears to partly explain the opposite decisions in the two cases. Indeed, Gaddafi was captured 10 months before Al-Senussi. Since a State wishing to challenge the admissibility of a case must, in conformity with Article 19 (5) of the ICC Statute, make the challenge 'at the earliest opportunity', Libya filed

---

29 *Ruto* Admissibility Judgment, above n 17, [41].

30 *Kenyatta* Admissibility Judgment, above n 17, [40].

31 *Gbagbo* Admissibility Decision, above n 17, [81].

32 Heller, 'Radical Complementarity', above n 11, 641.

33 *Prosecutor v Ruto (Dissenting Opinion of Judge Anita Usacka, Judgment on the appeal of the Republic of Kenya against the decision of Pre-Trial Chamber II of 30 May 2011 entitled 'Decision on the Application by the Government of Kenya Challenging the Admissibility of the Case Pursuant to Article 19(2)(b) of the Statute')* (International Criminal Court, Appeals Chamber, Case No ICC-01/09-01/11-307, 30 August 2011) [27].

34 *Gbagbo* Admissibility Decision, above n 17, [32], also clarifying that the expression 'time of the proceedings' does not refer to 'subsequent proceedings on appeal'.

35 For discussions on the inability and unwillingness parts of the admissibility determination, see, among many others, Akhavan, 'Complementarity Conundrums', above n 3; Kevin Jon Heller, 'The Shadow Side of Complementarity: The Effect of Article 17 of the Rome Statute on National Due Process' (2006) 17 *Criminal Law Forum* 255 ('The Shadow Side of Complementarity'); Frédéric Mégret and Marika Giles Samson, 'Holding the Line on Complementarity in Libya: The Case for Tolerating Flawed Domestic Trials' (2013) 11(3) *Journal of International Criminal Justice* 571.

its admissibility challenge in the *Gaddafi* case almost a year before it did in the *Al-Senussi* case.[36] Partly in consequence of this, its investigation was less advanced when the time came to submit its arguments before the Pre-Trial Chamber in *Gaddafi*. Since a State is not allowed to submit new arguments before the Appeals Chamber, even though the investigation may have developed between the two hearings, the Appeals Chamber is limited to assessing the reasonableness of the Pre-Trial Chamber's decision on alleged errors of fact,[37] and in this case it did not intervene. Apparently conscious of this, the Appeals Chamber seemed to suggest that Libya institute another admissibility challenge, implying that the situation could correspond to 'exceptional circumstances' referred to in Article 19 (4) of the Statute.[38] A similar situation occurred in the case against Simone Gbagbo. The Appeals Chamber confirmed the Pre-Trial decision on admissibility on the facts relevant at the time of submission to the Pre-Trial Chamber and, ironically, two months after Gbagbo had been convicted and sentenced in Côte d'Ivoire for domestic crimes, facts which were not taken into account on appeal[39] (she was also eventually acquitted in a separate trial for crimes against humanity almost two years later[40]).

As Akhavan rightly notes, there exists a great disequilibrium between the ICC's and its States Parties' clocks:

> The ICC clock tends to run too fast for states emerging from mass atrocities. The admissibility challenges of Libya in the cases of Saif Al-Islam Gaddafi and Abdullah Al-Senussi illustrate the realities of reconciling immediate global justice with the imperatives of local justice following mass atrocity. Striking the right balance between time and justice is at the root of an effective system of complementarity.[41]

---

36 Akhavan, 'Complementarity Conundrums', above n 3, 1051-2. The arrest warrants for both individuals had been emitted on 27 June 2011, together with that of late Muammar Gaddafi: *Prosecutor v Saif Al-Islam Gaddafi (Warrant of Arrest)* (International Criminal Court, Pre-Trial Chamber I, Case No ICC-01/11-14, 27 June 2011); *Prosecutor v Abdullah Al-Senussi (Warrant of Arrest)* (International Criminal Court, Pre-Trial Chamber I, Case No ICC-01/11-15, 27 June 2011); *Prosecutor v Muammar Mohammed Abu Minyar Gaddafi (Warrant of Arrest)* (International Criminal Court, Pre-Trial Chamber I, Case No ICC-01/11-13, 27 June 2011).

37 *Gbagbo* Admissibility Decision, above n 17, [39]. It will also intervene if an error of law 'materially affected the Impugned Decision'. Ibid [40].

38 *Gaddafi* Appeal Judgment, above n 21, [44]. Art. 19 (4) of the Rome Statute reads: 'The admissibility of a case or the jurisdiction of the Court may be challenged only once by any person or State referred to in paragraph 2.... In exceptional circumstances, the Court may grant leave for a challenge to be brought more than once'.

39 For a cogent critique, see Heller, 'Radical Complementarity', above n 11.

40 Human Rights Watch, *Côte d'Ivoire: Simone Gbagbo Acquitted after Flawed War Crimes Trial – First Lady's Acquittal Highlights ICC Process as Critical Path for Victims* (29 March 2017) <www.hrw.org/news/2017/03/29/cote-divoire-simone-gbagbo-acquitted-after-flawed-war-crimes-trial>.

41 Akhavan, 'Complementarity Conundrums', above n 3, 1043.

The test for admissibility thus leaves little space for States to develop their own prosecution strategies and adapt them to local post-conflict or ongoing conflict dynamics.

In other words, the admissibility criteria that embodies in law the idea of complementarity has developed in a way that may appear at odds with the very concept of complementarity, which emphasises States' duty in the international justice enterprise and respect for their sovereignty. If complementarity is to develop as 'praxis' and not only as 'mantra',[42] some adjustments might be needed both at the procedural and at the OTP's strategy levels.

B Complementarity: an incentive that creates a system of international criminal justice?

Regardless of the absence of a clear obligation in the Statute that would oblige States Parties to criminalise the core crimes nationally or to assert jurisdiction over such crimes on the basis of universality, the ICC complementarity scheme works as a strong incentive for legal reforms. Many observers argue that the impact of the complementarity principle on domestic legal systems – particularly if promoted 'proactively' by the court's organs – is the ICC's most promising contribution to the fight against impunity and to lasting peace and security.[43]

It seems that the 'ICC train' has indeed created a momentum toward a relatively broad embracement of universal jurisdiction for ICC crimes, and implementation of such crimes in national law. This must be based either on these States' view that it is an obligation flowing from the Statute, as some States have explicitly argued,[44] or on some popular assumptions about the existence of such obligations in the ICC Statute, which 'sometimes can have a [strong] impact on complementarity's catalysing effect'.[45]

The extent to which States have included the core crimes in their domestic criminal legislation and the manner in which they have done

---

42 Ibid 1045.
43 See, eg, William W Burke-White, 'Proactive Complementarity: The International Criminal Court and National Courts in the Rome System of Justice' (2008) 49 *Harvard International Law Journal* 53; MS Ellis, 'International Justice and the Rule of Law: Strengthening the ICC through Domestic Prosecutions' (2009) 1 *Hague Journal on the Rule of Law* 79.
44 See, eg, Dutch Explanatory Memorandum (*Memorie van Toelichting*) on the substantive implementing legislation (*Wet Internationale Misdrijven*) which states: 'Although not expressly provided for in the Statute, the majority of States – including the Kingdom – were always of the opinion that the principle of complementarity entails that States Parties to the Statute are *obliged* to criminalise the crimes that are subject to the International Criminal Court's jurisdiction in their national laws *and furthermore to establish extra-territorial, universal jurisdiction, which enables their national criminal courts to adjudicate these crimes even if they have been committed abroad by a foreign national*'. Kamerstukken II 2001/02, 28 337, No 3 (MvT), 2, 18 (emphasis added), cited in Jann K Kleffner, *Complementarity in the Rome Statute and National Criminal Jurisdictions* (Oxford University Press, 2008) 91.
45 Nouwen, above n 2, 43.

so is very uneven. Parliamentarians for Global Action document that 'as of 4 February 2014, only 65 countries have enacted legislation containing either complementarity or cooperation provisions, or both, into their domestic law'.[46] Amnesty International, in its 2012 latest updated preliminary survey of legislation around the world conducted to assist the Sixth Committee (Legal) of the UN General Assembly in its annual discussions of universal jurisdiction, found that 166 (approximately 86%) of the 193 UN Member States have defined one or more of the four crimes, but that definitions were 'seriously flawed' and inconsistent.[47] It further found that 147 (approximately 76.2 %) out of 193 States have provided for universal jurisdiction over one or more of these crimes.

Domestic specificity as regards criminalisation of the international offences is not prohibited and may in fact be inevitable, even desirable, to ensure that national law is able to operate effectively in its social, cultural and legal tradition contexts. However, the lack of clear obligations under the ICC Statute, and the gaps in other international law sources with respect to States' obligations regarding international crimes, as will be discussed below, certainly allow States to adopt a piece-meal approach to criminalisation and favour incoherent and unequal domestication of international norms, which affects the creation of a true 'system' of international criminal justice.

Aside from impact at the normative level, the ICC can obviously have broader implications for States' domestic capacity and will to prosecute international crimes, outside the strict framework of the admissibility procedures discussed above. Researchers have documented 'surprising impacts' or 'unintended positive complementarity' of the ICC in States under investigation, noting a correlated increase of domestic human rights prosecutions in the intermediate term. They argue that this relationship results 'from a "willingness game" between ruling coalitions attempting to feign commitment to human rights norms and reformer coalitions, who use the onset of ICC investigations as an opportunity to engage in human rights litigation'.[48] The 'will' to prosecute indeed can be formed by curious local dynamics, with the ICC acting overhead as a catalysing sort of ghost. The shadow presence of the ICC in States where it has opened 'preliminary investigations' arguably also stimulates domestic action. In Colombia, the ICC's relatively passive role

---

46 Parliamentarians for Global Action, *Implementing Legislation on the Rome Statute* <www. pgaction.org/programmes/ilhr/icc-legislation.html>. Note that implementing the cooperation provisions, unlike criminalising the offences, is compulsory under the Rome Statute, pursuant to Arts. 70 (4) (a) and 88.

47 Amnesty International, *Universal Jurisdiction: A Preliminary Survey of Legislation Around the World – 2012 Update* (9 October 2012) <www.amnesty.org/en/documents/ior53/019/2012/en/> 12-3.

48 Geoff Dancy and Florencia Montal, 'Unintended Positive Complementarity: Why International Criminal Court Investigations May Increase Domestic Human Rights Prosecutions' (forthcoming 2017) *American Journal of International Law* <https://ssrn.com/abstract=2736519>.

certainly influenced the peace process and, in particular, the ways in which special schemes of accountability were negotiated.[49]

The impact of international criminal justice on national legal systems can also relate to their capacity to conduct trials. The effect on capacity-building can come not only from the direct involvement of the institutions themselves but also through the blossoming transnational networks of nongovernmental institutions, United Nations actors, diplomatic missions, notably of major donor States, and humanitarian and development agencies. The resurgence of international criminal justice in the 1990s led to the emergence of a 'global compact' in which different actors promote the international norms and contribute to local reforms that take account of these norms, even more strongly and in a more organised way since the creation of the ICC. Collectively, they can have a noticeable impact in different local settings.

The positive complementarity approach of the Office of the Prosecutor involves encouragement for national proceedings, positive interaction with domestic actors, and 'acting as a catalyst with development organizations and donors' conferences to promote support for relevant accountability efforts'.[50] The limited resources of the ICC to build local know-how as regards prosecutions and trials for international crimes indeed suggest that this daunting challenge will need to be tackled in conjunction with other actors involved in post-conflict situations. Efforts should also be made to avoid the potentially damaging 'reverse legacy' effect – international or internationalised institutions competing with and diverting resources from national institutions, draining domestic capacity, or contributing to negative perceptions of the domestic legal system.[51] This should not mean investing less in international mechanisms, but rather that more resources should be provided to domestic justice systems in post-conflict settings as a general rule.[52]

49 Geoff Dancy and Florencia Montal, 'From Law versus Politics to Law in Politics: A Pragmatist Assessment of the ICC's Impact' (2016-2017) 32 *American University of International Law Review* 645, 688; see, more generally, *In the Shadow of the ICC: Colombia and International Criminal Justice: Report of the expert conference examining the nature and dynamics of the role of the International Criminal Court in the ongoing investigation and prosecution of atrocious crimes committed in Colombia* (May 2011) <http://sas-space.sas.ac.uk/3206/1/ICC%2C_Colombia_and_International_Criminal_Justice_Conference_Report.pdf>.

50 OTP, *Prosecutorial Strategy 2009–2012* (1 February 2010) <www.icc-cpi.int/nr/rdonlyres/66A8dcdc-3650-4514-AA62-D229D1128F65/281506/otpProsecutorial Strategy20092013.pdf> [17]; see also Art. 93 (10) of the Rome Statute; OTP, *Strategic Plan 2016–2018* (6 July 2015) <www.icc-cpi.int/iccdocs/otp/070715-OTP_Strategic_Plan_2016-2018.pdf>; OTP, *Strategic Plan June 2012–2015* (11 October 2013) <www.icc-cpi.int/iccdocs/otp/OTP-Strategic-Plan-2013.pdf>.

51 Office of the United Nations High Commissioner for Human Rights, *Rule-of-law Tools for Post-Conflict States: Maximizing the Legacy of Hybrid Courts* (2008) HR/PUB/08/2 <www.ohchr.org/Documents/Publications/HybridCourts.pdf> 15; see also Jane E Stromseth, 'Pursuing Accountability for Atrocities after Conflict: What Impact on Building the Rule of Law?' (2006–2007) 38 *Georgetown Journal of International Law* 251, 266, which provides examples of this potential tension from Rwanda, Sierra Leone and East Timor.

52 Office of the United Nations High Commissioner for Human Rights, above n 51, 15.

II Horizontal complementarity: the Swiss cheese of international law

A *Obligations to extradite or prosecute and the gaps in international law*

Obligations at international law with respect to ICL relate to three distinct but related concepts, namely the obligation to criminalise the offence in domestic law; the obligation to give national courts jurisdiction over the core crimes (prescriptive jurisdiction, which can be territorial or extraterritorial, including on the basis of universality); and the obligation to exercise jurisdiction, most often where a suspect is found on a State's territory, and that is embodied in the obligation *aut dedere aut judicare*, or the obligation to extradite or prosecute.

Several widely ratified treaties provide for these obligations. It may be apposite to clarify that the obligation *aut dedere aut judicare* is distinct from universal jurisdiction, but the two overlap to some extent. An *aut dedere aut judicare* obligation is a direction as to how to 'enforce' jurisdiction, which may or may not have been 'prescribed' on the basis of universality. As per the International Law Commission, 'when the crime was allegedly committed abroad with no nexus to the forum State, the obligation to extradite or prosecute would necessarily reflect an exercise of universal jurisdiction'.[53]

The obligation to extradite or prosecute is mandated for grave breaches of the Geneva Conventions and the first Additional Protocol,[54] and for apartheid,[55] enforced disappearances[56] and torture.[57] These treaties also mandate States to establish prescriptive jurisdiction on the basis of territoriality,

---

53 *Report of the Working Group on the Obligation to Extradite or Prosecute* (aut dedere aut judicare), UN Doc A/CN.4/L.829, [24] ('Report WG extradite or prosecute').
54 Articles 49/50/129/146, respectively, of the *Geneva Convention for the Amelioration of the Condition of the Wounded and Sick in Armed Forces in the Field*, opened for signature 12 August 1949, 75 UNTS 31 (entered into force 21 October 1950) (*Geneva Convention I*); *Geneva Convention for the Amelioration of the Condition of the Wounded, Sick and Shipwrecked Members of the Armed Forces at Sea*, opened for signature 12 August 1949, 75 UNTS 85 (entered into force 21 October 1950) ('*Geneva Convention II*'); *Geneva Convention Relative to the Treatment of Prisoners of War*, opened for signature 12 August 1949, 75 UNTS 135 (entered into force 21 October 1950) ('*Geneva Convention III*'); and *Geneva Convention Relative to the Protection of Civilian Persons in Time of War*, opened for signature 12 August 1949, 75 UNTS 287 (entered into force 21 October 1950) ('*Geneva Convention IV*') (collectively '*Geneva Conventions*'); and arts 85-87 of the 1977 *Protocol Additional to the Geneva Conventions of 12 August 1949, and relating to the Protection of Victims of International Armed Conflicts (Protocol I)*, opened for signature 8 June 1977, 1125 UNTS 3 (entered into force 7 December 1978) ('*Protocol Additional I*').
55 *International Convention on the Suppression and Punishment of the Crime of Apartheid*, opened for signature 30 November 1973, 1015 UNTS 243 (entered into force 18 July 1976) ('*Apartheid Convention*'), Art. V. Note that, as an exception, at Art. V, the exercise of jurisdiction is phrased in permissive terms ('may').
56 *International Convention for the Protection of All Persons from Enforced Disappearance*, opened for signature 20 December 2006, 2716 UNTS 3 (entered into force 23 December 2010), Arts 9-11.
57 *Convention against Torture*, above n 9, Arts 5-7.

active nationality, passive nationality and universality and to criminalise the offences in their domestic law. The Genocide Convention is more limited: it imposes prosecution obligations on territorial States and provides for a general duty with respect to extradition.[58] Various regional and international human rights treaties also provide for a general duty to repress serious violations of human rights that can be qualified as crimes against humanity.[59] Importantly, however, such human rights treaties provide very limited extra-territorial obligations and certainly do not oblige States to repress violations that have occurred on other States' territories.

The *aut dedere aut judicare* obligation creates a powerful tool to achieve justice. Interpreting the regime of the Convention against Torture, the International Court of Justice has confirmed that '[e]xtradition is an option offered to the State by the Convention, whereas prosecution is an international obligation under the Convention, the violation of which is a wrongful act engaging the responsibility of the State'.[60]

However, numerous atrocity crimes – most crimes against humanity, war crimes other than grave breaches, war crimes in non-international armed conflict and genocide – are not covered by a treaty obligation to extradite or prosecute.[61] A rule of customary international law to that effect may be emerging, but a safer view at the moment is that the existing rule is permissive rather than mandatory.[62]

As noted above, there is no explicit obligation in the ICC Statute to criminalise the crimes *qua* genocide, crimes against humanity and war crimes, to establish jurisdiction over the crimes and certainly no obligation to assert jurisdiction on the basis of universality. Neither does the Statute provide for an *aut dedere aut judicare* obligation, although it provides for obligations to arrest and surrender a person if so requested by the Court (art. 89) and for certain rules regarding competing requests, *i.e.*, where a State receives

---

58 *Convention on the Prevention and Punishment of the Crime of Genocide*, opened for signature 9 December 1948, 78 UNTS 277 (entered into force 12 January 1951), Arts V–VII.

59 *International Covenant on Civil and Political Rights*, opened for signature 19 December 1966, 999 UNTS 171 (entered into force 23 March 1976) Art. 2 (3); Human Rights Committee, *General Comment No 20: Replaces General Comment 7 concerning prohibition of torture and cruel treatment or punishment (Art. 7)*, UN Doc CCPR/C/GC/20 (10 March 1992) (amnesties are incompatible with the duty to investigate); Human Rights Committee, *General Comment No 31: The Nature of the General Legal Obligation Imposed on States Parties to the Covenant*, UN Doc CCPR/C/21/Rev.1/Add.13 (29 May 2004) [19] (disciplinary or administrative measures are not sufficient to satisfy the right to an 'effective remedy'); *American Convention on Human Rights*, opened for signature 22 November 1969, 1144 UNTS 123 (entered into force 18 July 1978) Art. 2; *Velasquez-Rodriguez (Honduras)* (Inter-American Court of Human Rights, Ser C, No 4, 1988) [166] (recognising a duty to punish); *Almonacid Arellano et al (Chile)* (Inter-American Court of Human Rights, Ser C, No 154, 2006); *Caso Gomes Lund y otros ("Guerrilha do Araguaia") (Brasil)* (Inter-American Court of Human Rights, Ser C, No 219, 2010).

60 *Belgium* v *Senegal (Judgment)* [2012] ICJ Rep 422 [95].

61 *Report WG extradite or prosecute*, above n 53, [20] (emphasis added).

62 *Final Report of the Working Group on the Obligation to extradite or prosecute (aut dedere aut judicare)*, UN Doc A/CN.4/L.844, [8]–[14].

a request from the Court for the surrender of a person and also receives a request from any other State for the extradition of the same person for the same conduct (art. 90).

Thus, at the present time, there appears to be a gap in international law concerning the obligation to prosecute or extradite over certain categories of atrocity crimes.

B *Some consequences of the gaps*

The developments in ICL in the last two decades and the adoption of the ICC Statute have spurred enthusiasm at the national level, and various States have made no distinction in their laws for the core crimes and have criminalised and provided for universal jurisdiction for all of them. In this context, one could think that the existence of a formal obligation would be unnecessary or even redundant. Indeed, why differentiate, at the execution stage, between crimes of similar gravity? In Canada, for instance, the two prosecutions thus far, of Désiré Munyaneza and Jacques Mungwarere for the genocide in Rwanda, concerned genocide and crimes against humanity as well as, in the case of Munyaneza, war crimes committed in a non-international armed conflict, making no distinction based on existing international obligations. Such prosecutions as well as numerous others worldwide would seem to signal a non-discriminatory vision. But the non-existence of formal obligations at international law has further impacts. The incoherent criminalisation of the core crimes in domestic legal orders was mentioned above and is certainly a direct consequence of the gaps in the obligations at international law.

I Influence on prosecutorial discretion

Another obvious consequence is that the existence of formal obligations could influence the exercise of prosecutorial discretion, favouring prosecutions where other conditions such as availability of evidence are met. It is presumed that faced with a treaty obligation, authorities will act with a view of not breaching it. Moreover, an international obligation to investigate and prosecute can be incorporated into domestic law, giving a legal basis (and more weight to victims and groups pressing for prosecution in a given case) to formally or informally dispute the decision of the authorities.

The example of South Africa is telling in this regard. The Constitutional Court recognised an obligation to investigate international crimes; a powerful judicial confirmation of the impact that genuine consideration of the State's responsibilities in the international fight against impunity can have in practice.[63] In addition to providing an enforceable criterion at the domestic

---

63 *National Commissioner of the South African Police Service v Southern African Human Rights Litigation Centre and Another* [2014] 30 SA [55]–[60] (Constitutional Court).

level, a State could also be held liable for an internationally wrongful act if it failed to respect its obligation to prosecute or extradite. The International Court of Justice case concerning Senegal and Belgium shows the power of such an international obligation at international law. Senegal had the obligation to prosecute (if it chose not to extradite), based on the Convention against Torture, and the international proceedings led to the historic trial of Hissène Habré on the basis of universal jurisdiction.

A contrario, where a State is confronted with a formal obligation in international law to prosecute or extradite, it can obviously not invoke the non-existence of such an obligation as a justification for inaction, a legitimate but often convenient argument to favour political, diplomatic or financial issues over principled contributions to the fight against impunity. If the cases of *Munyaneza* and *Mungwarere* in Canada, and dozens of cases elsewhere, are positive indications of the non-selective approach of the legal authorities to prosecute international crimes on the basis of universal jurisdiction, the political authorities, however, have not hesitated to exploit the gap, justifying the expulsions (not extraditions) of dozens of alleged war criminals from the country on the basis that 'Canada is not the UN. It's not our responsibility to make sure each one of these [alleged war criminals present in Canada] faces justice . . .'.[64] The absence of certain obligations at international law can also serve, as in Spain in 2014, as a justification to cut back on existing universal jurisdiction legislation, where in reality, political, diplomatic or ideological reasons are at play.[65]

Another related consequence that touches on a distinct aspect of prosecutorial discretion concerns the qualification of the crime that is eventually investigated and prosecuted in a given State. The absence of obligations with respect to some international crimes – and the consequent lack of implementation in domestic law – can force a prosecutor or an investigative judge to investigate a set of facts not as crimes against humanity or war crimes but, for instance, as terrorist acts. As an example, the changes brought to the universal jurisdiction legislation in Spain make it much more difficult to prosecute genocide, crimes against humanity and war crimes than to prosecute other types of crimes such as terrorism.[66]

Such restrictions influence the typification of serious violations of international law in domestic criminal trials – moving away from prosecuting 'human rights' crimes to an increased focus on 'international and national security crimes' – and consequently affect the resources invested at the national level to fight different categories of crimes. Trials held in different European countries

---

64 Laura Payton, 'War crimes prosecution not up to Canada, Toews says: 6th war crimes suspect in Canadian custody', *CBC News* (online), 3 August 2011 <www.cbc.ca/news/canada/war-crimes-prosecution-not-up-to-canada-toews-says-1.1065599> (citing the then Public Safety Minister).

65 *Ley Orgánica 1/2014, de 13 de marzo, de modificación de la Ley Orgánica 6/1985, de 1 de julio, del Poder Judicial, relativa a la justicia universal* (Exposición de motivos).

66 José Elías Esteve Moltó, 'The "Great Leap Forward" to Impunity: Burying Universal Jurisdiction in Spain and Returning to the Paradigm of Human Rights as "*domaine réservé*" of States' (2015) 13(5) *Journal of International Criminal Justice* 1121, 1131-2.

for crimes committed in Syria have indeed tended to be prosecuted as terrorism, although investigations are also ongoing for international crimes, and specialised units created to prosecute terrorism charges are typically much better resourced than those on crimes against humanity, genocide and war crimes.[67]

II Extradition: the missing limb of the horizontal enforcement system

Furthermore, the lack of obligations to extradite or prosecute at international law regarding many atrocity crimes has an under-reported consequence: it does not favour interstate cooperation, affecting mutual legal assistance and extradition. Extraterritorial prosecutions rely extensively on cooperation by the territorial State and effective mutual legal assistance may often be the deciding factor in a State's capacity to conduct trials (fair and impartial trials that also allow cooperation with the accused). Extradition is obviously a central element in the 'obligation to extradite or prosecute' and despite such central role, it is in fact rarely used, constituting, in our view, the missing limb of the international enforcement system. Apart from a recent surge of extraditions to Rwanda, after numerous years of refusals to do so, and a steady flow of a few extraditions to Bosnia, for example, there are very few extraditions for international crimes worldwide. This is partly due to the fact that the horizontal, or indirect, enforcement of ICL through State cooperation is weakly provided for in international multinational treaties.

Human rights treaties such as the Conventions against Torture and Enforced Disappearances provide for sophisticated regimes of mutual legal assistance and extradition, facilitating the implementation of the alternative obligation to 'extradite' or 'prosecute'. However, these treaties are of limited application. The ICC Statute contemplates an extensive vertical cooperation regime that has its own challenges, but it does not provide anything as regards horizontal cooperation to implement effectively the complementarity principle (except for a mention about competing requests, as noted above). Interstate cooperation thus relies almost exclusively on bilateral and regional treaties as well as domestic law. Despite the large number of such treaties, States where suspects are found often lack agreements with the State where the crimes were committed.[68] While the absence of a treaty is not necessary fatal (sometimes

---

67 In France, for instance, the *pôle anti-terroriste* is much better resourced then the *pôle pour les crimes contre l'humanité*. Agence France-Presse, 'Crimes contre l'humanité: en France, un pôle d'enquêtes bridé faute de moyens', *Justiceinfo.net* (online), 7 May 2016 <www.justiceinfo.net/fr/reperes/27225-crimes-contre-l-humanit%C3%A9-en-france,-un-p%C3%B4le-d-enqu%C3%AAtes-brid%C3%A9-faute-de-moyens.html>; cf Stop Djihadisme (gouvernement français), *Justice : des moyens supplémentaires pour lutter contre le terrorisme* <www.stop-djihadisme.gouv.fr/lutte-contre-terrorisme-radicalisation/mesures-lutter-contre-terrorisme/justice-moyens>.

68 See, eg, Maarten P Bolhuis, Louis P Middelkoop and Joris van Wijk, 'Refugee Exclusion and Extradition in the Netherlands: Rwanda as Precedent?' (2014) 12 *Journal of International Criminal Justice* 1115.

States can enter into *ad hoc* arrangements), it creates an extra hurdle and a justification to use other means less respectful of the spirit and letter of the *aut dedere aut judicare* idea, such as immigration measures. As an example, the lack of an extradition treaty with Rwanda for many years provided Canada with a justification for ignoring Rwanda's extradition request in the case of Léon Mugesera. Mugesera was eventually deported to Rwanda and was welcomed by the police who arrested him upon arrival. The removal constituted a disguised extradition, without the safeguards and mutual trust extradition entails.[69] In fact, Canada and other States (over)use immigration measures as a tool to ensure that they are not a 'safe haven' for perpetrators of international crimes, a practical way around the more expensive and cumbersome criminal law measures of prosecution and extradition, a state of affairs which the absence of obligations at international law contributes to maintaining.[70]

The ghost that is extradition in the horizontal enforcement system also impedes a reasonable exercise of universal jurisdiction based on subsidiarity, *i.e.*, the idea that universal jurisdiction plays as a default mechanism and should only be exercised if the territorial or active nationality States (the *forum conveniens*) are unable or unwilling to exercise their jurisdiction.[71] The mechanism to determine whether a territorial State is 'unable or unwilling' to investigate and prosecute a suspect present on a third State's territory so that universal jurisdiction could be exercised without hurting the principle of subsidiarity is an interstate affair: it's called extradition.

Extradition has its own rules, and there are a number of reasons why extradition to the territorial State will be impossible. There are issues of dual nationality and dual criminality but, most importantly, non-refoulement obligations and the ability of the custodial State to refuse extradition where the suspect would risk a flagrant denial of justice. Those considerations for instance have blocked extraditions to Rwanda for years, but they are the strict minimum, the basic reasons that will, in certain cases, put the custodial State in a well-justified position not to extradite. The perfect system would then heed the International Court of Justice's decision in *Belgium v. Senegal*, according to which, as noted above, prosecution is an obligation, extradition an option.

---

69 See other examples in Ward Ferdinandusse, 'Improving Interstate Cooperation for the National Prosecution of International Crimes: Towards a New Treaty?' (2014) 18(5) *ASIL Insights* <www.asil.org/insights/volume/18/issue/15/improving-inter-state-cooperation-national-prosecution-international>.

70 For Canada, see, eg, Fannie Lafontaine, 'The Prosecute or Expel Dilemma in Far-Away Lands: Alternative Universal Justice for Victims of International Crimes' in Jo-Anne Wemmers (ed), *Reparation for Victims of Crimes against Humanity: The Healing Role of reparation* (Routledge, 2014) Ch. 6.

71 For a full discussion, see Fannie Lafontaine, 'National Jurisdictions' in William A Schabas, *The Cambridge Companion to International Criminal Law* (Cambridge University Press, 2015) 155-77; Fannie Lafontaine, 'Universal Jurisdiction: The Realistic Utopia' (2012) 10 *Journal of International Criminal Justice* 1277.

Therefore, the importance of extradition cannot be underestimated, not only because it represents the legal framework applicable to State cooperation to ensure that justice is rendered *somewhere*, but also because it serves as the vehicle to alleviate concerns about State sovereignty raised by the exercise of universal jurisdiction. Filling the gaps in the international enforcement system is an important first step in providing national jurisdictions with the tools to contribute to closing the impunity gap.

Two initiatives that seek to alleviate some limitations of the current system are worth mentioning.[72] First, the International Law Commission decided in 2013 to include the topic 'Crimes against humanity' in its programme of work.[73] The draft Convention on crimes against humanity prepared by the Crimes Against Humanity Initiative[74] alleviates many of the concerns identified here as regards these crimes, issues that the International Law Commission agrees need to be discussed: it would oblige States to criminalise these crimes in their domestic law and establish jurisdiction, provide for an obligation *aut dedere aut judicare* and establish a sophisticated regime of State cooperation on mutual legal assistance and extradition. This convention would fill some of the gaps as regards the core crimes, but it would leave some of the other gaps unaddressed, particularly as regards genocide and war crimes committed in non-international armed conflicts. Numerous States have hence joined a second initiative to open negotiations on a multilateral treaty on mutual legal assistance for genocide, crimes against humanity and war crimes. Such an eventual treaty would provide for a sophisticated regime of extradition and mutual legal assistance to implement the core obligation to prosecute or extradite all atrocity crimes.[75] In any case, the need for a revamped and more comprehensive treaty system on the obligations of States regarding the prosecution of atrocity crimes is obvious, and the current initiatives – especially if developed in a coherent fashion – have much potential to fill some gaps in the 'horizontal' international law enforcement system.

III Conclusion

The future of international criminal justice partly lies in the strengthening and better understanding of the dynamic between the ICC and States in the prosecution of international crimes. It also lies in a stronger normative

---

72 Payam Akhavan, 'Whither National Courts? The Rome Statute's Missing Half' (2010) 8 *Journal of International Criminal Justice* 1245, 1248.

73 *Report of the International Law Commission on the Work of its sixty-fifth session (6 May–7 June and 8 July–9 August 2013)*, UN Doc A/68/10, Ch. XII, s A.2 and Annex B.

74 The Initiative was composed of a group of experts who drafted a proposed treaty: <http://crimesagainsthumanity.wustl.edu/>; see also Leila Nadya Sadat (ed), *Forging a Convention for Crimes against Humanity* (Cambridge University Press, 2011).

75 Ferdinandusse, above n 69; Gillian MacNeil, 'Eyeing the Gap: Extradition and MLAT Treaties for Core Crimes Prosecutions' on *International & Transnational Criminal Law* (25 January 2017) <http://rjcurrie.typepad.com/international-and-transna/2017/01/guest-blog-extradition-mlat-for-core-crimes.html>.

system to favour interstate cooperation towards the same objective. Beyond the evidence and the rhetoric, many challenges remain: international obligations are inconsistent; practical and political obstacles lead to scarce prosecutions; and extradition is underused. The next decades will require a move from an unduly State-centric 'no safe haven' idea to awareness that States must be proactive members of a global system with a common goal.

Sadly perhaps, the brutal geopolitical chaos related to the conflict(s) in Syria and the consequent current deadlock for any international mechanism might revive the once announced 'fall' of universal jurisdiction. Throughout 2016, authorities in Austria, Finland, France, Germany and Sweden have brought charges, and investigations are ongoing in Norway, Switzerland and The Netherlands, mostly against rebels.[76] European States have also recently opened investigations into alleged abuses by the Syrian regime.[77] The new *International, Impartial and Independent Mechanism to Assist in the Investigation and Prosecution of Persons Responsible for the Most Serious Crimes under International Law Committed in the Syrian Arab Republic since March 2011*, established in December 2016 by the General Assembly, as well as numerous States and NGO initiatives to collect evidence, provide a glimpse of hope that international justice might, once again, represent a form of belated – important yet insufficient – response to our collective failure to prevent or stop atrocity crimes.

Further reading

Dancy, Geoff and Florencia Montal, 'Unintended Positive Complementarity: Why International Criminal Court Investigations May Increase Domestic Human Rights Prosecutions' (2017, forthcoming) *American Journal of International Law* <https://ssrn.com/abstract=2736519>.

Heller, Kevin Jon, 'Radical Complementarity' (2016) 14 *Journal of International Criminal Justice* 637.

Nouwen, Sarah MH, *Complementarity in the Line of Fire: The Catalysing Effect of the International Criminal Court in Uganda and Sudan* (Cambridge University Press, 2013).

Schabas, William A, *The International Criminal Court: A Commentary on the Rome Statute* (Oxford University Press, 2nd ed 2016).

Stahn, Carsten, 'Admissibility Challenges before the ICC: From Quasi-Primacy to Qualified Deference?' in Carsten Stahn (ed.), *The Law and Practice of the International Criminal Court* (Oxford University Press, 2015) 228.

---

76 TRIAL International *et al*, above n 8, 3.
77 See, eg, David Bosco, 'Can Spanish Courts Find Justice for the Victims of Syria's Atrocities?', *The Washington Post* (online), 4 April 2017 <www.washingtonpost.com/news/democracy-post/wp/2017/04/04/can-spanish-courts-find-justice-for-the-victims-of-syrias-atrocities/?utm_term=.48e66072be87>; Pauline Brosch, 'Here's how German courts are planning to prosecute Syrian war crimes', *The Washington Post* (online), 4 April 2017 <www.washingtonpost.com/news/democracy-post/wp/2017/04/04/heres-how-german-courts-are-planning-to-prosecute-syrian-war-crimes/?utm_term=.98c39afdd3c4>.

14

THE INFLUENCE OF INTERNATIONAL HUMAN RIGHTS LAW ON INTERNATIONAL CRIMINAL PROCEDURE

Yvonne McDermott

I Introduction

The fully-fledged legal disciplines of international human rights law and international criminal law both emerged from the aftermath of the Second World War. The Universal Declaration of Human Rights was signed on 10 December 1948,[1] less than two years after the conclusion of the International Military Tribunal at Nuremberg,[2] and just one day after the adoption of the Genocide Convention which defined the crime of genocide under international law and mentioned that it should be tried as a crime domestically or 'by such international penal tribunal as may have jurisdiction'.[3] As such, it is clear that both bodies of law share a 'common ancestry'.[4]

The Nuremberg Principles adopted by the UN General Assembly in 1946 recognised not only that those accused of crimes under international law should be brought to justice, but also that persons charged with such crimes had the right to a fair trial.[5] This emphasis on the rights of the accused

---

1 *Universal Declaration on Human Rights*, GA Res 217A (III), UN GAOR, 3rd sess, 183rd plen mtg, UN Doc A/810 (10 December 1948).

2 *France and ors v Göring and ors (Judgment and Sentence)* [1946] 22 IMT 203, 1 October 1946.

3 *Convention on the Prevention and Punishment of the Crime of Genocide*, opened for signature 9 December 1948, 78 UNTS 277 (entered into force 12 January 1951) Art. VI.

4 William A Schabas, 'International Criminal Law and Tribunals and Human Rights' in Scott Sheeran and Nigel Rodley (eds), *Routledge Handbook of International Human Rights Law* (Routledge, 2013) 215.

5 *Affirmation of the Principles of International Law recognized by the Charter of the Nürnberg Tribunal*, GA Res 95, UN GAOR, 1st sess, UN Doc A/RES/95 (11 December 1946) Principles I and V.

has continued through the lifetimes of the international criminal tribunals established since the end of the twentieth century, and has had a notable bearing on the rules of procedure and evidence adopted and amended by these tribunals. By today, a fully-fledged discipline known as 'international criminal procedure' has emerged, as evidenced by the large number of monographs and other works dedicated to procedural frameworks in international criminal trials.[6]

This chapter examines the extent to which international human rights law has influenced the development of international criminal procedure. It begins with a discussion of whether the international criminal tribunals are formally bound by international human rights standards. It then discusses the institutional interplay between international criminal tribunals and international human rights courts, before providing a number of areas of international criminal procedure where international human rights law has had a formative influence. Overall, this chapter demonstrates that, while human rights law standards are not strictly binding on most of the international criminal tribunals, human rights law has exerted a remarkable influence over the moulding and interpretation of international criminal procedure.

II Are international criminal tribunals bound to respect human rights law?

Given the influence that international human rights law has had on international criminal procedure, it is apposite to examine whether the tribunals consider themselves formally bound to respect human rights law, or whether human rights standards are seen as merely persuasive. One of the most common arguments in favour of the proposition that international criminal tribunals must respect human rights law refers to the tribunals' core aims of promoting respect for the rule of law, and their status as international institutions. Given that the *ad hoc* international criminal tribunals were created by the United Nations Security Council, and the United Nations has a role in ensuring states' compliance with international human rights law, some authors have argued that it is obvious that United Nations-created bodies would be bound by those same human rights standards.[7] In this tone,

---

6 Kai Ambos, *Treatise on International Criminal Law, Vol. III: International Criminal Procedure* (Oxford University Press, 2016); Göran Sluiter *et al* (eds), *International Criminal Procedure: Principles and Rules* (Oxford University Press, 2013); Yvonne McDermott, *Fairness in International Criminal Trials* (Oxford University Press, 2016); Christoph Safferling, *International Criminal Procedure* (Oxford University Press, 2012); Christoph Safferling, *Towards an International Criminal Procedure* (Oxford University Press, 2001).
7 Fausto Pocar and Linda Carter, 'The Challenge of Shaping Procedures in International Criminal Courts' in Linda Carter and Fausto Pocar (eds), *International Criminal Procedure: The Interface of Civil Law and Common Law Legal Systems* (Elgar, 2015) 1, 8.

the Secretary General of the United Nations noted at the creation of the International Criminal Tribunal for the Former Yugoslavia (ICTY) that it was 'axiomatic' that the tribunal would fully comply with the standards set out in the International Covenant on Civil and Political Rights (ICCPR).[8] This line of reasoning has been followed in a number of international criminal decisions, where the tribunals have considered themselves 'bound to uphold' an accused's rights as enshrined in Article 14 of the ICCPR.[9] This obligation is more explicit for the International Criminal Court (ICC), which has a statutory obligation to interpret and apply its applicable law 'in accordance with internationally recognized human rights'.[10] The ICC has held that human rights underpin every aspect of the Statute.[11] In addition, human rights law can constitute a source of applicable law under the Court's Statute, falling under Article 21(1)(b) ('applicable treaties and the principles and rules of international law') or Article 21(1)(c) ('general principles of law') of the Court's Statute.[12]

A related argument in favour of finding that the international criminal tribunals are obliged to respect international human rights law relates to the principle of equality of treatment. In *Hadžihasanović*, the ICTY noted that the relevant states of the former Yugoslavia had become party to the European Convention of Human Rights, and that as such, it behoved the tribunal to ensure that the defendants before it received treatment that was no less favourable to what they would be entitled in their home states.[13]

---

8 *International Covenant on Civil and Political Rights*, opened for signature 16 December 1966, 999 UNTS 171 (entered into force 23 March 1976).

9 *Galić v Prosecutor (Judgement)* (International Criminal Tribunal for the Former Yugoslavia, Appeals Chamber, Case No IT-98-29-A, 30 November 2006) (Pocar) [2]. See also *Rutaganda v Prosecutor (Judgement)* (International Criminal Tribunal for Rwanda, Appeals Chamber, Case No ICTR-96-3-A, 26 May 2003) (Pocar; *Semanza v Prosecutor (Judgement)* (International Criminal Tribunal for Rwanda, Appeals Chamber, Case No ICTR-97-20-A, 20 May 2005) (Pocar); *Prosecutor v Tadić (Decision on the Prosecutor's Motion Requesting Protective Measures for Victims and Witnesses)* (International Criminal Tribunal for the Former Yugoslavia, Trial Chamber, Case No IT-94-1-T, 10 August 1995) [25]-[27].

10 *Rome Statute of the International Criminal Court*, opened for signature 17 July 1998, 2187 UNTS 90 (entered into force 1 July 2002) Art. 21(3).

11 *Prosecutor v Lubanga (Judgment on the Appeal of Mr. Thomas Lubanga Dyilo against the Decision on the Defence Challenge to the Jurisdiction of the Court pursuant to article 19 (2) (a) of the Statute of 3 October 2006)* (International Criminal Court, Appeals Chamber, Case No ICC-01/04-01/06-772, 14 December 2006) [37].

12 Annika Jones, 'Insights into an Emerging Relationship: Use of Human Rights Jurisprudence at the International Criminal Court' (2016) 16(4) *Human Rights Law Review* 701, 711.

13 *Prosecutor v Hadžihasanović (Decision Granting Provisional Release to Enver Hadžihasanović)* (International Criminal Tribunal for the Former Yugoslavia, Trial Chamber II, Case No IT-01-47-T, 19 December 2001) ('*Hadžihasanović Provisional Release Decision*'); *Prosecutor v Blagojević (Decision on Vidoje Blagojević's Application for Provisional Release)* (International Criminal Tribunal for the Former Yugoslavia, Trial Chamber II, Case No IT-02-60-PT, 22 July 2002) [23]-[25].

Moreover, it is clear that the fair trial provisions of the tribunals' Statutes are closely modelled on international human rights law, with most Statutes' fair trial provisions comprising an almost verbatim reflection of Article 14 of the ICCPR.[14] Given the 'legislative influence'[15] of these human rights standards on international criminal tribunals' Statutes, it surely stands to reason that the case law of the courts that interpret such standards should also have a persuasive influence. In *Furundžija*, the ICTY read a right to a reasoned opinion into the fair trial provisions of the Statute, even though no such right was explicitly included in Articles 20 or 21 of the Statute, on the basis that the European Court of Human Rights had established that the right to a reasoned opinion was 'a component of the fair hearing requirement'.[16] Similarly, in *Rwamakuba*, the ICTR found that although there was no explicit right to an effective remedy for violations of a defendant's rights, 'this right undoubtedly forms part of customary international law', and it listed a number of regional and international human rights instruments in support of this interpretation.[17]

On the other hand, it could be argued that the tribunals are not expressly bound by human rights law, given that they cannot sign up to be party to human rights treaties in the same way as states can. To this end, Judge Shahabuddeen has argued that human rights obligations do not apply 'lock, stock and barrel' to international criminal tribunals.[18] Similarly, it could be argued that the fact that international criminal tribunals are not subject to an external supervisory body, as the states that are party to those human rights treaties are, renders any application of human rights law to international criminal law and procedure essentially a voluntary exercise.[19]

A further distinct argument on the non-binding nature of international human rights on international criminal tribunals relates to the seriousness of

---

14 Krit Zeegers, *International Criminal Tribunals and Human Rights Law* (Springer, 2016) 63. See further *Hadžihasanović Provisional Release Decision*, above n 13; *Prosecutor v Kanyabashi (Decision on the Defence Motion on Jurisdiction)* (International Criminal Tribunal for Rwanda, Trial Chamber II, Case No ICTR-96-15-T, 18 June 1997) [44]; *Prosecutor v Norman (Decision on the Application for a Stay of Proceedings and Denial of Right to Appeal)* (Special Court for Sierra Leone, Appeals Chamber, Case No SCSL-2003-08-PT, 4 November 2003) [18].

15 Erik Møse, 'Impact of Human Rights Conventions on the Two *ad hoc* Tribunals' in Morten Bergsmo (ed), *Human Rights and Criminal Justice for the Downtrodden – Essays in Honour of Asbjorn Eide* (Martinus Nijhoff, 2003), 207.

16 *Prosecutor v Furundžija (Judgement)* (International Criminal Tribunal for the Former Yugoslavia, Appeals Chamber, Case No IT-95-17/1-A, 21 July 2000) [69].

17 *Prosecutor v Rwamakuba (Decision on Appropriate Remedy)* (International Criminal Tribunal for Rwanda, Trial Chamber III, Case No ICTR-98-44-T, 31 January 2007) [40]–[41].

18 *Galić v Prosecutor (Judgement)* (International Criminal Tribunal for the Former Yugoslavia, Appeals Chamber, Case No IT-98-29-A, 30 November 2006) (Shahabuddeen) [19].

19 Salvatore Zappala, *Human Rights in International Criminal Proceedings* (Oxford University Press, 2005) 164.

the crimes with which the defendants are charged. Even though international human rights law makes clear that provisional release awaiting trial should be the rule, not the exception,[20] the international criminal tribunals were slow to realise the right to liberty pending trial, in part, it seems, due to the nature of the crimes alleged.[21] This perspective also arose in *Tadić*, where the Appeals Chamber likened the ICTY to a military tribunal, given the severity of international crimes.[22] This argument on military tribunals was unconvincing, given that military tribunals are expected to respect the right to a fair trial as much as a 'regular' tribunal.[23] However, states are permitted to derogate from human rights (including the right to a fair trial) in times of emergency, and this has led to some suggestions that the derogability of human rights treaties mean that international criminal tribunals cannot be bound by these standards as a matter of customary international law.[24] By contrast, Sluiter has convincingly argued that derogation is specific to states in times of emergency, and cannot be imported to international criminal procedure.[25]

International criminal procedure, however, cannot be based entirely on the standards derived from human rights law, given that a margin of appreciation is offered to states in implementing human rights standards. To this end, human rights standards have been said to be 'indeterminate', insofar as human rights courts do not set out a prescriptive list of procedures that ought to be followed, and a margin of appreciation is offered to states in incorporating human rights to their own legal systems.[26] However, as the ICC noted in *Lubanga,* international human rights case law offers guidance when the international criminal tribunal has to determine whether

20 See below, part 4.A.
21 *Prosecutor v Delalić (Decision on Motion for Provisional Release filed by the Accused Zejnil Delalić)* (International Criminal Tribunal for the Former Yugoslavia, Trial Chamber, Case No IT-96-21-T, 25 September 1996) [19].
22 *Prosecutor v Tadić (Decision on the Prosecutor's Motion Requesting Protective Measures for Victims and Witnesses)* (International Criminal Tribunal for the Former Yugoslavia, Trial Chamber, Case No IT-94-1-T, 10 August 1995) ('Tadić Protective Measures Decision') [28].
23 Human Rights Committee, *General Comment No 32: Right to Equality before Courts and Tribunals and to Fair Trial,* 90th sess, UN Doc CCPR/C/GC/32 (23 August 2007).
24 Tadić Protective Measures Decision, above n 22, [61].
25 Göran Sluiter, 'International Criminal Proceedings and the Protection of Human Rights' (2002-2003) 37 *New England Law Rev* 935, 938.
26 Frédéric Mégret, 'Beyond "Fairness": Understanding the Determinants of International Criminal Procedure' (2009) 14 *UCLA Journal of International Law and Foreign Affairs* 37; Compare, however, the ECtHR in *Schatschaschwili v Germany (Judgment)* (European Court of Human Rights, Grand Chamber, Application No 9154/10, 15 December 2015) [108] ('the Court reiterates that, while it is important for it to have regard to substantial differences in legal systems and procedures, including different approaches to the admissibility of evidence in criminal trials, ultimately it must apply the same standard of review under Article 6 §§ 1 and 3 (d) irrespective of the legal system from which a case emanates').

an action contravenes international human rights standards, or merely a domestic procedural norm.[27]

Thus, the correct approach to the question of whether international criminal tribunals are bound by human rights law is probably that taken by the ICTR in *Barayagwiza*, where it noted that regional human rights treaties and the related jurisprudence developed under those treaties 'are persuasive authority which may be of assistance in applying and interpreting the Tribunal's applicable law'.[28] Human rights jurisprudence 'may have a persuasive effect', but is not formally binding on the tribunals.[29] International criminal tribunals (aside from the ICC, as mentioned above) are not expressly bound by international human rights law, but this body of law is undoubtedly a source of inspiration and guidance for ensuring the rights of the accused and solving particular procedural issues that arise in practice. Human rights standards may also constitute customary international law and/or general principles of law, which are secondary sources of applicable law before the international criminal tribunals.[30] In practice, as shall be shown below, human rights law has had a significant influence over the character and development of international criminal procedure.

III The interplay between human rights courts and international criminal tribunals

A number of cases have sought, unsuccessfully, to bring international criminal tribunals based on the continent of Europe within the remit of the European Court of Human Rights (ECtHR)'s adjudicatory functions. In *Milošević*, the ECtHR determined that Slobodan Milošević's claim was inadmissible, as he had not exhausted domestic remedies (despite the fact that those remedies had little prospect of success, as acknowledged by the Court).[31]

ICTY defendant Naletilić took his case against Croatia before the ECtHR, claiming that the Tribunal was not impartial or independent and as such, Croatia violated his rights by transferring him to the jurisdiction of

---

27 *Prosecutor v Lubanga (Decision on the Confirmation of Charges)* (International Criminal Court, Pre-Trial Chamber I, Case No ICC-01/04-01/06-803, 29 January 2007) [69].

28 *Barayagwiza v Prosecutor (Decision)* (International Criminal Tribunal for Rwanda, Appeals Chamber, Case No ICTR-97-19-AR72, 3 November 1999) [40].

29 *Prosecutor v Bizimungu (Decision on Prosper Mugiraneza's Fourth Motion to Dismiss Indictment for Violation of Right to Trial without Undue Delay)* (International Criminal Tribunal for Rwanda, Trial Chamber II, Case No ICTR-99-50-T, 23 June 2010) [6].

30 *Rome Statute*, Art. 21(1); *Prosecutor v Kupreškić (Judgment)* (International Criminal Tribunal for the Former Yugoslavia, Trial Chamber, Case No IT-95-16-T, 14 January 2000) [591].

31 *Milošević v Netherlands (Admissibility Decision)* (European Court of Human Rights, Second Section, Application No 77631/01, 19 March 2002) 801, 805 ('the existence of mere doubts as to the prospect of success of a particular remedy which is not obviously futile is not a valid reason for failing to exhaust domestic remedies').

the Tribunal.[32] The ECtHR distinguished between 'extradition', where a risk of a flagrant denial of a fair trial may give rise to a case under Article 6 of the ECHR,[33] and, in this case, 'the surrender to an international court which, in view of the content of its Statute and Rules of Procedure, offers all the necessary guarantees including those of impartiality and independence'.[34] This reasoning is somewhat unconvincing, given that the difference between extradition to stand trial in a domestic court and transfer to stand trial in an international criminal tribunal is not immediately obvious. Moreover, the ECtHR's assertion that the Tribunal's statutory framework contains protections for the right to a fair trial, and that therefore, by implication, there can be no concerns about the fairness of its proceedings, can be contrasted with its position on states, who usually have enshrined the right to a fair trial into domestic constitutional or legal frameworks but who nevertheless can be found to have violated that right on a practical examination of the facts. We might compare the ECtHR's position in this case with that taken in *Abu Qatada*, for example, where the Court noted that the guarantees provided under Jordanian law had very little 'real practical value', in light of its examination of the state's practice.[35] It is clear that the ECtHR was unwilling to carry out such a practical assessment of the ICTY's practice, and was content instead to accept the guarantees enshrined in the Tribunal's Statute and rules at face value.

Later, the ECtHR's position that it did not have jurisdiction to examine the acts of international tribunals situated in the territory of a state party became even more explicit.[36] Again stressing that 'the basic legal provisions governing . . . [the ICTY's] organisation and procedure are purposely designed to provide those indicted before it with all appropriate guarantees', the Court stressed that it was not obvious that the international legal responsibility of the host state was engaged simply by virtue of the fact that the international tribunal was located on its territory.[37] Similarly, in a case concerning a witness before the ICC who sought asylum in the Netherlands, the ECtHR found that the fact that the witness was deprived of his liberty on the territory of the state pursuant to an international agreement did

---

32 *Naletilić v Croatia (Admissibility Decision)* (European Court of Human Rights, Fourth Section, Application No 51891/99, 4 May 2000) ('*Naletilić Admissibility Decision*').

33 *Othman (Abu Qatada) v United Kingdom* [2012] I Eur Court HR 159, [258]; *Bader and Kanbor v Sweden* [2005] XI Eur Court HR 75, 87; *Soering v United Kingdom* (1989) 11 Eur Court (ser A) HR 439, [113].

34 *Naletilić Admissibility Decision*, above n 32, 3.

35 *Othman*, above n 33, [278].

36 *Galić v Netherlands (Admissibility Decision)* (European Court of Human Rights, Third Section, Application Nos 22617/07 and 49032/07, 9 June 2009).

37 Ibid.

not 'bring questions touching on the lawfulness of his detention within the "jurisdiction" of the Netherlands'.[38]

Thus, it is clear that the ECtHR has distanced itself from any role in adjudging upon the adherence of international criminal tribunals to human rights standards, preferring instead to declare that it is evident from the tribunals' legal frameworks that the rights of the accused will be respected, and that such questions would, in any event, fall outside of its jurisdiction. To date, no other international human rights court has been asked to assess a claim submitted by an individual tried or detained by an international criminal tribunal.

Despite refusing to hear the claims of individuals detained by international criminal tribunals, the ECtHR has not viewed its role as existing in a vacuum in relation to the burgeoning body of jurisprudence developed by these tribunals. In several hundred cases to date, the ECtHR has referred to the law or practice of international criminal tribunals in reaching its decisions. In *Marguš v. Croatia*, for example, the ECtHR referred to the drafting history of the ICC Statute and Article 20 of the Statute on *ne bis in idem*, as well as the case law of the Special Court for Sierra Leone, before determining that amnesties for international crimes contravene states' obligation to prosecute and punish such crimes.[39] The ECtHR has also had reference to international criminal law in its discussions on sentencing,[40] and the elements of crimes against humanity,[41] genocide,[42] and torture.[43]

However, it is no exaggeration to say that there has been an 'asymmetry of influence',[44] with the international criminal tribunals referring much more frequently to human rights courts than vice versa, and with human rights law having a much deeper influence on international criminal law (especially international criminal procedure) than international criminal law has on human rights.[45] In practice, the international criminal tribunals have rarely expressly

---

38 *Djokaba Lambi Longa v Netherlands (Decision)* (European Court of Human Rights, Third Section, Application No 33917/12, 9 October 2012).

39 *Marguš v Croatia* [2014] III Eur Court HR 1; see also *Zolotukhin v Russia* [2009] I Eur Court HR 291.

40 *Vinter and ors v United Kingdom* [2013] III Eur Court HR 317; *Kafkaris v Cyprus* [2008] I Eur Court HR 223; *Murray v Netherlands (Judgment)* (European Court of Human Rights, Grand Chamber, Application No 10511/10, 26 April 2016).

41 *Korbely v Hungary* [2008] IV Eur Court HR 299.

42 *Vasiliauskas v Lithuania (Judgment)* (European Court of Human Rights, Grand Chamber, Application No 35343/05, 20 October 2015).

43 *Al-Adsani v United Kingdom* [2001] XI Eur Court HR 79.

44 Sergey Vasiliev, 'International Criminal Tribunals in the Shadow of Strasbourg and Politics of Cross-Fertilization' (2015) 84 *Nordic Journal of International Law* 371.

45 Solomon T Ebobrah, 'International Human Rights Courts' in Cesare PR Romano, Karen J Alter and Yuval Shany (eds), *The Oxford Handbook of International Adjudication* (Oxford University Press, 2013) 225.

derogated from international human rights law in their jurisprudence on the rights of the accused, and they have deferred extensively to the case law of the ECtHR in particular in this regard,[46] as shall be shown in greater detail in part IV.

IV Practical examples of human rights law's impact on international criminal procedure

This section illustrates that the international criminal tribunals have been heavily influenced by the case law of international human rights bodies, in particular the ECtHR, in developing their procedure. We might question why the ECtHR has made such a particular impact upon international criminal procedure. This can likely be attributed to the extensive jurisprudence of the ECtHR on Article 6 of the ECHR, which accounts for some 90% of the Court's cases, or possibly to the fact the ECtHR is geographically closer to many of the tribunals in The Hague.

The ICC is rather distinct from the *ad hoc* tribunals, insofar as it is formally bound, by virtue of Article 21(3) of its Statute, to interpret the law in a manner that is consistent with international human rights law. To this end, human rights law has, unsurprisingly, had a more explicit influence over the ICC's jurisprudence than its predecessors. In *Katanga and Chui*, the Court found that Article 21(3) effectively trumped other Articles of the Statute where the application of the other statutory provision would contravene international human rights law.[47] The ICC has gone beyond the limits of its Statute on a number of occasions to meet the standards of international human rights law. For example, in *Lubanga*, the Court determined that the accused had the right to pre-trial disclosure, and granted a stay of proceedings, despite that remedy not being included in the Statute, on the grounds that the Court was subject to international human rights law.[48] In *Ntaganda*, the accused's right to family life was considered in deciding on the proportionality of restricting the accused's communications.[49] In *Lubanga*, the ICC

46 Nicolas AJ Croquet, 'The International Criminal Court and the Treatment of Defence Rights: A Mirror of the European Court of Human Rights' Jurisprudence?' (2011) 11 *Human Rights Law Review* 91, 92.

47 *Prosecutor v Katanga and Chui (Decision on an Amicus Curiae application and on the "Requête tendant à obtenir présentations des témoins DRC-D02-P-0350, DRC-D02-P-0236, DRC-D02-P-0228 aux autorités néerlandaises aux fins d'asile" (Articles 68 and 93(7) of the Statute))* (International Criminal Court, Trial Chamber II, Case No ICC-01/04-01/07-3003, 9 June 2011) [73].

48 *Prosecutor v Lubanga (Judgment on the Appeal of Mr. Thomas Lubanga Dyilo against the Decision on the Defence Challenge to the Jurisdiction of the Court pursuant to Article 19 (2) (a) of the Statute of 3 October 2006)* (International Criminal Court, Appeals Chamber, Case No ICC-01/04-01/06-772, 14 December 2006) [35]–[39].

49 *Prosecutor v Ntaganda (Decision Reviewing the Restrictions Placed on Mr Ntaganda's Contacts)* (International Criminal Court, Trial Chamber VI, Case No ICC-01/04-02/06-1494, 7 September 2016) [35].

relied extensively on ECtHR jurisprudence in determining the meaning of the Court's 'substantial grounds to believe' evidentiary standard for the confirmation of charges.[50]

More specifically, there are a number of distinct areas where human rights law has had an obvious role in shaping international criminal procedure. Two such areas are particularly noteworthy, namely the law and procedure on provisional release pending trial (4.1), and on the examination of witnesses (4.2).

A Provisional release

In the early days of the *ad hoc* tribunals, an accused person was required to demonstrate 'exceptional circumstances' before they could be considered for provisional release.[51] Despite a change to the ICTY Rules of Procedure and Evidence in 1999,[52] provisional release continued to be the exception and not the rule,[53] and it was for defendants to prove that they would not pose a risk of flight or witness intimidation.[54] This position of release as an exceptional measure stood in contrast to human rights standards; the ICCPR expressly demands that detention in custody pending trial 'shall not be the general rule',[55] while regional human rights treaties declare a right to trial without undue delay or to release pending trial.[56] In *Krajišnik*, the ICTY Trial Chamber considered that the length of the accused's detention 'although long, does not exceed the periods which the European Court of Human Rights has found reasonable'.[57] By contrast, Judge Robinson, in his dissenting opinion to that decision, opined that the ECtHR's principle that mandatory detention on remand was *per se* incompatible with the Convention

---

50 *Prosecutor v Lubanga (Decision on the Confirmation of Charges)* (International Criminal Court, Pre-Trial Chamber I, Case No ICC-01/04-01/06-803, 29 January 2007) [38].

51 International Criminal Tribunal for the Former Yugoslavia, *Rules of Procedure and Evidence*, UN Doc IT/32/Rev.16 (2 July 1999).

52 International Criminal Tribunal for the Former Yugoslavia, *Rules of Procedure and Evidence*, UN Doc IT/32/Rev.17 (17 November 1999).

53 *Prosecutor v Brdanin and Talić (Decision on Motion by Momir Talić for Provisional Release)* (International Criminal Tribunal for the Former Yugoslavia, Trial Chamber II, Case No IT-99-36-T, 28 March 2001) [18].

54 *Prosecutor v Tadić (Decision on Miroslav Tadić's Application for Provisional Release)* (International Criminal Tribunal for the Former Yugoslavia, Trial Chamber, Case No IT-95-9-T, 4 April 2000); *Prosecutor v Krajišnik (Decision on Momčilo Krajišnik's Notice of Motion for Provisional Release)* (International Criminal Tribunal for the Former Yugoslavia, Trial Chamber III, Case No IT-00-39&40-PT, 8 October 2001 [12].

55 *International Covenant on Civil and Political Rights*, opened for signature 16 December 1966, 999 UNTS 171 (entered into force 23 March 1976) Art. 9(3).

56 *European Convention for the Protection of Human Rights and Fundamental Freedoms*, opened for signature 4 November 1950, 213 UNTS 222 (entered into force 3 September 1953) Art. 5(3); *American Convention on Human Rights*, opened for signature 22 November 1969, 1144 UNTS 123 (entered into force 18 July 1978) Art. 7(5).

57 *Prosecutor v Krajišnik (Decision on Momčilo Krajišnik's Notice of Motion for Provisional Release)* (International Criminal Tribunal for the Former Yugoslavia, Trial Chamber III, Case No IT-00-39&40-PT, 8 October 2001) [22].

was equally applicable to the international tribunal.[58] He noted that, even though the international tribunal's lack of a police force to enforce warrants may require some adjustments to the interpretation of the law:

> [C]are must be taken lest these adjustments go so far that their effect is to nullify the rights of an accused person under customary international law. There is no legal basis for interpreting the ICCPR as though it provided one set of rights applicable at the municipal level, and another set applicable at the international level.[59]

Judge Robinson therefore recommended that the amended Rule 65 should be interpreted as placing a burden on the prosecution to show that the criteria for provisional release set out in that Rule were satisfied, rather than requiring the accused to prove that he or she would appear for trial and would not pose any danger to any person if released.[60] His reference to international human rights standards clearly fits within the equality of treatment theory set out above in part 2 – the principle underpinning this approach is that the individual should receive the same respect for their universal human rights (principally the right to a fair trial), regardless of the forum in which they are tried. Contrary to Judge Robinson's recommendations, later case law continued to place the burden of proof on the accused in relation to Rule 65, and provisional release remained relatively rare, especially before the ICTR and SCSL, where it was difficult to find a state willing to host an accused person while on provisional release. However, the fact that the amendment of Rule 65 of the ICTY's Rules of Procedure and Evidence was enacted in 1999 (and followed by the ICTR in 2003[61]) precisely to bring the Tribunal's Rules in line with international human rights standards highlights the influence of human rights law on international criminal procedure.

More recently, the Rules of Procedure and Evidence were amended again to temper the right to provisional release without trial. In 2011, an amendment was inserted to add that the 'existence of sufficiently compelling humanitarian grounds may be considered in granting such release'.[62] This amendment followed from a decision in *Prlić et al*, where the prosecution successfully appealed a decision to provisionally release the accused at an advanced stage of proceedings, namely after a decision on a Rule 98*bis* ('no case to answer') motion

---

58 Ibid, *Dissenting Opinion of Judge Patrick Robinson*, [7]–[8].
59 Ibid [10].
60 Ibid [18].
61 International Criminal Tribunal for Rwanda, *Rules of Procedure and Evidence*, UN Doc ITR/3/Rev.13 (27 May 2003).
62 International Criminal Tribunal for the Former Yugoslavia, *Rules of Procedure and Evidence*, UN Doc IT/32/Rev.46 (20 October 2011) r 65(B).

had been delivered.[63] The Appeals Chamber found that the Trial Chamber had erred in considering the defendants' requests to be based on humanitarian grounds capable of justifying a short period of provisional release.[64] Since that decision, the ICTY read Rule 65(B) as requiring evidence of 'sufficiently compelling humanitarian grounds' if the case was at an advanced stage, although some Trial Chambers evidenced discomfort with this new requirement, particularly on the basis of its apparent incompatibility with international human rights law.[65] A later Trial Chamber decision in *Prlić et al* relied extensively on human rights law, particularly the case law of the ECtHR, in determining that the particular accused, who had been in detention for a period of over five years by that stage, was not obliged to show humanitarian grounds justifying his release.[66] The wording of the Rule amendment reflects this more rights-compliant formulation, insofar as it does not require the accused to prove sufficiently compelling humanitarian grounds, but that such grounds can be taken into account.

The ICC Statute, by contrast to the legal framework of earlier international criminal tribunals, contains an explicit right to provisional release pending trial.[67] In the *Bemba* case, Judge Trendafilova explicitly embraced the principles that detention should be the exception and not the rule,[68] and that allegations of witness interference must be substantiated,[69] thus reflecting human rights standards that the ICTY and other tribunals were criticised for ignoring. In a dissenting opinion to a decision denying former Côte d'Ivoire President Laurent Gbagbo provisional release, Judge Ušacka relied extensively on the case law of the ECtHR in supporting her opinion that this decision lacked sufficient reasoning.[70] Thus, human rights law continues to

---

63 *Prosecutor v Prlić (Decision on Prosecution's Consolidated Appeal against Decisions to Provisionally Release the Accused Prlić, Stojić, Praljak, Petković and Ćorić* (International Criminal Tribunal for the Former Yugoslavia, Appeals Chamber, Case No IT-04-74-AR65.5, 11 March 2008).

64 Ibid [21].

65 *Prosecutor v Stanišić (Decision Denying Mico Stanišić's Request for Provisional Release during the Upcoming Summer Court Recess)* (International Criminal Tribunal for the Former Yugoslavia, Trial Chamber II, Case No IT-08-91-T, 29 June 2011) (Robinson) [16]–[19].

66 *Prosecutor v Prlić (Decision on Slobodan Praljak's Motion for Provisional Release)* (International Criminal Tribunal for the Former Yugoslavia, Trial Chamber III, Case No IT-04-74-T, 21 April 2011) [36].

67 *Rome Statute*, Art. 60.

68 *Prosecutor v Bemba (Decision on the Interim Release of Jean-Pierre Bemba Gombo and Convening Hearings with the Kingdom of Belgium, the Republic of Portugal, the Republic of France, the Federal Republic of Germany, the Italian Republic, and the Republic of South Africa)* (International Criminal Court, Pre-Trial Chamber II, Case No ICC-01/05-01/08-475, 14 August 2009) [77].

69 Ibid [73].

70 *Prosecutor v Gbagbo (Judgment on the appeal of Mr Laurent Koudou Gbagbo against the decision of Pre-Trial Chamber I of 13 July 2012 entitled "Decision on the 'Requête de la Défense demandant la mise en liberté provisoire du président Gbagbo")* (International Criminal Court, Appeals Chamber, Case No ICC-02/11-01/11-278, 26 October 2012) [8]–[14].

bear value as an interpretative tool, even where the standards included in the Court's legal framework seem to be more protective of human rights standards than the human rights tribunals themselves.

B Examination of witnesses

Human rights law has also had a bearing on evidentiary matters in international criminal law, particularly when the tribunals are faced with such issues as witness anonymity and unavailability.[71] The *ad hoc* tribunals, as is widely known, moved from a strict preference for live testimony in court towards a more liberal approach towards the admissibility of written witness statements over the course of their lifetimes, an approach largely driven by efficiency concerns.[72] In justifying their apparent departure from stringent protection of the right to confront witnesses, the tribunals have relied extensively on human rights law.

In its well-known decision on witness protection measures, the ICTY's Trial Chamber in *Tadić* cited the ECtHR's decision in *Kostovski v Netherlands*[73] no fewer than eight times. In *Kostovski*, the ECtHR held that the applicant's rights had been violated when he had not been given 'an adequate and proper opportunity to challenge and question a key witness against him'.[74] Perhaps remarkably, this decision was used as the basis for the Trial Chamber's drawing of a seemingly obverse conclusion in *Tadić*, when it found that anonymous witnesses might be permissible, in limited circumstances.[75] The apparent irony in this use of *Kostovski* to reach this conclusion was noted by the ICTY's former President, Antonio Cassese, who wrote that:

> The Majority Opinion of the Trial Chamber was, of necessity, selective in its reliance on the *Kostovski* case. Indeed, it must be borne in mind that the finding of the majority ... was that fair trial guarantees were not violated with anonymous witnesses, whereas the finding of the European Court in *Kostovski* was that such guarantees were violated.[76]

71 See further Yvonne McDermott, 'Absent Witnesses and the Right to Confrontation' in Triestino Mariniello and Paolo Lobba (eds), *Judicial Dialogue on Human Rights: The Practice of International Criminal Tribunals* (Brill/Nijhoff, 2017) (forthcoming).
72 Patricia M Wald, 'Dealing with Witnesses in War Crime Trials: Lessons from the Yugoslav Tribunal' (2002) 5 *Yale Human Rights & Development Law Journal* 217, 227; Peter Murphy, 'No Free Lunch, No Free Proof' (2010) 8 *Journal of International Criminal Justice* 539.
73 *Kostovski v Netherlands (Judgment)* (European Court of Human Rights, Plenary, Application No 11454/85, 20 November 1989).
74 Ibid [41].
75 *Tadić Protective Measures Decision* (International Criminal Tribunal for the Former Yugoslavia, Trial Chamber, Case No IT-94-1-T, 10 August 1995) [85]–[86].
76 Antonio Cassese, 'The International Criminal Tribunal for the Former Yugoslavia and Human Rights' [1997] *European Human Rts Law Rev* 329.

More recently, in granting deferred disclosure of prosecution witnesses' identities to the defence, the ICC relied extensively on the ECtHR's case law, which has found that the right to disclosure of evidence is not an absolute right, but that counterbalancing measures must be put in place to protect the rights of the accused in an adversarial criminal trial.[77]

One of the ECtHR's most controversial recent decisions on the right to examination of witnesses in circumstances where a key witness is unavailable was the 2012 Grand Chamber judgment in *Al-Khawaja and Tahery*.[78] Prior to this case, the accepted jurisprudence of the ECtHR determined that where a conviction had been based solely or to a decisive degree on the testimony of a witness whom the defendant has not had the opportunity to examine or have examined, this would normally be a breach of Article 6.[79] However, the Grand Chamber in *Al-Khawaja and Tahery* determined that the 'sole or decisive' rule should be interpreted flexibly in light of the need to assess 'the overall fairness of the proceedings, namely to weigh in the balance the competing interests of the defence, the victim, and witnesses, and the public interest in the effective administration of justice'.[80] This decision has been criticized as eroding the rights of the accused.[81] Nevertheless, it was instructive in the SCSL's Appeals Judgment in *Taylor*, where the Appeals Chamber noted that

> the Grand Chamber of the ECtHR held that reliance on an uncorroborated hearsay statement as the sole or decisive basis for a conviction is not precluded as a matter of law and does not *per se* violate the accused's right to a fair trial.[82]

The Appeals Chamber went on to conclude, rather dangerously, that it was not *per se* impermissible to base a conviction solely on uncorroborated hearsay evidence.[83] The SCSL's interpretation of *Al-Khawaja and Tahery* arguably goes beyond the Grand Chamber's ruling. It is worthy of note that the Grand Chamber's ultimate conclusion was that Tahery's Article 6 rights had been breached, but that Al Khawaja's had not.[84] The difference between

---

77 *Prosecutor v Katanga and Chui (Public redacted version of the Decision on the Protection of Prosecution Witnesses 267 and 353 of 20 May 2009)* (International Criminal Court, Trial Chamber II, Case No ICC-01/04-01/07-1179, 28 May 2009) [32]–[33].

78 *Al-Khawaja and Tahery v United Kingdom* [2011] VI Eur Court HR 191.

79 *Kostovski v Netherlands*, above n 73, [41]–[45].

80 *Al Khawaja and Tahery*, above n 78 [146].

81 Laura Hoyano, 'What Is Balanced on the Scales of Justice? In Search of the Essence of the Right to a Fair Trial' (2014) *Criminal Law Review* 4.

82 *Prosecutor v Taylor (Judgment)* (Special Court for Sierra Leone, Appeals Chamber, Case No SCSL-03-01-A, 26 September 2013) [85].

83 Ibid [90].

84 Al Khawaja and Tahery, above n 78, 257.

the two cases was that Tahery's conviction had been based on the untested testimony of the 'sole witness who was apparently willing or able to say what he had seen', and the defence was unable to call any other witness to contradict his evidence,[85] whereas the written statement of the key witness in Al Khawaja's case was supported by another complainant, whose testimony bore strong similarities to that of the unavailable witness, and by the evidence of two friends in whom she had confided before her death.[86] The *Taylor* Appeal Judgment did not discuss these nuances in the Grand Chamber's judgment, instead preferring to emphasise the general principle that convictions based solely or to a decisive extent on untested witness testimony are not automatically in breach of the right to a fair trial. The Grand Chamber's emphasis that 'where a conviction is based solely or decisively on the evidence of absent witnesses, the Court must subject the proceedings to the most searching scrutiny'[87] was not mentioned; instead, the Appeals Chamber noted that the Trial Chamber should 'carefully evaluate the reliability of such evidence and bear in mind the safeguards designed to ensure fairness'[88] in basing a conviction on such evidence.

This example illustrates that the influence of international human rights law can have a negative impact on the rights of the accused, as well as a positive impact as illustrated by part 4.A above on provisional release. International human rights courts should be mindful of the potential broader deleterious effects that any dilution of established principles of the right to a fair trial might have, not merely for the applicant before them, but for other defendants before courts who rely on their jurisprudence. The case law on the right to confrontation highlights the international criminal tribunals' ability to mould precedents from human rights case law to support their conclusions, even where the human rights case(s) in question do not apparently offer such support.

V Conclusion

This chapter discussed the influence of human rights law on international criminal procedure. It argued that, while some persuasive arguments have been raised to support the idea that international criminal tribunals are bound to respect human rights law, it is more appropriate to say that human rights is a persuasive authority before the tribunals. The only exception to this rule is the ICC, which is formally bound to interpret its Statute and Rules in a manner that complies with human rights law, by virtue of Article 21(3) of its Statute.

---

85 Ibid [162].
86 Ibid [156].
87 Ibid [147].
88 *Prosecutor v Taylor (Judgment)* (Special Court for Sierra Leone, Appeals Chamber, Case No SCSL-03-01-A, 26 September 2013) [90].

The fact that the ECtHR has declined to consider complaints of individuals who find themselves in the hands of international criminal tribunals situated on the territory of state parties is significant, because it shows that the relationship between these two bodies of law is not hierarchical. Human rights courts and international criminal tribunals can borrow from one another's jurisprudence, but they are by no means bound to do so. In practice, human rights courts have referred less extensively to international criminal law than international criminal tribunals have referred to human rights law.

Two particular areas highlighting the influence of human rights law on international criminal procedure were discussed in detail; the law and practice on provisional release and the law and practice on the right to confrontation. Any number of distinct components of the right to a fair trial could have been chosen for this analysis, and all would have highlighted the influence of human rights law on international criminal procedure.[89] The two examples chosen illustrate that human rights law can have a positive effect on protecting the rights of accused persons before international criminal procedure, as was the case with the right to provisional release, or can be used (and possibly abused) as a justification when derogating from those rights, as evidenced by our discussion on the right to confrontation of witnesses. It is imperative that observers of international criminal tribunals continue to fully interrogate the extent to which their procedural standards are truly in conformity with the right to a fair trial, as extensively developed by the law of international human rights bodies.

The influence of international human rights law on international criminal procedure is unlikely to wane any time soon, particularly in light of the ICC's interpretative obligation under Article 21(3), as the ICC becomes the main international criminal tribunal in existence. It will be interesting to see whether future decisions of the human rights tribunals will draw more extensively on international criminal law. A greater symbiosis between the two bodies of law would be welcome in developing a clearer understanding of what the right to a fair trial requires under international law.

Further reading

Croquet, Nicolas AJ, 'The International Criminal Court and the Treatment of Defence Rights: A Mirror of the European Court of Human Rights' Jurisprudence?' (2011) 11 *Human Rights Law Review* 91.

Jones, Annika, 'Insights into an Emerging Relationship: Use of Human Rights Jurisprudence at the International Criminal Court' (2016) 16(4) *Human Rights Law Review* 701.

---

89 Other aspects so influenced include: the right to trial by an independent and impartial tribunal; the rights to interpretation and translation, and the principle of legality/*nullum crimen sine lege*.

Mariniello, Triestino and Paolo Lobba (eds), *Judicial Dialogue on Human Rights: The Practice of International Criminal Tribunals* (Brill/Nijhoff, 2017).

McDermott, Yvonne, *Fairness in International Criminal Trials* (Oxford University Press, 2016).

Schabas, William A, 'International Criminal Law and Tribunals and Human Rights' in Scott Sheeran and Nigel Rodley (eds), *Routledge Handbook of International Human Rights Law* (Routledge, 2013) 215.

Sluiter, Göran *et al* (eds), *International Criminal Procedure: Principles and Rules* (Oxford University Press, 2013).

Vasiliev, Sergey, 'International Criminal Tribunals in the Shadow of Strasbourg and Politics of Cross-Fertilization' (2015) 84 *Nordic Journal of International Law* 371.

Zappala, Salvatore, *Human Rights in International Criminal Proceedings* (Oxford University Press, 2005).

Zeegers, Krit, *International Criminal Tribunals and Human Rights Law* (Springer, 2016).

15

'AND WHERE THE OFFENCE IS, LET THE GREAT AXE FALL'

Sentencing under international criminal law

Mark A. Drumbl[1]

I Introduction

This chapter explores *how* and *why* international criminal courts and tribunals punish the individuals they convict of international crimes. To be sure, 'the great axe' is no longer in vogue amid transnational circles, as it had been throughout Shakespeare's England – or Hamlet's Denmark – where it fell and beheaded for all sorts of infractions and betrayals. International institutions now punish primarily through imprisonment. Although the Nuremberg IMT, the progenitor of much of modern international criminal law (ICL), did deploy the axe of the death penalty, it also ushered in an era that exhorted, notwithstanding being 'flushed with victory and stung with injury', that the 'four great nations . . . stay the hand of vengeance'.[2] The death penalty lingers, assuredly, within some national legal frameworks. The Bangladesh International Crimes Tribunal, for example, in November 2013 sentenced two individuals *in absentia* to death by hanging for their involvement in the murder of pro-independence activists during Bangladesh's 1971 war of independence from Pakistan. Twenty-two defendants sentenced to death by Rwandan national courts for their role in the genocide were publicly executed in 1998. Rwanda, however, abjured the death penalty in 2007. Among a number of factors that precipitated this

---

1 The quotation in the title is from Claudius in William Shakespeare, *Hamlet*, Act 4, Scene 5. Parts of this chapter draw from and update the author's contributions to *The Elgar Companion to the International Criminal Tribunal for Rwanda* (2016) Ch. 14 and *The Elgar Companion to the International Criminal Court* (forthcoming). Many thanks to Shahram Dana for input and to Barbora Holá for sharing and guiding me through all her data.

2 Justice Robert H Jackson, *Opening Statement before the International Military Tribunal, Nuremberg*, The Robert H. Jackson Centre <www.roberthjackson.org/speech-and-writing/opening-statement-before-the-international-military-tribunal/>.

development was the ICTR's refusal to refer cases to the Rwandan national courts in satisfaction of the UN's completion strategy so long as the death penalty (and subsequently life imprisonment with special conditions – *i.e.* solitary confinement) remained on the books in Rwandan national law.[3] In this regard, the ICTR – which closed its doors at the end of 2015 – perhaps served as a 'gentle civilizer'[4] paradoxically draining the harshest of sentences for those individuals found to have committed the gravest of offences.

'Civilising' how international institutions punish nonetheless must synergise with the reality that sentencing matters greatly for many constituencies. Victims care about what ultimately happens to persons convicted of serious international crimes. Many victims call for long, hard sentences; while others are unmoved by any sentence at all. And others may wish to preserve their own humanity through a more modest repressive scheme or may incline, like Nietzsche, to '[d]istrust everyone in whom the impulse to punish is powerful'.[5] As the popular plebiscite on the Colombian peace agreement acidly revealed in October 2016, voters who live amid violence may be more willing to barter punishment for peace while those who live further away may be vexed by such deals. The bottom line is that sentencing fulfils important narrative functions and addresses moral questions of responsibility and payback. Sentencing can also serve as a venue to individuate differentiations among perpetrators, in particular within the context of group crimes, and thereby inject granularity into the attribution of fault.

The sentencing of international crimes is also emerging as a jurisprudentially systematised area. This is not to say that it is a jurisprudentially satisfying area, to be clear, and much work remains to be done. But it is systematised in that international judges reference the work of other international courts and tribunals in their sentencing jurisprudence. Although the need to individualise the penalty means that previous sentencing practices provide only limited assistance,[6] a sentencing practice is emerging within international institutions. This practice occurs despite the formal absence of the doctrine of *stare decisis* and proof that the affirmed penal norm in fact constitutes a general principle of law. This cross-stitching also takes place notwithstanding variations among the mandates and directives of various international institutions as enunciated by their enabling instruments.

3 Cf *Prosecutor v Uwinkindi* (*Decision on Prosecutor's Request for Referral to the Republic of Rwanda*) (International Criminal Tribunal for Rwanda, Case No ICTR-2001-75-R11, 28 June 2011).

4 This phrase of course is Martti Koskenniemi's, see Martti Koskenniemi, *The Gentle Civilizer of Nations: The Rise and Fall of International Law 1870–1960* (Cambridge University Press, 2001).

5 Friedrich Nietzsche, *Thus Spoke Zarathustra* (1883) pt 2, Ch. 29.

6 See *Prosecutor v Thomas Lubanga Dyilo (Decision on Sentence)* (International Criminal Court, Appeals Chamber, Case No ICC-01/04-01/06 A 4 A 6, 1 December 2014) [77].

This Chapter proceeds through several steps. First: to synthetically summarise the governing legal texts of representative international institutions, specifically, the International Criminal Court (ICC), the United Nations Mechanism for International Criminal Tribunals (UNMICT, replacing the ICTR and ICTY), and the Special Court for Sierra Leone (SCSL), with a view to setting out the sentencing parameters and the factors to which judges turn in assessing the gravity of the offence, on the one hand, and individualising factors, on the other, which are commonly referred to as aggravating and mitigating circumstances. Second: to review sentencing practice and quantum, enforcement of sentences, and consistency in sentencing. Third: to touch upon penological aspirations so as to interrogate the ability of custodial sentences to attain their ideologically avowed retributive and deterrent goals. A brief conclusion follows.

II Positive law instruments of international courts and tribunals

With the thinnest of exceptions that relate to the administration of justice,[7] contemporary international courts and tribunals prosecute and punish only natural persons. Legal persons, such as corporations, are not cognisable as subjects of ICL. This gap persists despite considerable evidence of how corporate involvement fosters, facilitates, and fuels mass atrocity.[8] One inchoate regional instrument, the 2014 Malabo Protocol pertaining to the proposed International Criminal Law Section of the African Court of Justice and Human Rights, contemplates corporations ('legal persons') as potential defendants and addresses the penalties they may receive.[9] That said, the

---

7 In July 2016, the Special Tribunal for Lebanon (STL), referencing Lebanese law, entered a guilty verdict on a contempt charge against Akhbar Beirut S.A.L., a corporation that hosted a newspaper and website. See further Ekaterina Kopylova, 'Akhbar Beirut S.A.L. Guilty of Contempt, STL Found: One Small Verdict for a Tribunal, a Giant Leap for International Justice?' on *Opinio Juris* (4 August 2016) <http://opiniojuris.org/2016/08/04/akhbar-beirut-s-a-l-guilty-of-contempt-stl-found-one-small-verdict-for-a-tribunal-a-giant-leap-for-international-justice/> (noting also that 'the plain reading of the Rome Statute [. . .] does not preclude the institution of Article 70 proceedings against a corporation – for destroying, tampering or interfering with the collection of evidence, as may be the case'). The STL has jurisdiction over 'persons' but Article 3 of its Statute references only 'individual criminal responsibility'.

8 For one of the most penetrative accounts, see Annika Van Baar and Wim Huisman, 'The Oven Builders of the Holocaust: A Case Study of Corporate Complicity in International Crimes' (2012) 52 *British Journal of Criminology* 1033.

9 *Malabo Protocol*, Art. 46C(6) specifies: 'The criminal responsibility of legal persons shall not exclude the criminal responsibility of natural persons who are perpetrators or accomplices in the same crimes'. The International Criminal Law Section of the African Court of Justice and Human Rights can impose 'prison sentences' and/or 'pecuniary fines' (Art. 43A(2)) and in

future of this institution, its viability, and the effect of the Malabo Protocol on the substantive content or practice of ICL remains highly uncertain.

The enabling instruments of international criminal courts and tribunals offer little in the way of specific guidance when it comes to how much time convicts should serve in prison. The ICC can sentence an offender to up to 30 years' imprisonment, with a possibility of 'life imprisonment when justified by the extreme gravity of the crime and the individual circumstances of the convicted person'.[10] The Rome Statute lacks any minimum sentence or individualised sentencing range for specific crimes or modes of liability. The same dynamic arises with the ICTY, ICTR, and UNMICT. A convict may be incarcerated for a term up to life. Since there is no mandatory minimum sentence, ICTR and ICTY judges have the power to impose any sentence ranging from one-day imprisonment to life imprisonment for any crime within their jurisdiction.[11] The Special Tribunal for Lebanon (STL) also is able to issue a life sentence. But not all international penal institutions have that capacity. The Statute of the SCSL, for example, formally precludes life sentences and stipulates that juvenile offenders (persons between fifteen and eighteen years of age) are to be treated with clemency so as to encourage their rehabilitation.[12] The SCSL's first Chief Prosecutor, David Crane, elected not to indict any juvenile, however, so this framework never was deployed. Two other internationalised tribunals, the Extraordinary Chambers in the Courts of Cambodia (ECCC) and the Special Panels for East Timor, proceed somewhat differently. The ECCC's foundational instruments establish a minimum sentence of five years' imprisonment and a maximum sentence of life imprisonment (with the possibility of combining this with seizure of personal and real property acquired by criminal conduct, which is to be returned to the state). The East Timor Special Panels punish through a fixed term of imprisonment, capped at 25 years for a single crime.

addition thereto may 'order the forfeiture of any property, proceeds or any asset acquired unlawfully or by criminal conduct, and their return to their rightful owner or to an appropriate Member state' (Art. 43A(5)). To date, the Malabo Protocol has received no ratifications.

10 See also *Rome Statute of the International Criminal Court*, opened for signature 17 July 1998, 2187 UNTS 90 (entered into force 1 July 2002) Art. 77(1). See also Art. 76(1), which reads: 'In the event of a conviction, the Trial Chamber shall consider the appropriate sentence to be imposed and shall take into account the evidence presented and submissions made during the trial that are relevant to the sentence'.

11 A contrast thereby arises between the ICTR's discretion and the domestic *gacaca* legislation in Rwanda which had deployed comprehensive sentencing guidelines keyed to the categorisation of the offence and whether or not (and when) the accused tendered a guilty plea. The domestic *gacaca* legislation also contemplated community service as a remedy, unlike international sentencing practice.

12 *Agreement between the United Nations and the Government of Sierra Leone on the Establishment of a Special Court for Sierra Leone*, signed 16 January 2002, 2178 UNTS 137 (entered into force 12 April 2002) annex ('*Statute of the Special Court for Sierra Leone*') ('SCSL Statute') Art. 17; Special Court for Sierra Leone, *Rules of Procedure and Evidence* (adopted 16 January 2002) r 101.

The Rome Statute does not refer to the national sentencing practices of the situation country. Here, the *ad hocs* proceed differently. Their Statutes require them to have recourse to the general practice regarding prison sentences in the courts of the former Yugoslavia and Rwanda, respectively. This provision does not imply an obligation to conform to the relevant national practice, though there is an obligation to consider such practice or to take it into account.[13]

The *ad hoc* tribunals, SCSL, East Timor Special Panels, STL, and the ICC follow a similar 'formula' when it comes to sentencing. This is to begin by assessing the 'gravity' of the crime and then to consider the 'individual circumstances of the convicted person'.[14] The ICTR has held that the gravity of the offences committed is 'the deciding factor in the determination of the sentence'.[15] Although sentences in similar cases are instructive, these antecedents are not binding as benchmarks.[16] The time the convicted person has spent in detention upon an order of the international court or tribunal then is to be deducted, along with the time spent in detention during trial.[17] Sentence is to be pronounced in public and, wherever possible, in the presence of the accused.[18] Moreover, sentence is to be joint, that is, cumulative of all the convictions.[19] In the case of the *ad hoc* tribunals, defendants are mostly

---

13 See, eg, *Prosecutor v Semanza (Judgement)* (International Criminal Tribunal for Rwanda, Appeals Chamber, Case No ICTR-97-20-A, 20 May 2005) [345], [347], [377].

14 *Rome Statute*, Art. 78(1); SC Res 955, UN SCOR, 49th sess, 3453rd mtg, UN Doc S/RES/955 (8 November 1994) annex (*'Statute of the International Criminal Tribunal for Rwanda'*) (*'ICTR Statute'*) Art. 23(2); SC Res 827, UN SCOR, 48th sess, 3217th mtg, UN Doc S/RES/827 (25 May 1993), as amended by SC Res 1877, UN SCOR, 64th sess, 6155th mtg, UN Doc S/RES/1877 (7 July 2009) (*'ICTY Statute'*) Art. 24(2); SC Res 1757, UN SCOR, 61st sess, 5685th mtg, UN Doc S/RES/1757 (30 May 2007) annex (*'Agreement between the United Nations and the Lebanese Republic on the establishment of a Special Tribunal for Lebanon'*) ('STL Statute') Art. 24; Special Panel for Serious Crimes (East Timor), *On the Establishment of Panels with Exclusive Jurisdiction over Serious Criminal Offences*, UN Transnational Administration in East Timor, UN Doc UNTAET/REG/2000/15 (adopted 6 June 2000) regs 10.1-10.2.

15 *The Prosecutor v Nyiramasuhuko et al (Judgement and Sentence)* (International Criminal Tribunal for Rwanda, Trial Chamber II, Case No ICTR-98-42-T, 24 June 2011) [6189].

16 Ibid [6190].

17 *Prosecutor v Siméon Nchamihigo (Judgement and Sentence)* (International Criminal Tribunal for Rwanda, Trial Chamber III, Case No ICTR-01-63-T, 12 November 2008) [383]. Judges shall, when imposing penalty upon a convict, take into account 'the extent to which any penalty imposed by a national court on the same person for the same act has already been served'. *ICTR Statute*, Art. 9(3); *ICTY Statute*, Art. 10(3); SC Res 1966, UN SCOR, 64th sess, 6463rd mtg, UN Doc S/RES/1966 (22 December 2010) annex (*'Statute of the International Residual Mechanism for International Criminal Tribunals'*) (*'UNMICT Statute'*) Art. 7(3).

18 *Rome Statute*, Art. 76(4). Article 76(2) requires the Chamber to hold a sentencing hearing if requested by the Prosecutor or the accused, or to hold one on its own motion.

19 *Rome Statute*, Art. 78(3).

convicted on multiple counts but only one global sentence is issued.[20] While this approach of totality/globality is economical, it also shrouds many of the factors that influence the determination of sentence and complicates matters when the Appeals Chamber revisits sentence in light of quashing, substituting, or adding convictions. Thus far at the ICC (four convictions at the time of writing), a specific sentence has been given as to each charge for which a conviction was entered, and then a global sentence was issued matching the most severe among these concurrent sentences.

The ICC Rules of Procedure and Evidence indicatively list some factors to consider in sentencing, including explicitly enumerated aggravating and mitigating factors.[21] These are, non-exhaustively: the extent of the damage caused, in particular the harm caused to the victims and their families; the nature of the unlawful behaviour and the means employed to execute the crime; the degree of participation of the convicted person; the degree of intent; the circumstances of manner, time, and location; and the age, education, social, and economic condition of the convicted person. Turning to mitigating factors as individualised circumstances, the Rome Statute non-exclusively indicates: 'substantially diminished mental capacity or duress' and 'the convicted person's conduct after the act, including any efforts by the person to compensate the victims and any cooperation with the Court'. Aggravating circumstances are enumerated in Rule 145(2)(b) as:

(i) Any relevant prior criminal convictions for crimes under the jurisdiction of the Court or of a similar nature;
(ii) Abuse of power or official capacity;
(iii) Commission of the crime where the victim is particularly defenceless;
(iv) Commission of the crime with particular cruelty or where there were multiple victims;
(v) Commission of the crime for any motive involving discrimination [. . .];
(vi) Other circumstances which, although not enumerated above, by virtue of their nature are similar to those mentioned.

No ordering principle is provided as to the relative weight to attribute to any of these factors; 'one or more aggravating circumstances' may justify the imposition of life imprisonment.[22] Whereas aggravating factors need to be proven beyond a reasonable doubt, factors in mitigation need to be

---

20 Barbora Holá, *Sentencing of International Crimes: Consistency of Sentencing Case Law* (2012) 4 *Amsterdam Law Forum* 3, 9.
21 International Criminal Court, *Rules of Procedure and Evidence*, Doc No ICC-ASP/1/3 (adopted 9 September 2002) rr 145(1)(c), 145(2).
22 Ibid r 145(3).

established only on the balance of probabilities, and do not need to be directly connected to the offences charged.

The enabling instruments of the *ad hoc* tribunals are more parsimonious when it comes to the factors to consider in determining gravity and individual circumstances.[23] Rule 101 (common to both *ad hoc* tribunals) requires Trial Chambers to take into account mitigating and/or aggravating circumstances. With one exception (substantial cooperation by the offender), Rule 101 does not enumerate such circumstances. The Statutes of the ICTY and ICTR however each additionally provides that following governmental or superior orders may be considered a mitigating circumstance if justice so requires.[24]

That said, the jurisprudence of the *ad hocs* has generated a large number of aggravating and mitigating factors. These, in turn, have informed the jurisprudence of the ICC. It has been held that an aggravating factor only can increase the sentence if that factor did not form an element of the actual offence.[25] Preserving differentiations between elements of the crime, factors that pertain to gravity, and aggravating factors can be tricky. The due process rights of the defendant and the principle of legality indeed require vigilance in this regard so as to avoid double-counting.

The following aggravating circumstances have arisen in the jurisprudence of both *ad hoc* tribunals: the breadth of the crimes (*e.g.*, numbers of victims) and the suffering inflicted; the youth of the victims or their general vulnerability; the nature, degree, and form of the perpetrator's involvement (active role, principal perpetrator, secondary/indirect involvement, or aider and abettor); premeditation and discriminatory intent; abuse of a leadership position or a position of stature; promoting an environment of impunity; depraved motivations, zeal, great effort, and enthusiasm in committing the crimes; and deportment of the accused during trial.[26] At the SCSL, Liberian leader Charles Taylor – 64 years old – was sentenced to 50 years. In sentencing, the Trial Chamber emphasised as aggravating factors the extraterritoriality of Taylor's acts (that is, he meddled in Sierra Leone from his perch in Liberia) and also, in

---

23 The SCSL was required to consult ICTR sentencing practices. *SCSL Statute*, Art. 19(1). The Rules of Procedure and Evidence of the ICTR apply *mutatis mutandis* to the conduct of proceedings before the Special Court for Sierra Leone. *SCSL Statute*, Art. 14(1). Upon the SCSL's closure, a residual mechanism also was established to supervise the institution's ongoing legal obligations which include administrative and archival management, witness protection, and fulfilment of prison sentences.

24 *ICTY Statute*, Art. 7(4), *ICTR Statute*, Art. 6(4). This does not relieve the accused from criminal responsibility.

25 *Prosecutor v Deronjić (Judgement on Sentencing Appeal)*, (International Criminal Tribunal for the Former Yugoslavia, Appeals Chamber, Case No IT-02-61-A, 20 July 2005) [106]–[107], [127].

26 *Prosecutor v Kayishema (Judgement)* (International Criminal Tribunal for Rwanda, Trial Chamber II, Case No ICTR-95-1-T, 21 May 1999) [17] (sentence influenced by the fact one of the defendants repeatedly smiled and laughed while genocide survivors testified).

particular, his status as Head of State. The SCSL has noted, in contradistinction with other institutions, that accessorial perpetration (*i.e.* aiding and abetting) does not necessarily mean a lower sentence than direct perpetration.[27]

Commonly referenced mitigating factors include: whether and when the accused pled guilty and/or admitted guilt (a very significant factor); substantial cooperation by the offender with the prosecution; the remote or tangential nature of the convict's involvement in the crime; voluntary surrender; remorse; the youth, advanced age, health, and other personal circumstances of the offender (including whether married and with children); the extent to which the offender was subject to duress, orders, or coercion; the good character of the offender; the chaos of constant armed conflict; that the offender did not have a previous criminal record for ordinary common crimes; and assistance to victims. Human rights violations, moreover, suffered by the offender during pre-trial or trial proceedings may also count in mitigation.[28] The SCSL has insisted that mitigation should not be granted based on the perceived 'just cause' (for example the Civil Defence Forces' backing of the democratically elected government) for which a convict may have fought.[29]

Trial Chamber judges are given considerable discretion in determining the length of sentence.[30] The Appeals Chamber nonetheless exercises a monitoring function: its primary task is to review whether a trial chamber

---

27 *Prosecutor v Taylor (Appeal Judgement)* (Special Court for Sierra Leone, Appeals Chamber, Case No SCSL-03-01-A-1389, 27 September 2013) [663]–[670]. Shahram Dana argues that Taylor's responsibility should be seen as that of an 'enabler'. See ASIL, 'Punishment and Sentencing in International Criminal Law' (12 April 2014) <https://www.asil.org/blogs/punishment-and-sentencing-international-criminal-law>.

28 *Prosecutor v Kajelijeli (Judgement and Sentence)* (International Criminal Tribunal for Rwanda, Trial Chamber II, Case No ICTR-98-44A-A, 23 May 2005) (the original multiple sentences (two life sentences and 15 years) were decreased to a single sentence of a fixed term of 45 years, less time served in detention, owing to Appeals Chamber *proprio motu* finding of 'serious' violations of Kajelijeli's fundamental rights during his arrest and detention in Benin). See also *Prosecutor v Nahimana (Judgement and Sentence)* (International Criminal Tribunal for Rwanda, Trial Chamber I, Case No ICTR-99-52-T, 3 December 2003) [1106]–[1107].

29 *Prosecutor v Fofana and Kondewa (Appeal Judgement)* (Special Court for Sierra Leone, Appeals Chamber, Case No SCSL-04-14-A, 28 May 2008) [532]–[535].

30 *Renzaho v Prosecutor (Judgement)* (International Criminal Tribunal for Rwanda, Appeals Chamber, Case No ICTR-97-31-A, 1 April 2011) [606]; *Setako v Prosecutor (Judgement)* (International Criminal Tribunal for Rwanda, Appeal Chamber, Case No ICTR-04-81-A, 28 September 2011) [277]; *Prosecutor v Kvočka et al (Judgement)* (International Criminal Tribunal for the Former Yugoslavia, Appeals Chamber, Case No IT-98-30/1-A, 28 February 2005) [668]–[669], [715] (recognising there is 'no definitive list of sentencing guidelines', that 'sentencing is essentially a discretionary process on the part of a Trial Chamber', and concluding that 'the Trial Chamber has discretion as regards the factors it considers in mitigation, the weight it attaches to a particular mitigating factor, and the discounting of a particular mitigating factor'); *Ngirabatware v Prosecutor (Judgement)* (Mechanism for International Criminal Tribunals, Appeals Chamber, Case No UNMICT-12-29-A, 18 December 2014) [255].

made any discernible errors in sentencing.[31] In principle, across international penal institutions, appellate judges will not interfere with the trial judges' sentencing discretion merely because they might have made a different ruling. That said, the Appeals Chamber also can revisit the quantum of sentence by altering the actual convictions (or acquittals) entered by the Trial Chamber; though in other instances, entering acquittals or convictions on some of the charges upon appeal has not affected the length of the sentence.

In addition to imprisonment, Article 23(3) of the ICTR Statute and Article 24(3) of the ICTY Statute allow judges to 'order the return of any property and proceeds acquired by criminal conduct, including by means of duress, to their rightful owners'. *De facto*, however, these remedies have not been deployed, in large part owing to the indigence of convicts. The ICC also can impose fines and order forfeiture (of proceeds, property, and assets derived directly or indirectly from the crime), in addition to imprisonment, but these remedies shall be imposed only if imprisonment is insufficient and with regard to the convict's financial capacity and motivation.[32] These remedies were declined in the *Lubanga* and *Katanga* cases owing *inter alia* to the convict's indigence – a recurrent theme in international criminal prosecutions. The Rome Statute, however, breaks new ground in that it also permits reparations to be made to victims.[33] Pursuant to Article 75(1),

> the Court may, either upon request or on its own motion in exceptional circumstances, determine the scope and extent of any damage, loss and injury to, or in respect of, victims and will state the principles on which it is acting.

It 'may make an order directly against a convicted person specifying appropriate reparations to, or in respect of, victims, including restitution, compensation and rehabilitation'.[34] Importantly in light of the indigence phenomenon, however, the ICC can also make reparative orders through the Trust Fund for Victims, which also supports collective projects that run separately from any conviction.[35] The Fund is to be capitalised by compensation

---

31 Examples of discernible error at the *ad hoc* tribunals include when the Trial Chamber weighs extraneous or irrelevant considerations, or fails to weigh (or sufficiently weigh) relevant considerations, makes clear factual errors, or when the Trial Chamber judgment is unreasonable or plainly unjust.

32 *Rome Statute*, Art. 77(2).

33 *Rome Statute*, Art. 75.

34 *Rome Statute*, Art. 75(2).

35 *Rome Statute*, Art. 79(2); International Criminal Court, *Rules of Procedure and Evidence*, r 98. The *Lubanga* proceedings also gave rise (in August 2015) to the issuance of an Appeals Chamber decision establishing the principles and procedures to be applied to reparations.

orders entered against convicts (in theory) and also by voluntary grants from organisations and governments (in actuality, with 34 donor countries so far).[36] The Trust Fund however disclaims any punitive orientation and operates within a restorative paradigm. Hence, it is not part of the ICC's penalty schematic. The Fund has supported projects in Northern Uganda and the Democratic Republic of the Congo, including vocational training, counselling, reconciliation workshops, and reconstructive surgery.

Each of the enabling instruments of the ICTY, ICTR, and SCSL permit sentences to be pardoned or commuted and early release to be granted.[37] So, too, does the Rome Statute: Article 110(3) states that when the convict has served two-thirds of the sentence, or 25 years in the case of life imprisonment, the Court shall review the sentence to determine whether it should be reduced. Any possible sentence reduction can only be applied to the remaining one-third of the sentence. A sentence reduction may be issued if the Court determines the existence of one or more of the following factors: (1) 'early and continuing willingness' of cooperation by the convict; (2) the convict's 'voluntary assistance . . . in particular providing assistance in locating assets subject to orders of fine, forfeiture or reparation which may be used for the benefit of victims'; or (3) other factors 'establishing a clear and significant change of circumstances sufficient to justify the reduction of sentence, as provided in the Rules . . .'.[38]

Rule 223 of the ICC Rules of Procedure and Evidence also is germane to early release proceedings. This Rule provides that judges shall take into account a number of additional criteria to those enumerated in Article 110, namely: (a) the conduct of the sentenced person while in detention, which shows a genuine dissociation from his or her crime; (b) the prospect of the resocialisation and successful resettlement of the sentenced person; (c) whether the early release of the sentenced person would give rise to significant social instability; (d) any significant action taken by the sentenced person for the benefit of the victims as well as any impact on the victims and their families as a result of the early release; and (e) individual circumstances of the sentenced person, including a worsening state of physical or mental health or advanced age.[39]

In the case of the ICTR, 'imprisonment shall be served in Rwanda or any of the States on a list of States which have indicated to the Security Council their willingness to accept convicted persons, as designated by the [ICTR]'. The Statute

---

36 See <www.trustfundforvictims.org/sites/default/files/imce/summary_EN_LR_ONLINE. pdf>.

37 *ICTR Statute*, Art. 27; *ICTY Statute*, Art. 28; *SCSL Statute*, Art. 23; *STL Statute*, Art. 30; Special Panel for Serious Crimes (East Timor), *On Transitional Rules of Criminal Procedure*, UN Doc UNTAET/REG/2000/30 (adopted 25 September 2000) reg. 43.1.

38 *Rome Statute*, Art. 110(4).

39 See generally *Prosecutor v Germain Katanga (Decision on the review concerning reduction of sentence of Mr Germain Katanga)* (International Criminal Court, Appeals Chamber, Case No ICC-01/04/01/07, 13 November 2015).

of the ICTY makes no reference to any specific state. Individuals convicted of crimes by the ICTR and ICTY therefore serve their sentences in states that have concluded enforcement agreements with the ICTR or with the UNMICT.

ICTR Statute Article 27 (substantively similar to that of ICTY Statute Article 28) governs pardon or commutation of sentences. It reads as follows:

> If, pursuant to the applicable law of the State in which the convicted person is imprisoned, he or she is eligible for pardon or commutation of sentence, the State concerned shall notify the International Tribunal for Rwanda accordingly. There shall only be pardon or commutation of sentence if the President of the International Tribunal for Rwanda, in consultation with the judges, so decides on the basis of the interests of justice and the general principles of law.

The ICTY adopted a 'rule of thumb' to permit eligibility for early release upon completion of at least two-thirds of the sentence, despite the fact that this benchmark did not reflect the municipal law of all enforcing states.[40] This is the ICC's benchmark, as well. Persons convicted by the East Timor Special Panels also had the right to be released from prison after two-thirds of their sentence was served as long as they behaved well while in custody and the release would not threaten public safety and security.[41] In assessing applications for pardon or commutation of sentence, the ICTY is to consider the gravity of the crimes, the treatment of similarly-situated prisoners, the convict's demonstration of rehabilitation, and substantial cooperation with the prosecution. ICTY judges have ruled that the prospect of early release should not factor into the determination of the length of the sentence.[42] In other words, it would be improper to gross up the length of sentence to absorb the possibility of early release.

Article 26 of the UNMICT Statute permits convicts to petition for pardon or commutation of sentence. Eligibility hinges upon the law of the state in which the convict is serving sentence. The petition, however, is to be made to the UNMICT president, who also renders the decision. Rule 151 of the UNMICT Rules of Procedure and Evidence identifies a number of illustrative factors that the UNMICT president shall take into account in

---

40 Roísín Mulgrew, *Towards the Development of the International Penal System* (Cambridge University Press, 2013) 57–58. In the case of the SCSL and ICTR, Mulgrew notes that neither 'have pre-determined points for release eligibility'. Ibid 59.

41 *Prosecutor v Mau (Judgement)* (Special Panels for Serious Crimes, District Court of Dili, Case No 08/C.G/2003/TD.DIL, 23 February 2004); *Prosecutor v Gusmão (Judgement)* (Special Panels for Serious Crimes District Court of Dili, Case No 07/C.G./2003, 28 February 2003).

42 *Prosecutor v Dragan Nikolić (Judgement on Sentencing Appeal)* (International Criminal Tribunal for the Former Yugoslavia, Appeals Chamber, Case No IT-94-2-A, 4 February 2005) [97].

such determinations. These are: the gravity of the crime or crimes for which the prisoner was convicted; the treatment of similarly-situated prisoners; the prisoner's demonstration of rehabilitation; and any substantial cooperation on the part of the prisoner with the prosecutor. In addition, the president may consider the interests of justice and the general principles of law; any other information that he or she considers relevant; along with the views of any judges of the sentencing chamber who are UNMICT judges.[43] The UNMICT has affirmed the two-thirds benchmark from the ICTY and would apply that consistently among both ICTY and ICTR convicts.

The UNMICT now supervises and enforces all sentences in accordance with international standards of detention and the applicable law of the enforcing State. Conditions of imprisonment must be compatible with relevant human rights standards.

II Sentencing practice, quantum, and enforcement

As of the time of writing, the ICC has sentenced four convicts: Lubanga, Katanga, Bemba, and al-Mahdi. They received sentences of 14, 12, 18, and 9 years respectively.

Jean-Pierre Bemba Gombo was the former Vice-President of the DRC and had led one of that country's more powerful militia groups. He was found guilty for his role as commander in failing to prevent or punish rape, murder, and pillage by his troops in the Central African Republic (CAR) in 2002 and 2003. The *Bemba* case is noteworthy as being the first at the ICC to focus on sexual and gender-based violence against women, men, and children and, in terms of modes of liability, to invoke command responsibility. Witnesses testified as to the many effects of rape upon survivors, including the longitudinal and intergenerational impact thereof, and the specific social effect of rape in the CAR (in terms of social reintegration), including the rape of men. The Chamber found that the number of victims was substantial; the degrees of damage caused to the victims, their families, and communities was 'severe and lasting;' and ultimately found that the crimes were of the 'utmost, serious gravity'.[44] The Chamber also engaged in a detailed discussion of aggravating circumstances when it came to the crimes of rape. Specifically, it referenced the defenceless nature of the victims and the cruelty of the acts.

---

43 Mechanism for International Criminal Tribunals, *Practice Direction UNMICT/3 – Practice Direction on the Procedure for the Determination of Applications for Pardon, Commutation of Sentence, and Early Release of Persons Convicted by the ICTR, the ICTY, or the Mechanism* (5 July 2012) [9].
44 *Prosecutor v Bemba (Decision on Sentence pursuant to Article 76 of the Statute)* (International Criminal Court, Trial Chamber III, Case No ICC-01/05-01/08, 21 June 2016) [40].

Ahmad al-Faqi al-Mahdi, a radical Islamist, was sentenced in 2016 to nine years in a case emerging out of the Mali situation.[45] Al-Mahdi had pleaded guilty. He was charged in relation to his role in demolishing nine historic shrines and the door of a renowned mosque (Sidi Yahia) in Timbuktu, Mali, which constituted conduct proscribed by Rome Statute Article 8(2)(e)(iv).[46] Al-Mahdi's prosecution and sentencing was the first for the ICC with regard to the war crime of destruction of cultural heritage. In terms of the gravity of the crime, the judges noted that crimes against property are generally of lesser gravity than crimes against persons, but also underscored the symbolic value, religious salience, and affective attachment generated by the Timbuktu shrines. The sentencing judges explicitly linked the crime to human suffering.

Thomas Lubanga, a rebel leader in the DRC, was convicted as a co-perpetrator of the war crime of conscripting and enlisting children under the age of 15 years and using them to participate actively in hostilities in a non-international conflict. His was the ICC's first conviction and sentence. The special vulnerability of children was recognised in sentencing him to fourteen years. Germain Katanga, also a DRC rebel leader, was convicted as an accessory to one count of murder as a crime against humanity and to four counts of war crimes (murder, attacking a civilian population, destruction of property, and pillaging) for a 2003 attack and sentenced to 12 years' imprisonment. Katanga was given credit for his efforts in decommissioning child soldiers within armed forces.

The ICTY has finalised 82 sentences.[47] Five of these are life sentences (6% of the total). Among the 77 determinate sentences, the median term is 15 years and the mean term is 15.54 years. The minimum determinate sentence is 2 years in length and the maximum life sentence is 40 years. It should be noted, in addition, that 11 other individuals are being tried, re-tried, or their cases remain under appeal either at the ICTY or at the MICT.

The ICTR has finalised 59 sentences. Seventeen of these are life sentences. Among the 42 determinate sentences, the median sentence is 25 years and the mean sentence is 24.67 years. The shortest determinate sentence issued by the ICTR is 6 years, while the maximum is 47 years. Owing to the comparatively larger number of life sentences awarded by the ICTR (28.9 % of the total), Barbora Holá concludes that including the life sentences (coded at a value of 100) in the median calculations would increase the median sentence to 30 years. In *Nchamihigo* an ICTR Trial Chamber held that:

---

45 *The Prosecutor v Ahmad al Faqi al Mahdi (Judgement and Sentence)* (International Criminal Court, Trial Chamber VIII, Case No ICC-01/12-01/15, 27 September 2016).

46 This provision criminalises intentionally directing attacks against buildings dedicated to religion, education, art, science, or charitable purposes, historic monuments, hospitals, or places where the sick and wounded are collected, which are not military objectives.

47 All of the ICTR and ICTY data are compiled and analysed by Barbora Holá and shared with the author on 7 January 2017 (tables on file with the author).

[A] sentence of life imprisonment is generally reserved for those who planned or ordered atrocities and those who participated in the crimes with especial zeal or sadism. Offenders receiving the most severe sentences also tend to be senior authorities.[48]

The Appeals Chamber in *Nchamihigo* (a defendant who had been a deputy prosecutor, so not a senior authority within the government) ultimately reversed some of the convictions and substituted a term sentence of 40 years. Life sentences, however, have been routinely imposed against senior government authorities, along with persons who did not hold government positions (such as a tea factory director and high-level official in the *Interahamwe* militia).

Recent empirical work drawn from ICTR and ICTY sentencing practice has flatly found that 'mitigating factors have no significant effect on overall sentence length', while factors that relate to gravity of the crime and aggravating factors do constitute significant predictors of sentence length.[49] On this latter note, this one study found that, contrary to the statements made by international criminal tribunals denying a hierarchy of crimes,[50] sentencing reveals the existence of such a hierarchy, with genocide yielding the longest sentences, followed by crimes against humanity and then war crimes.[51] Moreover, among aggravating factors, acting with sadism or personally committing the crime resulted in significant sentencing enhancement.[52] This study also found that 'defendants who directly ordered crimes were sentenced to longer terms than those who did not and that rank or political position is a significant predictor of sentence: the higher the rank, the longer the term'.[53]

The SCSL has sentenced its nine convicts to an average term of nearly 39 years and a maximum term of 52 years.[54] Although the SCSL cannot issue a life sentence, such hefty term sentences *de facto* equate life imprisonment. The East Timor Special Panels had convicted 84 individuals (arising out of 55 trials) before ceasing operations (after funding ran out) on May 20, 2005. The Special Panels issued a broad range of terms of imprisonment: from 11 months to 15 years for ordinary crimes and from 2 to 33 ⅓ years for extraordinary international crimes. Mean and median sentences issued by the Special Panels for international

48 *Prosecutor v Siméon Nchamihigo (Judgement and Sentence)*, (International Criminal Tribunal for Rwanda, Trial Chamber III, Case No ICTR-01-63-T, 12 November 2008) [388].
49 Joseph W Doherty and Richard H Steinberg, 'Punishment and Policy in International Criminal Sentencing: An Empirical Study' (2016) 110 *American Journal of International Law* 49, 72–73.
50 *Prosecutor v Mrkšić & Šljivančanin (Judgement)* (International Criminal Tribunal for the Former Yugoslavia, Appeals Chamber, UN Doc ICTY-IT-95-13/1-A, 5 May 2009) [375].
51 Doherty and Steinberg, above n 49, 72.
52 Ibid.
53 Ibid.
54 Alette Smeulers, Barbora Holá and Tom van den Berg, 'Sixty-Five Years of International Criminal Justice: The Facts and Figures' (2013) 13 *International Criminal Law Review* 7, 22. Sentences in the *RUF*, *CDF*, and *AFRC* cases are being served in Rwanda.

crimes were 9.9 and 8 years, respectively. The length of Special Panel sentences shrinks, however, when the effects of conditional release and Presidential Decrees (pardons) are considered. In addition to pleading guilty, the East Timor Special Panels cited similar aggravating and mitigating factors to those in the ICTR and ICTY. A review of the Special Panels' jurisprudence reveals considerable attention paid to vulnerability of victims, superior responsibility, and political context[55] as aggravating factors; and, as mitigating factors, remorse, personal/ family circumstance, and position as a subordinate/coercive environment. The Special Panels had occasionally referred to traditional indigenous principles in sentencing, such as *adat* (taking responsibility/paying respect to authority).

Individuals convicted by the *ad hoc* tribunals randomly serve sentence in a large number of jurisdictions that have concluded agreements with the tribunals. So, for example, ICTY convicts have been incarcerated in Germany, Austria, Spain, Italy, Denmark, Finland, Norway, the United Kingdom, Sweden, Portugal, Estonia, and France; ICTR convicts have been incarcerated in Mali, Benin, Italy, and Sweden. Róisín Mulgrew aptly describes this situation as one of 'warehousing':[56] little coordination arises when it comes to the terms and conditions of imprisonment. What is more, little thought is given over to the nature of rehabilitative and reintegrative programmes. Perhaps individuals convicted of collective international crimes should be mainstreamed with individuals convicted of ordinary common crimes who serve their sentences in national jails. Their criminality, after all, is often a matter of conformity to social norms rather than departure from social norms, a point which is addressed in the next section of this chapter when the penological goal of deterrence is set out. On the other hand, perhaps these convicts have special needs and should be segregated.

After release, moreover, former convicts experience vastly different fates. Some return to their home jurisdictions where they are celebrated as heroes, while others slink into destitution and anonymity, and others are unable to return home because of fear of persecution there. Turning to the ICTY: 56 convicts have already been released, which represents 68% of those finalised cases convicted of substantive crimes. At the ICTR, 20 convicts have been already released, which represents 34 % of those convicted of substantive crimes.[57] One particularly disturbing phenomenon at the ICTR is that seven acquitted individuals and three released convicts reside in a safe house in Arusha, Tanzania.[58] They do not yet have anywhere else to go. They fear to

---

55 *Prosecutor v Beno (Judgement)* (Special Panels for Serious Crimes, District Court of Dili, Case No 4b/2003, 16 November 2004) [20], noting that 'particularly despicable . . . is that the accused . . . committed these crimes against his fellow-countrymen in the interest of a foreign power that was illegally occupying his home country'.

56 Mulgrew, above n 40.

57 In addition, there are two contempt cases. Data compiled and analysed by Barbora Holá (on file with the author).

58 Patrick W Hayden and Katerina I Kappos, 'Current Developments at the Ad Hoc International Criminal Tribunals' (2014) 12 *Journal of International Criminal Justice* 367, 390.

return to Rwanda. These individuals (some of whom were acquitted over a decade ago) need to be relocated – a point which the ICTR president has repeatedly raised. Other released ICTR convicts have remained in Mali, where they had served their sentence, in that they too express fears for their personal safety were they to return to Rwanda.

At the ICC, Lubanga's application for early release was denied in 2015. Although the judges found there to be a prospect for his resocialisation and successful resettlement in the DRC, they rejected the application in the circumstances at the time. On December 19, 2015, Lubanga was transferred to a prison in the DRC to serve his sentence. The DRC is the first state designated by the ICC to enforce the imprisonment of convicts pursuant to Article 103 of the Rome Statute. Katanga's application for early release, which was not opposed by the Prosecutor, was granted (a reduction in sentence of three years and eight months).[59] Katanga, who also returned to the DRC, will apparently be retried there by a military tribunal on charges of war crimes and crimes against humanity despite the fact that his time with the ICC will have been served and early release granted. The ICC Presidency determined in April 2016 that these domestic proceedings may go ahead.[60] While ICC officials may consider the crimes charged in national prosecutions to be different from those that sustained the international convictions, in reality they do form part of a very similar underlying conduct, thereby triggering concerns over double jeopardy and raising questions why the ICC prosecuted at all in light of the DRC's evident willingness and ability to do so.

III Penological aspirations

International criminal judges gesture towards important rationales when they impose sentences. Retribution and general deterrence are the two most prominently cited punishment goals.[61]

---

59 *Prosecutor v Katanga (Decision on the review concerning reduction of sentence of Mr Germain Katanga)* (International Criminal Court, Appeals Chamber, Case No ICC-01/04/01/07, 13 November 2015).

60 For critique of this outcome, see Patryk Labuda, 'Complementarity Compromised? 'The ICC Gives Congo the Green Light to Re-Try Katanga' on *Opinio Juris* (21 April 2016) <http://opiniojuris.org/2016/04/11/complementarity-compromised-the-icc-gives-congo-the-green-light-to-re-try-katanga/>.

61 *Prosecutor v Bemba (Decision on Sentence pursuant to Article 76 of the Statute)* (International Criminal Court, Trial Chamber III, Case No ICC-01/05-01/08, 21 June 2016) [10], citing also *Prosecutor v Katanga (Decision)* (International Criminal Court, Trial Chamber III, Case No CC-01/04-01/07, 23 May 2014); *Prosecutor v Popović et al (Appeal Judgement)* (International Criminal Tribunal for the Former Yugoslavia, Appeals Chamber, Case No IT-05-88-A, 30 January 2015); and *Case 001 Kaing (Appeal Judgement)* (Extraordinary Chambers in the Courts of Cambodia, Supreme Court Chamber, Case No 001/18-07-2007-ECCC/SC, 3 February 2012); *Prosecutor v Stakić (Judgement)* (International Criminal Tribunal for the Former Yugoslavia, Appeals Chamber, Case No IT-97-24-A, 22

Although there are many divergent schools of retributivism, what retributivists generally share is an understanding that the infliction of punishment rectifies the moral balance, in particular, through condemnation of the criminal conduct.[62] Simply put, punishment is what the perpetrator deserves. Punishment, therefore, is to be proportionate to the extent of the harm caused by the crime and also to the perpetrator's degree of intentionality. When it comes to extraordinary international criminality, however, tension may arise, in particular at the lower ranks of offenders, insofar as crimes of terrible gravity may in fact be committed by persons with low intent – the phenomenon of administrative or occupational massacre within a totalitarian apparatus. How to proceed in such instances? In *The Unbearable Lightness of Being*, Milan Kundera invokes, from the classics,

> Oedipus, who did not know he was sleeping with his own mother, yet when he realized what had happened, he did not feel innocent. Unable to stand the sight of the misfortunes he had wrought by 'not knowing', he put out his eyes and wandered blind away from Thebes.

Mapping Oedipus onto the Prague Spring, and the voice of Tomas, the defrocked surgeon, Kundera perseveres:

> When Tomas heard communists shouting in defense of their inner purity, he said to himself. As a result of your 'not knowing', this country had lost its freedom, lost it for centuries, perhaps, and you shout that you feel no guilt? How can you stand the sight of what you've done? How is it you aren't horrified? Have you no eyes to see? If you had eyes, you would have put them out and wander away from Thebes!

To which one might note that Kundera was wrong about the centuries. But he was right, one might argue, that ignorance of one's contribution to the harm, contributions delivered daily – routine contributions, a job – might fade as a defence if the harm becomes of sufficient magnitude and gravity.

In any event, the ICTY Appeals Chamber has emphasised that 'retribution should not be misunderstood as a way of expressing revenge or vengeance'.[63] Rather, it has conceived of the retribution as the 'expression of condemnation

March 2006) [402], stating that 'the Appeals Chamber notes that the jurisprudence of the Tribunal and the ICTR consistently points out that the two main purposes of sentencing are deterrence and retribution'; *Prosecutor v Marqués et al* (Special Panels for Serious Crimes, District Court of Dili, Case No 09/2000, 11 December 2001) [979].

62 See generally HLA Hart, *Punishment and Responsibility* (Clarendon Press, 1968) 234–235.
63 *Prosecutor v Kordić and Čerkez (Judgement)* (International Criminal Tribunal for the Former Yugoslavia, Appeals Chamber, Case No IT-95-14/2-A, 17 December 2004) [1075]; *Prosecutor v Katanga (Decision)* (International Criminal Court, Trial Chamber III, Case No ICC-01/04-01/07, 23 May 2014) [38].

and outrage of the international community'.[64] The ICC proceeds similarly. In this regard, retributive motivations wander in the direction of expressivism. The expressivist punishes to strengthen faith in rule of law among the general public, as opposed to punishing simply because the perpetrator deserves it or will be deterred by it. From an expressivist perspective, punishment proactively embeds the normative value of law within the community.[65] This in theory leads to positive general prevention.

General deterrence considers that the purpose of prosecuting and punishing individuals who commit mass atrocity is utilitarian in nature, that is, to dissuade others from offending in the future. Specific deterrence implies that punishing the offender will deter that one offender from reoffending. When the activity of international criminal justice institutions is taken as a whole, the focus of deterrence remains oriented towards general deterrence. From a deterrence perspective, punishment is inflicted because of the consequentialist effect of reducing the incidence of crime: 'The generality of men are naturally apt to be swayed by fear rather than reverence, and to refrain from evil rather because of the punishment that it brings than because of its own foulness'.[66]

On occasion, international judges also refer to other penological rationales including rehabilitation,[67] incapacitation, and reconciliation. These rationales, however, are not particularly salient. Reconciliation overall has not received much more than lip-service, although it arose in the *Katanga* judgment where the convict's *post hoc* efforts to demobilise and disarm child soldiers were affirmatively lauded (and recognised) as a mitigating factor.

Whether the sentencing practices of international institutions attain their avowed penological goals remains an unsettled question. The evidence is mixed regarding whether and to what extent punishing a perpetrator dissuades other perpetrators, either in the same region or elsewhere, from offending, in particular in the case of collective discrimination-oriented crimes such as

---

64 *Prosecutor v Nikolić (Judgement)* (International Criminal Tribunal for the Former Yugoslavia, Trial Chamber I, Case No IT-02-60/1-S, 2 December 2003) [86].

65 On expressivism generally, see Mark A Drumbl, 'Collective Violence and Individual Punishment: The Criminality of Mass Atrocity' (2005) 99 *Northwestern University Law Review* 539; Robert Sloane, 'The Expressive Capacity of International Punishment: the Limits of the National Law Analogy and the Potential of International Criminal Law' (2007) 43 *Stanford Journal of International Law* 39.

66 Aristotle, *Nicomachean Ethics*, book 10, Ch. 9.

67 Rehabilitation is among the more frequently referenced among this group of subjacent objectives, but is often described as not deserving of undue weight (*Prosecutor v Milutinović et al (Judgement)* (International Criminal Tribunal for the Former Yugoslavia, Trial Chamber, Case No IT-05-87-T, 26 February 2009) [1146]) or as something to be de-emphasised because of the international nature of the sentencing institution (*Prosecutor v Fofana and Kondewa (Sentencing Judgment)* (Special Court for Sierra Leone, Trial Chamber I, Case No SCSL-04-14-T, 9 August 2007) [28]).

genocide and persecution. A recent study conducted under the auspices of the International Nuremberg Academy grappled with the inherent difficulties in measuring deterrence, in the first place, and then correlating it with the interventions of international courts and tribunals. Entitled *Two Steps Forward, One Step Back*, this excellent study found some unsystematised and impressionistic evidence of deterrent effect within ten post-conflict case-studies.[68] It also identified a number of challenges to deterrence, specifically, selectivity in prosecutions (when only one 'side' is prosecuted), witness security, and also the perceived severity of sentencing.

The likelihood of getting caught is more influential than any other factor in discouraging criminal conduct. Yet the likelihood of getting caught and prosecuted by an international institution in cases of atrocity crimes sadly remains low. In terms of retribution, the severity of a prison sentence may never be able to reciprocate the gravity of egregious international crimes. Meting out just deserts in such cases ominously suggests the abandonment of core principles of international human rights law (whether in terms of the length of sentence or conditions of confinement). Many ICTY and ICC convicts received sentences that were not any longer than those routinely meted out to ordinary common criminals in many national justice systems. But, on the other hand, just how meaningful is the harshest of sentences in the case of the most invidious of crimes? In her thoughtful work on retributivism, Erin Germantis neatly pulls in Dostoyevsky, from *The Brothers Karamazov*: 'What do I care for a hell for oppressors? What good can hell do?'[69]

IV Conclusion

The theory and practice of sentencing international crimes will face new wrinkles in the future. One wrinkle is the reality of (re)nationalisation of prosecution and punishment. The *ad hocs* are shuttered or about to shutter. UNMICT's work mostly is managerial. The ICC (initially created to complement national initiatives) struggles to manage its workload and increasingly faces financial and legitimacy challenges. The inexorable drift of the future, it seems, will be towards greater involvement of national actors in the prosecution and punishment of international crimes. Will sentencing practices and penological theories operationalised at the international level migrate into national contexts? Is this desirable? Will these practices circulate, and then

---

68 Jennifer Schense and Linda Carter (eds), *Two Steps Forward, One Step Back: The Deterrent Effect of International Criminal Tribunals* (International Nuremberg Principles Academy, 2016).

69 Erin Germantis, 'Is Retributive Justice a Sound Penological Theory in the Context of Genocide? What Is the Alternative?' (student paper, Monash University, Faculty of Law, November 2016) 1, citing Fyodor Dostoyevsky, *The Brothers Karamazov*, trans. Constance Garnett (Modern Library, 1950) 24.

recirculate, ultimately to become a general practice among states when it comes to crimes such as genocide, crimes against humanity, and war crimes? Although overburdened and stretched in its capacity, paradoxically, the ICC Office of the Prosecutor now seeks to expand its focus by turning to crimes such as environmental destruction and land-grabbing. Would the rationales for sentencing in these instances be similar or different?

Among the aims of this book is to capture the dynamics and hydraulics of internationalisation and transnationalisation. These processes map onto sentencing as well. As the boundaries between international crimes, on the one hand, and transnational crimes, on the other, become increasingly porous, questions arise whether the aspirations for sentencing should also become consistent. Is the perpetrator of corruption, of human trafficking, or of terrorism 'like' the *génocidaire*?

And, finally, how do penological aspirations intersect with the increasing presence of victims in criminal proceedings? The ICC is a court yet also connects to an avowedly 'restorative' framework that involves reparations. Can one institutional regime coherently manage these multiple roles? Perhaps it would be wiser to fully diversify how to imagine responses to mass atrocity by more vigorously invoking truth commissions, reintegrative rituals, and expertise from disciplines other than law? Such diversification would oblige the courtroom and jailhouse to relax its controlling grip, and cede its exalted status, over the process of post-conflict justice. Perhaps the time has come to gaze beyond 'the great axe'.

Further reading

Drumbl, Mark A, 'Collective Violence and Individual Punishment: The Criminality of Mass Atrocity' (2005) 99 *Northwestern University Law Review* 539.

Holá, Barbora, *Sentencing of International Crimes: Consistency of Sentencing Case Law* (2012) 4 *Amsterdam Law Forum* 3.

Doherty, Joseph W and Richard H Steinberg, 'Punishment and Policy in International Criminal Sentencing: An Empirical Study' (2016) 110 *American Journal of International Law* 49.

Mulgrew, Róisín, *Towards the Development of the International Penal System* (Cambridge University Press, 2013).

16

THE ROLE OF VICTIMS

Emerging rights to participation and reparation in international criminal courts

Stephen Smith Cody and Eric Stover

I Introduction

Victims' rights are now a mainstay of international justice. In recent decades, legal reforms have provided a range of rights and entitlements to survivors of mass atrocity. The most profound change has taken place at the International Criminal Court (ICC), the first international court to explicitly recognize the right of victims to express their views and concerns and receive reparations following criminal convictions.[1] But victim-oriented innovations can also be found in regional courts, hybrid or mixed courts, and national courts.[2] In this chapter, we use the term "victim participation" as an umbrella term to include victims of serious international crimes who participate in trial proceedings either as victim-witnesses; civil parties (in French, '*parties civiles*') in the civil law tradition; or as "victim participants" as defined in the Rome Statute of the ICC.[3]

---

1 Susana SáCouto and Katherine Cleary, *Victim Participation before the International Criminal Court* (War Crimes Research Office, American University Washington College of Law, 2007); Susana SáCouto and Katherine Cleary, 'Victims' Participation in the Investigations of the International Criminal Court' (2008) 17(1) *Transnational Law & Contemporary Problems* 74; Marcus T Funk, *Victims' Rights and Advocacy at the International Criminal Court* (Oxford University Press, 2010).

2 Charles P Trumbull IV, 'The Victims of Victim Participation in International Criminal Proceedings' (2008) 29 *Michigan Journal of International Law* 777; Valentina Spiga, 'No Redress without Justice: Victims and International Criminal Law' (2012) 10(5) *Journal of International Criminal Justice* 1377; Eric Stover, Mychelle Balthazard and Alexa Koenig, 'Confronting Duch: Civil Party Participation in Case 001 at the Extraordinary Chambers in the Courts of Cambodia' (2011) 93(882) *International Review of the Red Cross* 503.

3 *Rome Statute of the International Criminal Court*, opened for signature 17 July 1998, 2187 UNTS 90 (entered into force 1 July 2002) ('*Rome Statute*'); Rule 85 of the ICC's Rules of Procedure and Evidence (RPE) states: '(a) "Victims" means natural persons who have

The recent shift towards expanding the rights for victims in court proceedings has generated considerable debate among court personnel and scholars alike.[4] Advocates for greater victim participation call attention to the constructive influence victims can have on investigations and trials.[5] Victims, they argue, can aid in identifying sources of evidence, help triangulate testimonial evidence with documentary and physical evidence, and build a more veracious official record of atrocity crimes.[6] Victim participation also brings survivors' stories and concerns into the cloistered chambers of judges and lawyers, who often live and work far from the places affected by violence.[7] Victims link international legal proceedings to local histories of violence and suffering.[8]

Meanwhile, critics argue that victim participation, if not handled properly, can violate the rights of the accused to a fair trial, interfere with prosecutorial strategies, and cause trial delays as a result of victims testifying in court or victims' lawyers making motions to judges.[9] Still others express trepidation that victims' narratives of violence create added pressure for convictions and threaten to lower de facto standards of culpability.[10] Victim participation

suffered harm as a result of the commission of any crime within the jurisdiction of the Court; (b) Victims may include organizations or institutions that have sustained direct harm to any of their property which is dedicated to religion, education, art or science or charitable purposes, and to their historic monuments, hospitals and other places and objects for humanitarian purposes'. International Criminal Court, *Rules of Procedure and Evidence*, Doc No ICC-ASP/1/3 (adopted 9 September 2002) Rule 85 <www.icc-cpi.int/iccdocs/PIDS/legal-texts/RulesProcedureEvidenceEng.pdf>.

4 Mariana Pena and Gaelle Carayon, 'Is the ICC Making the Most of Victim Participation?' (2013) 7(3) *International Journal of Transitional Justice* 518; Carsten Stahn and Sara Kendall, *Contested Justice: The Politics and Practice of International Criminal Court Interventions* (Cambridge University Press, 2015); Eric Stover and Harvey Weinstein (eds), *My Neighbor, My Enemy: Justice and Community in the Aftermath of Mass Atrocity* (Cambridge University Press, 2004).

5 Jo-Anne Wemmers, 'Where Do They Belong? Giving Victims a Place in the Criminal Justice Process' (2009) 20(4) *Criminal Law Forum* 395; REDRESS, *Representing Victims before the ICC: Recommendations on the Legal Representative System* (April 2015) <www.redress.org/downloads/publications/1504ReprentingVictims.pdf>.

6 Spiga, above n 2; Christine Chung, 'Victims' Participation at the International Criminal Court: Are Concessions of the Court Clouding the Promise?' (2008) 6(3) *Northwestern Journal of International Human Rights* 459; Hans-Peter Kaul, 'Victims' Rights and Peace' in Thorsten Bonacker and Christoph Safferling (eds), *Victims of International Crimes: An Interdisciplinary Discourse* (Springer, 2013) 223.

7 Claire Garbett, 'The Truth and the Trial: Victim Participation, Restorative Justice, and the International Criminal Court' (2013) 16(2) *Contemporary Justice Review* 193.

8 Anna Byrson, 'Victims, Violence, and Voice: Transitional Justice, Oral History, and Dealing with the Past' (2016) 39 *Hastings International and Comparative Law Review* 299.

9 Miriam Cohen, 'Victims' Participation Rights within the ICC: A Critical Overview' (2008) 37 *Denver Journal of International Law and Policy* 381; Mirjan Damaska, 'What Is the Point of International Criminal Justice?' (2008) 83(1) *Chicago-Kent Law Review* 329.

10 Mirjan Damaska, 'The Competing Visions of Fairness: The Basic Choice for International Criminal Tribunals' (2010) 36 *North Carolina Journal of International Law and Commercial Regulation* 365.

can also drain limited court resources. To realize victims' formal rights court staff must depend on cooperation from national and local officials, develop effective outreach and education programmes, and recruit competent legal counsel—all of which can be costly. These practical challenges can be insurmountable in some post-conflict situations or where accused perpetrators retain significant power.

Since the mid-1990s, international criminal justice has moved away from exclusively punitive approaches to more restorative ones, including truth commissions, lustration programmes, and reparations processes. These restorative mechanisms have greatly expanded the ability for victims to have their voices heard and acknowledged. But greater victim recognition and participation raises several critical questions: Who should be considered a victim? What obligations do courts and other justice mechanisms have to victims? When do such obligations begin and end? And what roles should judicial officials play, if any, in addressing victims' needs beyond their participation in criminal proceedings? We cannot answer all of these questions here. Rather, we examine the evolution of victims' rights and the development of a troubling gap between what victims expect from international criminal courts and what these courts can deliver.

We begin by describing the role victims have played in war crimes trials from Nuremberg and Tokyo to the ICC. We find that greater attention to victim inclusion has expanded opportunities for survivors to join international criminal cases and to seek reparations, but rarely has it met their expectations of what justice means and should deliver. Victims who participate in trials express frustration at the length of investigations and proceedings, the number of collapsed cases or acquittals, and the lack of victim-support services.[11] While international criminal trials are unlikely to satisfy critical and diverse needs of survivors of mass violence, they can still provide victims with recognition and acknowledgment and act as a springboard for social mobilization. When paired with broad national and international efforts to support, protect, and restore communities affected by mass violence, international trials can make valuable contributions to social reconstruction in post-conflict settings.

II The role of victims from Nuremberg to The Hague

Little, if anything, is known about the experiences of victims and witnesses who testified before the International Military Tribunal in Nuremberg (Nuremberg tribunal) and the International Military Tribunal for the Far East (Tokyo tribunal) or the hundreds of national war crimes trials which

---

11 Stephen Smith Cody *et al*, *The Victims' Court? A Study of 622 Victim Participants at the International Criminal Court* (Human Rights Center, University of California, Berkeley, School of Law, 2015).

followed in their wake. What is known is largely anecdotal, based on accounts given to the press by past witnesses. A handful of dramatists have written plays using documentary materials from the Nuremberg and Tokyo trials, but it doesn't appear as if they interviewed or drew on the post-trial observations of any victim-witnesses.[12] Nor are there any empirical studies in the English literature of victim-witnesses and their perceptions of the trial process.[13]

What explains this paucity of information about the role of victim-witnesses in the trials following the Second World War? To begin with, the architects of these tribunals had little interest in showcasing the suffering of victims in any pronounced way. Allied forces in both Germany and Japan were more intent on vilifying the German and Japanese leaders in the eyes of their own people—and of those they had conquered—than in creating a forum for victims to tell their story.

In his opening statement at the first Nuremberg trial, the chief prosecutor, Justice Robert J. Jackson, told the judges: "We will not ask you to convict these [defendants] on the testimony of their foes. There is no count in the Indictment that cannot be proved by books and records."[14] As such, Jackson developed a strategy of *symbolic* justice—one that would prove German crimes *not* from the mouths of witnesses but from the Third Reich's own voluminous archives.[15] By the end of the trial, Jackson had entered four thousand Nazi documents as trial exhibits, along with eighteen hundred still photographs.

As for witnesses, Jackson decided to call only thirty-three witnesses, of whom only a few were survivor-witnesses. Most of the witnesses appeared before the court not to relate individual instances of war crimes but to testify to the "collective, systematic, and bureaucratic activities of massive and complex organizations that executed criminal policies from the highest levels of government."[16] While survivor testimony would have humanized the trial, Jackson feared it could also be viewed as too horrific to be believed. He also feared that the defence might challenge victim-witnesses about the

---

12 Ian Buruma, *The Wages of Guilt: Memories of War in Germany and Japan* (Farrar, Straus, and Giroux, 1994) 138-176.

13 This section draws on several works published previously by one of the authors: Eric Stover, *The Witnesses: War Crimes and the Promise of Justice in The Hague* (University of Pennsylvania Press, 2005); Stover, Balthazard and Koenig, above n 2; and Eric Stover, Victor Peskin and Alexa Koenig, *Hiding in Plain Sight: The Pursuit of War Criminals from Nuremberg to the War on Terror* (University of California Press, 2016).

14 Drexel A Sprecher, *Inside the Nuremberg Trial: A Protector's Comprehensive Account* (University Press of America, 1999).

15 Telford Taylor, *The Anatomy of the Nuremberg Trials: A Personal Memoir* (Alfred A. Knopf, 1992) 148.

16 David Cohen, 'Beyond Nuremberg: Individual Responsibility for War Crimes' in Carla Hesse and Robert Post (eds), *Human Rights in Political Transition: Gettysburg to Bosnia* (Zone Books, 1999) 53.

cooperation, both direct and indirect, that some Jewish leaders gave to the Nazi administration, and thus undermine the prosecution's case.[17]

At the Tokyo tribunal, a number of victim-witnesses appeared on the stand, especially during the prosecution's presentation of the horrendous crimes committed in Nanking. But, as Japanese historian Yuma Totani points out, they were few in number. "The common practice," Totani writes:

> was to limit the number of witnesses and to rely on documentary evidence, seemingly in consideration of the constraints as well as the logistical problems in locating and bringing witnesses from overseas. When the Allied prosecutors did bring in witnesses, they did so sparingly. The average number was one or two per episode of war crime, and only for singularly important cases.[18]

Most of the documentary evidence at the Tokyo trial was taken from the national-level war crimes trials that were held contemporaneously in the Pacific theatre. Relying on this huge volume of material and limited testimonial evidence, the prosecution managed to complete its presentation in only six weeks.[19]

While scores of victims and witnesses testified in national trials throughout Europe and the Pacific in the wake of the Second World War, it wasn't until the trial of the SS officer Adolf Eichmann in an Israeli court in 1961 that a forum was created almost exclusively for survivors of mass atrocities. The Eichmann trial marked the advent of what the French sociologist Annette Wieviorka calls an "era of testimony" in war crimes trials that continues to this day. She points to the pedagogical and commemorative role performed by the scores of prosecution witnesses, many of whom were Holocaust survivors, as having lit, in the words of the court's chief prosecutor, Gideon Hausner, "a spark in the frigid chamber which we know as history."[20]

It was through the Eichmann trial, writes the American historian Deborah Lipstadt, that "the story of the Holocaust . . . was heard *anew*, in a profoundly different way, and not just in Israel but in many parts of the Jewish and non-Jewish world."[21] This new narrative, told through the stories of survivors, was heard beyond Israel's borders largely because of the growth of television outlets around the world. During the eight-month trial, cameras recorded every moment, allowing television networks to dispatch daily updates to their viewers worldwide.

17 Robert H Jackson, *The Nürnberg Case* (Alfred A. Knopf, 1957) 10.
18 Yuma Totani, *The Tokyo War Crimes Trial: The Pursuit of Justice in the Wake of World War II* (Harvard University Asia Center, 2008) 121.
19 Ibid 114-115.
20 Annette Wieviorka, *L'ère du témoin* (Plorn, 1998) 97.
21 Deborah E Lipstadt, *The Eichmann Trial* (Schocken Books, 2011) 192-194.

The American legal scholar Lawrence Douglas would later describe the Eichmann trial as a "form of group therapy," a ritual of national catharsis that was both pedagogic and transformative, enabling Israelis to commemorate the Holocaust and develop a new "national identity [as] the Israeli as a self-sufficient warrior."[22] Douglas recognized that the prosecutors may have manipulated the testimonies of Holocaust survivors for didactic and even nation-building purposes, but he argued that the cathartic aspects of the proceedings far outweighed any distortions of the criminal process.

But not all observers of the Eichmann proceedings thought this victim-centred approach to justice was necessarily a good thing. Writing for *The New Yorker*, Hannah Arendt betrayed her impatience with the "endless sessions" of survivor testimony, much of which, she said, "had no or only the slightest connection with the deeds of the accused."[23] Arendt argued that while every effort must be made during criminal proceedings to acknowledge the suffering of victims, it must not be forgotten that:

> a trial resembles a play in that both begin and end with the doer, not with the victim .... In the center of a trial can only be the one who did—in this respect, he is like the hero in the play—and if he suffers, he must suffer for what he has done, not for what he has caused others to suffer.[24]

In other words, vindicating the victims must be subordinated to the requirements of a fair trial in which the accused—and he alone—remains the protagonist.

In recent decades, France has received the most attention for its use of victim participation, or *parties civiles*, in war crimes trials. The trials, which took place between 1983 and 1998, were of three alleged Nazi war criminals and sympathizers: Klaus Barbie, head of the Gestapo in Lyon; Paul Touvier, leader of a Vichy-run paramilitary group under the direction of Barbie; and Maurice Papon, a police official in the Prefecture of Bordeaux. Similar to the Eichmann trial, the three accused were tried by domestic courts applying domestic laws, although they referred to and/or applied principles of international law.

In the 1987 Barbie case, the court defined the term 'victim' fairly broadly, thereby establishing an expansive foundation for civil party participation in the Papon and Touvier trials that followed. Victims in the Barbie trial included

---

22 Lawrence Douglas, *The Memory of Judgment: Making Law and History in the Trials of the Holocaust* (Yale University Press, 2001) 109.

23 Hannah Arendt, *Eichmann in Jerusalem: A Report on the Banality of Evil* (Penguin Books, 1977) 261.

24 Ibid.

not only the direct objectives of systematic racial and religious persecution [i.e. Jews and other groups sent to Auschwitz and other concentration camps], but also those who opposed such persecution by any means. Thus, [even] Resistance members, as soldiers fighting Nazism ... could be deemed victims of crimes against humanity.[25]

Barbie's trial, like the Eichmann proceedings, was a huge media event. Day after day, the French media ran stories focusing on the testimonies of civil parties—Jews and resistance fighters alike. This media coverage forced French society to reexamine what up until then had been a taboo topic; namely, the role of Vichy France during the Occupation and its hushed majority, the thousands of "bystanders, " though neither active collaborators nor active resisters, who had turned a blind eye to the suffering of their fellow citizens.[26] Many civil parties told wrenching stories about how their neighbours— French men and women like themselves—had watched, fearful and silent, while the Gestapo broke into their homes or nabbed them on the streets. Some spoke about the horrors they had witnessed in Nazi concentration camps, and how they had returned, penniless and dispossessed, to France. Known as the "Zebra men and women," they were greeted, according to the cultural historian Alice Y. Kaplan, not "as heroes but as embarrassing reminders of France's shame and guilt during the Occupation."[27]

Like the Barbie trial, the Touvier and Papon proceedings were notable for their extensive civil party participation—and equally controversial. Touvier and his attorneys, for example, faced not only the public prosecutor but also a bevy of thirty-four civil party lawyers representing victims and victims' groups. As with the Eichmann trial, many of the civil parties had nothing to say about Touvier and Papon and their alleged crimes, and only a few were able to draw any direct link between the fate of their family members and the actions of the former Nazi collaborators.[28]

The establishment of the UN ad hoc international criminal tribunals for Rwanda and the former Yugoslavia in the mid-1990s brought new challenges for victims and witnesses and court personnel who interacted with them. Neither the tribunals' statutes nor their Rules of Procedure and Evidence provided victims and witnesses with specific "rights." Instead, court documents referred to witness services as "entitlements." In the early

25 Michael E Tigar *et al*, 'Paul Touvier and the Crime Against Humanity' (1995) 30 *Texas International Law Journal* 285, 295.

26 Jane Kramer, 'Letter from Europe', *The New Yorker* (New York), 16 May 1985, 141.

27 Alice Y Kaplan's introductory remarks in Alain Finkielkraut, *Remembering in Vain: The Klaus Barbie Trial and Crimes against Humanity* (Columbia University Press, 1992) xv.

28 Nancy Wood, 'The Papon Trial in an "Era of Testimony"' in Richard J Goslan (ed), *The Papon Affair: Memory and Justice on Trial* (Routledge, 2000) 97.

years, both tribunals were strapped for cash, which meant their Victims and Witnesses Sections (VWS) were unable to provide their clients with adequate support services, let alone employ in-country representatives who could deal immediately with problems, such as witness intimidation, when they arose. Court personnel were also woefully unschooled in the cultural, political, and social histories of the former Yugoslavia and Rwanda.[29]

In 1998, four years after the establishment of the Yugoslav tribunal and at a point when the number of trials and witnesses had become significant, the VWS began distributing a brochure in Serbo-Croatian to prospective witnesses.[30] The brochure described the tribunal's mandate, the role of witnesses, and their entitlements, including travel arrangements, protective measures, and other pertinent information, yet it made no mention of any rights afforded victims and witnesses. Under the section on protection measures, the onus of raising the issue of protection was placed on the potential witness, who may not have fully grasped the risks of testifying in a public forum thousands of kilometres away from their homes. The brochure also did not provide witnesses with notice of any entitlement to information about the conviction and subsequent appeals hearings, imprisonment, and release of the accused. There was also no mention of any form of reparations as Rule 106 of the Tribunal's Rules of Evidence and Procedure stipulates that victims can only claim compensation before domestic courts in the former Yugoslavia against those who have been convicted before the tribunal.[31] Tribunal prosecutors and investigators, as well as defence attorneys, were supposed to give the brochure to potential witnesses, but, according to witness section staff, most witnesses never received it. Many witnesses only learned about the full range of protective measures once they came to The Hague, and they usually acquired the information from other witnesses at their hotel or at the tribunal.[32]

Fortunately, the budgets of both tribunals increased in the early 2000s. Since then, significant strides have been made to provide victims and witnesses with better services. While little empirical research has been conducted about the attitudes and opinions of victims and witnesses who have testified at the Rwandan tribunal, a pilot survey of 300 prosecution and defence witnesses at the Yugoslav tribunal found that most respondents had had a positive experience in testifying and interacting with the court. The survey,

---

29 Stover, *The Witnesses*, above n 13, 136-141.
30 A copy of the brochure, titled *Information for Witnesses Testifying before the International Criminal Tribunal for the Former Yugoslavia*, is on file at the Human Rights Center, School of Law, University of California, Berkeley.
31 Kimi King *et al*, *Echoes of Testimonies: A Pilot Study Into the Long-Term Impact of Bearing Witness before the ICTY* (University of North Texas and the Victims and Witnesses Section at the International Criminal Tribunal for the former Yugoslavia, 2016) 20.
32 Stover, *The Witnesses*, above n 13, 136-137.

conducted over a two-year period, 2013–2015, also found that a number of witnesses had "faced social, economic, and other repercussions as a result of their testimony, and there was a small, but critical group of witnesses who faced security threats before and after they testified." The respondents were generally supportive of the tribunal and felt they were treated fairly, "but were less favorably disposed toward the punishments meted out by the Tribunal, as well as critical that the trials have taken so long."[33]

The increased participation of victims—whether as victim-witnesses or as civil parties—in war crimes trials since the Eichmann proceedings has generated a fierce debate in international legal circles. On one side are the moralists like Lawrence Douglas who believe war crimes trials "must be seen not simply as a procedural device whose legitimacy is governed by rules generated within the system of legality itself, but as a complex ritual" that can shape collective memory of horrible events and transform and educate both individuals and societies.[34] On the other are the legal purists like the writer Ian Buruma who argue that court proceedings must be above all else a "system of rules and procedures" that should never be bent or altered to satisfy wider social or political goals. Writes Buruma:

> Just as belief belongs in the church, surely history education belongs in school. When the court of law is used for history lessons, then the risk of show trials cannot be far off. It may be that show trials are good politics ... but good politics don't necessarily serve the truth.[35]

Since the early 1990s, a number of national and international victims' rights and human rights organizations have lobbied to ensure that victims' participatory rights be embedded in the founding documents of the ICC and other international criminal tribunals. The evolution of victims' rights resulted from a confluence of forces, including the success of domestic victims' rights movements and the growth of human rights norms worldwide that promoted victim-oriented justice. Meanwhile, these demands for expanded victim participation rights, reparations, and alternative justice mechanisms, such as truth commissions and state reparation programmes, called into question mandates centred solely on accountability and punishment. Given the opportunity to voice their concerns, victims expressed diverse and conflicting ideas about what they expected from the practice of international justice.

33 King *et al*, above n 31, 9.
34 Lawrence Douglas, *The Memory of Judgment: Making Law and History in the Trials of the Holocaust* (Yale University Press, 2001) 112-113.
35 Buruma, above n 12, 142.

III The rise of victims' rights

Victim participation is not a new phenomenon. Victims have long enjoyed substantive roles in criminal trials in most civil law jurisdictions—which predominate in continental Europe, Latin America, many parts of Africa and Asia. Because the judge in the civil law tradition actively controls the trial's direction and questioning of witnesses, victims may be granted an assortment of rights, including the right to seek compensation by applying to join the criminal prosecution as a civil petitioner. Victims may also benefit from legal representation, present evidence, cross-examine witnesses, and make closing statements in cases pending before civil law judges.[36]

Yet, victims' roles in common law prosecutions have been more limited, at least until victims' rights movements emerged in the United Kingdom and United States during the 1960s. Responding to the demands of advocacy groups, legislators in these countries enacted laws to protect and compensate crime victims, especially victims of rape and child abuse.[37] These early domestic movements, in sharp contrast to the international advocacy that followed them, tended to align with law and order agendas. However, new laws, coupled with new research on the psychological effects of trauma,[38] helped generate secondary waves of legislation, which instructed prosecutors and law enforcement officers that victims of crime should be regarded as *active and engaged participants in*—and not merely *auxiliaries to*—the criminal justice system. Previously sidelined victims could now have more opportunities to express diverse and complicated social agendas that extended beyond vengeance to forms of reparative justice, including reparations and the construction of memorials.

During the same period, the accretion of case law, developed by regional human rights courts, interpreted human rights conventions to confer legal standing on victims. The European Court of Human Rights, for example, now holds that victims have a right to be kept informed of trial proceedings, provided with information about the investigation and trial, and allowed access to relevant documents to ensure meaningful participation.[39]

Speaking of the new centrality of victims in domestic proceedings criminologist David Garland writes:

---

36 See Vivian Grosswald Curran, 'Globalization, Legal Transnationalization and Crimes against Humanity: The Lipietz Case' (2008) 56(2) *American Journal of Comparative Law* 376.

37 In common law countries, New Zealand adopted the first victims' compensation law in 1963, followed by England in 1964. See William Doerner and Steven Lab, *Victimology* (Routledge, 7th ed, 2015) 19.

38 See, eg, Judith Lewis Herman, *Trauma and Recovery: The Aftermath of Violence: From Domestic Abuse to Political Terror* (Basic Books, 1992).

39 See Raquel Aldana-Pindell, 'In Vindication of Justifiable Victims' Right to Truth and Justice for State-Sponsored Crimes' (2002) 35(5) *Vanderbilt Journal of Transnational Law* 1399, 1419-1422, 1434-1436.

The new political imperative is that victims must be protected, their voices must be heard, their memory honoured, their anger expressed, their fears addressed .... The victim is now, in a certain sense, a much more representative character, whose experience is taken to be common and collective, rather than individual or atypical.[40]

The victim, according to Garland, has returned to the core of criminal justice policy: "Specific victims are to have a voice—making victim impact statements, being consulted about punishment and decisions about release, being notified about the offender's subsequent movements."[41]

Such changes are captured in the Declaration of Basic Principles of Justice for Victims of Crimes and Abuse of Power, adopted in 1985 by the UN General Assembly. The declaration sets out basic principles of justice, including the right of victims to have access to the judicial process and to receive reparations, and establishes an inclusive definition of victims that recognizes individual survivors, their dependents, and groups of victims. Victims are defined as:

[P]ersons who, individually or collectively have suffered harm, including physical or mental injury, emotional suffering, economic loss or substantial impairment of their fundamental rights, through acts or omissions that are in violation of criminal laws operative within Member States, including those law proscribing criminal abuse of power.[42]

This victim-oriented approach contrasts with the Nuremberg and Tokyo tribunals where prosecutors largely presented harms as offences against humanity as opposed to violations directed at individual victims.[43] In contrast, the founders of more recent international courts, including the International Criminal Court and the Extraordinary Chambers in the Courts of Cambodia (ECCC), have responded to domestic movements and changing global norms by adopting more expansive procedural rights for victims. The idea that victims have participation and reparation rights in international criminal proceedings has emerged as a widely accepted belief in the field of international criminal justice.[44]

---

40 David Garland, *The Culture of Control: Crime and Social Order in Contemporary Society* (University of Chicago Press, 2001) 11.

41 Ibid 12.

42 *Declaration of Basic Principles of Justice for Victims of Crimes and Abuse of Power*, UN Doc A/RES/40/34 (29 November 1985) A.1.

43 Conor McCarthy, *Cambridge Studies in International and Comparative Law: Reparations and Victim Support in the International Criminal Court* (Cambridge University Press, 2012) 38.

44 Peter Dixon and Chris Tenove, 'International Criminal Justice as a Transnational Field: Rules, Authority and Victims' (2013) 7(3) *International Journal of Transitional Justice* 393.

The ECCC, for example, allows victims to act as civil parties in trials against accused Khmer Rouge leaders. A civil party is an actual party to the criminal proceedings and thus shares many of the same procedural rights as the defence and prosecution.[45] The Court's Internal Rules permit civil parties to testify at the ECCC without being called by the prosecution or defence, to participate at different stages of the trial, and to give commentary on collective and moral reparations. Civil parties can also question witnesses, experts, and the accused, subject to the approval of judges.

In the ECCC victim participation has depended, however, on support from international organizations, foreign governments, and Cambodian human rights groups. These organizations have undertaken victim outreach and education programmes to inform victims of their rights, sponsored community meetings to discuss proceedings, and assisted victims who have sought to complete applications to participate in cases. The Transcultural Psychosocial Organization, a local mental health organization, maintains a hotline for victims, provides psychological counselling for victims inside and outside of the courtroom, and, if summoned by the presiding judge, a staff member sits next to anyone who becomes agitated or overly emotional on the witness stand.

The ECCC expansion of victim participation also has raised concerns about procedural fairness and the financial costs of victim-oriented justice. Prosecutors and defence attorneys complained that lawyers for the civil parties failed to coordinate the participation of their clients in proceedings, which resulted in delays and repetitive questions. They also accused civil parties of acting as second prosecutors. As a consequence, ECCC judges narrowed the scope of victim participation during the 'Duch' trial, and eventually prohibited civil parties from questioning the accused, challenging witness character, or making submissions on sentencing, which resulted in civil party boycott for several days.[46]

Despite these limitations, victims generally characterized their participation in the 'Duch' trial as positive.[47] But many expressed complicated feelings about the process and judicial outcomes.[48] Civil party lawyers objected to their

---

45 The Court draws a distinction between victims as complainants and victims as civil parties. A complainant is any person who witnessed or became aware of a Khmer Rouge crime and chooses to submit a complaint to the court prosecutors.

46 Elisa Hoven, 'Civil Party Participation in Trials of Mass Crimes' (2014) 12(1) *Journal of International Criminal Justice* 81; John D Ciorciari and Anne Heindel, *Hybrid Justice: The Extraordinary Chambers in the Courts of Cambodia* (Ann Arbor, 2014).

47 Stover, Balthazard and Koenig, above n 2.

48 Phuong Pham *et al*, 'A Population-Based Survey on Knowledge and Perception of Justice and the Extraordinary Chambers in the Courts of Cambodia' (Survey Report, Human Rights Center Berkeley, June 2011) <www.law.berkeley.edu/files/HRC/Publications_After-the-First-Trial_06-2011.pdf>; Phuong N Pham *et al*, 'Victim Participation and the Trial of Duch at the Extraordinary Chambers in the Courts of Cambodia' (2011) 3(3) *Journal of Human Rights Practice* 264.

restricted role in proceedings. A number of civil parties expressed deep disappointment with the ultimate 'Duch' sentence as well as with their inability to obtain reparations.[49] The first trial at the ECCC underscored the tension between greater victim inclusion and the judicial mandate to ensure fast and fair trials for the accused. Victims acting as civil parties were given opportunities to voice concerns, which complicated trials and caused judges and prosecutors to limit their role in proceedings. These challenges, of meaningful victim participation, also emerged at the ICC.

IV International Criminal Court

From the first days of the Rome Statute negotiations—the deliberations that created the ICC—a number of civil society organizations, victims' rights organizations, and delegations lobbied for a progressive vision of victim participation.[50] They advanced new provisions that aspired to the welfare and recovery of individual victims. Although ICC trial standards and procedures mostly reflected adversarial common law hostile to full-fledged victim participation, they also included several legal innovations aimed at granting victims unprecedented rights. These rights became defining features of the new court as articulated in Article 68(3), the statute's major provision on victims.[51] It reads:

> Where the personal interests of victims are affected, the Court shall permit their views and concerns to be presented and considered at stages of the proceedings determined to be appropriate by the Court in a manner which is not prejudicial to or inconsistent with the rights of the accused and a fair and impartial trial. Such views and concerns may be presented by the legal representatives of the victims where the Court considers it appropriate, in accordance with the Rules of Procedure and Evidence.[52]

Article 68(3) signalled a major departure from previous criminal tribunal mandates. In just a few sentences it granted a range of new participation rights and also required the court to protect and support victims and witnesses who participated in cases.[53] Article 75 went even further and directed the court to "establish principles relating to reparations to, or in respect of,

---

49 Stover, Balthazard and Koenig, above n 2.

50 Fanny Benedetti, Karine Bonneau and John L Washburn, *Negotiating the International Criminal Court: New York to Rome, 1994-1998* (Martinus Nijhoff, 2014).

51 For discussion, see Sergey Vasiliev, 'Article 68(3) and Personal Interests of Victims in Emerging Practice of the ICC' in Carsten Stahn and Göran Sluiter (eds), *The Emerging Practice of the International Criminal Court* (Brill, 2009) 638.

52 *Rome Statute*, Art. 68.

53 *Rome Statute*, Art. 68(1): 'The Court shall take appropriate measures to protect the safety, physical and psychological well-being, dignity and privacy of victims and witnesses'.

victims, including restitution, compensation, and rehabilitation."[54] Victims—for the first time in international criminal cases—had a right to voice their concerns and receive compensation.

This novel approach was a significant victory for victims' rights advocates who had drafted the language on victim participation and lobbied in closed door sessions for its inclusion in the final statute.[55] The successful adoption of Articles 68 and 75 also suggested a general burgeoning of victims' rights in international justice. After the passage of the Rome Statute, mechanisms of international criminal justice had to explicitly address restorative justice and the role of victims in proceedings. Hailed as the first "victims' court," the ICC drafters reimagined international justice and invited future courts to embrace victim-centred rules and procedures.[56]

Aspirational law, however, must confront practical realities, and victim participation soon confronted logistical and material challenges. Rome delegates had relied on constructive ambiguities to craft the consensus on victim participation, and this left ICC judges with the monumental task of translating broad mandates into clear and concise rules. In the early cases, judges developed *sui generis* models of victim participation, experimenting with different approaches to outreach, legal representation, and communication. Some judges, for example, ordered victims to submit individual applications to chambers while others adopted a more collective approach that appointed legal representatives to specific groups.[57]

Mass atrocity cases can generate a huge number of victims, making it infeasible to include large numbers of them as witnesses or victim participants.[58] Victim participation, by necessity, must be a representational project whereby lawyers are appointed to represent groups of victims. These legal representatives act as advisors and conduits of information to their clients, as well as their advocates in The Hague.[59] Since many victims and their organizations cannot afford lawyers, the ICC must also pay for their representation, which, in turn, limits the number of appointments because of the costs entailed. But independent of costs and logistical hurdles, victim representation raises

54 *Rome Statute*, Art. 75.

55 Cherif Bassiouni, 'Negotiating the Treaty of Rome on the Establishment of an International Criminal Court' (1999) 32 *Cornell International Law Journal* 443; Chris Tenove, *Justice and Inclusion in Global Politics: Victim Representation and the International Criminal Court* (PhD Thesis, University of British Columbia, 2015).

56 Eric Stover *et al*, 'The Impact of the Rome Statute System on Victims and Affected Communities' (Paper presented at The Review Conference of the Rome Statute, Kampala, Uganda, International Criminal Court, 30 May 2010).

57 See Cody *et al*, above n 11.

58 For example, in the case against Jean-Pierre Bemba the ICC received more than five thousand individual applications. See ICC Working Group on Lessons Learnt, 'Report on Cluster D(1): Applications for Victim Participation to the Study Group on Governance' (25 August 2015).

59 See REDRESS, above n 5.

a number of other issues: Who counts as a victim? How should victims be grouped? What professional credentials are sufficient to act as a victims' lawyer? Should victims be able to select their own lawyers?

Since January 2006, ICC judges have begun to restructure and consolidate the process of victim participation in light of the material and logistical challenges.[60] They have also raised concerns about the quality of victims' legal representation and the level of assistance available to conflict-affected communities.[61] Writes Elizabeth Evenson of Human Rights Watch:

> The court's responsibilities relevant to impact extend beyond those assigned to the OTP [Office of the Prosecutor]. These include the Registry's outreach programmes to make court proceedings accessible to affected communities. It also includes its efforts to facilitate rights guaranteed under the Rome Statute, the ICC's founding treaty, for victims to participate in court proceedings and to seek reparations. Assistance projects carried out by the Rome Statute's Trust Fund for Victims to provide physical and psychological rehabilitation, as well as material support, can have an important and immediate effect on the lives of some victims.[62]

Organized political interference and intimidation have further undermined efforts to consult and provide meaningful legal representation to ICC victims. In Kenya, where former ICC Chief Prosecutor Luis Moreno-Ocampo brought charges against the President, Uhuru Kenyatta, and the Deputy President, William Ruto, for mobilizing ethnic gangs during the post-election violence of 2007-2008, victims have faced near constant intimidation. According to the current Chief Prosecutor Fatou Bensouda:

> There was a relentless campaign to identify individuals who could serve as Prosecution witnesses in this case and ensure that they would not testify. This project of intimidation preceded the start of our investigation in Kenya, intensified in the weeks leading up to the beginning of the trial, and continued throughout the life of the case.[63]

---

60 Fiona McKay, 'Victim Participation in Proceedings before the International Criminal Court' (2008) 15(3) *Human Rights Brief* 2.

61 Stephen Smith Cody, Susana SáCouto and Chris Tenove, 'Victims at the ICC: What Is the Way Forward?' on Mark Kersten *Justice in Conflict*, 10 December 2014 <http://justicein conflict.org/2014/12/10/victims-at-the-icc-what-is-the-way-forward/>; International Federation for Human Rights, *FIDH Comments on the ICC's Registrar's ReVision Proposal in Relation to Victims* (18 November 2014) <www.fidh.org/IMG/pdf/letter_registar_icc.pdf>.

62 Elizabeth Evenson, 'Making Justice Count: Lessons from the ICC's Work in Côte d'Ivoire' (Report, Human Rights Watch, August 2015) <www.hrw.org/report/2015/08/04/making-justice-count/lessons-iccs-work-cote-divoire>.

63 *Statement of the Prosecutor of the International Criminal Court, Fatou Bensouda, regarding Trial Chamber's decision to vacate charges against William Samoei Ruto and Joshua Arap*

Kenyan victims had expressed optimism about the prospects for justice and accountability when the court opened investigations in 2010, but their faith in the court began to wane as prosecutions faltered and then collapsed. A total of 839 victim participants eventually joined the ICC case against Kenyatta, while 954 victim participants registered to participate in the ICC case against Ruto.[64] Victim participants in both cases made clear that they wanted to tell their stories, provide evidence, and seek collective and individual reparations.[65] Still, many were too afraid to speak out against the accused. "Prosecution witnesses in this case have been under siege," Bensouda declared in 2015, after the abduction and murder of Mr. Meshak Yebei, a Kenyan man who had previously been under the ICC's protection.[66] Many who initially provided accounts of the violence during the investigations stage subsequently recanted their stories and refused to cooperate further with the court. A climate of fear in Kenya made meaningful victim participation impractical. Writes Bensouda: "The hurdles we encountered in our efforts to investigate and prosecute have frustrated the course of justice for the victims in this case and this must be a matter of profound regret."[67]

Despite the challenges seen in Kenya, few practitioners of international criminal law have retreated from the idea that victims should have a meaningful stake in international criminal prosecutions. Many view victim participation as essential to the legitimacy, effectiveness, and truth-making of international criminal proceedings.[68] It's also evident from recent convictions that victim contributions to criminal investigations, judicial processes, and legal decision-making can enhance public support for criminal trials and willingness of affected communities to accept legal outcomes.[69]

At the same time, international courts must acknowledge their own limitations. As several recent studies have shown, law and legal accountability

Sang without prejudice to their prosecution in the future (6 April 2016) <www.icc-cpi.int/Pages/item.aspx?name=otp-stat-160406>.

64 Human Rights Watch, 'ICC: Kenya Deputy President's Case Ends: Witness Interference Undermined Trial' (5 April 2016) <www.hrw.org/news/2016/04/05/icc-kenya-deputy-presidents-case-ends>.

65 Cody *et al*, above n 11.

66 Alexa Koenig, Stephen Cody and Eric Stover, 'After Kenya, Lessons for Witness Protection' (ABA-ICC Project, *Arguendo*, 1 June 2015) <www.international-criminal-justice-today.org/arguendo/after-kenya-lessons-for-witness-protection/>.

67 Bensouda, above n 63.

68 Spiga, above n 2; Jonathan Doak, *Victims' Rights, Human Rights and Criminal Justice: Reconceiving the Role of Third Parties* (Hart, 2008); Carolyn Hoyle and Leila Ullrich, 'New Court, New Justice? The Evolution of "Justice for Victims" at Domestic Courts and at the International Criminal Court' (2014) 12(4) *Journal of International Criminal Justice* 681; Claire Garbett, 'From Passive Objects to Active Agents: A Comparative Study of Conceptions of Victim Identities at the ICTY and ICC' (2015) 15(1) *Journal of Human Rights* 40; REDRESS, above n 5; Sofia Stolk, 'The Victim, the International Criminal Court, and the Search for Truth' (2015) 13(5) *Journal of International Criminal Justice* 973.

69 For example, victims' groups played essential roles in the investigation, prosecution, and convictions of Chadian dictator Hissène Habré and war criminal Jean-Pierre Bemba Gombo.

will inevitably disappoint those seeking justice after mass atrocity.[70] Criminal prosecutions alone will not heal the social macerations of conflict or repair inter-community relations, though they may aid in those processes. International criminal law is not a panacea for war-torn societies. At best, it can provide limited acknowledgement and recognition to those who have suffered horrendous crimes.[71]

V Conclusion: leveraging victims' rights

The expansion of victims' rights has ignited discussion about the proper substantive and procedural boundaries of international criminal law. What responsibilities do international criminal courts have to promote victim-oriented or reparative justice? And are they equipped to do so? How do courts determine who is an eligible victim? How do they structure victim participation programmes? What obligations do courts have to support and protect victims who participate in cases? These are hard questions without universal answers. Yet, underlying these questions is recognition that survivors of mass atrocity are not simply the principal beneficiaries of legal accountability. They are vital participants. The rise in victims' rights signals a change in the orientation of international criminal interventions. Once organized and carried out exclusively by international elites—distinguished judges, diplomats, influential lawyers—international criminal justice now explicitly acknowledges the contributions of victims to criminal investigations, prosecutions, and reparations.[72]

Victims' rights also have transformed meanings of justice. For most of legal history, prosecutors and judges have presumed that victims' interests aligned with their accountability goals. Victims rarely commented on investigations, legal process, substantive law, or prosecutorial strategies, particularly in common law jurisdictions. It was enough that courts promised victims retribution and punishment. A victim might testify as a witness and answer discrete questions posed by lawyers, but they had few opportunities to influence investigations, tell their stories, advocate for specific charges, or make filings with judges. Judgements were handed down to silent communities. However, as victims and their organizations became more influential, they began to push back on narrow conceptions of punitive justice. They contested the idea that legal accountability was the sole means of obtaining justice; they demanded restorative justice, transformative justice, reparative, and gender

---

70 See, eg, Cody *et al*, above n 11; and Stover and Weinstein, above n 4.
71 Rosalind Shaw and Lars Waldorf, 'Introduction: Localizing Transitional Justice' in Rosalind Shaw, Lars Waldorf and Pierre Hazan (eds), *Localizing Transitional Justice: Interventions and Priorities after Mass Violence* (Stanford University Press, 2010) 3.
72 Thomas M Antkowiak, 'An Emerging Mandate for International Courts: Victim-Centered Remedies and Restorative Justice' (2011) 47 *Stanford Journal of International Law* 279.

justice as constitutive of post-conflict justice.[73] The result has been a more pluralistic and inclusive vision of justice that increasingly reflects restitutive norms, and even forgiveness. Yet law can be ill-equipped to discharge such manifold desires.

The evolution of victims' rights has created great expectations that international courts can—and should—satisfy the needs of survivors. But the expansion of formal participation rights has not always translated into meaningful justice for victims. Many victims who participate in international criminal trials have expressed frustration with the lack of communication, the glacial pace of proceedings, and the absence of material support or reparations.[74] Given the scale of atrocities and the insufficiency of resources, international courts, even when steadfast in their desire to include victims, can struggle to live up to victim expectations and needs. Even the best-run courts can fall short. For this reason, court personnel must identify partner organizations willing to marshal specific services for affected communities, such as psychosocial care, educational and vocational programmes, and resettlement for displaced families.

Thousands of victim participants require basic nutrition, medical, and mental health care to ensure their meaningful participation in legal cases. The ICC's Trust Fund for Victims, and other victim-based nongovernmental organizations and foundations, are essential to link victims' groups with medical providers, counsellors, non-governmental organizations, state parties, or regional bodies willing to support justice projects that extend beyond the scope of criminal prosecutions. These auxiliary institutions can also collaborate with victims' legal representatives to lobby for state or voluntary international reparations programmes.

Effective victim participation depends not only on resource allocation from courts themselves, but also collaboration with bridging organizations that can supplement court efforts. State agencies, international donors, and victim-related support organizations are key actors in efforts to improve victim participation through both legal complementarity and local capacity building. Such efforts to complement victim participation programmes can help to overcome the inevitable limits of criminal courts, which frequently lack the institutional capacity and local knowledge necessary to effectively engage in more broadly defined transitional justice work. International criminal justice alone cannot reach the multitude of harms in communities affected by mass violence, even if law offers the best mechanism to prevent future cycles of violence.

The cultivation of external partnerships can also assuage the disappointment felt by many victims who look to judicial institutions for more than

---

73 See Hoyle and Ullrich, above n 68.
74 Cody *et al*, above n 11.

they can deliver. Accountability efforts must not be allowed to cabin victims' pursuit of other forms of social, political, and economic justice. In fact, the mandate for victim inclusion present in most modern international criminal courts requires courts to encourage, and at times even facilitate, broader transitional justice efforts aimed at supporting survivors and reinforcing the value of victims' voice after violence. Meaningful victim participation requires that basic needs, including psychosocial support, be met. Therefore, victim-oriented justice implies responsibilities for the well-being, welfare, and protection of victims, even when criminal courts as stand-alone institutions lack the capacity to fully satisfy those responsibilities.

In conclusion, the growth of victims' rights, from the Nuremberg and Tokyo trials to the ICC, has redirected attention from legal accountability to victim inclusion and reparative justice. New rights, rules, and regulations in international criminal courts elevate victims from onlookers to participants in post-conflict decision-making. Yet while these changes have transformed legal proceedings, they seldom satisfy victims' expectations of justice. Legal accountability can provide acknowledgement, and at times even redress, to survivors, but criminal prosecutions are not a panacea for the diverse needs of victims. Criminal trials must be part of broader national and international efforts to support, protect, and restore communities affected by mass violence.

Further reading

Doak, Jonathan, *Victims' Rights, Human Rights and Criminal Justice: Reconceiving the Role of Third Parties* (Hart, 2008).

Funk, Markus T, *Victims' Rights and Advocacy at the International Criminal Court* (Oxford University Press, 2010).

Loftus, Elizabeth, *Eyewitness Testimony* (Harvard University Press, 1979).

McCarthy, Conor, *Reparations and Victim Support in the International Criminal Court* (Cambridge University Press, 2012).

Moffett, Luke, *Justice for Victims before the International Criminal Court* (Routledge, 2014).

Shaw, Rosalind, Lars Waldorf and Pierre Hazan, *Localizing Transitional Justice: Interventions and Priorities after Mass Violence* (Stanford University Press, 2010).

Stover, Eric and Harvey M Weinstein (eds), *My Neighbor, My Enemy: Justice and Community in the Aftermath of Mass Atrocity* (Cambridge University Press, 2004).

INDEX

Uniting for Peace Resolution 163
Universal Declaration on the Human
Genome and Human Rights 103
Universal Declaration of Human Rights
105, 280
universal jurisdiction principle 50, 261–2
universalism 23–4

Vagi, V. 24
Van Schaack, B. 190
Vergès, J. 23
Versailles Peace Conference 16–17, 18,
20, 21, 25
vertical complementarity 7, 262–71
victim-based organizations and
foundations 334
victim-centred humanity 97–8
victims 7, 8, 317–35; consoling 11–12;
history of the role of 319–25; ICC
317, 327, 329–33; leveraging victims'
rights 333–5; rise of victims' rights
326–9
victims' rights movements 326

war crimes 5–6, 38, 109–29;
accountability 120, 121–2;

compliance and deterrence
122–7, 128; distinction and
proportionality 116–21; establishing
a war crime 111–15; history of ICL
13, 14–15, 16–17, 109–11; ICC
111, 123, 124–5, 127, 128, 243;
relationship between IHL and
ICL 115–20
weapons: fully autonomous 118–22,
127–8; newly developed 115
Webber, J. 65
Werner, W. 255
Western imperialism 54, 234
Wieviorka, A. 321
Wilhelm, Kaiser 16, 21
Williams, A. 15
witness intimidation 331–2
Women's Caucus for Gender Justice
133–4, 141
Women's Initiatives for Gender Justice
142–3

Yebei, M. 332
Yugoslavia 201, 203; ICTY *see*
International Criminal Tribunal for
the former Yugoslavia

CPSIA information can be obtained
at www.ICGtesting.com
Printed in the USA
BVHW042031061218
534980BV00009B/45/P